Read! Write! Work!

Harcourt, Inc.

Read! Write! Work!

William G. Thomas and Liz Swiertz Newman

Harcourt College Publishers

Fort Worth Philadelphia San Diego New York Orlando Austin San Antonio
Toronto Montreal London Sydney Tokyo

Publisher	Earl McPeek
Acquisitions Editor	Stephen Dalphin
Developmental Editor	Michell Phifer
Project Editor	Laurie Bondaz
Art Director	Garry Harman
Production Manager	Cindy Young

ISBN: 0-15-507279-X
Library of Congress Catalog Card Number: 99-61037

Address for Domestic Orders
Harcourt College Publishers, 6277 Sea Harbor Drive, Orlando, FL 32887-6777
800-782-4479

Address for International Orders
International Customer Service
Harcourt Inc., 6277 Sea Harbor Drive, Orlando, FL 32887-6777
407-345-3800
(fax) 407-345-4060
(e-mail) hbintl@harcourtbrace.com

Address for Editorial Correspondence
Harcourt College Publishers, 301 Commerce Street, Suite 3700, Fort Worth, TX 76102

Web Site Address
http://www.hbcollege.com

Harcourt College Publishers will provide complimentary supplements or supplement packages to those adopters qualified under our adoption policy. Please contact your sales representative to learn how you qualify. If as an adopter or potential user you receive supplements you do not need, please return them to your sales representative or send them to: Attn: Returns Department, Troy Warehouse, 465 South Lincoln Drive, Troy, MO 63379.

Printed in the United States of America

9 0 1 2 3 4 5 6 7 8 066 9 8 7 6 5 4 3 2 1

Harcourt College Publishers

Dedicated
To All Beginning Writers.
"You can't wait for inspiration.
You have to go after it with a club."
~Jack London

Harcourt, Inc.

Contents

PART TWO: Writing Techniques   99

Harcourt, Inc.

Harcourt, Inc.

Preface

READING AND WRITING EXERCISES FOR THE JOB-MINDED

Sometimes a student asks why it's necessary to study English when what he or she wants to be is a tradesperson, a technician, or an artisan. *Read! Write! Work!* answers that question. If you're in college to pass time, to please your parents, or to socialize, this textbook is not for you. It's for serious students who want to focus on reading and writing as the direct path to getting the jobs they want.

The book emphasizes the connection between *having good skills* and *getting and keeping a job.* To give you a head start on other job applicants, the authors combine language lessons and information on the *life skills essential for job readiness,* as named in the SCANS (Secretary's Commission on Achieving Necessary Skills) list. *Read! Write! Work!* intends to help you *get* to work—to make you better qualified than those who don't see the *connection* between having English and life skills and getting the job.

Many students arrive in college "grammatically challenged." Their reading and writing abilities are not good enough for the classes they have to take nor for the jobs they want to get. Good news! It's not too late to get up to speed on basic English grammar—and you'll enjoy the process. The SCANS lessons prepare you for circumstances you'll encounter on the job. The professional articles apply to situations people face daily in the "outside" world. The student stories and essays show what good skills are, and they encourage you to improve your own skills. The writing techniques chapters will help you express yourself. The exercises are designed to give you enjoyable practice in using good English. You'll have fun recognizing and fixing "boneheads"—those written blunders that plague us all: misspellings, wrong word choices, sentence fragments and run-on sentences, misused pronouns and verbs, and comma and apostrophe errors.

The textbook serves in a manner that is entertaining, inspiring, and productive for you who are in college to prepare for your chosen job. You'll accomplish a lot of work in a short time. Whatever your job destination, you *can* get there from here. Study *Read! Write! Work!* now—so you can read, write, and work later. It's your job—both the time you spend on your education and its eventual goal.

Work: Something made greater by ourselves and in turn that makes us greater.
~Maya Angelou

FEATURES OF THE BOOK

SCANS FOCUS

In 1992, the U.S. Department of Labor issued a series of reports known as SCANS (Secretary's Commission on Achieving Necessary Skills). The primary report, "Learning a Living," provides guidelines for educators in secondary schools and vocational colleges. With the goal of high performance by graduates, the report emphasizes the necessary *everyday skills* students must master—in addition to knowledge in their chosen fields—in order to succeed in the U.S. workforce.

We've incorporated the SCANS competencies within the writing technique chapters of the book to show how they serve in the workplace. As you consider the necessary skills, you can assess your own readiness to apply them in your chosen vocations. In addition, the complete "Definition of SCANS Know-How" appears in the appendix of the book.

BASIC WRITING TECHNIQUES

This book helps to teach you the *practical skills* of (1) understanding what you read and (2) expressing yourself through writing. We'll present ten different writing techniques you can use in approaching an assignment: Storytelling *(Narration)*, Drawing Word Pictures *(Description)*, Giving Meanings *(Definition)*, Using Examples *(Illustration)*, Making Categories *(Classification)*, Showing Similarities and Differences *(Comparison and Contrast)*, Discussing Reasons for Results *(Cause and Effect)*, Listing the Steps *(Process)*, Dialogue *(Written Conversation)*, and Influencing People *(Persuading and Convincing)*. After we describe each technique, we'll give you an assignment to practice that particular writing technique.

We provide examples of the technique in both a student-written paper and a professionally written paper. Additionally, as an entertaining but real challenge, we give a "bonehead" version of the technique for you to edit and rewrite. To top it all off, we even include GrammarWorks to help you review the mechanics of writing. The ten writing techniques are shown in the box below.

BASIC WRITING TECHNIQUE

Storytelling *(Narration)*
Drawing Word Pictures *(Description)*
Giving Meanings *(Definition)*
Using Examples *(Illustration)*
Making Categories *(Classification)*
Showing Similarities and Differences *(Comparison and Contrast)*
Discussing Reasons for Results *(Cause and Effect)*
Listing the Steps *(Process)*
Dialogue *(Written Conversation)*
Influencing People *(Persuading and Convincing)*

EXAMPLES OF STUDENT WRITING

The student papers are the product of assignments for reading and composition classes similar to the class you're attending. The students represent a broad cross-section of vocational interests and ages and multicultural backgrounds. All student authors have granted permission to include their efforts as examples of quality classwork.

Just as you will improve in this class, the student authors improved their skills in English grammar, correct language structure, punctuation, and writing techniques in their English classes. To practice using what they learned, they chose a topic that interested them from the selection following each lesson on a writing technique. Whether or not the *topics* of the student papers interest you, note how the students have implemented the writing techniques. The object of including student-written papers is to show you how students applied the learned techniques to written assignments. After each of these student-written examples of technique, there is a set of questions to affirm that you understood what they tried to communicate. Reading the examples of good writing by students like yourselves should help you use the skills you gain to write quality compositions of your own. One of your papers might qualify for the next edition of this textbook!

EXAMPLES OF WRITING IN THE WORLD OF WORK

In this speedily changing world, the written word guides us in our ever-increasing comprehension of the work environment. Every vocational field has written rules and regulations, manuals of instruction, and informational journals and magazines. Successful individuals consult professionally written articles to provide on-going education in their chosen job fields.

In many chapters of *Read! Write! Work!* we've included a professional article from a trade magazine or journal. These are the types of articles you'll read in the real world of work. The authors are not called *professional* because they make their living by the written word. Rather, they're *professionals* in their fields, people who practice the craft they're writing about. The information they offer often applies to various job fields. The articles have been selected because they're well written, they're of general interest, and they serve as examples of the particular writing technique explored in the chapter in which they appear. They're down-to-earth and practical, and they bear witness to the continually evolving changes in the workplace. As with the students' articles, there is a set of questions following each professionally written article to affirm that you've thoroughly digested the material.

SPECIAL FEATURE—*BONEHEADS!*

This GrammarHound symbol signals that, with a little digging, you can find a "bonehead." What's a bonehead? *A bonehead is a careless mistake.* Throughout *Read! Write! Work!* we use boneheads to help you recognize and correct mistakes. We *all* make careless mistakes, even when we really know better. Making a bonehead mistake doesn't mean we're dumb. The GrammarHound's boneheads are taken from actual published writing, which shows that people who edit newspapers, install street signs, and paint business banners all make spelling, sentence structure, and other grammatical mistakes—just like students who write papers. It's not life threatening. *Don't worry.* As you learn to recognize mistakes that others have made, you'll make fewer mistakes.

English is a hard language to learn. It's natural to make mistakes. Many of us speak English as a second language. Some of us had big holes in our learning experiences in elementary or secondary school. We missed learning parts of English grammar or spelling or sentence structure. Some of us have words we misspell all the time, like "impliment" [a bonehead]. It is *implement,* a noun meaning *tool* or a verb meaning *to put into use.* That's why the authors decided to emphasize boneheads all the time. As you recognize the mistakes, you'll more easily remember the right way to put a sentence together. You'll avoid misspellings and wrong word choices, fragments and run-ons, and you'll write in clear, complete thoughts. We think you'll enjoy learning with this special feature of *Read! Write! Work!*

GRAMMARWORKS!

These short lessons provide fast and simple ways to help you review and remember the basic elements of good grammar, punctuation, and word use. Each GrammarWorks table is followed by an exercise to help you reinforce what you have learned by practicing with the lesson at hand.

To reinforce the GrammarWorks lessons, we repeat the following list throughout the book. We think it will help you recognize and avoid making the Big Eight Bonehead grammar mistakes: (1) Words Misspelled, (2) Words or Caps Incorrect, (3) Sentence Fragments, (4) Sentence Run-Ons—Spliced or Fused, (5) Pronouns Confused, (6) Verbs Misused, (7) Commas Misplaced, and (8) Apostrophes Abused.

Harcourt, Inc.

```
                            ●
┌─────────────────────────────────────┐
│           THE BIG EIGHT              │
│           BONEHEADS!                 │
│                                      │
│   ■ Words Misspelled                 │
│   ■ Words or Caps Incorrect          │
│   ■ Sentence Fragments               │
│   ■ Sentence Run-Ons, Spliced or Fused│
│   ■ Pronouns Confused                │
│   ■ Verbs Misused                    │
│   ■ Commas Misplaced                 │
│   ■ Apostrophes Abused               │
└─────────────────────────────────────┘
```

WRITING STANDARDS FOR ENGLISH

English skills assessment is far more than a cumulative grade based upon a semester's work. In college English courses, students progress from their skills level at the beginning of the class to a higher skills level at the end. Therefore, rather than the average of all grades from the beginning to the end of the semester, *the final grade represents the student's level of achievement upon completion of the course.* There is no penalty for starting at a low skills level; your grade depends solely upon the skills level you achieve.

In Chapter 12, we describe five levels of writing skills. This information enables you to understand where you stand at any given point of assessment and what you must accomplish to advance to a higher level. It's important to recognize the benefit of this grading system: *Consistent performance at a higher level at the end of the semester will be rewarded.* Just as a track athlete attains a "PR" (personal record) rather than an average of times or distances, improvement in English language comprehension and writing ability results in a higher final grade for this course.

COMPUTER LITERACY

Today's technology demands that entry-level workers be able to use a computer in their everyday activities. We encourage you to learn and apply computer word-processing skills as an integral writing tool. To familiarize you with this important technology, we provide an introduction to computers in Chapter 13. We suggest that computer literacy be pursued either individually or as a laboratory exercise as part of this course.

ACKNOWLEDGMENTS

We wish to acknowledge the following student contributors, former users of early versions of *Read! Write! Work!* We are happy to honor them by publishing them here: Dedrick Brown, Minnie Choi, Connie A. Coleman, Phong B. Diep, José de Dios, Maria M. Evans, Rosa Granados, Mimie Hanson, Shakei Quinn, Margarita Reyes, Marco Rivera, Kyra Sapp, Lon Spencer, Frank Stovall, and Gerardo Vasquez.

Our special thanks go to Charles Denova, PhD, for writing "Computer Fundamentals" specifically for this book. Dr. Denova is widely recognized as one of the nation's leading advocates of human resources planning and development. His experience includes over thirty-five years as a practicing manager and key human resource specialist with several Fortune 500 companies, and high school, junior college, and university teaching. The authors are very grateful for his generous contribution in preparing this beginner's guide to computer literacy.

We would like to acknowledge the following reviewers who gave us invaluable advice for shaping the manuscript: Ben Larson, York College; Robin Ramsey, Albuquerque Technical and Vocational Institute; Kathleen Rice, Ivy Tech State College; and Joseph Thweatt, State Technical Institute, Tennessee.

We also thank those who facilitated our refinement and preparation of the manuscript. Academic contributors include Los Angeles Trade Technical College faculty: Dean Sharon Tate, Craig J. Barnett, Nancy Berkhoff, Val Cooper, Ralph Guthrie, Pamela Jo Herbert, Charles Lunt, Robert Wemischner, and Adrienne Zinn. The authors appreciate the editorial support and assistance of Sharon Markenson, Carolyn McCarthy, Mark Owen Regan, Lee Newman, and Diane Thomas.

Finally, we acknowledge the hard-working students who use our book. We designed it especially to teach you English skills while helping you move toward your chosen career. Welcome to reality. Welcome to the world of work. Welcome to *Read! Write! Work!* Enjoy it!

Ready? *Let's get to work!*

William G. Thomas and Liz Swiertz Newman

Wm. G. Thomas, Ed.D., is a professor of English at Los Angeles Trade Technical College and a freelance writer. He has co-authored or edited seven books and has numerous newspaper, journal, and magazine credits. He returned to teaching after an administrative career in higher education, including CEO positions at Johnston College, College of the Tehachapis, and New Dimensions of Los Angeles, and deanships at UCLA, Cal State Northridge, and the Los Angeles Community Colleges.

Liz Swiertz Newman is a writer of fiction and nonfiction, manuscript editor, and self-proclaimed "grammar cop." She has served as executive secretary and report writer in the world of work. She completed her B.A. requirements forty years after she started college, following a busy interval filled with family, career, and world travel. She is currently working towards her MFA in creative writing.

Preparing Yourself

Chapter 1

WHY READ? WHY WRITE?

THE PURPOSE OF THE TEXT

The objective of *Read! Write! Work!* is to provide a user-friendly format to help you improve your communication skills. Reading and writing are inseparable. The better you read, the better you will write. In this book, students and professionals in their job fields illustrate the writing techniques you will learn. By reading their examples, you will see how to use each writing technique to communicate your thoughts. By applying what you learn to your assignments, your writing will improve. A craft like writing requires skill, and there's no getting around it: Skill requires practice. This book will provide plenty of prompts and exercises to help you practice.

A SUCCESSFUL EMPLOYER, OR OLD-TIME HIRING PRACTICES

Centuries ago, Sir Walter Raleigh, a famous British explorer, sailed the seven seas in search of gold, tobacco, furs, and other treasures. Because almost everyone jumped ship when his vessel returned to England, he needed a new crew before every voyage. This is how he recruited employees to handle the heavy sails, swab the decks, and perform the hundreds of other backbreaking tasks.

Around two o'clock on the morning of departure, Raleigh's strongest loyalists would drive a large, horse-drawn cart to a British public drinking house (a "pub"). They'd bop a few drunks on the head, dump them into the cart, and carry them aboard ship. The new crew members would wake up on board several miles out to sea and spend a sober year or two doing whatever the captain wanted. Most of the seafarers couldn't read or write. Many didn't even speak English. They didn't need to. Raleigh only needed to use them from the neck down. They just had to know their jobs and do them—or else.

WORKING FROM THE NECK UP, OR WILL YOU USE YOUR MIND OR YOUR BODY?

Fortunately, employers have changed their recruiting methods since Raleigh's day. They're looking for people who *can* use that priceless computer that we call the human brain. They pay good wages to those who *can* read, write, and compute numbers, and who have skills in their chosen fields. Why do *you* need to read and write well? Your future career success will depend on how well you understand what you read and how well you write what you think. You'll be competing for the available jobs with people who have good reading and writing skills. People who lack these skulls—uh-oh, a bonehead blunder!—skills, won't get good jobs.

WHY NOT LEAVE SCHOOL NOW AND GO TO WORK?

On a pleasant September day, Scott, age eight, announced to his father that he wanted to drop out of school. "Okay," his dad said, to Scott's complete surprise. "You can quit." He smiled at his son's expression of disbelief. "What are you going to do with all that spare time?"

Scott was ready. "Oh, I'll ride my bike, eat Big Macs, go swimming in the neighbor's pool, kick back at the movies, watch TV—all that fun kind of stuff."

"Where will you get the money for McDonald's and the movies?" his father asked.

"I'll get a job," Scott responded.

His father started itemizing reasons why Scott might have trouble finding a job. Scott couldn't read the paper. He hadn't even heard of the classified ads. He'd never written a letter to his aunt in New York, much less to a prospective employer. What kind of job was he qualified for? Scott said maybe he'd just hang out at home and eat peanut butter sandwiches. Then his father asked, "Without a job, how are you going to pay the rent?"

DEPARTMENT STORE JOB ADVERTISEMENT

Team Leaders Wanted!

The team leader position provides hands-on experience in merchandising, stock placement, customer service, selling, and leadership. Team leaders are our future storeline executives. You will play an active role in developing your road to success. Through on-the-job development process, team leaders participate in a variety of key functions.

- **Initiate active roles** in recruiting, staffing and scheduling, reviewing associates, and client development.
- **Maintain merchandise standards** through daily stock movement, processing of goods, merchandising, and sale/event set up.
- **Insure department customer service objectives** by helping to schedule lunches/breaks, serving as selling role models, and suggesting staff increases or decreases.
- **Serve as staff resources** in customer service, policies/procedures, and selling standards.
- **Provide guaranteed customer satisfaction** through customer accommodations/conflict resolution in absence of manager.
- **Assist manager** in training new associates/existing associates in new merchandise, policies, and procedures while on the floor.

Qualifications include demonstrated leadership skills, an understanding of general business concepts, the ability to effectively organize and communicate, strong analytical and quantitative skills, customer service experience, and solid academic achievement. Candidates must be flexible and willing to accept positions throughout our geographical area.

"Rent? What rent?" the bemused boy replied.

"If you don't go to school, you have to support yourself as well as pay for all the fun stuff," said his dad. "That means clothing, food, entertainment, and rent. Get the picture?"

"Stop! Stop! I've heard enough!" Scott said loudly. "I'll stay in school—but only long enough to learn to read."

Scott wisely remained in school. He learned to read—and *well*. The more he read, the more he learned; the more he learned, the "smarter" he became. So he finished elementary school and junior high school. He kept reading and learning—through high school, college, and to grad school for his Master's Degree in business administration. He spent one of his graduate years in Spain, where he learned to read and write in Spanish. Today, Scott is in international marketing, selling synthetic fiber to Third World countries. He's even added Portuguese to his language resources. Would this have happened if he had quit school at six or sixteen, or if he had stopped learning at twenty-six?

From a newspaper. *This notice makes some careers seem twice as attractive as others. What word would you delete?*

What College Freshmen Want to Be When They Grow Up:
- Management
- Executive
- Engineer
- Physician
- Engineer
- Teacher

COULD YOU COMMUNICATE WITH A MARTIAN?

How do you express thoughts out loud to another person? You talk, of course! Talk is speaking our thoughts in words that make sense to another person. The words we exchange bring images to the "mind's eye." Illustrations are examples that help get our points across, and we want to show how important communication is to functioning on an everyday basis, so here's an example of a situation in which only *spoken* words won't work.

You're walking down Second Avenue in New York City when you notice a person who looks lost. He's wearing Sun Ray glasses and an outfit that's a cross between a Giant's uniform and a surfer's wet suit. You wave. The guy waves back. You smile and say, "Nice day." He smiles and says, "Aklmjl." You say, "I don't understand." He says, "Opkpqwe opok." You realize you have a communication problem. A dog walks by. You point at it and say, "Dog." Your new friend says, "Dog." Then you draw a stick figure dog on a piece of paper and write the letters d-o-g. Underneath that, the spaceman writes g-l-e-b. You point to the dog and say "gleb." You are on your way to communicating. You hope you can both remember the new words and images. He'll need to be able to speak and read and write English if he's going to stick around, and you'll be able to write the first Martian/English dictionary.

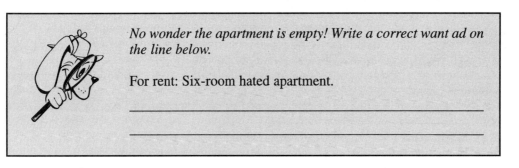

No wonder the apartment is empty! Write a correct want ad on the line below.

For rent: Six-room hated apartment.

_____

_____

WE LEARN OUR LANGUAGE THE SAME WAY

Most children talk before they read. They first say such words as *Mama, Daddy, no,* and *hot* before they work up to a Disney term like *Hakuna Matata*. The kids can't read or write yet, but they can sure talk. They add to their vocabularies, or learned words, as they explore their world. They learn the alphabet song, then they learn to recognize the letters, and then they start to put letters on a paper in patterns that form words. D-O-G places an image in their minds that looks like a four-legged animal with a waggly tail. Soon they can check books out of the library and read an entire story about a wooden puppet whose nose grew when he told a lie. Words become sentences. Sentences become stories. Stories expand children's knowledge of the world.

THE IMPORTANCE OF READING

Reading is an important aspect of communication. Reading is the act of deciphering letters that have been formed into words, and then into sentences, paragraphs, articles, and books. We read the mail—whether greeting cards or letters from the Internal Revenue Service. We read movie titles, menus, training manuals, operating instructions, fashion magazines, job advertisements, and articles about whether the Dodgers won or lost. We read street names, "Don't" signs, and traffic tickets. All our lives, we'll depend on reading for information. Reading expands our knowledge of the world.

Harcourt, Inc.

READINS THE PITS

That title's a "bonehead"! Write it correctly here: _____

The thought is right, but the spelling is wrong! Reading is the pits. You've got to start at rock bottom and climb your way up the reading trail to get to the top. Each level of reading success leads you to a new height of understanding and knowledge.

Reading reveals worlds that you might never enter yourself. You experience the thrills and dangers of the astronaut when you read *Apollo Thirteen.* You understand the Asian community in Los Angeles when you read Lisa See's *On Gold Mountain.* You share the passion of Martin Luther King Jr. when you read his speeches.

Reading not only expands your mind. It opens up parts of it you didn't realize you owned: creativity, imagination, visioning. The unknown becomes the known.

READING + WRITING = WORKING

THE CHANGING WORK WORLD

One thing you can count on in the world of work is *change.* Hammers have been replaced by devices that shoot nails into the boards they're connecting. Fashion designers no longer sketch out their new patterns; they input data into their computers and formulate three-dimensional drawings of their creations. Machine tooling has been automated. Modern food preparation, cooking, and storage methods have turned restaurant kitchens into processing laboratories. Modern data reproduction methods have made printing presses with movable type obsolete. Computers have generated the Information Age, and, throughout your career, you'll be affected by it.

You need to think now in technological terms about the world of work waiting for you. Like a computer, your mind continually processes information and stores knowledge for when you need to make use of it. You will continually confront *new* written information that must be understood, analyzed, and synthesized. To keep up in your field, you'll have to *read!* The following are examples of reading and writing requirements in the real world.

AUTO MECHANICS NEED TO READ AND WRITE!

Fortunately, the computer is still unable to repair a car. There aren't even robots invented for car repair. Although smog tests, tune ups, and mechanical problem diagnoses can be accomplished electronically, we still need good human mechanics. Say your car's engine has been missing badly. You take it into a garage near work for inspection. A man in a greasy, blue jumpsuit approaches you. "What's the problem, buddy?" he asks. You tell him about the car's irrational behavior and perhaps add that it sounds like, "b-b-b-umba, b-b-b-umba," and so on. "That sounds like the carburetor," the mechanic says. "I can fix it for $2,000." "Wait a minute. That's impossible!" you say. "Why?" asks the mechanic. "My car doesn't have a carburetor. It has a fuel injection system," you say. "Oh, I didn't know that," says the surprised mechanic.

Would you leave a wounded vehicle with *that* car doctor? No, you wouldn't—because no mechanic like that would have a job in the first place! No, you'd take your car to Jake Garabejian. The receptionist where you work says that Jake consults journals on the newest auto models and repair techniques. Lots of her friends have used Jake. He's familiar with technical manuals on every moving part of every automobile type—Japanese, German, British, or American, convertible, sedan, or van. Jake consults parts catalogues to figure up his repair estimates and writes down the costs of materials and labor. Jake has to read to order his supplies and equipment, and he has to write to respond to that occasional customer who has a complaint. Auto mechanics can only succeed in their jobs if they can read and write.

You have to be careful where you put your modifiers! Rewrite the sentence below.

For sale: Antique desk suitable for lady with thick legs and large drawers.

_____

_____

FASHION DESIGNERS NEED TO READ AND WRITE!

The style-conscious woman knows what colors are popular and what's the fashionable length of a skirt this year. The style-conscious man knew when grunge was no longer cool. Neither one wants to see the same clothing on the racks year after year. Fashion is a constantly changing business. At Nordingdale's, will they see a bunch of last year's styles made in fabrics that were popular two years ago? Of course not! Yong Lee, the head buyer who purchases the merchandise, would never order from a manufacturer who uses dated patterns and whatever material is on hand. She would soon be looking for a new job.

As long as Yong's been in the fashion trade, she has kept up with what's *new*. She knew about fabrics treated with Teflon and Tencel before the buyer at SearsMart, and about Vivienne Tam's stretchy, nylon mesh outfits that miraculously don't wrinkle and only need to be dipped in water to be cleansed. Yong is talking to a designer about some ideas she got from reading travelogues and history books. Publications abound in the fashion world. *Women's Wear Daily* is to the fashion trade what *The Wall Street Journal* is to the stock market. Even when you're the designer *setting* the styles, you have to keep up with the trade magazines to know what materials to work with and what the consumers want. You have to read and write to place orders for fabrics and fill orders for merchandise. The fashion world depends as much on written words as on drawings.

CARPENTERS NEED TO READ AND WRITE!

Charlie Alexander's a carpenter. He restores old buildings in the inner city. Charlie dropped out of school at the age of ten and worked around his farm community doing odd jobs to help his widowed mother. At eighteen, he joined the Navy. "Funny," Charlie says, "but I spent my whole four years in the Navy on dry land. When I was in boot camp, we lived in these old barracks. If something needed fixing, I'd grab a hammer or screwdriver and fix it. Word got around that I was pretty handy, and right away, they put me on the maintenance crew as a carpenter." When Charlie was discharged, he moved to Los Angeles. He thought it would be easy to get a job there, but it wasn't. "You see, I never learned to read well enough to study for the carpenters' union exam." He couldn't read the job ads in the newspapers or even fill out a job application.

"I was desperate," Charlie says. "I had to go back to school to learn how to read and write." The GI Bill helped Charlie through night school and two years of community college. "I never knew what I'd been missing," Charlie related to his college English teacher. "My life changed through all I discovered by reading. Writing about what I've read has led me to writing about myself, my feelings, my dreams and desires. Every day is an exciting new experience." Charlie, a very busy carpenter now, continues his schooling at night. "I keep taking courses just for my own enjoyment."

NURSES NEED TO READ AND WRITE!

You wake up in the emergency room, and you remember being in an automobile accident. You can't feel any sensation in your legs. A woman dressed like a nurse walks in. She picks up your chart. You ask, "How badly am I hurt?" She responds, "It says *spin-ale lac . . . lacta-tions* or something like that." Fortunately you're only dreaming.

Nurse Linda and Nurse Allen read the doctor's instructions and write notes on your changing condition. They laugh when you tell them about that dream. Linda says they verify a medication against the written instructions three times before administering it to any of their patients. Allen says nurses have to read all the time—about new methods of caring for sick people, rules and regulations, news about AIDS and cancer research, the minutes of countless meetings, and nurses' journals. They say nurses have to write, too—reports on the progress of their patients, logs of their activities while they're on duty, and recommendations on how to improve patient procedures and nursing conditions. In fact, all nurses have to pass reading and writing proficiency tests before they can obtain their nurses' licenses. As you recover, you're happy they passed the tests.

From a Los Angeles area newspaper. *This little poem has a dozen mistakes a computer spellcheck wouldn't find. Write the correct words on the lines to the right.*

Spellbound

I have a spelling checker.
It came with my PC.
It plainly marks four my revue (2) _____
Mistakes I cannot sea. (1) _____
I've run this poem threw it, (1) _____
I'm sure your please too no, (4) _____
Its letter perfect in it's weigh, (3) _____
My checker tolled me so. (1) _____

DESKTOP PUBLISHERS NEED TO READ AND WRITE!

Suppose your fiancée is a great sprinter and you want to marry her before someone at the Olympic Trials runs off with her. The wedding is a month away, and you need invitations. You grab the Yellow Pages and call the first desktop publisher that catches your eye. You give the person at the other end of the phone all the information—the date, church, and so forth, carefully spelling everything: the bride's name, Josie Ann Washington; the groom's name, Philip Andrew Bailey. One week later, you reject invitations for the wedding of "Joanne Warshindon" and "Andre Bialy."

Harcourt, Inc.

From a magazine story. *The run-on sentence also contains a misused pronoun. Rewrite the sentence, inserting the correct pronoun and fixing the comma splice errors.*

"McIntyre glowered at the phone, sport coat in hand. It was unusual for he and Schrunk to talk directly like this, usually they missed each other, usually they left messages."

_____

_____

Juno Jackson, the woman who takes care of your company's business cards, agrees to a rush job. She even calls you to confirm the spelling of your name. Juno uses a desktop publishing system with spellcheck, but she carefully proofreads her final copy before sending it to press. She knows that the computer might pass over a wrong usage. For example, *too*, *to*, and *two* are all correct words, but they mean different things. If Juno doesn't read well, a small mistake can mean the work has to be redone at her company's expense. (Incidently, Josie and Philip got their invitations in time. You'll see the Washington-Baileys at the next Olympics.)

Desktop publishers have more to read than just what they're supposed to reproduce. They have to read journals and magazine articles on copying and printing techniques, color transfers, copyright regulations—and other professional publications, two. (See, what did we tell you? The computer spellcheck didn't find *that* bonehead error!) They also have to write cost estimates and reports, and answer customer requests in writing.

CHEFS NEED TO READ AND WRITE!

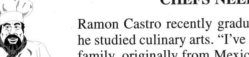

Ramon Castro recently graduated from a Texas community college where he studied culinary arts. "I've always loved to cook, and I come from a large family, originally from Mexico," Ramon said. "From the time I was a little boy, I helped my mom in the kitchen. I could make tortillas and salsa from scratch before I could hit a baseball. When I was growing up, I had all kinds of jobs: baling hay, milking cows, cleaning out stables—all jobs where I didn't have to think. When I was twelve, I got work in a restaurant washing out all the cookware, and when I was fifteen, I became the cook's assistant." Ramon's café specialized in Mexican-style food. "I told the cook I wanted to become a famous chef, and he sent me to his friend, a chef at the biggest hotel in Brownsville," Ramon reminisced. "He asked me what kinds of ethnic foods I could cook, and I didn't know what he was talking about. He explained that great chefs master the cooking techniques of every major cuisine in the world: French, Italian, Greek, Japanese, Chinese—every culture you can think of. 'You have to go to school, young man,' the master chef told me."

Ramon wasn't a reader when he enrolled to study culinary arts. "I had to become one, though. I read about every method and style of cooking that exists. I studied menus and lists of ingredients and how different herbs and sauces affect the flavor of food. I poured through magazines, reading trade articles on restaurant management and travel articles on the best places to eat in the world. I'm still learning. I'm still going to be a famous chef someday, but I have to keep studying." His reading and writing skills will determine whether Ramon stays a cook's helper or achieves his real goals.

From a newspaper's Sunday Magazine section. *Here's an example of the need for proofreading in the world of fashion. The following caption appeared with a photograph showing a stunning model wearing a bulky* white *sweater and slacks. Rewrite the caption correctly below.*

Michael Kors' wool wide-leg pants [$$$] and ribbed wool turtleneck sweater [$$$], available in black only.

OFFICE WORKERS NEED TO READ AND WRITE!

Before the advent of the computer, the only equipment needed in an office to communicate with the outside world was a telephone and a typewriter. What do you see now in a typical office? Everyone's sitting in front of a keyboard and looking at a monitor, reading and writing what's on that screen. Just for that computer, you've got hard disks, floppy disks, zip disks, zip drives, hard drives, hardware, software, CDs, word-processing, graphics, scanners, and modems. E-mail replaces "snail mail." Every one of the computer components, features, and programs has a thick manual and/or on-screen Help file. These days, you can hardly use the telephone without written directions. Voice-mail replaces answering machines. Don't forget copy machines, fax machines, sorters, shredders, and beepers. Every "time-saving" device comes with written instructions—and a different warranty.

"I got this job because I know how to operate the word-processing software they use here, along with most of the machines," reports Bernice Simmons, who works in what she terms the Office of the Future. "I'm as much a technician as a secretary these days, and I learned my skills by reading. I read everything that comes into this four-lawyer office," she says. Bernice opens and sorts the mail, distributes newsletters about changes in law, regulations, and statutes, and receives faxes with court appearance data. She transcribes dictation from an audiocassette to the word-processing program. Bernice says, "Sometimes the lawyers say, 'Send so-and-so a letter about such-and-such,' and I have to compose it from those limited instructions. I also keyboard the attorneys' handwritten legal tablet pages onto the computer—and I usually have to correct my bosses' grammar and spelling! My daily job makes me feel like a communication machine, but I love it—and I'm good at it."

FACTORY WORKERS NEED TO READ AND WRITE!

Fred Gallagher is fifty years old and has worked in the Southern California defense industry his entire career. When asked recently how factory work has changed over the years, Fred smiled a knowing grin. "I wasn't around when Henry Ford was building Model As, but he's credited with developing the assembly line method where parts were added piece by piece until the last stage in the process when the completed car was driven off the line. People were like machines. They each performed one task, and it was pretty boring," he says. "Nowadays, machines have mostly replaced people. Toolmakers, machinists, welders, and engineers take care of the machines.

"I help build radar systems for airplanes. I have to follow blueprints, write up structure and specification sheets, quote proper documentation, and write progress reports.

I even take the minutes at departmental meetings. I have to subscribe to manufacturing journals and magazines to keep up-to-date, or I'll be obsolete—like those Model As. Look at it this way. There's always a pilot out there, flying through murky weather or darkness, who's depending on whether or not I know what I'm doing. There's no place for poor readers or writers in my business."

IT ALL ADDS UP TO THIS . . .

Why read? Why write? It is, indeed, your *job*. It's your job in school, and it determines whether or not you get the job when you're out of school.
   Let's get to work!

THE MATH IS EASY!

Reading + Writing = Your Job
Knowledge + Effort = Success

ClassWorks!   *In-Class Assignment*

Exercise your writing skills! Write for 15 minutes on the following topic.
   Why is it important to read and write in your chosen vocational field?
   If you are undecided as to your career, write four reasons why someone in one of the following career fields must know how to read and write: police officer, postal clerk, salesperson, dental technician, or ambulance driver.

WE USE LANGUAGE TO COMMUNICATE OUR THOUGHTS

LANGUAGE

Language has three aspects: words that are thought, words that are expressed, and words that are understood. The objective of education is to improve our abilities to think, to express ourselves, and to understand and be understood by others. Words expressed and understood are the products of thought. The purpose of *writing* is to present our thoughts to others. The writing process is not complete until the paper is read.

LANGUAGE

- Words Thought
- Words Expressed
- Words Understood

THE PAPER

Whether a paragraph, an essay, or a research report, any written assignment is referred to by the generic term, *paper*. Every written work—essay, story, article, speech, letter, poem, or research paper—has a **structure** and a **purpose.** All papers have a **beginning,** a **middle,** and an **end.** All papers assigned are intended to illustrate a lesson studied in the book.

Words, sentences, and paragraphs are the building blocks you'll use to write your papers. You'll combine words to form sentences, combine sentences to form paragraphs, and combine paragraphs to create stories, essays, and longer papers.

THE WORD

Each word is like a puzzle piece. It can take many words to complete one thought picture. The words you know are stored in your vocabulary. You find new words in what you hear and what you read, as well as in two important reference books: the *dictionary* and the *thesaurus.*

The **dictionary** is used to check the spelling, the meaning, and the pronunciation of words. You are expected to consult a dictionary when you read words you don't understand or when you don't know how to spell a word. In your written assignments, you will be expected to spell words correctly and use them appropriately.

The **thesaurus** is used to find the closest word possible to the meaning you wish to express or to find new words to express your thoughts. You will be expected to learn new words and avoid repetition of overused words. With a good vocabulary, your ideas become interesting sentences, paragraphs, and essays.

THE SENTENCE

A sentence expresses a complete thought. It also has a beginning, a middle, and an end. A sentence begins with a capital letter, contains a subject and verb, and ends with a period, a question mark, or an exclamation point.

Example: The boy *(subject)*   threw *(verb)* the ball *(object)*   .*(period)*

| **Beginning** | **middle** | **end (punctuation)** |

Write a short sentence here. Place the subject first and the verb second.

| **Beginning** | **middle** | **end (punctuation)** |

Phrases and Clauses

A **phrase** is a fragment of a sentence. Phrases amplify meaning but do not express a complete thought. In the following example, see the two underlined phrases.

Sentence: *Marian walked*   <u>*across the street*</u>   <u>*to buy some ice cream.*</u>
Phrases: *across the street*   *to buy some ice cream.*

Write a short sentence with a phrase in it, and underline the phrase.

A **clause** always contains a subject and a verb. It can also contain phrases. There are two types of clauses, *independent* and *dependent.* (We do not count Santa Claus, who spells his name differently.) An **independent clause** is a complete sentence; it expresses a complete thought and can stand alone. A **dependent clause** cannot stand alone because it *depends* upon the independent clause to complete its meaning.

Sentence: *Judy and Sharon rented a movie that starred Jodie Foster as a riverboat gambler.*

Independent clause (complete thought): *Judy and Sharon rented a movie*

Dependent clause (incomplete thought): *that starred Jodie Foster as a riverboat gambler.*

Write an independent clause here.

_____

Three Types of Sentences: Simple, Compound, and Complex

Simple Sentence   A simple sentence expresses only one complete thought.

> *I like animals.*
> *Tannis and her husband live in the mountains.*

Write a simple sentence here.

_____

Compound Sentence   A compound sentence contains two or more complete thoughts (independent clauses), connected by a comma and a conjunction or, sometimes, by a semicolon. The common conjunctions that connect two independent clauses are *and, but, or, nor,* and *yet.*

> *Bill likes dogs, but Diane likes cats. Bill likes dogs; Diane likes cats.*
> *Judy and Sharon rented a movie,*   and   *it starred Jodie Foster and Mel Gibson.*
>   Independent clause   conjunction   independent clause

Write a compound sentence here.

_____

Complex Sentence   A complex sentence completes one or more thoughts and contains at least one *independent* and one *dependent* clause. The conjunctions that connect an independent clause and a dependent clause are: *who, whom, that, which, as, because, if,* and *since.*

> *Clark,*   *who is very fit,*   *works at a health club.*
>   Dependent clause
> *In his garden, Grandpa grows lilacs,*   *which are Grandma's favorite flowers.*
>   Independent clause   dependent clause

Write a complex sentence here.

_____

You'll use complete sentences in the development of paragraphs, essays, and papers.

THE PARAGRAPH

A paragraph is one group of closely related sentences. A paragraph has a beginning, a middle, and an end. Most often, the first sentence expresses the topic—what the paragraph will tell about. The middle sentences develop that topic. And the final sentence summarizes that topic. You'll be expected to use three or more paragraphs in the construction of your papers.

In the blanks that follow, complete the sentences about paragraphs.

The first sentence of a paragraph _____ the topic.

The middle sentences _____ that topic.

The final sentence _____ that topic.

THE ESSAY

An essay uses paragraphs to develop a single topic. The essay also has a beginning, a middle, and an end. The beginning paragraph is the topic paragraph. It contains a sentence expressing the purpose of the paper, the *thesis*. The beginning paragraph is therefore sometimes called the thesis paragraph because it states what the essay will show or prove. The middle paragraphs develop and support the topic. The ending paragraph summarizes the middle paragraphs and draws a conclusion about the thesis of the first paragraph. You'll use this structure for all of the essays you write.

In the blanks that follow, complete the sentences about essays.

The first paragraph of an essay is called the _____ or the _____ paragraph.

The thesis states _____.

The middle paragraphs of an essay _____ and _____ the topic.

The ending paragraph _____ the middle paragraphs and

_____ about the thesis.

THE REPORT

The report consists of a number of pages that describe solutions to different problems or lead readers to specific conclusions, based on information found in outside sources such as books, magazines, or personal interviews. While *other* papers may express the thoughts, opinions, and experiences of the *writer*, the research report draws upon the findings of people with expert knowledge of the subject. Chapter 11 explains how to organize, document, and write a report.

TIPS ON EDITING

EDITING SHORT AND LONG "BONEHEAD BLUNDERS"

When editing the boneheads, your own work, or another student's work, follow these guidelines. As you read the material, look for misspellings, wrong words or wrong capitalizations, sentence fragments or run-on sentences, wrong verb forms and pronouns, and comma and apostrophe errors.

- **Circle misspellings.** Any combination of letters that does not represent the word intended is considered a misspelling, including words not found in the dictionary, misused words, and words with missing or misused capital letters. When you look in a dictionary to check the spelling, always check the meaning also, to be sure you have the word you want. (You can check the word's pronunciation at the same time.)
- **Place an X at the beginning of sentence fragments.** Watch for sentence fragments, which are strings of words that do not represent a complete thought. Often they contain a subject and verb but are *dependent* clauses, requiring other, *independent* clauses to make their meaning complete.
- **Place an X at the beginning of run-on sentences.** A run-on sentence is one in which two or more independent clauses are connected without appropriate punctuation. An independent clause is a complete thought. To recognize run-on sentences, look for these symptoms: complete thoughts connected with a conjunction but no comma; complete thoughts with no separation at all between them (a fused sentence); and complete thoughts separated by a comma used as a conjuction (a comma splice). Depending on the sentence, you can correct the

Harcourt, Inc.

error by inserting a period, or a comma and a conjunction, or a semicolon between the independent clauses, or by making two or more complete sentences.

- **Underline wrong verb forms and pronouns.** Any verb is considered a wrong verb when it is misspelled, is the wrong tense, or doesn't agree with its subject in person and number. Any pronoun is considered wrong if it doesn't agree with its antecedent or its verb.
- **Underline places with comma and apostrophe errors.** The comma and the apostrophe have specific rules for their use. Any uses of commas and apostrophes that do not fit into the rules are errors. We will explain these rules for you later.

You'll want to avoid these eight most commonly made mistakes when writing your papers.

THE BIG EIGHT BONEHEADS!

- Words Misspelled
- Words or Caps Incorrect
- Sentence Fragments
- Sentence Run-Ons, Spliced or Fused
- Pronouns Confused
- Verbs Misused
- Commas Misplaced
- Apostrophes Abused

You will learn about sentence construction, parts of speech, and punctuation in the GrammarWorks tables in sections 1 and 2 of the book.

THE BONEHEAD PARAGRAPHS

Bonehead paragraphs illustrate how *not* to fulfill a writing technique assignment. The following example of a bonehead paragraph includes the "Big Eight" bonehead mistakes listed in the box above. Review the types of mistakes to look for, and then identify them in the following paragraph, "Chewing Gum Is a Bad Habit."

A BONEHEAD PARAGRAPH

**CHEWING GUM IS A BAD HABIT
BY SHARON DENTINE**

(1) My cousin Gordon has many freinds they hang out at his house after work. (2) Playing cards. (3) Last week, we all went to a foreign movie, it's subtitles were in english. (4) I got my popcorn, and I stuck my gum under the seat. (5) I was sitting in the aisle seat but Gordon wanted to sit on the isle. (6) When I moved over and the seat flew up. (7) The gum stuck on his knew pants'. (8) He kept swaring at me until the usher come and tolled him to be quit. (9) I'm not never going to the movies with Gordon again. (10) If a person really wants to watch a foreign movie, you're better off going alone.

Edit the paragraph above. Search for the Big Eight Boneheads: circle misspelled words, wrong words, and wrong capitalizations. Put an X in front of sentence fragments,

Harcourt, Inc.

run-on, spliced, and fused sentences. Underline misused pronouns and verbs and the comma and apostrophe errors. Each sentence has a number. On the lines below, write what you've found wrong with each numbered sentence. (Write what you found wrong with sentence (1) on line 1, etc.)

1. _____
2. _____
3. _____
4. _____
5. _____
6. _____
7. _____
8. _____
9. _____
10. _____

Now you're ready to revise the paragraph. Write it in your own words on a separate piece of paper.

The following version of the paragraph is one possibility for the "final draft" version of the previous bonehead paragraph.

EXAMPLE: REVISION OF A BONEHEAD PARAGRAPH

CHEWING GUM IS A BAD HABIT
REVISION BY LOTTA I. DIAZ

My cousin Gordon has many friends. They hang out at his house after work playing cards. Last week, we all went to a foreign movie with English subtitles. I got my popcorn, and I stuck my gum under the seat. I was sitting in the aisle seat, but Gordon wanted to sit on the aisle. When I moved over, the seat flew up, and Gordon got the gum stuck on his new pants. He kept swearing at me until the usher came and told him to be quiet. I'm never going to the movies with Gordon again. If you really want to watch a foreign movie, you're better off going alone.

NOTE: The authors hope you enjoy learning what NOT to do from the "bonehead paragraphs" and the real-world bonehead blunders throughout the book.

With a little more thought to the ad, the man might get hired! Below, rewrite the ad to fit the job-hunter's meaning.

Man, honest, will take anything.

_____

USING READING TO DEVELOP WRITING SKILLS

THE COMMUNICATION TWINS: WRITING AND READING

Writing and reading coexist. Writing is meant to be read. Every time you write, or rewrite, you're creating something brand new. Whatever you write— a letter, a story, or a paper for your sociology class, no one else would write the same thing the same way. No one else has *your* particular experience, talents, and skills. Because of your own personal background, you bring an individual approach to what you *read* also. You construct the meaning from what you read plus what you already know. Whoever reads your paper will view it through their life experiences.

HOW READING HELPS YOUR WRITING

Reading good quality writing can improve your own writing. Why? Because the more you read, the more aware you become of writing techniques, and the better you become at expressing what you want to communicate. Almost unaware, you absorb the methods that good writers use to support the points they want to make.

TECHNIQUES FOR WRITTEN COMMUNICATION

Reading helps you recognize the tricks of the writing trade. The best writers carefully plan their work. They use specific ways of organizing a paper called *techniques, strategies,* or *rhetorical approaches,* that help readers understand what they're trying to say. In this book, we call these ways of organizing a paper **techniques.** We'll show you ten of them: telling stories (narration), drawing word pictures (description), giving meanings (definition), using examples (illustration), making categories (classification), showing similarities and differences (comparison and contrast), listing the steps (process), discussing reasons and results (cause and effect), influencing people (persuading and convincing), and dialogue (written conversation).

All of the student papers and professional articles used in this book are examples of these different techniques or approaches to writing. You can follow these models to develop your own writing skills. They will help you to form your own ideas and provide support for them. Remember, the bonehead paragraphs show you how *not* to use a particular technique.

From the Sports section. *Here's a sentence that forgot what it set out to accomplish! On a separate piece of paper, list the key points the writer is trying to convey. Then write a better paragraph than this writer did.*

Her [Venus Williams'] first Wimbledon experience need not begin and end with her first-round loss Saturday, a gloomy but dry day in which officials crammed a full slate of matches and, in an effort to catch up after losing two days to rain, decided to schedule play today, only the second time in tournament history the gates of the All England Club will have been opened on the middle Sunday.

READING HAS MULTIPLE VALUES

Reading helps you in countless ways. It improves and expands your vocabulary. It teaches you good grammar and syntax (placement of words in a sentence). As you read more complex materials, you find that you can think in more precise and abstract terms and express yourself more capably. Reading enables you to relate a new subject to one you already know something about. Reading expands knowledge. Reading helps you find answers to your questions and to formulate new questions. With practice, you can learn to skim and scan a written work so you can go right to the information you're seeking. Good readers retain much of what they read and call upon the information stored in their memories as they need it. Reading is, indeed, a valuable skill.

READING HAS MANY BENEFITS!

It Helps You:
- Improve and expand your vocabulary
- Learn good grammar and syntax
- Express yourself more capably
- Think in precise and abstract terms
- Relate subjects to what you already know
- Expand your knowledge
- Find answers to questions

WHAT ELSE IS READING?

- **Reading is saving time.** You can tell from looking at a title and a page of written words whether the material contains what you want to know.
- **Reading is enlightening.** As you learn new things, you enhance your life experience.
- **Reading is a challenge.** You seek to understand the writer's message.
- **Reading is interpretive.** When you appraise what you read, and agree or disagree, you strengthen your thought processes.
- **Reading is stimulating.** Reading can make you want to go places, do things, and write about your experiences.
- **Reading is entertaining.** Appreciating and enjoying well-crafted writing is like listening to good music or looking at beautiful paintings.
- **Reading is *fun!***

OBJECTIVES OF A GOOD READER

You've probably run into very good readers in your classes. They're not necessarily nerds, but they're usually good students. They understand and remember what they read, and they use the ideas to help in their own writing and school endeavors. They use reading as a study skill.

Gloria Goodreader has definite purposes in mind when she reads. She wants to learn about the authors' main ideas. She wants to identify writers' techniques as models for her own writing. She's become a good reader to improve her vocabulary and to expand her experiences. Gloria reads to study information for a test, to learn how to save money buying a car, to find out where to apply for a job, and to accomplish many other things.

Good readers don't look at assigned reading as a chore; they look upon all reading as one of the many pathways to their own future success.

GOOD READERS HAVE A PURPOSE IN MIND!

- They read to learn the author's ideas and the techniques used to express them.
- They read to improve their vocabularies and to expand their experience.
- *They read to succeed!*

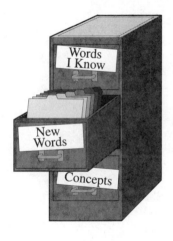

CHARACTERISTICS OF A BAD READER

Bad readers don't really care about reading. Ralph Rotten-reeder resents his reading assignments and usually doesn't complete them. Ralph also has too many distractions. He tries to read while watching TV or listening to a sports talk show on the radio. He takes frequent time-outs to talk with his friends on the telephone. He'll do anything to put off reading an assignment, even take out the trash!

If he attempts an assignment at all, he skims the material as fast as he can, usually at the last possible moment, hoping to remember the overall idea—because he can't be bothered to make notes. He never uses the dictionary to look up words he doesn't understand. If his college English teacher questions him about a writer's message, he always misses the author's major point.

Is Ralph preparing for success, or for failure? Do you suffer from any of his reading shortcomings?

BAD READERS DON'T CARE!

- They don't realize that reading assignments benefit them.
- They are distracted by TV and friends and anything else.
- They rush through the reading assignments and miss the point.
- *They snooze, they lose!*

READING TO DEVELOP VOCABULARY

WHAT'S THE PURPOSE OF A BROADER VOCABULARY?

An expanded vocabulary is not intended to make us appear highfalutin.* New words help us *think*. As you increase the number of words you understand, you become better able to express your feelings and ideas clearly. We store these words until we need them in the filing cabinets of our brains. They are the tools that help us put new ideas together.

New words clarify and shorten the messages we send to others in speech and writing. *Clarify* means *make clear*. Having strong,

---

*If *highfalutin* is unfamiliar to you, it means pretentious or haughty. There! You've just expanded your vocabulary.

Harcourt, Inc.

sharp, and specific words in your vocabulary rather than weak, vague, and general ones provides you with an increasingly greater ability to communicate your meaning to others. People with good vocabularies aren't showing off. They're just expressing themselves precisely. A good vocabulary is like the marquee at the movies. The marquee tells what's going on inside the theater; a good vocabulary tells what's going on inside the mind of the speaker or writer.

From a magazine article on riding mountain bikes. *Where's a spell checker when you need one? Write the incorrectly spelled word below.*

CRUISING DOWNHILL: Keep butt back, out of saddle, with thights resting against rear part of saddle, waist and arms bent.

WHAT IMPACT DO YOU HAVE WITH LIMITED SKILLS?

Marvella Green is head of a college nursing program. She says she was deeply embarrassed recently when one of her students gave a speech to a group of visiting high school students. Ms. Green said, "When Marcus opened his mouth, out came examples of his inadequate vocabulary and very poor grammar. He said, 'Me and the nursing students and faculty is stoked you guys is here.' Although Marcus is smart and knows his nursing, his speech made him seem rather ignorant. I wanted to sneak away from the auditorium so I wouldn't have to admit he was one of our students."

Your vocabulary must mature as you mature. It must be appropriate to the circumstances—as formal or casual as your audience. For you to be taken seriously in your job, your skills must reflect that you take your job seriously.

From a booklet about self-publishing. *Mistakes are distracting and confusing to readers. Edit the sentence to insert the missing word.*

Such authors do not have a proven track record of past successes, nor do they a name that is readily identifiable to the average consumer.

CAN WE UNDERSTAND NEW WORDS WITHOUT A DICTIONARY?

You can often tell what a word means by the words around it. "I could tell the fender was fixed with Bondo because it looked like frozen metal bubbles had dropped on the garage floor." If you never heard the word *Bondo* before, you now have an idea that it's a liquid metal material used to repair a dented fender.

Here comes another word whose meaning is revealed in its context. "At work, Hector is *ubiquitous*. As a line supervisor in the shoe factory, every day he follows one basketball shoe through the whole process of construction, from raw material to finished product. He asks about everybody's families, makes announcements on the loud speaker, posts notices on the bulletin board, talks on the phone, and receives and sends faxes. That guy is here, and he's there—all at the same time." Do you have an idea of what *ubiquitous* means? Hector is *everywhere*!

If authors think their readers might have trouble understanding a word, they often help define it. "He opened the *valve* for the front lawn sprinklers. The water stored inside the plastic pipe pushed out from the pressure of the water behind it, so the crab grass got plenty to drink." You can guess that a valve regulates the flow of fluids.

DEFINING WORDS FOR THE READER

Often a writer tells the reader the meaning of a word to make certain the reader understands. The following examples show how writers define their meaning for readers.

- They took a wrong turn into a *cul-de-sac*, a dead-end street with a big circle for turning around.
- By reading, you are having experiences *vicariously*; that is, you are living them through the actions of the characters in the book.
- Some concepts are *incomprehensible*; they can't be understood even when a writer defines them.
- Her name was *Alma*, which is Spanish for soul.

In technical writing for a specific vocational field, you will sometimes use words that have different meanings from their normal use outside that particular field. If the writer has introduced the terms properly, the readers will interpret the meanings properly. Because we have had new terms explained to us, we are aware of multiple meanings of words. An *uninvited rodent* in the housewife's kitchen is different from *the mouse attached to a computer.* A *spider* crawling up the bathroom wall is not the same as a *bug that's a bacterial infection.* A *piece of wood* isn't the *stick* you're referring to in *an automobile's gear-shift mechanism.*

When writers don't attempt to make such terms understandable to the reader, they are accused of using *jargon*—words specific to a field that exclude others from understanding their meaning.

From the Business section. *Would someone who drops a letter from the end of a word be so careless as to drop a zero from the end of an amount of money? Edit the sentence below, writing the correct word above the misspelled word.*

First Nationwid Bank bought Cal Fed Bancorp for $1.2 billion in 1996. Operations are centered at First Nationwide's San Francisco headquarters.

READING FOR COLLEGE, READING FOR LIFE

READING TO DEVELOP STUDY SKILLS

When you're studying, you're trying to *learn* something—to remember information for the time when you need to recall it. In reading to learn, mastering this three-part study skill will be worth your while: (1) previewing, (2) reading, and (3) summarizing major points. Such reading is entirely different from reading a mystery novel or the autobiography of a figure skater just for pure enjoyment.

First you **preview** the material. This involves both **skimming** and **scanning.** When you *skim* material, you glance through it for key points. It's very helpful for the reader to first look at the title of a paper and then *skim the material to locate the main ideas* in the document to understand what it is about. When you *scan,* you examine material more closely, though still not thoroughly. Because an author supports major points with facts, arguments, expert judgment, and other materials, a reader can *scan the material to look for details* that strengthen the points being made. With the morning newspaper, you might *skim* an article about last night's local NBA game to see who scored the most points or whether your favorite player contributed. You might *scan* a reference book to see whether it contains support information for your research paper. Good readers are often able to skim and scan at the same time.

Next, you **read** the text; that is, you try to understand what the author's intent is in every written passage. If you own the book you are reading, you might underline or highlight certain words, phrases, or sentences that are most pertinent to the subject. You can also write key words in the margins so that later you can scan the marginal notes to find that information again.

Finally, you **summarize** the information. Make brief notes, either in the margins of your book, on separate paper or cards, or on audiotape. You select the most important material and condense it in your own words. Referring to your notes helps activate your memory of the material.

Previewing, reading, and summarizing help you remember material through repetition and review, whether you're preparing for a test or for other reference needs.

READING TIPS

- **Preview**
  Skim for main ideas
  Scan for details
- **Read**
  Highlight key words
- **Summarize**
  Note major points

WRITING WILL MAKE YOU WANT TO READ MORE

The main purpose of this book is to encourage you to become a better writer so that you will enjoy writing as an important way to express yourself. You'll find that writing more will also increase your desire to read more. You'll want to figure out how different writers hold your attention. How do they organize and arrange their sentences into paragraphs? What writing techniques do they use in presenting their information?

While you are reading the student and professional material in this book, see if there are writers whose work you particularly like. Try to determine what styles they use, what kinds of voices they express in their writing, what kinds of moods they create, and the reasons that you find their stories interesting. Try to duplicate the qualities of those writers in your own efforts. Find published authors whose work interests you. Ask your friends, your teachers, and your coworkers about their favorite writers. Check books out of the library. In expanding your reading horizons, the terrain is unlimited.

From the Sports section. *Was it the letter writer or copy editor who made the pronoun mistake in this Letter to the Editor? Correct the pronoun mistake.*

My 100-pound twenty-one-year-old stepdaughter not only completed the same boot camp two weeks before your arrived, she finished as an honor grad.

READING TO EXPAND YOUR IMAGINATION

Nonfiction is pretty cut-and-dried. You can obtain factual information from many different sources: newspapers, books, journals, manuals, and personal experience. Fiction comes directly out of the writer's mind. **Fiction** consists of stories that authors make up in whole or in part from their imaginations. While some element(s) may be factual, fiction is *not* about what *really* happened to *real* people, but about fictitious characters in sometimes improbable situations. Fictional stories are usually narratives consisting of six basic elements:

- The *plot* or story line
- The *characters* who take part in the story
- The *scenes* or incidents in which the characters are involved
- The *settings* where the action takes place
- The *mood* of the story—whether morbid, happy, educational, adventuresome, romantic, or ridiculous
- The *theme* or meaning the author wants to convey

WRITTEN MATERIAL IS EITHER FICTION OR NONFICTION

Does the writing express facts or does it represent someone's unleashed imagination? You'll have the opportunity to write both fiction and nonfiction for class assignments.

Nonfiction writing is based on fact, opinion, or experience. In a vocational major and on the job, most of what you'll read will be nonfiction.

In **fiction** writing, the author tests his imagination. He makes up a story out of his head. The story may be based on fact, but he interweaves the facts with characters and incidents that are make believe. Cartoons, fairy tales, romance novels, and spy stories spring primarily from the authors' imaginations.

One of the jobs of a reader is to distinguish between *fact* and *fiction!*

PARTS OF A FICTIONAL STORY

- Plot
- Characters
- Scenes
- Setting
- Mood
- Theme

Imaginative writings include novels or book-length stories, short stories, dramatic plays, and musical theater. One of the great joys of reading is to use these journeys of fantasy as an escape from the reality of our lives. Good fiction grabs your attention on the first page, so that you might burn the roast you're cooking for dinner or neglect to answer a ringing telephone because you're so wrapped up in what you're reading.

When *reading* fiction, you often "identify" with one of the characters in the story. You take on the feelings of that personality as you read the book. You experience events that might never happen to you in real life. You gain knowledge of how people work and think and live. Identifying with a character in a book can enhance your reading enjoyment.

When *writing* fiction, you become *all* of the characters: the heroine *and* the handsome man she saves from the flaming superstructure; the detective *and* all the suspects who might have killed the wealthy computer company executive; the dog *and* the master whose life it saves. You can be someone you're not and do things you would never really do. It's all there in your mind, just waiting for you to write it out. Practicing fiction writing can really stimulate your creativity.

WRITING TIPS: HOW TO MAKE YOUR WRITING INTERESTING

- *Grab* the reader's *attention*!
- *Plan* ahead; use good *organization*.
- *Select* suitable *writing techniques*.
- *Develop* your own writing *style*.
- *Find* your *writer's voice*.
- *Set* an appropriate *mood*.
- *Find* written *models* to follow.

Clearly, this modeling agency isn't a model for good grammar! Rewrite the ad on a separate sheet of paper.

We are auditioning this week only! Children ages four to seventeen years, start your children in print, commercials and film. Our clients are featured in ads for Target. Macy's, Nordstrom and many others.

LEARNING GRAMMAR THROUGH READING

Grammar consists of the rules that have evolved for spoken and written language. In every culture, the members understand one another because of their agreement as to what their words mean—and what the order of the words, the pauses, and the inflections mean. Following the proper grammar rules is like following the traffic laws. Both sets of regulations were developed to help people know what to do and when to do it. Just as red lights and stop signs tell pedestrians and drivers where to stop and for how long, punctuation marks tell readers where the writer's thoughts pause or stop.

In this book, we'll review some of the most important grammar rules. But the truth is, your most accessible "grammar book" is anything you read in quality books and magazines. But beware of those bonehead blunders! As you are reading along, if the words were to say, *"Them; are a person who know everythink about your grammer what there be to know,"* you would know right away that much is wrong with the construction, verb use, punctuation, spelling, and so on that the writer has used. You would certainly doubt the person's credibility as an author. Now, how do you suppose you learned to recognize that? You learned by listening to people who *speak right* and by reading the works of people who *write right.*

As you read, pay close attention to the flow of the words. If they flow well, it is because the writer has chosen the proper word order and punctuation to channel the words. As you read, you know automatically where the narration ends and the dialogue begins because you have learned that quotation marks set off the "spoken words" in writing. *You know so much more grammar than you realize.* Give yourself the chance to learn more. The GrammarWorks! exercises at the end of most chapters of the book will help you.

THE BOTTOM LINE

Not being able to express yourself *well* diminishes people's respect for your skills in your chosen profession. You don't want to cause someone to want to sneak away because you can't express yourself skillfully. You don't want to make "bonehead" mistakes. Of course not, or you wouldn't be here. Take advantage of the everyday lessons you find while reading, and be the one to hold your audience spellbound.

Without good speaking, writing, and reading skills, you may not even *get* an audience. *Let's get to work!*

GRAMMARWORKS! The "Big Eight" Boneheads

1. WORDS MISSPELLED
Tips: Look words up in the dictionary. Learn spelling rules. Look for the root of the word.

PROBLEM	INCORRECT	SPELL THE WORDS CORRECTLY HERE.
Incorrectly	writting, amoung, bussiness	_____
spelled word	definately, shelfs, enviorment	_____

2. WORDS MISUSED, CAPITALS MISSING OR MISUSED
Tips: Avoid mistakes by paying attention as you write and by proofreading your finished work.

PROBLEM	INCORRECT	WRITE THE CORRECTED SENTENCE HERE.
Misuse of	Dot and Phil *where*	_____
words and	driving *thru texas*	_____
capital letters	last *Winter.*	_____

3. SENTENCE FRAGMENTS
Tips: A sentence contains a complete thought. A fragment might belong with the sentence before it or after it. You might need more words, or fewer words, to express your complete thought.

PROBLEM	INCORRECT	WRITE A COMPLETE SENTENCE HERE.
Incomplete	When you have something	_____
thought	to say and you want people	_____
	to understand you.	_____

GRAMMARWORKS! The "Big Eight" Boneheads (continued)

4. RUN-ON SENTENCES, FUSED SENTENCES, COMMA SPLICES, CONFUSING SENTENCES
Tips: If there is more than one complete thought, separate the thoughts with a *comma plus a conjunction,* not just a comma. Try making one of the thoughts a *dependent clause.* If a sentence is confusing, make two (or more) sentences. Don't just throw commas at long, rambling sentences!

PROBLEM	INCORRECT	CORRECT THE RUN-ON SENTENCE HERE.
Too many thoughts with incorrect connections	I wrote my essay, that has four paragraphs it's about environmental problems, the teacher will like it.	_____ _____ _____ _____

5. PRONOUN MISUSE
Tips: Be consistent! Do you have a good reason to change from talking about *him* or *her* to talking about *you* or *we?* Does the pronoun agree in person and number with the noun ahead of it?

PROBLEM	INCORRECT	WRITE THE CORRECTED SENTENCES HERE.
Pronouns don't agree with each other or with ante-cedents	A person should go to a doctor for their check up. They will check your heart, your lungs, and so forth.	_____ _____ _____ _____ _____ _____

6. VERB MISUSE—NONAGREEMENT, WRONG VERB TENSE OR VERB FORM
Tips: Keep verbs near their subjects so subjects and verbs will agree in person (first, second, or third) and number (singular or plural). Verb tense tells when the action occurs. Study verbs forms!

PROBLEM	INCORRECT	WRITE THE CORRECT SUBJECT/VERB COMBINATIONS IN THE PRESENT TENSE.
Verb is not same person or number as subject	*Mel don't* know if *you wants* to come when *he be going* or after Sooze *has went.*	_____ _____ _____ _____

GRAMMARWORKS! The "Big Eight" Boneheads (continued)

7. COMMA MISUSE OR NONUSE

Tips: Commas mark where a writer or reader would naturally pause. Commas separate clauses, words in a series (put one before the *and*), and elements in dates and addresses. They also set off direct address, appositives, and introductory, parenthetical, and unnecessary phrases and clauses.

PROBLEM	INCORRECT	ADD SEVEN COMMAS, AND LIST THE REASONS HERE.
Words, phrases, or clauses are not set off	Mo on Friday May 1 Bo (3) and Jo will eat party and (2) stay with us and we'll (1) need extra food you know.(1)	_____ _____ _____ _____

8. APOSTROPHE MISUSE OR NONUSE

Tips: The apostrophe ['] is most commonly used to indicate either possession* or contraction. To show *possession* (belonging or ownership), add apostrophe s ['s] to the person, place, or thing that has possession. Be careful with plurals! To show *contraction* (two words combined, with one or more letters of the second word omitted), put an apostrophe ['] in place of the missing letters.

POSSESSION PROBLEMS	INCORRECT POSSESSION USAGE	USE POSSESSIVE APOSTROPHES CORRECTLY. WRITE THE FIVE ITALICIZED WORDS, CORRECTLY MOVING, ADDING, OR OMITTING THE APOSTROPHE IN EACH.
An apostrophe is omitted, misplaced, or added in error	The *ladie's* and *gentlemens'* hats blocked *Vics'* view of the *clowns antic's* at the circus.	_____ _____ _____ _____

CONTRACTION PROBLEMS	INCORRECT CONTRACTION USAGE	USE CONTRACTION APOSTROPHES CORRECTLY. WRITE THE THREE ITALICIZED WORDS, CORRECTLY MOVING, ADDING, OR OMITTING THE APOSTROPHE IN EACH.
An apostrophe is omitted, misplaced, or added in error	*Were* learning where to place the contraction apostrophe. It *does'nt* take long to memorize *it's* correct usage.	_____ _____ _____ _____ _____

---

*Possessive personal pronouns do *not* use an apostrophe: *his, hers, its, ours, yours, theirs,* and *whose.*

A common mistake is to confuse *its* (the possessive form of *it*) with *it's* (the contraction of *it is*). Other words misused as contractions are *your* for *you're, there* for *they're,* and *well* for *we'll.*

ClassWorks!	***In-Class Assignment***
	*Exercise your writing skills! Write for 15 minutes on one of the following topics.* I am a good reader because . . . I am a bad reader because . . .

Chapter 2

ORGANIZING YOUR WRITING PROJECTS

Harcourt, Inc.

ORGANIZING YOUR ENGLISH WRITING ASSIGNMENTS

When confronted with a new or large project, any of us can be overwhelmed at first. It's natural to experience the feeling that we don't know where to start. To make writing papers less intimidating to students, the big new project of *English Assignment Due* is broken into seven small manageable tasks.

ONE WRITING PROJECT, SEVEN EASY STEPS!

1. Have a topic.
2. Gather basic information.
3. Decide on a writing technique.
4. Plan a structure.
5. Prepare the first draft.
6. Prepare the second draft.
7. Prepare and submit the final draft.

THE SEVEN STEPS

1. HAVE A TOPIC

In this English class, your writing assignments will include both single paragraphs and essays of three or more paragraphs. Whether you're writing a paragraph, an essay, a paper, or a report, the organization is basically the same. The first thing you need before beginning an assignment is a **topic.** In college classes, teachers usually assign general items to write about. This book offers "prompts" to get you going. A **prompt** is a suggestion or cue to help a student select a topic to write about. We encourage you to write about subjects that have something to do with you or your chosen career. When you write about your job field, you will learn more about various aspects of your vocation and improve your English language skills at the same time. It's very important that you stick to the topic itself and not wander off and write about unrelated issues or situations. For example, if you're writing about your own life (an autobiography), you wouldn't use most of your paper to describe your two sisters. All of the information you include in a written paper should relate directly to the major subject about which you are writing.

From a restaurant advertisement. *A bit of redundancy on the menu . . . . Does this ad make you wonder what day their* Saturday *brunch is? Rewrite the notice below.*

SUNDAY CHAMPAGNE BRUNCH
EVERY SUNDAY 11:30–3:00 PM

_____

_____

What If You Can't Think of Something to Write About?

It's always best to write about a subject with which you are already familiar: yourself, your job, members of your family, early childhood experiences, embarrassing moments, your love for your child, your bedroom, or your favorite food. The list can be endless, so don't waste valuable time searching for a topic when you should already be at work writing. Pick a topic quickly and run with it. One way to accomplish this is to take a blank piece of paper and write down anything that pops into your mind. After you have five to ten items, choose one. Then start jotting down ideas about that single item to begin to organize your paper.

Every Paper Needs a Title

Other than letters, everything you write should have a title. Like a newborn baby, your original creation deserves a special name. Selecting a *topic* is not the same thing as selecting a **title** for your paper. You can choose the title either before you start writing your paper, during the writing, or after you finish. Titles draw immediate attention to your writing. A good, catchy title gives a very good idea of what a paper is about and makes a reader want to know more. Titles should be centered on the page, with either all the letters capitalized or just the major words capitalized.

If you were writing about your college's Financial Aid office, you could choose from among many possible titles: *Money–You Can't Go to School without It; The College's Money Tree; Financial Aid Answers Financial Need;* or *The Bucks Start Here!* Browse through a magazine, a newspaper, or a Best Sellers list and see which titles grab you. Writers select titles from various sources, such as song lyrics, Bible quotations, and from nursery rhymes. An essay about the movie *Godzilla* could be *Face-Off with the Lizard.* An essay about a wonder drug for psychopathic liars could be *Pinocchio Drug Shortens Noses.*

Notice how each of these titles is aimed at sparking a reader's immediate desire to read further. You can use your creative ability to select attention-getting titles for your papers. Remember, your writing is your brand new creation. Your title should be something that shouts out the subject of your paper so people will want to read it.

WAYS TO GATHER IDEAS FOR PAPERS

- Freewriting
- Brainstorming
- Clustering or Mapping
- 5 Ws and an H
- Journal Keeping

---

2. GATHER BASIC INFORMATION: PREWRITING

Once you have selected a topic, or subject, there are five useful ways to gather ideas before you begin writing: freewriting, brainstorming, clustering or mapping, "the 5 Ws and an H," and the journal method.

Freewriting   In *freewriting,* you just start writing about anything that comes into your head. Don't stop to think! Just keep writing. Don't worry about punctuation or spelling; you can always fix that later. Write for five to ten minutes and then read what you've put down on paper, underlining any parts you may want to include in your assignment—whatever seems intelligent or expresses your meaning well. Pertinent humor often enlivens a paper.

FREEWRITING EXAMPLE

My Crummy Car
(It's okay for it to be boneheads at this point in the project.)

My furst car was the worse one every made it always ran out of gas and I had more flat tires than money in my pocket. It got about ten miles per gallon and the drivers' seat was just a big spring sticking up. It was so rusty and dented that people kept telling me I bought it from the Demolition Derby. It was a Dodge with a softtop that leaked like crazy when it rained. No one wanted to ride with me cause it was always breaking down."

The author of this *freewriting* piece already has enough information to underline the items he wants to include in the structuring and drafting of his paper. He'll eliminate the errors as he polishes the assignment.

Brainstorming   Brainstorming, or making an "idea list," is a perfect way to collect lots of ideas from which you can later choose the ones you want to include in your paper. Like freewriting, you want to jot down as many ideas as possible. But instead of writing a paragraph about the topic, you make a list of every idea that pops into your head. If you used this method to write about your lousy car, it would look like the following example.

BRAINSTORMING EXAMPLE

breaks down	*windows don't go up or down*
uses too much gas	*tail pipe exhaust smoky*
rusty and dented	*no passengers*
springs show through seat covers	*girlfriend hates it*
bald tires	*no insurance*
roof leaks	*uses too much oil*
no seat belts	*transmission grinds*
engine is noisy	*fuel pump leaks*

The author of this set of *brainstorming* ideas can go back and choose just the specific information he wants in his paper.

Clustering or Mapping   You might want to use an organizational method called clustering, or mapping, which is another common way to get your thoughts from your head to a piece of paper. In *clustering,* you start out with the main subject, considering it to be like the trunk of a tree, and then you branch out, or cluster, drawing associations around the main topic and between subtopics.

Let's take the Crummy Car topic again.

Clustering or Mapping Example

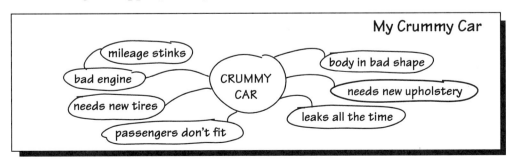

As other details, ideas, or examples come to mind, you make new clusters. From the results, you can select the items you want to include in your paper.

5 Ws and an H   With this method, which news reporters have used since newswriting began, you ask six basic questions about the topic you've selected: *Who? What? Where? When? Why?* and *How?* Using the car topic, the following example is one way to gather ideas for a paper.

---

5 WS AND AN H EXAMPLE

My Crummy Car
Who?   Me
What?   My '88 Dodge convertible needs new tires, upholstery, body work, a new engine, and a
          paint job.
Where?   In my garage.
When?   Once I get some money, I'll start fixing it up.
Why?   It gets flats, the springs are showing, it's dented, the engine doesn't work most of the
          time, and it looks awful.
How?   By working at fast food joint.

This method gives you a new slant on the story, since your main subject becomes what is needed to get the car fixed and how much it will cost.

Journal Keeping   Many writers keep journals or diaries about their daily experiences and activities. They want a record they can refer to later when they write a detailed account about an event, an idea, a romantic situation, or a travel experience. *Journal keeping* is also a good way for writers to develop their opinions about the government, politics, friendships, or whatever interests them. Journals are very private. They should be read only by the person keeping them. They can be kept in tablets, small books, or loose-leaf notebooks. Usually, you write down the month, date, and year, and off you go—with no rules or regulations.

JOURNAL EXAMPLE

Monday, March 23
Got up. Had bacon and eggs. Called Stella to wake her up for work. I should buy her an alarm clock for her birthday. Went to see if my car would start. It didn't. Called George to see if he could bring a jumper cable over. We got the damn thing going, but it started spurting gas all over the place. A hole in the gas line. I cut up an old inner tube and wired it around the hole.

And so on . . .   Any of these methods of prewriting should help you get a good start on your writing assignments. Practice each one to find which suits you the best.
Good luck! *Let's get to work!*

ClassWorks! *In-Class Assignment*

The prewriting techniques are freewriting, brainstorming, clustering, and 5 Ws and an H.

Using one of them, practice prewriting on the topic, "The Unmet Needs of Students at My College."

Prewriting helps you get an idea for a *topic sentence.* Write the topic sentence for a paper on unmet student needs.

_____

_____

_____

All students discover the prewriting method that works best for them. The following paper shows how one student author fulfilled the assignment to write an essay telling how he organizes his writing projects. You'll see he has a method all his own!

Lon Spencer was a student in Freshman English when he wrote this account of how he organizes his papers. He is now an officer with the Los Angeles Police Department.

Lon Spencer   Spencer 1
English 101-10:00
Organizing Papers
Sept. 5, 1997

                        A Writing Rebel

    To be frank, I don't follow any steps or use an outline
when I write an essay or a thesis paper. Neither do I
brainstorm nor utilize a formal writing strategy. In the 1952
silver screen classic, *Rebel without a Cause,* James Dean
portrays a surly teenager who stands up and clashes against a
conservative society. I like to think of myself as a "James
Dean of writing." I write the way I want to, not the way that
I was taught throughout my schooling. Teachers were always
telling me, "Listen, young man, if you continue to write this
way, you are going to run right into trouble." Of course, I
couldn't care less what they told me, and I continued to use
my own method of writing (if you want to call it that). The
way I write is very unorthodox, time consuming, and difficult.
I am not sure if it is the best way to write, but so far it
has worked for me.

    When I write, I first plant my buttocks on the swivel chair
in front of my Macintosh. I squirm around until I find

a comfortable position and then gaze at the glowing monitor, waiting for an idea to blossom from the garden of my mind (and, believe me, this garden is in dire need of water and sunlight). I wait and I wait, sometimes as long as an hour, just staring at the monitor like a drooling zombie out of a Roger Corman movie. Then, all of a sudden, BAM! An idea explodes in my head, and I strike at the keyboard faster than lizards catch flies! What happens next is difficult to explain. I sort of hop in the back seat of my brain and let my imagination do the driving. Out of nowhere, my mind is flooded by a monstrous tidal wave of creativity. My imagination hurls out hundreds of different views and different ways to write my assignment. The ideas come to me like children flocking to an ice cream truck on a scorching summer afternoon. I collect all of the ideas in my head, organize them, and figure out where and when they will fit into my paper. I guess I draw a mental picture of what my paper should look like, and that's when I type it up on the computer. From there on, I fall into this trance when I am typing. As I ferociously punch away at the keys, I am oblivious to everything around me.

For instance, the other day I was on my Mac, and my "typing trance" had me in a full Nelson. When my mom asked me to join the family for dinner, I did not budge from my seat because I was so transfixed in my writing assignment. Persistently, my mother called me several more times, and still I did not move. Finally, after growing weary of yelling my name, my mom stormed in, grabbed me by the ear, and pulled me out of the room! Can you picture this? A five-foot-two, one hundred and ten pound, forty-five-year-old woman dragging her six-foot-one, one hundred and sixty-five-pound, eighteen-year-old son by the ear? It was hilarious, despite the pain my ear had to endure. Basically, you have to go to extreme measures to pull me away from a writing assignment.

When I finally have my rough draft on the screen in front of me, I read it over. As I make changes, I think of more ideas to improve my paper, making it more fun to read. I just throw those new ideas into my assignment. When I have finally smoothed over all the blemishes and it looks as good as Sophia Loren, I know it is time to print that sucker up!

Well, I have shown you how Lon Spencer, the Rebel of Writing, constructs an essay. It's pretty wacky, huh? I'm positive that I am doing something wrong when I write, but

Spencer 3

even if I am, I am still having bundles of fun writing. To
me, that's the important thing. Well, sooner or later, someone
will point out to me what is wrong with my writing, and they
will try to correct my rebellious ways. Too bad they don't
know I couldn't care less.

WORK! WORK! WORK!

THIS EXERCISE HELPS BUILD COMPREHENSION SKILLS.

1. Lon's topic sentence is the opposite of what he has proved. Would you advise Lon to change his strategy for writing a paper? Why or why not?

   _____

2. Lon uses many colorful phrases to express himself. What does he mean by his "typing trance"?

   _____

3. Lon clearly enjoys writing. He says he doesn't care whether people like his method, but does he care whether people *like what he writes?*

   _____

4. What does he say that makes you believe that?

   _____

From a letter soliciting funds to support "Heal the Bay." *Can you find the incorrect word usage? Draw a line through the incorrect word and write the correct word above it.*

People who love our beaches and bay will be thrilled to know

we've received more reports of dolphin and sea lion

sitings than ever before.

---

3. DECIDE ON A WRITING TECHNIQUE

You have a topic; you've collected ideas to support the purpose of your paper; you've written a topic sentence (your thesis). Now what? Do you start writing? No, not yet! What happens next can take only a few minutes, but it's very important to the whole process of preparing your paper. You must settle on an approach or technique to use in writing your first draft. You will make your choice from the following techniques: telling stories (**narration**), drawing word pictures (**description**), giving meanings (**definition**), using examples (**illustration**), making categories (**classification**), showing similarities and differences (**comparison and contrast**), listing the steps (**process**), discussing reasons and results (**cause and effect**), influencing people (**persuading and convincing**), and dialogue (**written conversation**). We will explore these techniques in detail in future chapters.

Right now, in your early writing practice, it's best to select just one technique and use it as the single approach to writing your first draft. Later on, with more writing experience, you might find that combining these techniques can help you better communicate your thoughts to your readers.

Like a lawyer needs a particular strategy for a specific case, or a choreographer needs a particular arrangement of movements to tell a specific story in dance, a writer needs a particular approach for a specific subject. In the planning stage, each writer has a goal in mind and chooses the method that will best fulfill it. In writing the first draft of your paragraph or paper, you'll want to choose the technique that will best implement your plan or outline. After you decide on one approach, before you type or write your title and topic sentence, write down your objective at the top of a blank piece of paper. Look at it frequently to serve as a reminder of your chosen technique or approach.

Below are some assignment objectives. On the blank lines, fill in the technique you think the writer will use. Choose from the following: telling stories (narration), drawing word pictures (description), giving meanings (definition), using examples (illustration), making categories (classification), showing similarities and differences (comparison and contrast), listing the steps (process), discussing reasons and results (cause and effect), influencing people (persuading and convincing), and dialogue (written conversation).

"Tell the story about Aunt Grace graduating from college." _____

"Make the paper vivid by drawing word pictures." _____

"Tell what the word *loyalty* really means to me." _____

"Give examples of the teacher's instructional methods." _____

"Divide the store's departments into categories, and write about each of them in turn."

_____

"Explain how Macintosh and PC computers are similar." _____

"Name each stage of construction in building a house and tell how long each one takes." _____

"Explain why Tony got himself evicted." _____

"Convince the reader that a Consumer Sales Tax should replace income taxes."

_____

"Pretend I'm five years old, talking with my mother about my first day at school."

_____

You'll be using all of these techniques in your book assignments, starting with storytelling. This brief introduction to the writing techniques will help you recognize them as they appear in later chapters.

> ### WHICH WRITING TECHNIQUE SHALL I USE IN MY PAPER?
>
> - Storytelling
> - Drawing word pictures
> - Giving meanings
> - Using examples
> - Making categories
> - Showing similarities and differences
> - Listing the steps
> - Discussing reasons and results
> - Influencing people
> - Using dialogue

4. PLAN A STRUCTURE

You've selected your topic, gathered the basic information to include, and determined the best writing technique for your paper. Now, whether for a paragraph or an essay, you want a framework, or plan, for what you're writing. Your plan should include these elements: a topic sentence that states what the paper will show; the necessary supporting information that provides the body of the paper and communicates your message to your reader; and your conclusion—the outcome of the facts in the paper. The structure shows where you'll put all the facts, details, examples, and other information that you'll be expanding into your fully written paper.

The Purpose of the Paper

Every written paper has a purpose—a reason for being written. It's not just about completing an assignment for an English class, and it's not just about telling everything you know about a topic. *The purpose of each paper is to reach a conclusion about particular information so that it can be readily understood by the readers.* The purpose of a paper is called the **thesis.** It's what you want to communicate about the topic. As we've said before, a writer states this clearly in the first paragraph of the paper.

The Topic Sentence

The main idea or reason for the paper is contained in the **topic sentence** in the first paragraph. This sentence is called the **thesis.** The topic sentence communicates clearly, in a nutshell, what the paper is about. For instance, the topic sentence or thesis in your paper would be a statement that would follow these words (but don't use them in your thesis sentence):

My paper will show or prove that _____.

"substance abuse has dire consequences."

"wearing a nose ring symbolizes my individuality."

"the greatest challenge of my life is raising my daughter."

Each of these sample topic sentences portrays *what that paper will be about.* Topic sentences are important because they tell the readers about the main substance of the material they will be digesting. Topic sentences usually start a paper, but in some situations they might require a sentence or two of introduction, as in the following example on page 40:

My mother raised three daughters and four sons while working full time. My father was of no help to her. He was a drug addict. Watching how his addiction ruined the life of his wife and almost wrecked the lives of his seven children became my best lesson in what not to do with my life. *Addiction can ruin not only your own life but the lives of the people who love you.*

A topic sentence should be as specific as possible because it sets the paper in motion. The topic sentence provides subject matter, scope, and direction. Every paragraph in your paper will relate to this statement.

In an essay, the first paragraph is always the introductory paragraph that contains the topic sentence, which expresses the thesis of your paper; the middle paragraphs contain the supporting information; and the final paragraph is the conclusion, or summary, paragraph. It is wise to plan this structure for your paper before you write it, using some type of outline.

Outlining

Outlining is like assembling the skeleton for your paper-to-be. The outline is the underlying form for the fully fleshed out, well-organized body of your writing effort. You create the structure of your paper by sorting your initial ideas into groups of items that relate to one another, in support of your main topic. There are three ways to outline: the **short-form outline** (using words or short phrases), the **sentence outline** (using complete sentences), and the **step-sheet** (using either clauses or sentences). Short-form and sentence outlines work equally well for most papers. The step-sheet is particularly useful in fiction writing and in papers that give step-by-step information.

In the *short-form outline,* the writer uses alternating numerical and alphabetical characters to itemize the topics and subtopics.

EXAMPLE OF THE SHORT-FORM OUTLINE FOR A FIVE-PARAGRAPH ESSAY

1. **Topic Paragraph**
   Topic Sentence: *Before starting to restore a classic automobile, you must determine every item that needs upgrading.*
2. **Engine restoration**
   a. Electrical system
   b. Fuel system
   c. Mechanical system
   d. Exhaust system
3. **Body**
   a. Repair of damaged metal
   b. Repair of windows
   c. Fender replacement
   d. Paint job
4. **Finishing touches**
   a. Undercarriage
      (1) Replacement of tires
      (2) Adjustment of wheels, bearings, and struts
   b. Interior
      (1) Upholstery
      (2) Header
      (3) Carpeting
      (4) AM/FM radio replacement

---

continued next page

Harcourt, Inc.

5. Summary
  a. Priorities for repair
  b. Priorities for replacement

In the *sentence outline,* the writer uses one or more full sentences for each paragraph of the essay-to-be, later building upon them and adding to them as the paper is being written.

EXAMPLE OF THE SENTENCE OUTLINE FOR A FIVE-PARAGRAPH PAPER

1. Topic Paragraph
Topic sentence: *Before starting to restore your classic automobile, you must determine every item that needs upgrading.* The way to determine this is to look at the different parts of the automobile: the engine, the body, the undercarriage, and the interior. Then you have to determine the priorities.

2. The Engine Paragraph
Since the most important part of any automobile is the engine, without which it wouldn't move, the first set of problems I must consider are the electrical, fuel, mechanical, and exhaust systems.
First, I'll inspect the electrical system—the battery, ignition, generator, lights, fuses, gauges, AM/FM radio, and wiring.
Next, I'll troubleshoot the fuel system—the carburetor, then the fuel injector, and then the lines from the gas tank and around the engine.
To determine the extent of repair needed for the mechanical system—the engine, pistons, rings, drive shaft, and all movable parts will have to be taken apart.

3. The Body (expanded with sentences)
4. All Other Restorations Needed (expanded with sentences)
5. Conclusion (in sentences)
NOTE: Paragraphs three and four will follow the same format as for paragraph two. The outline for the fifth (or final) paragraph will contain the writer's conclusions and summary.

The *short-form outline* leads the writer through each point he or she wishes to make. The *sentence outline* provides start-up sentences to get the writing flowing. Either outline, done well, will result in a thorough and orderly paper.

 From the Sports section. *Long sentences often contain many errors, and they are confusing. This run-on sentence has a wrong verb form and a pronoun with no clear antecedent. We show one way to rephrase the sentence. On a piece of paper, write another way to state XX's meaning.*

"The guy did a great job for us," [XX] said. "There have been a lot of dramatic things happen in Cleveland the last five or six years and he was part of it."
Sample rephrasing: *A lot of dramatic things have happened in Cleveland in the last five or six years, and he was a part of the action.*

The *step-sheet* differs from a typical paragraph-by-paragraph outline. There are no rules in the step-sheet outlining method. Some writers include a great deal of detail; others use brief descriptions of ideas that will generate sentences in their minds when they write a first draft. The main difference is that items on a step-sheet are listed in steps in the exact order as the action in the paper will happen. Novel writers and storytellers quite often use a step-sheet to control their stories by describing the steps or incidents in the exact order as they imagine them happening. However, a step-sheet can be useful if you're writing about an experience you observed, such as an automobile accident, or about a process like making spaghetti. The purpose of a step-sheet is to keep events in the same order as they actually did or could happen. A logical sequence of steps provides a good guide for what you will write.

EXAMPLE OF STEP-SHEETING FOR FICTION

Marie meets Juan in algebra class at Hamilton High School.
M&J do homework together in library after school.
M watches J practice football.
M attends J's games.
M sees J break leg.
M carries J's books and helps him get to class.
J asks M to Senior Prom.
M's parents don't have money for dress.
Marie and mom get beautiful dress at Salvation Army store.
M gocs to prom with J.
Happy ending.

Step-sheeting shows a series of causes and effects that progress until the story's told. With a step-sheet, each clause will trigger sentences that develop into paragraphs that result in an interesting story with a satisfying ending. Once you have your outline or step-sheet, you're ready to begin writing your first draft.

ClassWorks!   *In-Class Assignment*

Prepare a five-paragraph *short-form* outline or *sentence* outline for an essay on this topic: "The Unmet Needs of the Students at My College."

Look at the thoughts you organized with the prewriting technique you used. Put the topic sentence that you wrote on the prewriting exercise at the top of your paper to help you focus on the purpose of your outline.

---

5. PREPARE THE FIRST DRAFT

Too many college students use their worst high school habits, such as writing an English paper the night before—or the same day—it's to be turned in. They don't perform the prewriting activities recommended in this book and in most college textbooks. They don't even identify a specific topic sentence, prepare a plan or outline, or have a technique in

 From the Sports section. *The writer seems to have forgotten about the other forty-nine states, and look how far the modifying phrase is from the pronoun it modifies! Rewrite the following long sentence, correcting the error and making it read more smoothly. One example is shown below. You might try using two sentences.*

[XX] had turned down opportunities to play overseas in hopes that another chance would come in the United State, waiting mostly in his native Montana for a call.

Example: *In his native state of Montana, [XX] waited for another chance to play for a United States team. Meanwhile, he turned down opportunities to play overseas.*

mind. They just sit down, write a paragraph or a string of paragraphs, and give the paper to their teacher. This is how papers full of bonehead mistakes are produced.

The whole idea of completing a polished, college-level assignment is to learn the proper sequences for the entire writing endeavor, from first idea to finished product. Preparation, germination (the sprouting seed of an idea), and development are equally important to a landscaper, an athlete, a successful shop owner, a fashion designer, a pediatric nurse, and a maintenance engineer. Success comes to those who have prepared well. Good preparation is *essential* to performing well.

Your first draft should contain all the main ideas you've collected and should follow the outline or step-sheet you've created. Your first paragraph will introduce your topic; paragraphs in the body of your paper will support the topic; and your last paragraph will summarize what you want your reader to learn from your creation. It's important to have a summary paragraph that ends the story or provides the reader with a satisfactory conclusion to the piece you've written.

The first draft is considered a "rough" draft. It's the initial version of what will eventually become your finished project—your third, or final, draft. Since the ideas are flowing out of your mind and you're putting them into sentence form, you may misplace a comma or omit or misspell words. Don't worry about that now. You want your ideas to flow easily. If English is not your first language, you might even include phrases in your native tongue that later you'll have to use a dictionary to translate. That's fine. Maybe your ideas come to you in very simple words, and you'll need a thesaurus to find the words you really want to use. Deal with that later, too. This is the time when you're releasing an outpouring of creative thought from your mind onto paper.

For now, think of yourself as a river, and of your overflow of ideas as a waterfall cascading down a mountain, landing in the deep pool that represents the paper you're writing. Don't stop that river of ideas from flowing. Remember, this is *your* original creation. This document cannot exist unless *you*—with your personal experience and knowledge, and the special way in which you express yourself—write it.

TIPS FOR REVISING DRAFTS

- Use a dictionary.
- Look for fragments and run-on sentences.
- Emphasize your major points.
- Be objective. Pretend you're the reader instead of the writer.

You can see typical first and second drafts on the following pages. The first draft shows editing notes, indicating changes to be made when the paper is revised (rewritten). The second draft has been revised and shows more editing notes for the final revision. The student's assignment was to write an autobiographical essay. As you pay attention to the paper through its drafts, you'll see that the big eight boneheads disappear.

Penalosa, Chad W.
10-28#5
First Draft Personal Story
Feb. 3, 1999

Title?

I have always ~~been one who~~ made drastic moves or decision without thinking about the consequences *(they)* ~~it~~ may cause. For me, what I sow I would reap. ~~It was~~ One sunny September day, ~~that~~ I made one of those decision, a major decision that would change my whole life. As I put on my wedding dress, doubts rushed through my mind. Would I regret this all my life, or would it be the life I'd always wanted? ~~I could talk to~~ No one *could help me* ~~every one around me was busy~~, besides I fell in love with my husband-to-be in such a short time, why would I need to hesitate now? I'd made my decision then. I knew that this was it. It was time to finally grow up and be an adult.

? As the strains of the wedding song filled the chapel, white roses garnered every corner, and candles *flickered* on the altar, I felt mixed emotions. It was the beginning of a new life for me, and scene from my past life flashed through my mind, *of* my childhood and my carefree life as a young adult. Yes, all this would change in just a few minutes, but it didn't seem to bother me. ~~all~~ I knew ~~was~~ that what I was doing was right. I was handed to my husband, and *he smiled* as he took my hand. All doubts were shed from my mind ~~he smiled at me~~ I knew then ~~everything would be okay and~~ that I could put my life into his hands ~~we would share life together side by side~~. The reverend talked about the importance of sharing life together as "one body, one soul" but still as two individuals.

~~Hands joined together and~~ Staring into my husband's eyes, I realized how much I loved him and that he now represented my future, ~~he would be~~ my inspiration to succeed, as well as the greatest love of my life. We made our vows, promising to be there through life's challenges and trials, ~~and~~ through happiness and tears.

Finally, as we sealed our vows with a kiss, I felt one journey had ended and another *had* began. New challenges would come along ~~I know~~, ~~and~~ *but* though ~~as young as~~ we may be *young*, we will pass each day, sharing life like we vowed. ~~I know~~ Nothing can hinder us from succeeding in our new ~~found~~ life together. Though we still have ~~such~~ a long way ahead of us, who needs to worry, we will always be each other's comfort *during* ~~at~~ life's greatest surprises.

Penalosa, Chad W.
English 28 - 10:00 a.m.
Group 5 - Assignment p. 69
Second Draft Personal Story
February 5, 1999

Sandcastles for Dreams

I have always made drastic moves or decisions without thinking about the consequences. One sunny September day, I made one of those decisions, a major decision that would change my whole life. As I put on my wedding dress, doubts rushed through my mind. Would I regret this all my life, or would it be the life I always *dreamed about* ~~wanted? I could talk to no one,~~ My family was not with me, ~~to comfort or ease my doubts~~ *to comfort me or* nor was anyone around to ease the turmoil of emotions that ~~brought this~~ *caused the* confusion inside me. ~~But~~ I fell in love with my husband-to-be in such a short time, Why would I hesitate now? I may be young, but I knew ~~it~~ in my heart I had already made the right decision. It was finally time to grow up and be an adult!

As the strains of the wedding song filled *the* chapel, the white roses and immaculate candles on the altar brought a wave of mixed emotions, sadness, joy, longing, and excitement. ~~But~~ More so, ~~it~~ *they* brought on love. It was the beginning of a new life for me. My childhood and carefree life as a young adult would be behind me in just a few minutes, but I knew I was doing something right. ~~I was handed to my husband and,~~ As *my husband* ~~he~~ took my hand, all doubts disappeared from my mind. He smiled at me, and I knew that I could put my life into his hands. The reverend talked about the importance of our new roles as "one body, one soul" but still as two different individuals. In my husband's eyes lay the promise of a bright future. A great surge of love warmed my whole being. ~~He now represents my inspiration to succeed, as well as~~ *for* the greatest love of my life. We made our vows, promising to be there through life's challenges and trials, and through all that represented*s* love and happiness.

Finally, as we sealed our vows with a kiss, *our* ~~one~~ journey ~~had ended; another journey~~ *together* began. We will encounter ~~more~~ *many* challenges along the way, ~~and young as we may be,~~ *but* we will pass each day side by side. People may insist that *the* dreams we make are but sandcastles easily washed *away* by the tides of time. I'm confident ~~we~~ *my husband and I* can prove all of them wrong. Though we ~~may~~ have a long way ahead of us, *we will* always have each other to share life's greatest surprises.

OK

BASIC EDITING NOTATIONS

You can use these marks to edit your own paper to make it easier to revise. You can also use them to edit the "boneheads" throughout this book.
Note: You will find examples of these marks in the edited drafts of Chad Penalosa's paper.

¶   Start new paragraph
^   Insert the letter, word, phrase, or sentence written above.
To show a misspelled word: either cross out the word and write the correct spelling above, or circle the word and write Sp? above (meaning, check the spelling).
To show that you want to move something: circle it and draw an arrow from there to where you want to move it.
To show that you want to omit something in the next draft: draw a line through it.

---

6. PREPARE THE SECOND DRAFT

The first task a writer has in preparing a second draft is **editing** the first draft; that is, marking corrections, deletions, and additions to the material on the first draft. If you don't know where to start, have someone helpful read your paper, or read it aloud yourself and hear what needs to be changed. Some English classes are organized into study groups or teams, and first drafts can be shared with members of the group. Before the paper is even turned in, misspelled words can be corrected, sentences that don't make sense or that sound awkward can be fixed, and ideas can be clarified and expanded. There's nothing wrong with getting someone else's opinion about your paper. That's not cheating. Writing is meant to be read and understood. It's still your paper, and you're still in charge of its final content and appearance. Be selective about making the changes others suggest; you can't please everyone, and you must remain true to your best instincts.

One of the reasons a draft should be double-spaced is to allow room for the writer to make **editing** notations, showing where to correct spelling and to add or rearrange words. As you prepare a new draft of your paper, adding your new ideas or changing your organization, you **revise,** or rewrite it. The second draft provides the opportunity to correct any mistakes you might have made in the first draft and to add new elements that will improve your paper.

- Use the dictionary to look up *any words that might be misspelled or misused.*
- Make sure you've avoided the big eight bonehead grammar mistakes, especially the two most common ones: *sentence fragments* and *run-ons.* A fragment is an incomplete thought punctuated as a sentence. A run-on is a sentence with too many topics or incorrect punctuation of multiple complete thoughts. These two errors can really mess up an otherwise well-written paper.
- Rethink your main points and decide if you've expressed them clearly. You can add, drop, or rearrange information.
- Try and look at the paper from a reader's standpoint rather than a writer's. Does the title make me want to read the paper? Is the topic sentence clear? Does the support of the main idea make sense, and does the organization carry me from point to point? Is everything in the paper essential to the main idea and to its purpose? Is the paper interesting? If not, why not? How can it be made better?

Write your second draft using the notations, corrections, and additions on the first draft to guide you. Include more new thoughts as you type the paper.

THE BIG EIGHT BONEHEADS!

- Words Misspelled
- Words or Caps Incorrect
- Sentence Fragments
- Sentence Run-Ons, Spliced or Fused
- Pronouns Confused
- Verbs Misused
- Commas Misplaced
- Apostrophes Abused

From the Sports section. *They were, was it?! Rewrite the awkward sentence, making the verb agree with the subject.*

An upset in the NCAA track and field competition were quickly forgotten by Amy Acuff in the USA championships.

_____

_____

_____

7. PREPARE AND SUBMIT THE FINAL DRAFT

Read over the second draft. Do you have any new thoughts to add to the paper? Does it flow well as you read it? Are the transitions (movements from thought to thought) clear and smooth between different times and places or from subtopic to subtopic? Do your descriptions of people, places, and things provide mental images? Do your verbs and adverbs project the action that is occurring? Are there any grammatical problems? Share your paper with a classmate, parent, or member of your class writing team. Ask the people who read it if it holds their interest. Ask if they have any ideas for further improvement.

The third or final version of your writing on a particular topic still may not be a masterpiece, but it should represent your best effort. If you've followed the initial steps carefully, you should have produced an interesting, well-organized, and *almost* mistake-free paragraph or essay. If you do this for every assignment, you can't help but succeed in your English class. More important, the skills you learn will carry you through the writing requirements in the world of work.

A properly formatted final-draft paper should look something like the student-written paper on the next page. You can see in the final version that a good paper that fulfills the assignment doesn't just *happen.*

Note: Assignments are to be submitted in double-spaced format, like the following essay.

Chad Penalosa is working on her nursing degree and is still as happily married as she was on her wedding day, which she writes about in the student paper on page 48.

Harcourt, Inc.

```
Penalsoa, Chad W.
Eng. 28-10:00a.m., Group 5
Assignment p. 69
Personal Story
February 7, 1999

                    Sandcastles for Dreams


     I have always made drastic moves or decisions without
thinking about the consequences. One sunny September day, I
made one of those decisions, a major decision that would
change my whole life. As I put on my wedding dress, doubts
rushed through my mind. Would I regret this all my life, or
would it be the life I've always dreamed about? My family
was not with me, nor was anyone around to comfort me or ease
the turmoil of emotions that caused the confusion inside me.
I fell in love with my husband-to-be in such a short time,
why would I hesitate now? I may be young, but I knew in my
heart I had already made the right decision. It was finally
time to grow up and be an adult!
     As the strains of the wedding song filled the chapel,
the white roses and immaculate candles on the altar brought
a wave of mixed emotions—sadness, joy, longing, and
excitement. More so, they brought on love. It was the
beginning of a new life for me. My childhood and carefree
life as a young adult would be behind me in just a few
minutes, but I knew I was doing something right. As my
husband took my hand, all doubts disappeared from my mind.
He smiled at me, and I knew that I could put my life into
his hands. In my husband's eyes lay the promise of a bright
future. A great surge of love warmed my whole being for the
greatest love of my life. The reverend talked about the
importance of our new roles as "one body, one soul" but
still as two different individuals. We made our vows,
promising to be there through life's challenges and trials,
and through all that represents love and happiness. Finally,
as we sealed our vows with a kiss, our journey together
began. We will encounter many challenges along the way, but
we will pass each day side by side.
     People may insist that the dreams we make are but
sandcastles easily washed away by the tides of time. I'm
confident my husband and I can prove all of them wrong.
Though we may have a long way ahead of us, we will always
have each other to share life's greatest surprises.
```

FORMATTING PAPERS

Following directions shows attention to detail, cooperation, and maturity, and it saves time. To complete an assignment and receive a grade on it, you must turn in a paper that complies with the instructions for the exercise—and turn it in on time. Understanding instructions is the responsibility of the student.

Whether you write in longhand or on a typewriter or computer, there's a universally accepted format for English assignments. This format prepares you for future written assignments in the world beyond college. The following items are necessary for a well-formatted paper.

Note: A "two-page paper" means two *typed, double-spaced* pages. A full page of text will contain 250 to 275 words. A 500-word assignment should consist of about two typed pages, properly formatted as specified below.

FORMAT FOR ALL HOMEWORK ASSIGNMENTS

- An acceptable paper is *typed* on 8-½-by-11-inch white paper, on one side only.
- Use a normal type style and size (called the font). A common computer font is Times New Roman regular, 12 point.
- There should be one-inch margins at the top, bottom, and sides of each page.
- In the upper left corner of the first page, put a single-spaced block. On four separate lines, put your name, the class name and time (and your group number, if applicable), the assignment page number, and the date.
- Double-space the rest of the paper. "Double-spacing" means there is a blank line after each line of typing (or handwriting).
- About one-fourth of the way down the page, center the title. You may capitalize all the letters in all the words of the title. Otherwise, capitalize the first and last words, all nouns, verbs, adverbs, adjectives, and prepositions of five or more letters. Either of the following is correct:

WRITTEN ON THE WIND or Written on the Wind.

- Double-space twice to begin the body of the paper.
- Indent every paragraph at least one-half inch but no more than one inch. (Do not double-space twice between paragraphs.)
- Number the pages at the top right, except for the first page, which doesn't need a number.

PROPER PAPER FORMAT

Type on white 8-½-by-11-inch paper.
Use one-inch margins and normal font.
Put name, class, time, assignment, and date in upper left corner.
Center title one-fourth of the way down the paper.
Double-space text and indent paragraphs.
Number the pages.
Count the words to be sure they're about equal to the amount of words assigned.

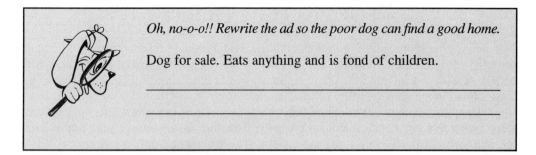

Oh, no-o-o!! Rewrite the ad so the poor dog can find a good home.

Dog for sale. Eats anything and is fond of children.

_____

_____

REVIEW OF THE STEPS THAT LEAD TO GOOD PAPERS

Following the seven steps in this chapter will help you produce strong papers. This review condenses the steps and puts them together so that you can easily refer to them while you're practicing the writing techniques.

SUGGESTED PREWRITING FORMAT

1. **Have a topic.** When selecting your topic, be sure it fulfills the exercise. You are responsible for understanding the assignment, so read the topic or question carefully.
2. **Gather basic information.** Use the one *prewriting method* that is easiest and most comfortable for you and works best for the assignment: *freewriting, brainstorming, clustering or mapping,* or *5 Ws and an H.*
3. **Decide on a writing technique.** Choose the best approach to writing your paper: telling stories *(narration)*, drawing word pictures *(description)*, giving meanings *(definition)*, using examples *(illustration)*, making categories *(classification)*, showing similarities and differences *(comparison and contrast)*, listing the steps *(process)*, discussing reasons and results *(cause* and *effect)*, influencing people *(persuading and convincing)*, or dialogue *(written conversation)*.
4. **Plan a structure.** Put the *purpose* of the paper into words. What is it you want to communicate about the topic to the reader? Write your *topic sentence,* the one sentence that tells the reader what your paper is about. Keep this in mind as you write your paper. Organize the ideas you want to include in your paper, using one of these methods: *short-form outline, sentence outline,* or *step-sheet outline.* Just as you need a map to drive around a large metropolitan city, you need a plan for your paper.

SUGGESTED DRAFTING PROCESS

1. **Prepare the first draft.** Follow your plan for writing your paper.
2. **Prepare the second draft.** Edit the first draft paper to indicate sentence structure problems, spelling, and punctuation changes. To prepare the second draft, revise the paper according to the editing notes you have made on the first draft.
3. **Prepare and submit the final draft.** Edit the second draft paper for overall organization, content, clarity, purpose, and for spelling and grammar mistakes. Give it your best effort. This is the draft you'll turn in to fulfill the assignment.

MENTAL CHECKLIST FOR PAPERS

In preparing your final draft, ask yourself the following questions.

Is my paper visual?
Yes, I have included word pictures that the reader can see in the mind's eye.

Harcourt, Inc.

Does the paper express my real feelings and opinions?
Yes, my own individual writer's voice comes through.

Do the details and facts lead the reader to understand my purpose, or is the paper too general?
I make my point clearly and include enough specific information to support it.

Is the dialogue appropriate? Would it (or does it) help my story?
I have dramatized the paper with some written conversation to make it more interesting.

Is the entire paper focused?
Yes, everything in the paper contributes to the point I'm trying to make.

Have I set the stage properly and given the necessary background?
Yes, I have answered the reader's questions as to who, what, where, when, why, and how.

ORGANIZATION IS THE KEY TO SUCCESS

When you organize your writing assignments according to the steps in this chapter, you'll create final drafts that will prompt satisfactory answers to the above questions. You'll be successful in this course and, more important, in the writing required in your future career.

Note: The authors believe students will find it worthwhile at this point to read chapter 12, Writing Standards for Developmental English. This chapter explains how instructors evaluate writing and determine grades.

Knowing what instructors look for gives students inside information that will help their writing significantly. Chapter 12 describes typical expectations in six areas of evaluation for student papers: significance of topic; organization and support of the topic; sentence use and structure; word use and vocabulary; use of outside sources; and English grammar.

GRAMMARWORKS! I. The Very Basics: Parts of Speech

SHE (PRONOUN) LOVES (VERB) SPINACH (NOUN).

NOUN	A *person* (**girl, mayor, Val Kilmer**), *place* (**Reno, stadium, beach**), *thing* (**book, dog, video**), or *idea* (**love, glamour, democracy**).
PRONOUN	A *substitute* for a noun. ***Subjective Pronouns:*** **I, you, he, she, it, we they. *Objective Pronouns:* me, you, him, her, it, us, them.**
VERB	Expresses *action or state of being* in the present (**give, eat**), past (**played, has gone**), or future (**will work, should be able**).
ADJECTIVE	*Describes a noun or pronoun.* **Kind** face, **blue** hat, **nice** car, **old** wallet, **funny** joke.
ADVERB	*Describes a verb* (leave **soon**, run **fast**), *adjective* (**bright** red, **quite** nervous), or other *adverb* (**very slowly, pretty far**).
PREPOSITION	*Introduces a phrase* that modifies another word in the sentence. **Over** his head, **before** dawn, **off** the road, **up** the tree, **in** the ocean, **out** the door.
	When the *object* of the preposition is a pronoun, *always* use an *objective* pronoun: **me, you, him, her, it, us, them.** Say: Sue was with **him** and **me** (or with **us**). Not: Sue was with **he** and **I** (or with **we**). **GrammarTool:** *Think plural!*

Harcourt, Inc.

GRAMMARWORKS! I. The Very Basics: Parts of Speech (continued)

CONJUNCTION   *Connects* two or more words, phrases, or clauses.
Jan **and** I went to Phoenix, **but** she did the driving **while** I slept **or** read.

ARTICLE   *Determines* whether a noun is specific **(the)** or nonspecific **(a, an).**
The box/**a** box, **the** man/**a** man, **the** orange/**an** orange.

The (article) **silly** (adjective) **girl** (noun) **really** (adverb) **loves** (verb) **very** (adverb) **fresh** (adjective) **and** (conjunction) **green** (adjective) **spinach** (noun) **on** (preposition) **her** (adjective) **ice cream** (noun).

Below each word in the following sentences, write the name for its part of speech. Select from noun, (noun), pronoun (pron.), verb, adjective (adj.), adverb (adv.), preposition (prep.), conjunction (conj.), or article (art.). You may use the abbreviations shown in the parentheses.

Example:	Raoul	met	his	brother	at	the	store.
	Noun	*verb*	*adj.*	*noun*	*prep.*	*art.*	*noun*

1. They   put   the   brown   bags   on   the   table.

2. Lois   and   I   cooked   dinner   for   everybody.

3. Roy   never   ever   eats   red   meat   or   cheese.

GRAMMARWORKS! II. The Very Basics: Parts of a Sentence

THE CLERK **(SUBJECT)** QUICKLY PUT **(PREDICATE)** EACH OF MY TEN ITEMS **(OBJECT)** ONTO THE SCANNER **(PREPOSITIONAL PHRASE),** WHICH DETECTS THE PRICES **(DEPENDENT CLAUSE).**

SUBJECT   *Topic* of the sentence: usually a noun **(Grace)**, a pronoun **(She)**, or a phrase consisting of the topic word and all its modifiers **(The efficient clerk).***

When the *subject* of the sentence is a pronoun, *always* use a *subjective* pronoun: **I, you, he, she, it, we, they, who.** Say: **He** and **I (we)** went. Not: **Me** and **him (us)** went. **GrammarTool:** *Think plural!*

PREDICATE   A verb and the words used to describe the *action* **(moved very quickly).**

OBJECT   A noun **(groceries)**, pronoun **(them)**, or phrase **(each of my items)** that *receives the action* of a verb.

When the *object* of the sentence is a pronoun, *always* use an *objective* pronoun: **me, you, him, her, it, us, them, whom.** Say: Jason saw **him** and **me (us).** Not: Jason saw **he** and **I (we). GrammarTool:** *Think plural!*

PHRASE   A *group of words* **[onto the scanner]** that enhances the meaning of another word. (The phrase in the brackets begins with a preposition.)

*****Modifiers** include articles, adjectives, and adverbs, which modify, or describe, words in sentences. (Refer to the preceding GrammarWorks on Parts of Speech.)

GRAMMARWORKS! II. The Very Basics:
Parts of a Sentence (continued)

CLAUSE	A *group of words that contains a subject and a predicate* [**which de-tected the prices**]. An *independent clause* is a complete thought and can stand alone as a sentence. A *dependent clause* is not a complete thought; it is a sentence fragment and cannot stand alone. (The clause in brackets, which begins with the word **which,** is a dependent clause.)

The silly girl (subject) **really loves** (predicate) **very fresh and green spinach** (object) **on her ice cream** (prepositional phrase), **which is usually chocolate** (dependent clause).

Below the words or groups of words in the following paragraph, identify their parts in the sentences: subject, predicate, object, phrase, independent clause, or dependent clause.

Example: At the store   where he was buying steaks,
　　　　　　Phrase　　　　　*dependent clause*
　　　　Raoul　　met　　Roy and Lois.
　　　　subject　　predicate　　　object

He　　invited　　them　　for dinner　　at our house,　　and they said yes.

The guys　brought　the food　into the kitchen.　Lois and I　made　dinner,

but Lois only ate the salad.　The guys,　who are always hungry,　were glad

because there was more for them!

Chapter 3

LOOKING WITHIN

IN THIS CHAPTER

PERSONAL STORY—AUTOBIOGRAPHY

STUDENT PAPER
"Nightmare in Hollywood" by Connie A. Coleman

PROFESSIONAL ARTICLE
"A Scrappy Entrepreneur" by Sharon Nelton

GRAMMARWORKS!
Many Kinds of Pronouns

GRAMMARWORKS!
Pronoun/Antecedent Agreement

FIXING A BONEHEAD PERSONAL STORY
"I Want to Do What I Love to Do" by Eloise Lookingood

Harcourt, Inc.

"I am the master of my fate:
I am the captain of my soul."

—"INVICTUS" BY W. H. HENLEY

PERSONAL STORY—AUTOBIOGRAPHY

OUR FAVORITE TOPIC—OURSELVES!

By now, we hope, you are eager to start writing! You'll get your feet wet by first writing about yourself. The above quotation is from a poem. Poetry quite often tells a **personal story.** In "Invictus," Henley tells that he is proud of himself for standing up to the trials of his life. Not all stories or poems written in the first person are autobiographical. Autobiography isn't a technique in itself. In writing about ourselves, we can utilize various techniques, but one feature distinguishes autobiography from all other writing: If *I* am writing the story, and it is about *me,* and I use first-person pronouns *(I, me, we, us, etc.),* that's **autobiography.** *Auto-* means self; *bio-* means life; and *-graphy* means writing. (A *biography* is about *someone else's* life.) Besides poetry, there are many other opportunities for writing about ourselves.

DIARIES AND JOURNALS

Two examples of autobiography are diaries and journals. A **diary** is usually a private, handwritten personal account of day-to-day events (such as *The Diary of Anne Frank,* written by a young victim of the genocide of Adolph Hitler). A **journal** often records things someone needs to remember (like names and impressions of places visited). Both diaries and journals can include experiences, feelings, and observations. "Putting it in writing" helps us focus on what we really feel. When we are hurt or angry, afraid or confused, writing about it helps us settle down and get our true feelings out. These "personal history books" are stories of one's growth and change. When older people reminisce, they often express regret for not having kept journals or diaries that recorded the personal experiences and world events of their lifetimes.

LIFE STORIES AND PERSONAL ESSAYS

Most of us think about ourselves or talk about ourselves quite a lot, but when it comes time to *write* about ourselves—we can't think of a thing to say. Your autobiography may be a **story** about what you've done or are going to do or an **essay** about what you think. Don't let your profound thoughts or brilliant observations slip away! Write a **personal essay** about whatever thrills you, amuses you, or makes you madder than a bad night's sleep. Remember that lesson you learned as a child that you like to tell your friends? Write down that **personal story.** You have a lot to say, and now's a fine time to start.

There are a few helpful guidelines for writing personal stories. Autobiographies are traditionally written in the **first person,** making full use of the first-person pronouns *I, me, my, mine, we, us, our, ours,* and so forth. They often include **dialogue** (written conversation), so you'll use quotation marks and follow the rules for dialogue punctuation. (We'll study quotation marks later, but you can consult the GrammarWorks! in chapter 10 now or whenever you want help with writing dialogue or writing quotations.) All set? Share your life! Have fun!

The following pages show examples of student and professional personal stories.

Harcourt, Inc.

The student author's assignment: Write an autobiographical essay. *Connie Coleman recently retired from the Los Angeles Metropolitan Transit System. He returned to school to complete his training as a cabinetmaker, which his responsibilities as a husband and father of three had interrupted in 1985.*

Coleman 1

Connie A. Coleman
Eng. 28-8:00
Autobiography
Aug. 26, 1999

Nightmare in Hollywood

What started out as a normal day in the life of a bus driver suddenly became something as suspenseful as the movie *Psycho*. It was my time of day, 4:00 in the morning. The street lights shone brightly, and the moon looked as close as if you could reach out and touch it. At that time of the morning, there isn't much traffic. The only thing on the streets were the stray pets, walking aimlessly. All was very peaceful.

My route, which began in Woodland Hills at the west edge of the San Fernando Valley, went through Hollywood and terminated in Inglewood. I started picking up familiar faces along the way, some smiling and speaking, others still half asleep, heading to their seats for a last doze before their stop. I liked that time of the morning because that was my personal time. I was in my own world, with no questions to answer, no traffic in my way—nothing to do except dream about retiring.

I arrived early at my stop at the corner of Hollywood Boulevard and Highland Avenue. I was waiting for the departure time, sipping my coffee and loading a few passengers, when something ahead caught my attention. I stared out the huge windshield, and I could just make out two figures running toward me in the middle of the street. They were four or five short blocks away, running in and out of the bright street lights. They ran very slowly, as if they had been running for some time. I was mesmerized by their behavior, as if I were watching a movie, and I couldn't take my eyes off them. They seemed to be playing tag. They would fall down, as if one was tackling the other, and then they would get up and start running again. This happened five or six times as they kept coming closer.

Finally I could see the two men clearly, in the headlights of the bus. They'd stopped running, breathing as if they had just completed the Los Angeles marathon. The sweat shone on their foreheads, and their clothes were dirty and torn. One of the men looked at me through the window, as if he needed help; the other man, standing straight and upright, stared at the anxious man angrily. The angry man was dressed in black, with a ski cap on his head. To my amazement, he held a very large and dangerous-looking knife in his hand. I became very concerned for the safety of my passengers at this time. I shifted gears and started to move the bus into the street when the other man screamed. "Please don't leave! He's going to kill me!"

His life was in my hands, and I had to make a decision. The tone and the fear in his voice made my heart feel mercy, but what about my passengers? I kept expecting someone to yell, "Open the door and let him in!" But no one on the bus seemed to be aware of what was happening. I felt as though I were alone at the movies. The only sound I heard was my own heart beating slowly, ever so slowly, waiting for something to happen. I finally made up my mind.

Cautiously and quickly, I opened the doors. To my surprise, only the man who had screamed for me to stop climbed aboard. The other man just watched us roll away. My new passenger took a seat close to the front of the bus, without uttering a word, as though there had been nothing wrong. I could feel his sense of comfort in his breathing. I slowly proceeded down Highland, leaving behind that dark, cold, fearsome experience.

As I glanced at him, the man seemed disoriented, tired, and relieved. After a few blocks, he said, "Thank you." I asked him if he was hurt, and he answered, "No." He made a call from a tiny cell phone and told me the police were on their way. Then he asked to be let out at Melrose to wait for the officers. Concerned for his safety, I urged him to stay on the bus a little longer, but he insisted he would be all right. I gave him the necessary information to contact my company in case I would be needed as a witness, or for any other assistance. As he exited the bus, I still wanted to help in some way, but I had to keep on schedule for my passengers, so I continued on my route. The whole day I could think only about what had happened.

Months later, I was contacted by my superiors and directed to appear in court concerning this incident, as a witness for the prosecution. The lawyers representing my company briefed me about what to expect when I gave my testimony. I sat in the back of the courtroom, but before I was called upon, the accused man pleaded guilty. I learned he

Harcourt, Inc.

Coleman 3

had been caught with the weapon by the police and had told
them he was despondent and emotionally distraught because his
fiancée had broken off their engagement. I left the courtroom,
knowing nothing would happen to the attacker, except
probation.

While walking to my car, I saw the man who had been
attacked. I walked up to him and asked if he knew me. He said
he did not remember me, and I said, "I'm the bus driver who
let you on the bus."

He took my hand and shook it firmly. "You saved my life,"
he said.

I felt good about being able to help another person.
"It's just another day in the life of a bus driver," I said.
I smiled and walked away.

WORK! WORK! WORK!

These exercises help build skills by prompting you to express your understanding of what you read.

Reading Comprehension

1. What does Connie mean when he writes that he likes the early morning hours because "that was my personal time"? _____

_____

2. Why didn't the assailant get on the bus? _____

_____

3. At what point did the author best exhibit his own personal standards? _____

_____

4. Have you ever had a extraordinary experience when using public transportation or any terrifying, "unreal" experience? Discuss. _____

_____

Writing Analysis

1. How can you tell this is an autobiographical story? Who is the narrator? _____

_____

2. What is the topic sentence of the essay? _____

_____

3. What writing "twist" did the author use to tie the beginning of the essay to the concluding paragraph? _____

_____

From the directions on a massage chair. *These instructions have quite a few boneheads. Circle and correct the three spelling mistakes, insert punctuation in the run-on sentence, and rewrite sentence 3 so the subject agrees with the introductory phrase.*

1. NOT RECOMMENDED FOR USE BY CHILDREN UNDER AGE 14 OR THE PHISICALLY DISABLED.
2. Do not put your hands or feet under the seat cushion and your pet is not allowed under the seat.
3. When changing the angle of the controller, a creaky sound may be head, but it is not a breakdown.
4. NO MEDICAL CLAMES ARE WARRANTED OR IMPLIED BY THE USE OF THIS PRODUCT.

_____

_____

In the following professional article, the writer supplements biographical information with autobiographical quotations from the person being interviewed.

A Scrappy Entrepreneur
by Sharon Nelton

recycle

When Marsha Serlin started United Scrap Metal, Inc., nineteen years ago, she did so with $200, a rented truck charged to her Sears card, and a sense—passed down from her father—that she could do anything she wanted to.

"I never knew I had a limit," says Serlin,

As it turned out, her father was right. Today, United Scrap, in Cicero, Ill., has 120 employees, more than 600 pieces of equipment, and annual revenues exceeding $40 million. And Serlin has become, if not a household name, a widely recognized figure in the world of small business. Last year she was named National Small Business Subcontractor of the Year by the U.S. Small Business Administration.

She is the first woman to win the subcontractor award, the thirtieth of which was given this year.

After years of keeping a low profile and getting customers by word of mouth, Serlin had hoped the publicity would bring the company more business. Instead, she got a marriage proposal and, she says, "a hundred calls from investment counselors and insurance salesmen."

Whoever coined the word "gutsy" must have had someone like Serlin in mind. Twenty years ago she had two small children, a marriage that would soon fall apart, and a small houseplant-installation business that she operated out of her home in Northbrook, Ill. "It was a thriving, nice little business, but not enough to support me," says Serlin.

She recalls that one of her male clients always seemed to be at home, which Serlin found unusual. She asked him what he did for a living, thinking that whatever it was, it "couldn't be a bad business—because this guy was never at work."

She learned that he was in the scrap business, and she decided that if she ever really needed money, that's the business she would go into.

When that time came, she called the client and said, "Teach me everything you know in twenty-four hours."

He agreed to help, but she was so naive, she says, that she showed up at his scrapyard wearing "a strapless sundress with a little jacket and a pair of sandals." These days she wears blue jeans, steel-toed boots, and a hard hat.

Serlin began knocking on doors of firms that might have scrap to sell, and she resold what she collected to larger scrap dealers. She soon found herself working sixteen hours a day six days a week and spending the seventh day doing paperwork.

It took her three years to work up the courage to ask her mentor what she was doing wrong. Why, she wondered, wasn't she at home as he had been when she met him? She learned that he had been so burned out from his business that he had taken six months off.

"I just imagined that I'd be home with my children after school and [be doing] all the other things mothers do raising their children," Serlin says.

She sees United Scrap as a recycling business. It purchases scrap—including metal, paper, and plastic—from other companies, such as Commonwealth Edison, an electric utility, and Andrew Corp., an Orland Park, Ill., electronics company. The materials are sorted, cleaned, chopped, baled, and resold to customers such as U.S. Steel and Alcoa to be remade into other products.

In Serlin's view, United Scrap acts as a partner with its clients, advising them, for example, on procedures that lead to better scrap management and helping them improve their bottom lines. And while the industry was fairly unsophisticated when Serlin started her company, she has kept up with technology, installing a computer system to track vehicles and materials.

"My customer is the No. 1 person," she says. "I do everything as though it were for me. I put myself into the shoes of the customer, and I say, "If I were him, what would I want from me?"

Serlin says she learned the business by asking questions: "If I didn't get the right answer, I'd go somewhere else. I didn't stop until I felt that I was doing the right thing."

As Serlin walks through her seven-acre scrapyard, it seems she knows every employee by name. Spread across the yard are pile after pile of scrap, ranging from discarded household items to highway signs and an old propeller. "We have metal as far as the eye can see," she says.

Serlin is working fewer hours now because her son, Brad, has taken over operations and sales. But only slightly fewer hours. That's in keeping with her work ethic. In fact, Serlin scoffs at the notion that luck played a part in her success. "People think that you're lucky," she says. "It's not luck. It's hard work."

Scrap-metal entrepreneur Marsha Serlin is the first woman to be named the nation's Small Business Subcontractor of the Year.

———————●———————

Exercise Related to the Professional Article from the World of Work

Reading Comprehension

1. In what type of business is Marsha Serlin? _____

2. What is her attitude towards her customers? _____

_____

3. To what does she attribute the success of her business and such honors as the National Small Business Subcontractor of the Year award? _____

_____

Writing Analysis

1. Is this a biographical or an autobiographical article? Discuss the differences between the two. _____

   _____

2. Intermingled throughout the article are quotations by Marsha Serlin. How do they help the flow of the writing? _____

   _____

3. Why does the author organize the twenty-year time span in reverse? _____

   _____

4. Would the story have been just as effective if the author had started twenty years in the past and built up to the subject's eventual success? _____

   _____

From a Neighborhood Watch newsletter. *Using the almost right word isn't good enough. Find the incorrectly spelled word and spell it correctly below. Are you sure?*

Recent cases that Detective [XXX] has completed include the arrest of a major methamphetamine trafficker, the seizer of three pounds of meth and $22,000 in cash . . . and the arrest of a cocaine abuser who was fascinated with firearms.

GRAMMARWORKS! Many Kinds of Pronouns

We've just talked about the first-person pronouns used in personal stories and essays (I, me, mine, etc.). There are many pronouns of differing kinds.

Pronouns often substitute for *nouns.* The two most common kinds of pronouns are *subjective* and *objective* pronouns.

SUBJECTIVE PRONOUNS	**I, you, he, she, it, we, you** (plural) **they, who.** These pronouns replace nouns that serve as *subjects;* they *perform* the action in the sentence. (**He** saw Erney drop the book, but **she** gave the book to Marla.)
OBJECTIVE PRONOUNS	**Me, you, him, her, it, us, you** (plural) **them, whom.** These pronouns replace nouns that serve as *objects;* they *receive* the action of the subject. (Ken saw **him** drop **it**, but the teacher gave **it** to **her.**)

Pronouns can also serve as *adjectives* and can also take the place of *phrases* and *clauses.* Here are six other kinds of pronouns.

POSSESSIVE DESCRIPTIVE PRONOUNS	**My, your, his, her, its, our, your, their, whose.** These pronouns serve as adjectives. (**His** wallet; **their** dog; **whose** child.)
POSSESSIVE PRONOUNS	**Mine, yours, his, hers, its, ours, yours, theirs.** These pronouns eliminate repetition by standing in for phrases. (Instead of "The comb is Jane's comb," we can say, "The

GRAMMARWORKS! **Many Kinds of Pronouns (continued)**

	comb is **hers.**" Instead of "The cassettes are their cassettes," we say, "The cassettes are **theirs.**")
REFLECTIVE PRONOUNS	**Myself, yourself, himself, herself, itself, ourselves, yourselves, themselves.** Reflective pronouns *emphasize* a noun or a pronoun. (A two-year-old child knows how to use emphasis: "I want to do it **myself.**" A boss, emphasizing his trust, says, "I know the information is correct because my secretary looked it up **herself.**") Emphasis should be used sparingly.
RELATIVE PRONOUNS	**Who, whom, whose, that, which.** These pronouns introduce clauses that *relate* to key elements of a sentence. (Jerry, **who** *manages the office,* left early. I don't know **whom** *I have to thank* for this refund check from the gas company. Sian, **whose** *grandmother is ninety-six,* expects to live a long life. Anne was impressed with the suit **that** *Mona wore.* Birdie printed her application in ink, **which** *is what the instructions said to do.*)
DEFINITE PRONOUNS	**This, that, these, those, here, there.** These pronouns refer to *specific* people, places, things, or circumstances. (**This** is my pen. **That** is what you get for not doing your homework. Shirley Jean liked **these** dishes, but she bought **those** instead. Leith moved **that** light over **here. There's** the cat!)
INDEFINITE PRONOUNS	**Both, several, some; all; another, each, every, one, none; either, neither; anybody, everybody, nobody, somebody; anyone, everyone, no one, someone; whoever, whomever; anything, everything, nothing, something.** These pronouns are nonspecific. Like all pronouns, it is essential to keep them close to the words they refer to so that your meaning is clear. **Both, several,** and **some** are plural pronouns. (**Both** [men] *want* to buy the car.) **All** can be singular or plural. (**All** *is* forgiven. **All** of his children *have* red hair.) The rest are singular pronouns. (**Anyone** can whistle. **Everything** is going to be all right.)

DON'T MAKE YOUR READERS GUESS WHAT YOU MEAN!

We know that a pronoun substitutes for a noun. But sometimes, instead of simplifying the communication of information, pronouns can cause misunderstandings. To avoid being misunderstood, the pronoun must follow closely after *the noun it replaces,* which is called **the pronoun's antecedent** (or referrent). An antecedent is something that goes before (*ante* means before; *cede* means go). When other nouns come between the antecedent noun and its pronoun, the meaning of the pronoun can be unclear. See the examples below.

*Jesse put my coat on the hook, but **it** fell off.*

The writer knows *it* means *my coat,* but the reader expects the pronoun to refer to the noun that directly precedes it (its antecedent), *the hook.*

*Bev and Don bought fresh tomatoes, garlic, and onions. **They** made a good pasta sauce.*

Does the writer mean *Bev and Don* cooked a good pasta sauce? Or that *fresh tomatoes, garlic, and onions* made the sauce good?

Zoe and Cho are always either fighting or kissing and making up. ***That*** *makes Neysa feel uncomfortable.*

What makes her uncomfortable—their fighting, their kissing, or their switching back and forth?

Pronouns must agree with their antecedents in number (singular or plural) and gender (masculine, feminine, or neuter). With animals, use *neuter pronouns (it, its)* when making general statements or when the animal's sex is unknown. The easiest way to make pronouns agree with their antecedents is to use plural nouns whenever possible. See the following example to avoid a common pronoun/antecedent error.

Incorrect: A person can forget where **they** put **their** keys.

Correct: People can forget where **they** put **their** keys.

Remember to keep all pronouns near their antecedents so that the meaning is clear!

GrammarWorks! Review

Circle all the pronouns in the following paragraph. You deserve an A+ if you find fifty of them!

Lisa asked Larry if she could borrow a dictionary. He said one was in his gym locker, but he couldn't remember its combination. So they went to the office to get it (the dictionary? or the combination?). There, the secretary said she needed to see some identification. He told her (the secretary? or Lisa?) to look in his backpack for his wallet. "Your hair looks better in this picture," said the secretary. "I cut it myself this time," Larry replied. "Well, you should go back to whoever cut it last time," she said. Larry said, "Meanwhile, can I just get what I came here for, which is my locker combination?" The secretary went to her computer. "Which program do I want?" she asked herself. "Several of them have similar names," she explained. "Here's the information! This is yours." She handed Larry a piece of paper with his combination on it. "Thanks, and I'm sorry to have troubled you," Larry said. "Oh, that's nothing. Some goofball forgot his combination and his locker number! Finals week is like that!" Larry came out of the gym without the dictionary. "The combination didn't work on my locker," he said. "Are you sure you went to the right one?" Lisa asked.

GRAMMARWORKS! Pronoun/Antecedent Agreement

Between you and me, it would be nice for us to agree! When a pronoun refers to a previous noun or pronoun, the previous noun or pronoun is its *antecedent*. Each pronoun that follows the antecedent and refers to it must "agree" with it in *person*, *number*, and *gender*.

- **Person** means the person speaking (first person: **I, we**), the person spoken to (second person: **you**), or the person spoken about (third person: **he, she, it, they**).
- **Number** means singular or plural.
- **Gender** means masculine (male), feminine (female), or neuter (neither masculine nor feminine, like a rock).

PRONOUNS THAT DO NOT AGREE WITH THEIR ANTECEDENTS	PRONOUNS THAT DO AGREE WITH THEIR ANTECEDENTS
PERSON DISAGREEMENT	PERSON AGREEMENT
The *old woman* in front of *me* is slow, but *you* shouldn't get impatient with *them*.	The *old woman* in front of *me* is slow, but I shouldn't get impatient with *her*.
When *you* say *you're* going to a party, *they* should be sure to show up.	When *you* say *you're* going to a party, you should be sure to show up.

GRAMMARWORKS! Pronoun/Antecedent Agreement (continued)

All the people voted *his* or *her* conscience.   *Each person* voted *his or her conscience.*

NUMBER DISAGREEMENT	NUMBER AGREEMENT
If *a person* doesn't look before crossing the street, *they* might get hit by a car.	A person who doesn't look before crossing the street might get hit by a car.
The guys on my baseball team all ordered *pizza. They were* really good!	The guys on my baseball team all really liked the pizza they ordered.
The *members* of my team argued about practicing, but *it* finally agreed.	The *members* of my team argued about practicing, but *they* finally agreed.

GENDER DISAGREEMENT	GENDER AGREEMENT
We have a boy dog. *It* always chases cars.	We have a boy dog. *He* always chases cars.
Everyone brought *their dog* to the park.	*They* all brought *their dogs* to the park.

SOLUTIONS! YOU CAN FIX AGREEMENT ERRORS IN ANY OF THESE WAYS:

- Change the *following* pronoun to agree with the antecedent;
- Change the *antecedent* noun or pronoun to agree with the *following* pronoun;
- Keep the pronoun *near* the antecedent so you won't make a mistake; or
- *Reconstruct the sentence* to avoid a possible problem in agreement.

In these sentences, either the pronoun doesn't agree with its antecedent or the pronoun's meaning is ambiguous. Correct the sentences, changing either the antecedent or the pronoun so they agree in person and number. Remember to place the pronoun near its antecedent.

1. If **we** don't watch where **we're** going, **you** could trip and fall. _____

2. A **person** should keep track of **their** expenses for when **they** do **their** taxes. _____

3. My **cat Buddy Boy** always loses **its** catnip. Have you ever heard of a **cat** losing **their** catnip? _____

4. My wife alphabetizes her spices and sorts my underwear by color. **It** drives me crazy. (What does *it* refer to or replace? One of these sentences needs to be rewritten, or the two sentences may be combined.) _____

5. They say when **people** go on a trip, **you** should take half the clothes and twice the money. _____

6. A **student** has to keep track of **your** schedules, **their** assignments, and what **we** need to do to graduate. _____

7. *See if you can find the problem in the following sentences, then rewrite just the second sentence.* Emily and Frank are hiking, and they've taken along all kinds of gear—canteens, food, jackets, books, horseshoes, and a TV and a VCR. **They**

shouldn't be on a hiking trip. (Clue: sometimes you *can't* use a pronoun and still make your meaning clear.) _____

_____

_____

From a free-movie-pass-with-dinner offer. *Rewrite the second sentence, fixing the subject/verb agreement.*

[A restaurant's] movie passes in Woodland Hills can be redeemed at the AMC-16 Theaters. . . . Tax, tip, and guest check minimums apply, and presentation of movie passes are based on the size of the party.

_____

_____

THE BIG EIGHT BONEHEADS!

- Words Misspelled
- Words or Caps Incorrect
- Sentence Fragments
- Sentence Run-Ons, Spliced or Fused
- Pronouns Confused
- Verbs Misused
- Commas Misplaced
- Apostrophes Abused

FIXING A BONEHEAD PERSONAL STORY
Read the paragraph and then follow the directions below.

I WANT TO DO WHAT I LOVE TO DO
BY ELOISE LOOKINGOOD

(1) Ever sence I was a little kid, I have always licked to shop for close. (2) My mother licks to shop, she use to take me shopping all the time. (3) I want to be a department store manager they get to boss everybody around. (4) The first time mom let me pick out what I was going to ware. (5) I choosed my Easter dress, which must of had about a million ruffles on it. (6) Her and me and my dad had went to a barbecue. (7) At our next door neighbors house. (8) She never gets over trying to wash out the barbaque sauce, because of the fluffy material. (9) I like to look nice and work with clothes. (10) When I finish this english class I'm going to apply for WalMarts' traning program.

Edit the paragraph above. Search for the Big Eight: circle misspelled words, wrong words, and wrong capitalizations. Put an X in front of sentence fragments, run-on, spliced, and fused sentences. Underline misused pronouns and verbs and the comma and apostrophe errors. Each sentence above has a number. On the lines below, write what you've found wrong with each numbered sentence. (Write what you found wrong with sentence (1) on line 1, and so on.)

1. _____
2. _____
3. _____
4. _____
5. _____
6. _____
7. _____
8. _____
9. _____
10. _____

Now you're ready to revise the paragraph. Write it in your own words on a separate piece of paper.

WORK! WORK! WORK!

Writing Practice

The following prompts will help you pick a topic to show what you've learned about writing personal stories.

"A job isn't finished until the paperwork is done."

Exercises in Writing a Personal Story or Autobiography

1. Write a three-paragraph personal story that starts with these words: *I decided to become a* (fill in the blank) _____ *because . . . "*

2. Write a three-paragraph personal story about an important moment in your life, a moment of change that involved at least one other person.

3. Write a three-paragraph autobiographical story about something funny, awful, or wonderful that happened to you at work, at school, or elsewhere.

4. Write a three-paragraph personal essay about something that really makes you mad.

WORK! WORK! WORK!

Lesson Review

The following exercise helps you recall what you learned in this lesson.

Fill In the Blanks Regarding Personal Story—Autobiography

1. If I am writing a story, and it is about _____, and I use _____-person pronouns, that's my personal story, or my _____.

2. People who keep a _____ or a _____ write personal stories regularly.

3. _____ tells what you personally think about some topic.

GrammarWorks! Review

Fill in the blanks about pronouns and pronoun/antecedent agreement.

1. The word that a pronoun follows and replaces is called its _____

    _____.

2. The two most common kinds of pronouns are _____

    _____.

3. Pronouns must agree with their antecedents in the following three ways:_____

    _____.

4. Some first-person pronouns are *I, me, my, mine.* Give the corresponding *third*-person pronouns for *she* and *he:* _____.

Circle the correct italicized words and cross out the sentence that uses a pronoun without a clear antecedent.

  Vicki and I/Vicki and me went to get batteries for our watches. The bus took *she and I/her and me* right to the mall. We went to get pretzels first, and *it was/they were* good! We met Chuck, *whose/who's* sister needed a battery for *her/his* Mermaid watch. Two boys *whom/that* we all like were selling batteries at Battery Shack, so of course *we three/us three* bought the batteries for our watches from Rick and Buck. They work!

Chapter 4

LOOKING FORWARD

IN THIS CHAPTER

JOB SEARCH CHALLENGES

JOB SEARCH CHALLENGES

THE PROCESS

Job search is not a complicated process. Basically, it requires six elements:

- a willing and qualified job candidate
- an available position
- a mailed request for an interview
- a resume[1] and cover letter
- an application form
- the job interview or interviews

A Willing and Qualified Candidate

A job seeker must desire to obtain a position in the area of employment best suited to his or her skills. Few people start at the top as presidents or chairpersons of boards. Many of you have never worked for salary or wages before. Accordingly, you must be *realistic regarding the level at which you can enter the job market and the speed with which you will be promoted.* The chief criterion, however, is your zeal to succeed in whatever undertaking you pursue, whether waitress, writer, window washer, or wardrobe waxer. You must know your availability, your capabilities and skills, your attitudes and values, your strengths and weaknesses. You must be *realistic about your entry-level earning power.*

One successful method of identifying your qualifications is to draft an outline of what you do well. Consider such factors as the positive features of your personality, how well you communicate with others orally and in writing, your dress and appearance, your skills, and what your paid and unpaid work experiences have taught you.

A willing candidate wants to know what qualities employers seek in a prospective employee. The SCANS skills and competencies described in chapters 5 through 10 provide this information in detail. In addition, the Appendix contains the SCANS "Know-How" definitions. As you study the SCANS lessons, keep in mind the *one* particular profession or career toward which you are presently directed. A number of exercises throughout this book will guide you to consider how you will use these life skills in the vocation you've chosen.

Are you a willing job candidate? Knowing where you eventually want to be in your career can help you select the employment routes you need to take you there. There are many good books on the job-search process. Consult some of them at the library. Better yet, compare them in a bookstore and buy yourself one!

An Available Position

Yes, this is the hard part. Is there a job out there for you? You won't know until you start looking. What are the job search resources? Newspapers, employment offices, friends, former employers, libraries, and teachers offer better potential for finding a desirable position than standing on a street corner with a sign saying "Will work for food."

Job Search Resources:

- The **classified ads** in newspapers are gold mines of employment information. Save money by exploring them at your local library, and copy carefully the information from the ads you want to follow up on.
- Most colleges have a **placement service.** Visit the staff and search the available job listings.

---

[1] Resume is from the French word meaning to sum up. That's why it's pronounced REH-zoo-may and why you might also see it spelled either *resumé* or *résumé* (with accent marks).

- If you're in a vocational or technical field, ask your **instructors** if they know of potential jobs or employers.
- Visit your state's **Human Resources Office.** Fill out forms, meet with a counselor, and be identified as a serious job seeker.
- Look for **"Help Wanted" signs** in the windows of businesses.
- Do you have **favorite places** where you like to do business, shop, or dine? No one will object if you inquire sincerely as to whether a job is available or will be available in the future.
- Inquire **where your friends or schoolmates are working.** Would they recommend you to their employers?
- Look on the Internet.

By all means, keep lists of possible jobs, places you want to work, and what happened where you've inquired. Keep at it. There is a job out there for you.

From a newspaper. *Avoid misspellings and wrong word choices on* your *job applications! Circle the ten errors and write them correctly below.*

JOB SEEKERS, BEWARE OF TYPOS!

"Excellant at people-oriented positi9ons and organizational problem solving."

"I have lurnt WorkPerfect 7.0, computor and spreadsheat programs."

"I never take anything for granite."

"To Home-Ever it concerns."

"Reason for leaving: maturity leave."

"Received a plague for Salesperson of the Year."

_____

_____

_____

A Mailed Request for an Interview

Unless the potential employer is a relative or your best friend, you're going to have to be interviewed to be considered for a job. Prospective employers want to know if you're qualified even before they interview you. A common way to provide an employer with information about yourself is to apply for a job through the mail. You write a letter requesting an interview, and you enclose a resume. A **job inquiry letter** is also know as a **cover letter** because it goes on top of the resume. We'll talk more about resumes later.

In the job inquiry, describe the position for which you are applying, tell how you found out about the job, and mention your strongest qualifications. In the last paragraph, request an interview and say when you are available to be interviewed. Address the letter and resume to a *specific individual,* often the personnel director or human resources manager at the place of prospective employment. You can telephone the business and say that you want to send a job inquiry and would like the name of the personnel director. It's essential that the letter you send be in a businesslike format, free of grammatical and spelling errors. Formatting for the letter and envelope is described in the next section.

Harcourt, Inc.

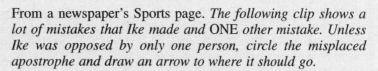

From a newspaper's Sports page. *The following clip shows a lot of mistakes that Ike made and* ONE *other mistake. Unless Ike was opposed by only one person, circle the misplaced apostrophe and draw an arrow to where it should go.*

"Ike XX was on his game last night. He dribbled the basketball off his foot instead of the floor; he passed the ball to Frank XXX's back; he slam-dunked in the wrong basket; he high-fived the referee after he got a foul called on him; and he went to the opponent's bench during the first timeout."

Format for the Cover Letter and Envelope

This information applies to all business letters. Type your letter, single-spaced, on 8-½-by-11 inch white paper. Allow at least a one-inch margin on all four edges of the paper. Your name and address may be centered at the top of the page or aligned against the right-hand margin. Use the two-letter postal abbreviation for the state (e.g., CA for California, MI for Michigan, etc.).

- Double-space between your address and the date. Write the date in this order: Month (capitalize and spell out), date, year. Example: September 14, 2001. Leave an inch of space.
- At the left margin, place the name and address of the person to whom you are sending the letter (the addressee). Put a comma after the person's name, to separate it from the person's job title. Capitalize all important words (e.g., Tina Tupper, Director of Personnel). If the title is especially long, omit the comma after the name and put the title on the line below the name.
- Double space between the company address and the *salutation* (e.g., Dear Ms. Tupper). Use a colon after the salutation.
- Indent each new paragraph one-half inch (indented form); or do not indent paragraphs, but double-space between them (block form).
- Double space between the final paragraph and the *complimentary close* (e.g., Yours truly or Sincerely). Use a comma after the complimentary close.
- Space four times before you type your name. You will sign your name, above your typed name, in this space.
- Make a copy for yourself of whatever you mail out.

Center your letter on the paper. If your letter is especially short, you may add extra spaces between the date and the addressee, or you may widen the margins to one and one-half inches.

SAMPLE COVER LETTER FOR JOB INQUIRY 1—INDENTED FORMAT

Your Street Address
City, State Zip Code
Telephone (for Messages)

Date

Name, Title of Contact at Prospective Employer Organization[2]
Company Name
Street Address
City, State Zip Code

Dear (Mr./Ms. Last Name):

(Reason for letter) I read your advertisement for a management trainee position in the *Chicago Tribune* last Sunday. I believe that I am very well qualified for the job.

(Why qualified) My current major at City College is business administration. I am a capable and enthusiastic student with a B-plus average. I have had sales positions in several small businesses and sold Kirby vacuum cleaners door to door. My resume is enclosed which describes my educational and work experience in more detail.

(Action to take[3]) I would like to arrange an interview with you or your representative at your earliest possible convenience. You can reach me at the telephone number above, or I will telephone your office within the next two weeks to verify the status of my application.

Sincerely,

(Sign your name)

Type Your Name

---

[2]If you don't know the name of the Personnel Director or Manager of Human Resources, call and ask the telephone operator at the organization.

[3]The purpose of the letter is to get the addressees to grant you an interview.

SAMPLE COVER LETTER FOR JOB INQUIRY 2—BLOCK FORMAT, BRUNO HASAGAWA

Your Name
Your Street Address
Your City, State Zip Code
Your Daytime Telephone Number
Fax Number and E-Mail Address (if available)

Date

Name
Title
Company Name
Address
City, State Zip Code

Dear Ms. or Mr. _____:

I am seeking employment as a management trainee in your restaurant chain. Throughout my college years, I earned my expenses by working at restaurants. I am currently employed part time at your location in Jacksonville, where I work as assistant night manager.

I am a graduating student at Seaside Technical College, majoring in restaurant management. I will be available for full time work next June. Enclosed is my resume and a reference from my manager, Ms. Page, who was Manager of the Year in 1998.

I would like to interview for your company training program. I will call you next week to see if you are accepting applications at this time. If not, I hope you will keep my letter on file for when you have an opening.

Sincerely,

Bruno Hasagawa

Fold your letter in thirds and send it in an envelope as wide as the paper. Address the envelope as shown below.

Your Name
Your Street Address
Your City, State   Zip Code

   The Person's Name, Job Title
   The Company's Name
   The Company's Street Address
   City, State   Zip Code

Use first class postage in the top right corner, and send your job inquiry on its way!

A Resume (pronounced REH-zoo-may)

A **resume** represents you when you're not there. It should be neat, informative, and grammatically correct. A resume is an outline describing your educational and employment history. It might also contain personal information, including your skills, hobbies, interests, and references. The sample resumes included in this section represent good resume form and content.

Personal Information   **Personal information** includes your name, address, and phone number, your date of birth, and other meaningful information. Any personal history that is pertinent to a particular job is essential to a resume. On the other hand, your age, marital status, whether or not you've been in jail, and your preference for cookie dough ice cream are probably not relevant—unless you're applying for a position that calls for an over-30, divorced ex-convict who likes ice cream. If a job requires special skills, like lifting, driving trucks, nursing the elderly, or lifesaving, it may be very important to mention your personal experience or certificates you've earned that show your qualifications.

Experience   Next comes your **school and work experience.** If you have a great deal of work experience, start with that. If not, begin with your educational background. State when and where you attended school, your major, and your grade point average (only if you have an A or B average). Although important to you, your accomplishments prior to high school are not usually important to a prospective employer. High school achievements are relevant only if you were a leader, an athlete, a scholar, or all of these. Your past and present college history is always relevant. List your educational accomplishments in reverse chronological order (the most recent years first), with the dates of beginning and ending attendance to the left of the school information. Employers are most interested in recent performance.

State your work experience in reverse chronology also. Make it easy for the employer to read, absorb, and use the information. Underline the position you held, name the company for which you worked, and give your supervisor's name and telephone number. *Do not omit the name and phone number of your supervisor.* Most important, include a brief list of your job duties and responsibilities. Don't list jobs where you worked only a few weeks! Longevity in a job speaks well of you. The duration of time you were employed in a position or with an organization is important. List the term of employment where it can be readily seen, to the left of the work description information.

Remember that not all work is paid work. Volunteer experience—such as organizing YMCA track meets, serving as secretary to a church choir, or preparing meals for a Senior Center—is quite valid.

Skills, Hobbies, and Interests   When are skills, hobbies, and interests important? Many of your strongest capabilities cannot be reflected in your education or employment background. Pertinent activities are worth mentioning. You may have successfully repaired all the mechanical problems of your old Chevy, or maybe you speak and write fluent Spanish as well as English. You've traveled to or lived in many distant lands. You've seen every play at the Mark Taper

Forum in the past five years. Garages, banks, travel agencies, or theater managers might be very interested in these "unpaid" activities.

References   The old saying, "It's not what you know, it's whom you know," holds water. Personal references are the people who can vouch for you, as well as for the information you give. Old family friends, former teachers, or previous employers who hold you in high regard are good resources. A valuable reference is an individual who has knowledge of your personality, abilities, interests, experience, of how you get along with people, and, especially, of whether you can be trusted. Trustworthiness is extremely important to employers. If you show you can be trusted with money, equipment, keys—even children, you have an inside lane to winning a position. It really helps to have references. List two or three people, with their phone numbers, and be sure to notify them that your potential employers might be in touch.

Employers are particularly impressed when a job applicant provides a letter of reference from a former employer or teacher. If you can obtain such a letter, you can use it over and over because it will be addressed "To whom it may concern." Provide a copy with each application you submit.

References can be provided later, and they should be acknowledged with a statement on your resume: "References provided on request." However, the object of the resume is to get an interview, and an employer is more likely to interview someone who provides references. Employers, eager to bring a good person into their organization, will call your references and ask them the questions not covered in your inquiry letter or resume. "Can I trust this person?" "How does she make decisions?" "Is he a good problem-solver?" "Would you hire her again?" An employer's ready access to people who can vouch for you increases your chance for a quick response to your inquiry. It's to your benefit to provide names and telephone numbers (even addresses and e-mail addresses), and your relationships to those who know you and your background well.

Not providing references might be interpreted as laziness on your part or fear that people won't speak well of you.

Career Goal   Finally, do you include your **career goal** at the top of the resume? It's up to you. If you're applying for an usher's position at CBS or bank teller employment at Bank of America, these types of companies start virtually everyone at the bottom. It would be advisable to express your interest in long-range employment on your resume. If, however, the position you seek is just to earn coin temporarily or to gain needed experience, your cover letter can attend to this subject quite adequately. Either way, you must convince the prospective employer that you are the one for this particular job.

NOTE: This is a good time to **visit your college career center.** Pick up a free copy of "Fifteen Tips on Writing Resumes" by Freda Graves or a similar resource, if available. Specially formatted computers or computer software programs can help you create your resume. More and more, the Internet is being used by job seekers.

From a small town newpaper. *A "compunym" is a mistake the computer doesn't find because it's a correctly spelled word— though it's the wrong word. Circle the word and write the correct word above it.*

Friends of library to hose used book sale February 8th.

SAMPLE RESUME 1, BRUNO HASAGAWA

```
BRUNO HASAGAWA              Ht: 5'4" Wt: 125
1234 West Fifth Street      Date of Birth: June 5, 1980
City, State Zip Code        SS# 557-50-xxxx
Telephone (for messages)    U.S. Citizenship
```

WORK EXPERIENCE

July 1998
to Present

Assistant Night Manager, Famous Restaurant Chain, Jacksonville.
Supervisor: Name, phone. Assistant night manager; order supplies; train personnel; maintain facility; and oversee total quality effort.

October 1997
to June 1998

Counter Service, McDonald's, Newport Beach.
Supervisor: Name, phone number. This was a part-time job where I prepared food, served customers, and assisted in the maintenance of the facility.

VOLUNTEER EXPERIENCE

1995—Present

Performed part-time services for deaf kids, including teaching them to ice skate.

EDUCATION

September 1999
to Present

Seaside Technical College GPA: 3.5
Major: Business Administration Minor: Computer Science AA Expected, June 2001

September 1997
to June 1999

El Camino College, Torrance
General Education Course

September 1994
to June 1997

St. Xavier's High School, Los Angeles
College Preparatory

Hobbies: [what you like to do] Play piano, figure skate, refinish furniture.

Interests: [what you like to watch or read about] Go to jazz concerts, read biographies.

Awards: Academic Decathlon team (two years), class representative (two years).

Special Skills: Good cook, quick to learn new things, good with people.

Travel: Mexico and Canada.

Languages: Fluent in American Sign Language, some Spanish.

References: Rev. Bruce Dunlap, clergyman: (xxx) 555-9786
Clarice Binghampton, neighbor (whose sons I baby-sat for six years): (xxx) 555-9812
Mrs. Deniese Johnson (taught her daughter to ice skate): (xxx) 555-4563

Personal Note: [Mentioning why you are unique is optional.]
My mother is deaf; I have helped her communicate since I was a child.

Harcourt, Inc.

The student author's assignment: Write your personal resume according to the guidelines in this chapter and Sample Resume 1.

Margarita Reyes has served as a volunteer with children and has worked in sales and administration. Her Liberal Arts A.A. degree will open many possibilities for this real "people person."

SAMPLE RESUME 2, MARGARITA REYES

Margarita Reyes
xxx East xxth Street, Los Angeles, CA 90011
(323) 111-2233

EDUCATION
1998–Present   Los Angeles Trade Technical College,
                  Los Angeles, CA
                  Liberal Arts Major
                  Graduation June 2000
                  A.A. Degree, G.P.A. 3.33

1996–1997   El Santo Nino Learning Center-G.E.D.
                  Los Angeles, CA

1996–1997   Manual Arts-Jefferson Community Adult School
                  High School Diploma
                  Los Angeles, CA

WORK EXPERIENCE
Present: Manual Arts-Jefferson High School CAS Teacher
                  Assistant, work in an individualized
                  independent lab with adults, give out books,
                  tests, grade papers, etc.
1996–1997   San Pedro Street School—School Volunteer
                  helped pre-kindergarten teacher and children
                  in various school activities.
1995–1997   Aster Fabrics—Administrative Assistant
                  Received-, shipped merchandise and filed
                  papers
1994–1995   Rodium Open Air Market—Salesperson, fabrics
1994   San Fernando Swapmeet—Salesperson, fabrics

ORGANIZATIONS/ACTIVITIES
San Pedro Street School—Volunteer
El Santo Nino Head-Start Program Volunteer, ongoing

```
SKILLS
Bilingual—English/Spanish
Excellent communication skills
Work well with children and adults in miscellaneous areas
Proficient in record keeping/basic computer knowledge


INTERESTS
Read Magazines, novels. Watch family programs.


AWARDS
Catholic Charities of Los Angeles
"El Santo Nino Achievement Award" (June 1997)


REFERENCES
Manual Arts-Jefferson High School   (323) xxx-9177
El Santo Nino, Mrs. Norman          (213) xxx-5246
Aster Fabrics, Charles or Carol     (213) xxx-6562
Rodium Open Air Swapmeet, Ms. Lee   (213) xxx-5069
San Fernando Swapmeet, Mr. Dale     (818) xxx-1699
```

Now Comes the Wait   Several days or weeks may pass before you receive an answer to your inquiry. If your letter interests or impresses the person you sent it to, you'll receive a telephone call to arrange an interview date and time.

A lack of interest in your inquiry is usually shown by a mailed response that is commonly termed a "rejection letter." Rejection is always difficult to take. You might feel that the cause relates to your own shortcomings. Most of the time, this is not the case. Even for some entry-level jobs, there are many applicants for each position, so that the person hired is often over-qualified. For higher-level jobs, many organizations promote only from within, but employment laws require that they publicize positions that have become available. In other situations, applicants are already known to employers, while you are a totally unknown entity. Another reason for rejection is that you simply might not be in the right place at the right time. Just keep trying!

If you don't get a response within two weeks, it's a good practice to follow up your letter with a phone call. Contact the office of the person to whom you wrote and say, "I just wanted to be sure you received my resume. Do you need any more information?" This suggests that you're genuinely interested in the position and are showing tenacity, a required qualification for many jobs. Don't criticize them for not responding! Do thank them for their time! Request a date by which you might call again, but don't be overly intrusive.

An Application Form

The moment of truth at last is here! Often, when you arrive for your job interview, you're handed an **application form** to complete. You might be given a pen and a clipboard with the application form, but always bring your own pen and paper to take notes. You might say to yourself, "I've included most of this information on my resume. Hasn't anyone read it?" *Of course* someone has reviewed your resume, or you wouldn't have been granted an interview!

Each organization has an application form that works best with its filing system. Fill out your application carefully and accurately. A neatly completed form helps the interviewer consult the information on it. Also, there are always questions on the form for which your resume *didn't* supply answers. These might include the following: your social security and driver's license numbers; whether you've ever been bonded (insured for handling valuables for a company); whether you are familiar with the organization's product or service, and so on. So do the drill and fill out each long, tedious form carefully. Write legibly, and answer each question truthfully and to the best of your ability. If there is a question that doesn't apply to you or your experience, print N/A (which means *not applicable*) on the space next to the question. In this chapter, we include a sample job application form you can practice on. (At the back of the book is a duplicate blank form you can complete and consult when filling out a company's application.)

Quite often, the completed application form is more important to the interviewer than your resume. To both you and the organization, it means you have your foot in the door.

 From a newspaper article on Old West furniture. *Did you ever hear of a* subject *of a preposition? There isn't such a thing. Circle the incorrect pronoun and write the correct pronoun above it.*

"'We thought it was cute,' Jack E. says of his first encounter with the western furniture that has become a passion for he and wife Sue Ane L."

How you deal with an **application** indicates your job preparedness. If you ask for a pen or pencil instead of having your own pen, you appear unprepared. If you do not have the names and phone numbers of your previous employers, you appear unprepared. If you can't just sit down and fill out the application, in a tidy and thorough manner, you appear unprepared.

Like it or not, your prospective employer will judge you on how you deal with the application process. Remember these procedures!

- **Follow the instructions on the application form.** Read through the application before beginning to write on it. If you can't follow instructions on an application, you could be judged unable to follow instructions on the job. If it says "last name first," *print your last name before your first name.* (This makes it easy to file the forms alphabetically.) If you make a small mistake, neatly draw a line through the error and write the correct information above it. If you put all your education information where your employment data belongs, ask for another blank form. *Don't try to be funny on the application!* If it asks for your desired salary, don't put down $1,000,000.00. Take the application seriously.

- **Print! Print neatly! Print in all capital letters!** Do not handwrite the application (unless there is a section, for instance, instructing you to say a few words about yourself in your own handwriting). These days, your application might be scanned into a computer for filing. The object of the application is to make information about you *readily and easily* available. If you write sloppily, you could be judged a careless person.

- **Have *all* information with you that could possibly be requested on the application.** Take a copy of your personal resume with you so that you can copy the information onto the application: your work history, including names and phone numbers of supervisors; your education history; and at least three personal references, including names, addresses, and phone numbers. Be sure you know your social security number. If you do not have the information with you, you could be judged as insincere in your interest to obtain a job with this company. Take copies of reference letters you have obtained in advance and any material that the interviewer might want to see (e.g., a portfolio of your work).

The Job Interview

All of your previous effort has been focused toward reaching the moment when you are face to face with the person who can hire you for the job you seek. You will want to prepare for the interview in advance—from selecting appropriate wearing apparel to researching the company. A well-groomed applicant shows businesslike behavior, serious intent, and respect for the interviewer and the interviewer's time. Not enough can be said for a well-prepared applicant with an understanding of the company to which he or she is applying. If you really want the job, research the company before interviewing. Well-prepared applicants take the time to study the company or service or product with which they will be working.

Preparation Pays Dividends   Look at informational brochures, annual reports, and newspaper archives.

- Talk to people who've worked for the company or who use its products or services.
- If possible, visit the organization before the interview. Even the exterior of a building can tell you a great deal about a company. A well-maintained, nicely landscaped place might house a better employer than a run-down building with broken windows.
- If you have a friend who works for the organization where the job is available, find out as much as possible about the specific job. Some successful job applicants find out who previously held the job and call to ask why that person left.

The more you know, the better you're prepared, the further you've explored than anyone else—plus your sincere desire to obtain the position, the better are your chances for being hired. These positive features will shine upon the interviewer through his arduous employee-search haze.

Does it seem logical that someone would spend money advertising in this way to people who can't read or write? Rewrite the ad below, possibly appealing to people who can read and write to help a friend who can't.

Illiterate? Write us today for help.

_____

_____

Words of Wisdom about Preparing for the Interview   Now you must charm whoever is across the table, convincing that person that no other candidate has the talent, the pizzazz, the appearance, the creativity, the knack, the calling, the potential, or the drive to succeed as well in this position as you. Believe it, and you can't help but receive serious consideration.

You will be judged on much more than what you have to say. Two things speak for you before you even open your mouth: what you wear and whether you're punctual. **Wear appropriate business clothing.** Of course, you will be neat and clean from hair to shoes. But what you're wearing won't make a shred of difference if you're late and they've already hired the person who had the appointment after yours. This is very important: **Be on time.** Plan to show up about fifteen minutes before the scheduled time. If you're delayed on the way, you'll still be on time. (If you're greatly detained, telephone and let the interviewer know.) Usually, your appointment will be set to allow time for you to fill out the application, but, by showing up early, you could be judged to be the kind of employee who will be punctual.

Face-to-Face at Last   When you meet your interviewer, offer to shake hands if that seems appropriate. Sit where indicated; sit straight but comfortably. Allow the interviewer to do the talking. Wait for him or her to finish what he or she is saying before you respond, and speak up. Answer questions honestly and thoughtfully. When you speak, show interest in the business relative to your foreknowledge of the company. The receptionist might have given you some material about the company to read. If you ask questions that were answered in the material, the interviewer might doubt your reading ability.

Usually, the interviewer asks if you have any questions. Ask any intelligent questions about the business, the job, and the opportunities for training and promotion. It's not a good idea to focus your questions on the "freebies" the company offers; however, in situations where you expect *long-term* employment, it is pertinent to inquire about health insurance, maternity and sick leave, the company's tuition reimbursement policy for continued education, and vacation time—especially if, for instance, lack of insurance would prevent you from taking the job.

In a large organization, several people might interview you. They'll compare notes as to your potential benefit as an employee. When each interview is over, thank the interviewer, and ask when the decision might be made.

Last Bit of Interview Advice   Whenever it seems appropriate, smile!

Do Your Written Homework   The sample cover letters, resumes, and application forms in this book will help you in the writing you must do for your job-search preparation. And remember, there are all kinds of guides and workbooks available for additional exploration of the job-search process.

Good luck!

EMPLOYMENT APPLICATION   *PLEASE PRINT ALL INFORMATION*

REYES,   MARGARITA   T.   RITA
LAST NAME   FIRST NAME   INITIAL   NICKNAME?

PERSONAL INFORMATION: Date_____

Address   xxx EAST xx^Th ST.   L.A.   CA   90011

Phone (323) 111 - 2233   Pager   —   E-mail Address   MREYES@〜

☐ Male ☒ Female ☐ Married ☐ Single   Social Security Number   557-50-xxxx

JOB SOUGHT   ☒ Part Time   ☐ Full Time

Position   TRAINEE   Salary Desired   Negotiable

Are you currently employed? Y   May we contact your current your current employer?   YES

EDUCATION (List in reverse chronological order. Include high school if pertinent.) ☐ Currently enrolled?

Name, City   L.A. TRADE TECH COLLEGE   Grade Average   3.33

Major Subjects Studied   LIBERAL ARTS   Year(s) 1998-2000

Awards, Degree, Certificates, Activities

Name, City   EL SANTO NIÑO LEARNING CTR   Grade Average   —

Major Subjects Studied   G.E.D.   Year(s) 1996-1997

Awards, Degree, Certificates, Activities   ACHIEVEMENT AWARD, CATH. CHARITIES AWARD

Name, City   MANUAL ARTS - JEFFERSON HIGH   Grade Average

Major Subjects Studied   COLLEGE PREP   Year(s) 1996

Awards, Degree, Certificates, Activities

VOLUNTEER EXPERIENCE

Place, City   SAN PEDRO ST. SCHOOL   Year(s) 1996-1998

Supervisor/Phone   MR. RIOS, PRINCIPAL   Activities   T.A. — (323) xxx-6353

Place, City   EL SANTO NIÑO HEAD START PROGRAM   Year(s) 1996-PRESENT

Supervisor/Phone   MS. NORMAN   Activities   T.A. — 213-xxx-5246

SKILLS AND INTERESTS

Hobbies and Crafts   READ, WATCH EDUCATIONAL T.V.

Skills and Languages   BILINGUAL - ENG/SPANISH, RECORD KEEPING,

Complete other side and sign application.

WORK WELL WITH KIDS.

FORMER EMPLOYMENT (List only current job and longest-held jobs, most recent first.)

Name, Address MANUAL ARTS - JEFF H COM. ADULT SCHOOL   Year(s) PRESENT

Supervisor's Name, Phone CLARE DAILY   (323) X xx - 9177

Duties T.A. in EDUC. LAB   Reason for Leaving —

Name, Address ASTER FABRICS   L.A.   Year(s) 1996 - 1997

Supervisor's Name, Phone CHARLES OR CAROL   (213) xxx - 6562

Duties ADMIN. ASST./CLERICAL SHIPPING + RECEIVING   Reason for Leaving MOVED

Name, Address RODIUM OPEN AIR MARKET   Year(s) 1994 - 1996

Supervisor's Name, Phone EVELYN LEE   (213) xxx - 5069

Duties SALES - FABRICS   Reason for Leaving NEEDED TO WORK MORE HOURS

REFERENCES (List three persons you've known more than one year and your association to them: business associates, educators, friends, etc. Do not list family members here.)

Name, Phone BOB PURVY - COUSIN   (818) xxx - 3030   Association COUSIN   Years LIFE-LONG

Name, Phone FATHER SERRA   Association PRIEST   Years 15 yrs.

Name, Phone BRIDGET RICHARDS   Association NEIGHBOR Years 4 yrs.

CLOSEST FAMILY MEMBER

Name, Phone TERESITA REYES   (323) xxx - 6630   Relationship MOTHER

The statements on this application are true to the best of my recollection. I authorize the employer or his/her agent to contact any of the parties whose names appear hereon.

Signature *Margarita Reyes*   Date

For company use only:
INTERVIEWER'S EVALUATION
☐ Punctual   ☐ Neat appearance   ☐ Courteous   ☐ Good Written Skills   ☐ Good Verbal Skills

REMARKS

Salary Discussed: Interviewer   Date

LN/Form 813

EMPLOYMENT APPLICATION   *PLEASE PRINT ALL INFORMATION*

LAST NAME	FIRST NAME	INITIAL	NICKNAME?

PERSONAL INFORMATION: Date_____

Address_____

Phone_____ Pager_____ E-mail Address_____

□ Male □ Female □ Married □ Single   Social Security Number_____

JOB SOUGHT   □ Part Time   □ Full Time

Position_____ Salary Desired_____

Are you currently employed?____ May we contact your current your current employer?____

EDUCATION (List in reverse chronological order. Include high school if pertinent.) □ Currently enrolled?

Name, City_____ Grade Average_____

Major Subjects Studied_____ Year(s)_____

Awards, Degree, Certificates, Activities_____

Name, City_____ Grade Average_____

Major Subjects Studied_____ Year(s)_____

Awards, Degree, Certificates, Activities_____

Name, City_____ Grade Average_____

Major Subjects Studied_____ Year(s)_____

Awards, Degree, Certificates, Activities_____

VOLUNTEER EXPERIENCE

Place, City_____ Year(s)_____

Supervisor/Phone_____ Activities_____

Place, City_____ Year(s)_____

Supervisor/Phone_____ Activities_____

SKILLS AND INTERESTS

Hobbies and Crafts_____

Skills and Languages_____

Complete other side and sign application.

FORMER EMPLOYMENT (List only current job and longest-held jobs, most recent first.)

Name, Address _____ Year(s) _____

Supervisor's Name, Phone _____

Duties _____ Reason for Leaving _____

Name, Address _____ Year(s) _____

Supervisor's Name, Phone _____

Duties _____ Reason for Leaving _____

Name, Address _____ Year(s) _____

Supervisor's Name, Phone _____

Duties _____ Reason for Leaving _____

REFERENCES (List three persons you've known more than one year and your association to them: business associates, educators, friends, etc. Do not list family members here.)

Name, Phone _____ Association _____ Years _____

Name, Phone _____ Association _____ Years _____

Name, Phone _____ Association _____ Years _____

CLOSEST FAMILY MEMBER

Name, Phone _____ Relationship _____

The statements on this application are true to the best of my recollection. I authorize the employer or his/her agent to contact any of the parties whose names appear hereon.

Signature _____ Date _____

For company use only:
INTERVIEWER'S EVALUATION
□ Punctual   □ Neat appearance   □ Courteous   □ Good Written Skills   □ Good Verbal Skills

REMARKS _____

_____

_____

_____

Salary Discussed: _____ Interviewer _____ Date _____

LN/Form 813

The student author's assignment: Write a job inquiry letter and include an autobiographical paragraph.
Kyra Sapp, a high school graduate majoring in office administration, is a single parent.

SAMPLE JOB INQUIRY LETTER, KYRA SAPP

1847 Some Street
Los Angeles, CA 90062
(xxx) 555-3311

March 17, 2000

Wanda Hiremee, Employment Director
Big Los Angeles Newspaper
Square One
Los Angeles, CA 90043

Dear Ms. Hiremee:

I'm applying for the Big Newspaper Intern Program. I read your advertisement for a trainee position in yesterday's edition of your paper.

I believe that I am very well qualified for the job. I graduated from Crenshaw High School where I majored in graphic arts. My training covered how to run the printing machines, shoot negatives, make plates, and operate the computers. My current major at Trade Technical College is graphic arts. I am a capable and enthusiastic student, maintaining a B-plus average. My enclosed resume describes my educational experience in more detail.

I would like to arrange an interview with you or your representative at your earliest possible convenience. You can reach me at the telephone number above, or I will telephone your office within the next two weeks to inquire about the status of my application.

Sincerely,

Kyra Sapp

WORK! WORK! WORK!

These exercises help build skills by prompting you to express your understanding of what you read.

Reading Comprehension

1. Name the two things Kyra mentioned of particular importance to the reader of her letter._____

2. What do you know about Kyra that isn't in her letter? _____

_____

Writing Analysis

1. In a business letter, what should be stated in the first paragraph? _____

_____

2. Briefly outline the paragraphs of this job inquiry letter. _____

_____

_____

_____

Often, when we're looking for a job, we wish we could know what the interviewer is thinking. The following professional article can help you look at your job-search steps from an employer's point of view.

Six Steps to Avoiding Hiring Mistakes
by Kathy Jenkins

Have you ever worked with a coworker who drives you crazy, can't perform their duties, is always depressed, or is chronically late? It's worse when you're the person who has hired the person with those traits and introduced him or her into a small shop filled with formerly contented employees. Although hiring always carries risk, there are some simple things you can do to maximize the chance that the next employee you hire is productive and well-suited for the job.

PHASE ONE: IDENTIFY THE NEEDED SKILLS

The sign business requires people with varied skills. You might be searching for an entry-level employee who can weed, coat out boards, keep the shop, clean and learn from the ground up. You might want help in design and layout. You might need an outdoor salesperson to drum up business. You might need a bookkeeper. I list these positions to reinforce the notion that each position for which you hire is a unique position. To fill the unique position, consider the following:

What talent is currently available in your shop? If you have two individuals who are quite talented with airbrush techniques, it won't be as important for the new hire to have airbrush skills. Knowing who possesses what ability in your current shop will require you to study skills and critically evaluate employee production.

- As you evaluate skills, don't be optimistic or give the benefit of the doubt. If you feel an employee is on the verge of acquiring a skill or you believe you can train someone to do something, keep that thought in the back of your mind. But sign production goes on today, not sometime in the future, and you need to assess your employees' abilities today in order to get an accurate read on what skills are missing.
- Break employee skills down into component parts. Anything you can notice about skill levels is important here. If your best employee really isn't good with customers, you've just identified a small gap that needs to be filled. Now, a new employee may not be one who will fill that slot, but it needs to be addressed all the same. Being realistic and as critical as you can will help you determine who you currently need to run optimally.
- This assessment doesn't have to be a formal, time-consuming process. As you work day-to-day, keep a critical eye and ear tuned to employees, noticing who does what well. This information will help you assign jobs, taking strengths into consideration, which will speed production and improve quality.

Write down, in specifics, what skills you need to hire. Don't be concerned if you've identified what seems like an impossible sequence of skills. If you really need a person who can use CorelDraw!™ software, and who likes to do cold-calling, so be it. Advertise for those skills. It is possible you'll find just who you need. It is more probable you'll find someone who has 80 percent of the skills you need, and you'll have to decide if you can live without the other 20 percent. We'll discuss that situation later. I do know that if you don't look for exactly who you need, you will certainly never find them.

PHASE TWO: PLACE THE AD

Place the ad in the local newspaper or trade journal and let the word out to your friends in the sign business. The safest person to hire is the person referred from your good friend in the business who has already worked with the new hire and knows what they're *really* like.

Ads don't have to be elaborate if you've done your homework. Newspapers charge by word or line, so edit your copy until you are succinct: "Sign designer with flair needed. Computer experience a must." An ad like this allows you to look for a person who thinks they have design skills, is creative, and computer literate. I emphasize that the person *thinks* they have those skills, because what they think and what you think may be different. Phase Three of the hiring process gets at testing those assumptions.

PHASE THREE: SCREENING CANDIDATES BY PHONE

Telephone screen as much as possible. Meeting someone in person takes a long time, unless you're willing to be impossibly rude. Candidates will want to come in and show you their portfolios. Before allowing this to happen, jot down a list of pre-qualifying questions you want to ask over the phone. For example, in our ad above, when a prospective candidate calls, ask them to detail what types of projects they've designed in the last year, what computer programs they feel comfortable with, what an example is of a recent creative solution they've devised. These three questions will get the person talking. You don't learn anything while *you're* talking. Listen carefully with a critical ear to what—and how—they are responding. Are you impressed with their most recent design efforts? Does the person know the computer program you have? Is their creative example something you believe is creative? Moreover, does the person exhibit a style you like? Open? Friendly? Helpful? Do they seem defensive? Self-aggrandizing?

Phone screening should allow you to weed out 50 percent to 75 percent of the applicants right away. You don't even have to have a reason not to extend an in-person interview. Just tell them that you'll be communicating by letter with everyone who will not be given an in-person interview.

If someone sounds promising, discuss the pay arrangements you're offering. If you want the person to work as a subcontractor for a few weeks before putting them on the payroll, say that. If you know the salary range is $10 to $12 per hour, depending on qualifications, reflect that. There is no sense wasting your time (and theirs) if your conditions are unworkable for the candidate.

PHASE FOUR: CONDUCT THE IN-PERSON INTERVIEW

Now you have a list of candidates who sound promising. Invite them in individually. Do some homework before they come. The sign business lends itself to demonstration so well that I'd recommend a two-part interview: oral and demonstration. When the person arrives, tell them you want to spend about twenty minutes chatting and then you'd like to see what they can do.

- Have a list of questions prepared. Ask them to describe examples of the skills you're looking for. Ask about some creative solutions the person has generated. You've touched on these during the phone screening but this time you'll be able to get more details or see whether the person can come up with additional examples. Be wary of the person who keeps cycling back to the one job that they designed which was creative and used the computer. Haven't they done any other jobs? A candidate should have a variety of jobs to talk about, or should be billing themselves as new and willing to learn.
- Ask to see their portfolios. Maybe you've actually seen their work around town. So much the better. Maybe you haven't, but you like what you see in the portfolio, and the style the person presents is compatible with what your shop puts out. If you mostly do dimensional gold lettering, and the person's portfolio is predominantly sandblasting, you might not have a good applicant fit. If their designs are 1970s retro in style, and you pride yourself on being avant garde, probe them to see if they can design the way you want and tell them they are not likely to be designing in their usual style. Ask if this will be a problem. Ask if they can do it. Ask if they even want to do it.
- Prepare a short task (in our example you might choose a design task which would take you about ten minutes) that requires them to demonstrate their skill. In the example, perhaps you would lead them to the computer, giving them a two-name logo that requires reworking. Tell them you'll give them twenty minutes, give them any design parameters you have, and let them go to work. Be prepared to understand that in twenty minutes they might not have anything you consider usable. They should have demonstrated, however, that they can use the program and that they can design under a realistic time-frame. You will see some ideas they have played around with and be able to see whether or not their raw material is useful.
- Thank them for their time and tell them you'll be getting back to them by letter. This is my personal preference because I hate making those "You didn't get the job" phone calls, and I'd rather write the bad news to them. If you don't mind, feel free to make any arrangements you want with the candidate about how you'll get back to them, and send them on their way.

Date

Name
Address
City, State

Dear (first name):

Thank you for your recent application and interest in the (specify) position we recently advertised for in the (insert name of newspaper or trade journal) on (insert date).

We received many applications for this opening and yours was not among those selected for an interview. We appreciate your interest in our shop and wish you good luck in your continued job search.

Sincerely,

Your name
Owner

Date

Name
Address
City, State

Dear (first name):

I appreciated your willingness to come by the shop for an in-person interview last week. I was impressed by your portfolio and the range of skills you can offer. Unfortunately, though you were a finalist for the position, you were not chosen to fill this position.

I wish you good luck in your continued job search. Thank you for taking an interest in (insert name of sign shop).

Sincerely,

Your name
Owner

PHASE FIVE: CHECK REFERENCES

You should now have two to five candidates you like, probably each for different reasons. Rank your preferences in order. Be sure to take everything you've learned into account. If you get a bad gut feeling about someone (they talked too much, fidgeted in their seat, told corny jokes), cut them off the list. If someone's skills seemed great as they talked about it—their portfolio looked good, but their demonstration was too slow—you've got a bigger problem. This means some of what they offered was good; some not so good. We can shed more light on this problem in the next step.

Having asked the candidate's permission, call references given to you by the top one or two candidates. Have in mind the questions you want to ask the referent. The referent is probably not going to want to spill the beans right off, so learn to read between the lines. In my example above where the candidate demonstrated some good qualities and some bad, ask the reference about the concerning qualities. You can ask questions like, "Did you find that he could make his deadlines?" "Was he able to work under pressure?" "How often did she have to do work over because the quality wasn't what you wanted?"

Ask referents open-ended questions. Questions that can't be answered with a Yes or No will provide more information that you might find useful. If you say, "Tell me about her creativity", you might get a response like, "She is so creative. Why, she plays the most elaborate practical jokes you've ever seen." This would not be a trait you would ordinarily even think of asking about, but open-ended questions might just elicit unexpected information that you will want to have.

Be alert for pauses and vague responses from the referent. If you ask, "Is this person sick often?" and the referent says, "Well, noooo . . .", be alert to follow up on what this means. You can say, "Can you tell me more?" or "You sound hesitant" or any comment that you think might elicit more information. Even if they say, "Well, I can't tell you any more about this topic," you know there is something problematic in that area.

Once you have the information from the references, you can make a judgment about how that person will fit in your shop. You aren't looking for a saint who has no questionable areas. You're looking for a person *you* can supervise. To give a personal example, I don't mind supervising people who get scattered and lose their focus. My management style fits well with allowing the person to sit down, talk through the options, and choose a plan. So if I'm choosing a candidate, and the references say the person gets rattled, I wouldn't necessarily rule them out since I feel confident I can manage that particular trait. But don't put me with a whiner—I don't handle that well. Are you getting the idea? Know yourself well enough to recognize what traits you can do well with and which ones to avoid.

PHASE SIX: WELCOME THE NEW EMPLOYEE INTO THE SHOP

If you don't do any of the other phases. Please consider doing Phase Six. It's that important! Once you've hired the individual, bring them into the shop and give them the "Welcome to My Shop" lecture. This is your chance to be The Boss. It doesn't matter whether or not your management style is heavy-handed or Boss-like. For this one interview, be Managerial.

People want to know there's someone in charge. If they're not running their own shop, they are telling you they want to work for someone. If it's you they're working for, they want to know you have at least a vague notion of how things are done around here. It's comforting to know there is a plan.

I suggest spending about half an hour with them, going over any procedures you'd like to see them do. These could include how you'd like them to keep track of their hours, how they should handle calling in sick, whether or not you pay for mileage, how the shop is organized, who handles phone calls when you're out of the office, who busy supplies that are running low, and the like. In this interview, you are imparting two pieces of information: the general procedures you'd like to see happening in your shop *and* that you're in charge and they should think of you in that way.

After taking any questions the new employee might have, tell them you'll have another one of these meetings in one month (or three months—whatever you think is reasonable). Use that meeting as a mini-performance review. Be sure to have several specific examples of things that are going well. Be generous in your praise—everyone tends to do more of the behavior that is getting them positive attention. Give any specifics concerning problem areas as well. You might say, "During the last month, I've been so impressed with your ability to work at a steady pace. You are dependable, and your phone manner is just what I'm looking for. I'm really enjoying your creative use of color, too. One thing I'd like you to focus on in the coming months is trying to improve your speed. I've noticed that your work is executed perfectly, but it's taking you about two hours longer than your coworkers to achieve that look. Are you noticing that things are taking you longer? Do you have any ideas of things you could do to increase speed without decreasing accuracy?" This will open up a give-and-take about things that might be done to allow the new employee to achieve your goals. You've also alerted them to the problem as you see it. This will allow you to continue to comment on the trait you've identified (lack of speed) as the weeks go by, enlisting the employee's help in solving the problem.

The rest of the time, you're free to have any management style you choose—even if your style is to not have a style. You can treat employees as buddies, you can have a beer after work with them—whatever you feel comfortable with and whatever gets you the results you want. I am convinced, however, that having these two meetings (one during the first week they're employed and one a reasonable amount of time later) will give you opportunities to catch and solve problems before they are such annoyances that they cause you to do something rash.

Being a manager is being in front of problems, working to head them off, and catching the ones that do crop up before they mushroom out of proportion. Hiring an employee is a big responsibility and firing someone is a nightmare. The steps I've outlined here should stack the deck in your favor.

Exercise Related to the Professional Article from the World of Work

Reading Comprehension

1. With what effective method of introduction does the author begin the article? _____

   _____

2. Name three of the six steps employers use in the hiring process.

   _____

_____

3. Who is the safest person to hire? _____

_____

4. What percentage of applicants can be weeded out by a telephone interview? _____

_____

Writing Analysis

1. What two types of business letters are included in the article? _____

   _____

2. The article begins with a question. Is this a useful way to begin an essay? _____

   _____

3. What is the topic sentence of the article? _____

   _____

_____

Sports sections of newspapers are good places to find mistakes! *Rewrite just the sentence fragment, making it a complete sentence.*

WESTWOOD—Perhaps it was the lateness of the hour, but for some reason the Harvard–Westlake High boys' basketball team didn't look sharp in the finale of the Martin Luther King Jr. Holiday Classic at Pauley Pavilion. At least for the first half.

_____

_____

Dear Applicant:

    I'm sorry to tell you that I can't hire you for the job you applied for today. You seem like a smart enough young man, but you just didn't have what an employer looks for in an applicant. I did hire someone today, and I can't help but compare you to that guy. I thought maybe if I told you the differences, it would help you get the next job you apply for.

- The person I hired dressed up for the interview. His clothes weren't new, but they were clean and neat, and his hair was washed and combed. You looked like you'd just finished playing soccer and were on your way to give your car a lube job. Serious job hunters make the extra effort to look their best.
- The person I hired filled out his application neatly and completely. Yours looked very sloppy and had a lot of misspelled words on it. You didn't even list phone numbers for your references. Employers take time away from their work to do interviews. Applicants who aren't prepared for their interview don't show respect for our time.
- The person I hired sat up and acted interested and eager to hear what I had to tell him. You slouched down in your chair with your arm over the back and acted bored with everything I talked about except the benefits, vacation time, and sick pay. Employers hire people who want to know what their responsibilities will be, not just what they'll get for showing up.
- The person I hired had no more experience than you, but he took the trouble to find out what business we're in. I was really surprised when you asked me what it is we do here. Employers like to think that an applicant is interested in the company's products or services.
- When I asked the person I hired about himself, he mentioned the subjects he takes in school and his interests in sports and cars. You said that you're sick of school, you like to hang out with your friends, and you don't care what kind of work you do so long as you make a lot of money. Employers look for applicants who have a positive attitude and a variety of interests.
- The person I hired also had a good answer when I asked him what kind of work he was looking for. He said he wanted a job where he could keep learning new things. You said you wanted a job where your girlfriend could work, too, so you could spend more time together. Employers think that, when you're on the job, your attention belongs on the work you do.

When I said I'd let you know, you slunk out of here like you knew you wouldn't get the job. Well, you were right. The funny thing is, I could have hired both of you today. Employers are always looking for young men and women interested in giving a full day's work for fair wages, eager to learn new tasks, and pleasant for others to work with. Perhaps if you take these differences into consideration, the next employer will refer to *you* as "The person I hired . . ."

Exercises Related to the Professional Article from the World of Work

Reading Comprehension

1. Why does the employer write the letter? _____

_____

2. Name three things the applicant did that made a bad

impression on the employer. _____

_____

_____

3. Name three things the person who got hired did to give a good impression to the employer._____

_____

_____

Writing Analysis

1. What makes the different comparisons easy to locate? _____

_____

2. Name three things missing from this letter that you would expect to find in a real letter. _____

_____

GRAMMARWORKS! I. What's the Difference?

ANXIOUS
Adjective/*anticipating something bad*
When I have to give a speech, I am **anxious** that I might forget it.

EAGER
Adjective/*anticipating something good*
I am **eager** to give this speech to introduce others to my views.

BREATH
Noun/*air inhaled into lungs*
Bad **breath** doesn't go over well in a job interview.

BREATHE
Verb/*take air into lungs and expel it again*
Abe likes to **breathe** the salty, fishy air of the sea.

CITE
Verb/*quote*
The preacher **cited** a Bible verse in his lesson.

SITE
Noun/*location*
Lee met the superintendent at the job **site.**

COSTUMER
Noun/*one who works with costumes (unusual outfits)*
We went to Rent-A-Costume, and the **costumer** helped us pick disguises for the masquerade party.

CUSTOMER
Noun/*a person who patronizes a business, a client*
It is a good business custom to act as if the **customer** is always right. Happy **customers** come back again.

EMPLOYEE
Noun/*person hired to do work for pay*
Josh's **employees** get their birthdays off, with pay.
[Tip: *ee* endings = the receiver of an action.]

EMPLOYER
Noun/*person who pays another to do work*
Reva's **employer** pays double wages for overtime.
[Tip: *er* and *or* endings = the doer of the action.]

FEVER
Noun/*elevated BODY heat*
Only a *sick body* has a **fever!**
A fever indicates infection or illness.

TEMPERATURE
Noun/*a measure of warmth or coldness*
Every *body* (and thing) has a **temperature**—an oven, a cabbage, the weather, a human ($98.6°\mp$), etc.

HEALTHFUL
Adjective/*free of illness-causing elements*
Even a **healthful** diet cannot ensure long life; however, an **unhealthful** diet can shorten life.

HEALTHY
Adjective/*of sound mind and body*
Olympic athletes must be very **healthy** to compete rigorously for many days.

GRAMMARWORKS! I. What's the Difference? (continued)

IMPLY	INFER
Verb/*suggest*	Verb/*draw a conclusion*
What Jedd said about Ed's salary **implied** that Jedd thought Ed was overpaid.	Zed had already **inferred** that Ed was overpaid because Zed always sees Ed loafing on the job.

Found in a notable newspaper. *Here's a seventy-two word sentence with multiple parentheses and a hard-to-find pronoun antecedent! On a separate piece of paper, break up the long sentence and place the pronouns nearer their antecedents.*

"The Hollywood Bowel announced its seventy-sixth summer season Tuesday with the news that the three-phase renovation of the Bowl begun in 1994 will be complete this summer (look for a new entrance plaza and box office, additional picnic areas and a new Bowl store), and it highlighted a summerful of music beginning in mid-June (the Playboy Jazz Festival) and stretching to the end of September (Fourth Annual Salsa and Latin Jass Festival)."

GrammarWorks! Review

Circle the correct italicized words in the following sentences. Each word above is used at least once.

1. I am *anxious/eager* to see if Luc got the job. He was nervous and *anxious/eager* about the interview.
2. The detective hired a *costumer/customer* to make him a disguise so good that even the regular *costumers/customers* at the coffee house where he hangs out wouldn't recognize him.
3. Dick can *cite/site* where it says in the warranty that he gets service on *cite/site*.
4. When Char had a *fever/temperature,* her *fever/temperature* was 102 degrees!
5. An *employee/employer* is the one who hires others. An *employee/employer* is the person hired.
6. If you eat *healthy/healthful* food, you're more likely to stay *healthy/healthful*.
7. If a newborn doesn't *breath/breathe* on its own, a quick spank will cause it to take a *breath/breathe*.
8. I *implied/inferred* from your inquiry that you want the job. That's what your letter *implied/inferred*.

GRAMMARWORKS! II. What's the Difference?

LOOSE	LOSE
Adjective/*not fastened, unrestrained*	Verb/*be deprived of, be defeated, misplace*
May's **loose**-fitting garment was elegant.	I'll **lose** my job if we **lose** the account!
[GrammarTool: *"Loose as a goose"* helps you remember the pronunciation and the two *o's*.]	[GrammarTool: *"Lose your shoes"* helps to remember the pronunciation and the one *o*.]

GRAMMARWORKS! II. What's the Difference? (continued)

ROLE
Noun/*a part played in a drama or a job at work*
Lisa plays the **role** of company ombudsman.

ROLL
Verb/*to turn end over end* +
Noun/*small bread*
The cat **rolled** a dinner **roll** across the table.

THAN
Conjunction/*introduces the second part of a comparison*
Gordon is older **than** Tracy is.
He'd rather read **than** watch TV.

THEN
Adverb/*at that time, next*
Walter read the want ads, and **then** he went to make some telephone calls to employers.

WERE
Verb/*plural past tense of verb* to be
Pierre and Lavonne **were** at the County Fair.

WHERE
Pronoun/*in what place; the place in which*
Show me **where** to put the invoices.

CENT
Noun/*one hundredth of a dollar*
Rose said she didn't have a **cent.**

SCENT
Noun/*odor, aroma, perfume*
The floral **scent** made me sneeze.

SENT
Verb (past tense of *send*)/*directed, dispatched*
The teacher **sent** Art to the nurse.

KNOW
Verb/*to be aware of or acquainted with*
Do you **know** the boss's name?

NO
Adverb signifying *negative*
Adjective signifying *not any*
No, Ho. I can give you **no** dough.

NOW
Adverb/*at this time*
The printer needs the copy **now** to do the job by Monday.

QUIET
Adjective/*silent, still*
The **quiet** boy read while we talked.

QUITE
Adverb/*very, rather*
I am **quite** sure you will like Jennifer.

QUIT
Verb/*stop, end*
Harry, **quit** biting your nails!

TO
Preposition/*toward*
Quan walked **to** the bus stop to meet his sister.

TOO
Adverb/*also, excessive*
I, **too** thought there was **too** much salt in the pasta

TWO
Noun or Adjective/*cardinal number*
Two can play tic-tac-toe, so let's get **two** pencils.

GrammarWorks! Review

Circle the correct italicized words in the following sentences. Each word above is used at least once.

1. If you need *to/too/two* reasons *to/too/two* find a job, that's one reason *to/too/two* many.
2. When you *loose/lose* weight, your old clothing becomes *loose/lose*.
3. When they were young, the older boy was taller *than/then* the younger one. *Than/Then* they grew up.
4. *Know/No/Now* that you called, at least you *know/no/now* that you have *know/no/now* new messages.
5. *Were/Where* have you been? We *were/where* worried. You *were/where* supposed to be here yesterday.

6. That's *quiet/quite/quit* a cut you have. *Quiet/Quite/Quit* wiggling and be *quiet/quite/quit* while the doctor examines it.
7. You have to play an active *role/roll* in your own future. Don't let chance *role/roll* over you.
8. I *cent/scent/sent* Juan for my favorite *cent/scent/sent* in cologne. It cost him a thousand *cents/scents/sents*.

FIXING A BONEHEAD JOB INQUIRY LETTER

Date: Never 12, 1999
FAX Memo to: DREAMJOB   213-555-$$$$
FAX from: KopyKlub   818-555-NO¢¢

MESSAGE: (1)To whoever it may consern:
(2)Im faxing you my ~~resmay~~ rezumae for tthe potion of office asst. (3)I'm a pepple person whom likes pepole alot. (4)Also i am a hard-working who is very carful and trussworthy.
(5)Plaese call me so I can interview you fro this job.
(6)Sinsurly, Alec Smart

Would you consider hiring this applicant, who made twenty mistakes in his job inquiry? Edit the memo, inserting improvements. Then, explain the mistakes in each numbered sentence on the corresponding numbered line below. We did the second one as an example. [You may use short forms in your explanations: s/b = should be, s/o = spell out.]

1. _____
2. *Example: Apostrophe s/b I'm. S/b no crossouts or typos (the). potion s/b position. s/o assistant.*

3. _____

4. _____

5. _____

6. _____

On a separate sheet of paper, rewrite the job inquiry letter.

THE BIG EIGHT BONEHEADS!

- Words Misspelled
- Words or Caps Incorrect
- Sentence Fragments
- Sentence Run-Ons, Spliced or Fused
- Pronouns Confused
- Verbs Misused
- Commas Misplaced
- Apostrophes Abused

WORK! WORK! WORK!
Writing Practice

This exercise helps build skills by prompting you to express your understanding of what you learned.

"A job isn't finished until the paperwork is done."

Exercises in Job Search Writing Skills

1. Write a one-page letter inquiring about a job in your field of study and referring to your enclosed resume. Address an envelope. You can consult the sample letters in this chapter as examples.

2. Write a one-page resume. This will accompany the cover letter you write to inquire about a job in your field of study.

3. Write out a list of questions you would ask your potential employer about the position you are seeking.

4. Many applications for employment ask you to write a paragraph or two about yourself. This helps a prospective employer get to know you and to see how you organize your thoughts. Write a one-paragraph personal story that would help an employer decide to hire you.

5. Fill out the blank application form in this chapter so that you can use it to complete a job application form at a place of potential employment.

WORK! WORK! WORK!
Lesson Review

The following exercises show what you've learned in this lesson.

Fill in the Blanks Regarding Job Search Techniques

1. Besides a willing and qualified job candidate and an available position, what four ingredients are required for the job process? _____
_____.

2. Before seeking a job, be realistic about three things: _____
_____.

3. A cover letter is a job inquiry that includes a _____
_____.

4. Five items to include in your resume are _____
_____
_____.

5. On interview day, don't forget to take a _____ and some
_____.

6. Some things you should know about the company in advance of the interview
   are _____
_____.

Writing Techniques

Harcourt, Inc.

Chapter 5

EXCHANGING INFORMATION

IN THIS CHAPTER

Harcourt, Inc.

SCANS FOUNDATION: READING, WRITING
SCANS COMPETENCY: PROCESSING INFORMATION

Among the skills necessary to hold a job are the abilities to acquire (get), evaluate (judge), organize (sort), maintain (update), interpret (understand), and communicate (share) information. You can't do a job without processing information.

To develop skills in getting information, we *read,* and we *think* about what we have read to be sure that we understand it and to judge if we believe it. To develop skills in sorting, updating, and sharing information we *write* our thoughts. We then *exchange* information by communicating it to others and getting feedback that we have been understood.

We will first practice these skills by exploring the two methods of communicating information known as narration (telling stories) and description (drawing word pictures).

Let's get to work!

SCANS FOCUS: READING AND WRITING—PROCESSING INFORMATION

NO ONE WILL ARGUE WITH THIS: WE ARE IN THE INFORMATION AGE

We're overloaded with information, and the faster we can get it—or give it—the better. Information we used to wait a week for can now be express-mailed, faxed, or e-mailed. Information we could only find by personally visiting a library, we can now get from a computer disk or on the Internet—the "information highway."

Like dinosaurs, we are fossils of an ancient age if we don't know how to get and give information quickly. The United States Department of Labor Secretary's Commission on Achieving Necessary Skills (SCANS) stresses that **processing information** is an essential job skill. That means you need to be able to handle information at every stage. But, what is involved in processing information?

YOU ALREADY KNOW WHAT YOU NEED TO KNOW!

How to Acquire (Get) and Evaluate (Judge) Information

At home, in school, or on the job you get and judge information daily.
- **Home.** You **acquire** information when you look in the television guide to see what is on at 8:00 P.M. You **evaluate** information when you decide what show you want to watch.
- **School.** You **acquire** information when you look at the schedule of college classes. You **evaluate** information to select what you need to take on days that are convenient for you.
- **Job.** You **acquire** information when you go to the storeroom to see if your office needs more supplies. You **evaluate** the information and decide to order fax paper.

How to Organize (Sort) and Maintain (Update) Information

Every day, you have occasion to sort and update information.
- **Home.** You **organize** information if you keep a photo album by year or a collection of tapes by type of music. You **maintain** information when your friend

gives you some old photos of the two of you trick-or-treating and you add them to the early album pages, or when you put your Country Western tapes back in the right box when you've finished listening to them.

- **School.** You **organize** information when you divide a loose-leaf notebook into different subjects. You **maintain** information when you put the syllabi and handouts in the right places.
- **Job.** You *fail* to **organize** information if you write down an appointment on the wrong day. You *fail* to **maintain** information if you don't cross off a canceled appointment and your boss drives fifty miles for nothing.

How to Interpret (Understand) and Communicate (Share) Information

You guessed it! You do it all the time.

- **Home.** You **interpret** information when you read a soup recipe and decide it'll be better if you reduce the salt, omit the parsley, and add garlic. You **communicate** information when you tell someone who's allergic to milk that there's no milk in the casserole.
- **School.** You've *failed* to **interpret** information when the teacher gives your paper back with "Follow directions!" written on it. But you did **communicate** the information that you didn't pay attention to the directions.
- **Job.** You **interpret** information when you see a new patient crying in the waiting room. You **communicate** your interpretation when you tell your boss, the dentist, that you think the new patient is either upset about something or afraid of dentists.

From a newspaper column. *Watch that subject/verb agreement! EITHER the subject OR the verb IS incorrect. Rewrite the portion of the sentence beginning with the word NEITHER.*

In the wake of the shooting, however, neither LaChasse nor the department were interested in rehashing old controversies.

_____

_____

JOBS REQUIRE INFORMATION SKILLS!

You're in college because you want to get a job you'll like. In the Information Age, it will not be enough to get by on your charm and good looks. Counting on your fingers or calling your grandfather to ask who was president in 1953 will not work at work. It will not be enough to have a ten-year-old encyclopedia or the yellowing paperback dictionary your mom made you carry in your backpack all through elementary school. All the bosses in the world will want *current* information. They will want it now.

You'd better know where to look it up fast! You'd better know what it means! You'd better know whether to alphabetize it or list it by date! You'd better be able to find it when you need it! You'd better be able to weigh that information and determine whether you need more. You'd better be able to communicate it clearly. And you'd better be able not just "to get by" but to read and write *well*. In addition, you'd better be *computer literate*—that means, able to do work on a computer and to find information on a computer. (We'll help you do that in chapter 13.) In this chapter, we'll show you two styles of communicating information: telling stories (narration) and drawing word pictures (description). By reading the stories and articles, and by doing the exercises, you'll practice your information-processing skills in a simple, straightforward manner.

In the information age, the people who can't understand what they read and who can't write so others understand them will have plenty of time, while they're job hunting (and hunting, and hunting) to think about how they wasted their educational opportunities.

There is no doubt about this: Employers will choose to hire the person who can *find, understand,* and *communicate* information.

Want Ad
General Office
Nexus International

Immediate opening for reliable self-motivated individual. Entry level will train. Gen ofc skills. Computer exp & Spanish a plus. Good reading, writing and communication skills. Responsible for the storing and finding of all company information: sales, production, legal, and personnel. Apply in person w/resume, salary require.

SCANS Focus Exercise

The following examples show opportunities for exchanging information on the job. Read the examples, and perform the exercise below.

Travel Agent: Uses an on-line computer terminal to seek and retrieve information relating to customers' requests, plans, and itinerary. Books and prints airline tickets.

Factory Work Supervisor: Records and maintains purchase requests and cost information on raw material. Requisitions needed materials. Keeps records of labor and materials.

Child-Care Aides: Compiles accurate written records, including all facets of the children's behavior and health, for the office and the parents.

Order-Filler: Checks inventory; sees there isn't enough stock to fill order and tells inventory control person. Informs customer of due date for back order.

Merchandise Shipper: Monitors inventory records; reports overages and shortages.

Cosmetologist: Stays current with new hair and makeup styles and techniques by reading magazines and trade journals and by attending fashion shows.

In-Class SCANS Exercise

The above examples show how information skills are involved in the jobs mentioned. Choose one of the following jobs and, on a separate piece of paper, give a brief example of how information skills apply to the work being done. For example, what kind of information is used on the job? How is it acquired, organized, and exchanged?

1.   Preowned car salesman
2.   Insurance agent
3.   Postal clerk
4.   Printer
5.   Your chosen career (Remember to name your chosen career in your answer.)

What a bargain! Some words have more than one meaning, and the intended meaning can be ambiguous depending on the placement of all the words. Below, rewrite the following ad so we know whether mood or machine is being adjusted.

We oil your sewing machine and adjust tension in your home for $1.

_____

_____

"Once upon a time . . ."

TELLING STORIES—NARRATION

THE STORYTELLER INFORMS AND ENTERTAINS

Telling stories is, perhaps, the most common approach to self-expression. A writer chooses that technique to supply information because everyone enjoys a well-told story. Since time began, adults and children have gathered to share stories of their experiences—to inform others, to entertain them, or maybe to *brag.* Spoken or written narration tells of events, usually in chronological order, to interest listeners or readers or to get some reaction from them. Usually the story is compressed to omit unimportant details, so that only interesting information remains. A written narrative can be as long as a book, as short as a joke, or as unstructured as a poem.

A STORY NEEDS . . .

A Plot.
Characters.
A Narrator.

THE BASIC ELEMENTS OF STORYTELLING

Whether nonfiction (true) or fiction (in whole or in part from the author's imagination), a narrative includes the **plot,** the **characters,** and the **narrator.** The plot is what happens in the story; the characters are the people (sometimes animals) who appear in the story; and the narrator is the storyteller. In all narratives, *someone* (the narrator) says that *something meaningful happened* (the plot) *to someone* (the main character).

A STORY NEEDS . . .

A Beginning.
A Middle.
An Ending.

To be complete, a story must have a **beginning** (the set-up for the story), a **middle** (what happens that leads to the climax, the fateful action in the story), and an **end** (the resolution, also called the summary—or the French term Hollywood uses, the *dénouement* (pronounced *day-new*-MAH). A joke is a story, and every joke leads us from the beginning (the set-up) to the end (the punch line).

IS THE NARRATOR . . .

Part of the Story?
Not Part of the Story?

THE NARRATOR'S POINT OF VIEW

The narrator, or storyteller, is the person from whose **point of view** the story is told. Of course, the *writer* is the narrator of the story, but the writer usually tells the story in one of two ways: from the *third person point of view*, using third person pronouns *(he, she, it, they)*; or from the *first person point of view*, using first person pronouns *(I, we)*. In the **third person,** which is the more common approach to storytelling, the narrator is *not* a part of the action and is *not* affected by the action. (In third person point of view, use first person pronouns only when characters speak, in dialogue set off by quotation marks.) In the **first person** point of view, the narrator is a *character* in the story and speaks of himself or herself, as well as others. For example, you may write a story about your friends in either first or third person.

> **First person: My** friend Erika likes to play practical jokes. One day **she and I . . .**
>
> **Third person:** A woman named Erika likes to play practical jokes. One day **she and her friend . . .**

FIRST PERSON

When the narrator is a character in the story, **use first person pronouns.**

I, me, my, mine;
we, us, our, ours.

Writing in the First Person Using the Pronoun *I*

When the narrator is a character in the story, the story is told from the **first person point of view.** When using the first person point of view, the narrator must be present in every scene, or the narrator must explain how he knows what happened when he was not present. The narrator does not know what goes on in the other characters' minds.

An example of a **first person** *nonfiction* **narrative** is the letter—*I* write *my* bank explaining how *I* think they messed up *my* checking account. An example of **first person** *fiction* **narrative** is the mystery story that is told by the *detective narrator.*

First person: Before **I** even looked at Georgia, **I** was attracted to her by the fistful of money she shoved in **my** face. "I'll take your case," **I** said.

> ### THIRD PERSON
>
> When the narrator is "invisible" and not part of the story, **use third person pronouns.**
>
> he, him, his; she, her, hers; they, them, their, theirs.

Writing in the Third Person as an Unidentified Observer of the Events

More often, the narrator is *not* a part of the story. A news article, which includes *who, what, where, when, why,* and *how* (the 5 Ws and an H), is an example of a **third person** *nonfiction* **story.** The unidentified narrator reports what happens without inserting his presence or his opinion. In a **third person** *fiction* **story,** the narrator serves as an unidentified observer, an invisible watcher who knows what all the characters are doing all the time.

This is how the fiction mystery story would look written in the third person.

Third person: Georgia stood at **Philip's** desk, shoving a fistful of hundred-dollar bills in **his** face. **He** hadn't earned so much money from **his** last five cases. "I'll take your case," **he** said.

> ### NARRATION . . .
>
> Has a Plan!
> Makes a Point!

NARRATION HAS A PLAN AND MAKES A POINT

In writing a narrative, you'll want to remember all these elements.

- Whether it's a true or fictional story, *something meaningful happens to someone.*
- The narrator tells the story *from a consistent point of view,* first or third person.
- In the **beginning,** the writer *sets up the characters and their problems.*
- In the **middle,** the story *flows forward in a logical order* that *leads the main characters to a decisive action (the climax).*
- In the **end,** the writer *answers all the questions* he placed in the reader's mind.

Three other features help make a good narrative. (1) A story is interesting because of its **conflict.** *The main character has to overcome obstacles to gain what he or she seeks.* (2) Characters are interesting because they **change or grow.** *What they experience makes them different at the end.* (3) A good storyteller recognizes that the audience is essential to the story and provides a good **payoff.** *The reader accepts the ending and is glad that he or she has spent the time reading the story.*

GOOD STORIES HAVE . . .

Conflict!
Characters that *Change*
because of What Happens!
A Good Payoff!

The following are examples of good student and professional storytelling.

The student author's assignment: Write about friendship using the storytelling technique.
Phong B. Diep is originally from Vietnam. He arrived in the United States several years ago with little knowledge of the English language.

```
Phong B. Diep                                    Diep 1
English 101-9:00
Storytelling
March 27, 1999
             That Is What Friends Are For

    It was only five in the afternoon, but the sun had long since
disappeared over the western horizon. On this moonless night,
Dean Barlow's old station wagon rumbled up the driveway of
his home and pulled to a complete stop next to the front
door. He let the engine idle for several moments before he
finally twisted the key out of the ignition. The engine died
out, but Dean slumped back into the driver's seat with no
intention of leaving the car just yet. He looked toward the
house. Dark and hungry, it awaited him to make his entrance,
and then it would swallow him up into eternal blackness.
Dean shook his head, trying to dislodge the irrational
thought.
    The day marked his thirty-fifth birthday, but he was
oblivious to the occasion because his life had ended six
months ago when his wife and eight-year-old daughter were
```

killed in a robbery at the local 7-Eleven. It left him
feeling empty and helpless, with nothing to live for. Life
goes on, but he had never known a moment of peace or
happiness since. His job was his only escape and distraction
from his inner turmoil. As a result, his loss turned into an
obsession.

Dean shunned his close friends and all people in
general, turning himself into a regular hermit. But at times
like these, he'd give anything just to have someone to talk
to or share a drink with. He glanced up at the rearview
mirror and stared longingly at the warm glows emanating from
some of the houses on the opposite side of the street. He
longed to be sitting under one of those glows, enjoying a
good dinner with his own family. Then he noticed the
unusually large number of cars parked along both sides of
the street. Ah, well, Dean sighed, someone is probably
giving a party or something. And he dismissed the thought.

Dean trudged heavily toward the front door and fumbled
in his coat pocket for the house keys. Surprisingly, the
door was unlocked, but it was no big deal. He was very
forgetful these days. Inside, without even bothering to turn
on a light, he started to take off his coat. All of a
sudden, lights from all over the house, as far as he could
see, were flicked on by invisible hands, causing a dull
throbbing in the back of his eyes. Faces popped out from
behind tables, chairs, doors, and sofas. They all screamed
"SURPRISE!" and he was attacked with paper confetti and
sprays of some kind of cold liquids. He stood wide eyed and
open mouthed as the people around him yelled out "HAPPY
BIRTHDAY!" The faces became familiar, and he finally
recognized them as his friends and neighbors. With the
innocence of a four-year-old, Dean whispered, "You guys
remembered my birthday . . . and you're giving me a party!"
An old buddy of his from high school yelled across the room
jovially, "Hey, that's what friends are for!"

For the first time in months, Dean detected a small glint
of happiness creeping into his heart. It felt good to be
loved and cared about. Maybe, just maybe, life would truly
go on for him after all. As for the time being, he was
determined to relax, enjoy the party, and maybe even learn
to be sociable again.

 **WORK! WORK! WORK!**

These exercises help build skills by prompting you to express your understanding of what you read.

Reading Comprehension

1. Why didn't Dean want to go inside his house? _____

_____

2. In a story, the main character changes in some way. What are the emotions Dean felt at the beginning, in the middle, and at the end of the story? _____

_____

_____

Writing Analysis

1. From whose point of view was the story told? _____

2. What is the purpose of the first paragraph? _____

_____

3. What is the purpose of the second paragraph? _____

_____

4. What is the "climax" of the story? _____

_____

The following professional article, in written narration, reflects the message that time marches on—to the tune of technology.

Changing Times
by Bill Bucci

Not long ago, Smith of Derby, the largest clock maker in Britain, was running out of time.

Over four generations, the company developed a reputation for quality and craftsmanship through creations such as the Great Clock in Saint Paul's Cathedral in London, and through major repair work on large clocks in Windsor Castle, Westminster Abbey, and Canterbury Cathedral. The company was even called upon to restore the oldest working clock in the world: the Salisbury Cathedral Tower clock, built in 1386.

"We've had a tradition of being the best right from the beginning," says Nick Smith, the company's group chairman and the great-grandson of John Smith, who founded Smith of Derby in 1856. "The first John Smith set new standards of reliability and longevity by using lighter weights in clock mechanisms, something that was rare at the time."

But in recent years, it became clear that tradition alone wasn't enough. Faced with rising costs, changing demand for clocks and growing competition, Smith of Derby found that many of its old methods were too labor-intensive and time-consuming.

"Our clocks were expensive," says Smith. "As we watched other clock companies dying out around us, we knew we'd have to overhaul our product line and change our manufacturing practices."

Smith, who calls himself a "bad accountant who had a fighting chance of being an entrepreneur," began doing just that. To better match products with customer needs, research and development specialists and salespeople were put in closer contact with each other. The company's managers scoured other industries for lower-cost production methods they could use in clock making. And they now subcontract the manufacture of many parts to outside companies with modern water- and laser-cutting equipment—techniques that provide more flexibility in terms of materials and design than the traditional casting and machining methods. "We can offer finely detailed features—say, all the feathers of a peacock on a weather vane—without having to resort to painting them on," says Smith." It looks a lot better and it's much less expensive to make."

Perhaps most critical was the movement of much of Smith of Derby's work to CAD. Using MicroStation software for design and layout work, the company was able to streamline operations—without sacrificing the tradition of quality that has long been its hallmark. For example, says Smith, before releasing designs for manufacturing, older artisans review the plans. "They have the kind of experience that's passed down from generation to generation of clock makers, and that can make all the difference. They'll say, 'If you use an exact fit, it will seize up very quickly with stone grit. But if you use a clock maker's fit, which leaves more space, the grit will drop through the other side of the gears.' So we'll adjust the design on the computer to factor in their practical know-how and wind up with a much more dependable product."

The advent of more modern methods has dramatically cut production time and labor costs. Clock design and manufacturing typically begins with loading initial client drawings directly into the computer—thereby avoiding the problem of things getting "lost in translation," says Smith. On the system, it's easy to scale drawings to actual size and modify them to the client's specific needs. "We consider aesthetics very important and match designs to the antiquity or modernity of a building. If we think we can improve on architects' designs or if they seek our advice, we make suggestions—especially with an eye to ensuring that the clock is easy to maintain and works reliably."

Most aspects of clock design utilize the computer: general layouts of tower clocks, steelwork for supporting platforms, stairways for access to service areas, clock faces, dials, hands and various types of wind vanes. Many standard internal mechanisms are stored in a MicroStation cell library, eliminating the need to redraw those parts for each job.

The company also has an extensive library of clock faces and hands it can customize to suit a specific client or match a building's architecture. When the on-screen design is complete, clients get printouts. Upon approval, CAM files, created from the MicroStation design, are sent on disk to the outside manufacturer, which uses the files to directly drive production.

In all, the process is much faster than it used to be. A case in point, says Chris Camm, design engineer, is the fifteen-foot Mickey Mouse clock—complete with Mickey's arms as the hands—installed three years ago in the main hotel at Euro-Disney near Paris. "It would have taken us months to make all the various colored-glass sections of the dial if we'd tried to do it manually. Using MicroStation, we digitized the material we got from Disney, selected the appropriate internal mechanisms and had everything approved in a few days. First, we test-cut the hands in plywood—they fit perfectly the first time. Then we went into production and laser-cut the entire dial—and all the colored glass—in two hours."

Harcourt, Inc.

The CAD system also has made repair work easier, especially on older mechanical clocks. (These historical clocks account for half of the company's business.) Camm typically traces a faulty part on a digitizing tablet, builds up the worn areas on-screen and produces a CAM file for manufacturing. "The result matches the original, except that now it's as good as new," Camm says. "Imagine trying to do that by hand."

Finally, says Smith, the technology has helped the company improve on tradition as well as uphold it. "We realized that we didn't have to make things as complicated as we had in the past. Now we can test redesigns on the computer before going into production, still get high quality and workmanship, and save money."

With more efficiency and lower costs, Smith of Derby has not only held its own in traditional markets, it has also been able to explore new opportunities. "We've expanded into custom markets that were closed to us because we were too expensive," says Smith. "In Chicago, we built the highest clock in the world. We supply floral clocks with moving figures and other customized clocks throughout the world. Our clocks harmonize with—and enhance—the architecture of modern office buildings, atriums, supermarkets, opera houses and other public places. It would have been very difficult, time-consuming and quite expensive to attain that kind of versatility without CAD/CAM."

That versatility is evident in Smith of Derby's ability to compete in a healthy mix of old and new areas. The company's recent projects include:

- Restoration of a 1765 clock in Charleston, South Carolina—the oldest clock in the United States. When another company electrified the clock, most of the original mechanism was scrapped. Using MicroStation, Smith of Derby successfully restored the clock using only the original frames, a few parts and historical records.
- The installation of auto-winding units for the quarter-chiming cage clock in Westminster Abbey and for a 1689 clock movement in Windsor Castle.
- Design and manufacture of a complex "automata" clock for a Stuttgart opera house. The elaborately designed clock has birds and animals that move and make sounds, and panels that open within the dial at certain hours.
- Design and manufacture of a custom clock for a mall in temple Court in Birmingham, England. The fifteen-foot diameter clock is in the shape of a pocket watch, compete with a chain of twenty-four links, each three feet long.

In another arena, Smith of Derby used its CAD system to grow revenues in the historic clock market, developing an automatic winder for old mechanical clocks that used to require weekly or even daily hand-windings. "Our auto-winding product is an add-on that retains the original clock-winding mechanism," says Smith. "That's particularly important in the United Kingdom, where we've taken a very conservationist approach to hand-wound clocks."

Today, Smith of Derby has more than 10,000 clocks installed in nearly fifty countries. In the United Kingdom, it services more than 4,500 public clocks a year. What does that all mean for the bottom line? "We don't like to give out sales figures because it tips off the competition," says Smith. "But I think the fact that we are seventy-five strong, and our closest competitor in the United Kingdom employs twelve people, speaks for itself. The changes we've made in recent years, including CAD/CAM, have helped make us the market leader.

"CAD/CAM gives us a way of communicating into the future, of continuing our tradition and making sure that priceless human skills are handed on as our people retire," Smith continues.

Perhaps the greatest benefit of the technology, he adds, is that it enables the company to respond quickly to changing demands. "It gives us that extra edge in terms of design and price flexibility. That's crucial because you never know what to expect in this business. One day we might be ministering to a fourteenth century clock, another day installing infrared controls for a polo clock. We even had an inquiry recently for an enormous clock in the mountains of Australia to be driven by solar power. It turned out to be too expensive for the client, but we knew we could have made the clock and it would have kept the right time. There's no limit now to what we can do."

───────●───────

Exercise Related to the Professional Article from the World of Work

Reading Comprehension

1. In what country is Smith of Derby located? _____

2. In moving from old planning methods, Smith now uses CAD. What does CAD mean? _____

3. Another credit to Smith is CAM. What does CAM mean? _____

_____

4. To what does Smith credit its success? _____

_____

_____

Writing Analysis

1. The author intentionally emphasizes time in the opening paragraph. Why? _____

_____

2. From what point of view is the article written? _____

3. What sentence expresses the *denouement* of the story? _____

_____

_____

GRAMMARWORKS! Verbs: Present, Past, and Beyond

When speaking of verbs, the word *tense* means time. The following illustration shows the tenses of *regular* verbs. See later tables for some commonly used *irregular* verb parts.

Regular verbs have three parts, including the root, for example, *to work.* To the root verb, we add *-ed* or *-ing* to form other tenses (or the other parts of the verb), for example, *worked, working.* You'll be surprised to know how many verb tenses you use! (The verbs in parentheses follow *third person singular* subjects [he, she, it].)

REGULAR VERBS LIKE *TO WORK*	PRESENT TENSE	PAST TENSE	FUTURE TENSE (*WILL* + PRESENT)
Simple	I, we, you, they do/don't work; he, she, it does/ doesn't work.	I, he, she, it, we, you they worked; I, he, she, it, we, you they did/didn't work	will/won't work

GRAMMARWORKS! Verbs: Present, Past, and Beyond (continued)

REGULAR VERBS LIKE *TO WORK*	PRESENT TENSE	PAST TENSE	FUTURE TENSE (*WILL* + PRESENT)
Progressive (means *in progress*) (Add form of **to be**.)	I am working; he, she, it is working; we, you, they are working.	I, he, she, it was working; we, you, they were working	will be working
Simple Perfect (Add form of **to have**.)	I, we, you, they have worked; he, she, it has worked.	had worked	will have worked
Progressive Perfect (Add forms of **to have** and **to be**.)	I, we, you, they have been working; he, she, it has been working.	had been working	will have been working

Two important verbs *help* form tenses of other verbs: **to have** and **to be.**
They are *irregular verbs* and their parts follow no pattern.

To form the *progressive* tense, use the proper form of **to be,** plus the *-ing* form of the main verb. For example, playing: **I am, he is ____; we, you, they are ____; I, he, she, it was ____; we, you, they were ____; will be ____.**

To form the *simple perfect* tense, use the proper form of **to have,** plus the *-ed* form of a main verb. For example, watched: **I, we, you, they have ____; he, she, it has ____; had ____; will have ____.**

To form the *present, past,* and *future progressive perfect* tenses, use the proper form of **to have,** plus *been* (of the verb *to be*), plus the *-ing* form of the main verb. For example, counting: **I, we, you, they have been ____; he, she, it has been ____; had been ____, will have been ____.**

GRAMMARWORKS! Forming Tenses of Regular Verbs

It's not as hard as it seems. There are just *four* kinds of present, past, and future tenses: **simple, progressive, simple perfect,** and **progressive perfect.**

THE FOUR KINDS OF TENSES OF REGULAR VERBS: HOW TO FORM THEM AND WHAT THEY EXPRESS

Simple Present: Use the root of the verb.
   Simple present is used to express a current action or condition.
Simple Past: Add *-ed* to the root of the verb.
   Simple past is used to express a past action.
Simple Future: Use **will** with the root of the verb.
   Simple future is used to express an expected or anticipated action.

Progressive Present: Use **am/is/are** with the *present* participle. Another word for participle is *part.*
   Progressive present expresses an ongoing action in the present time.
Progressive Past: Use **was/were** with the *present* participle.
   Progressive present expresses an ongoing action in the past time.
Progressive Future: Use **will be** with the *present* participle.
   Progressive future expresses an ongoing action in the future time.

GRAMMARWORKS! Forming Tenses of Regular Verbs (continued)

Simple Perfect Present: Use **have/has** with the *past* participle.
Present perfect expresses an action that has been completed or perfected in the present.
Simple Perfect Past: Use **had** with the *past* participle.
Past perfect expresses an action completed or perfected in the past.
Simple Perfect Future: Use **will have/has** with the *past* participle.
Future perfect expresses an action completed or perfected in the future.

Progressive Perfect Present: Use **have/has been** with the *past* participle.
Progressive present perfect expresses a progressive action that occurs in the present.
Progressive Perfect Past: Use **had been** with the *past* participle.
Progressive past perfect expresses a progressive action that occurred in the past.
Progressive Perfect Future: Use **will have been** with the *past* participle.
Progressive future perfect expresses a progressive action that will occur in the future.

GRAMMARWORKS! Tenses of the Regular Verb: *To Rain*

Here, in all its tenses, is the *regular* verb, **to rain.**
Root Word = **rain**   Present Participle = **raining**   Past Participle = **rained**

Note: Notice that the sentences express more complex thoughts as the verbs become more complex.

Simple Present, Past, and Future
It **rains** in winter.   It **rained** yesterday.   It **will rain** tomorrow.

Progressive (in progress) Present, Past, and Future:
It **is raining** right now.   It **was raining** as I was   It **will be raining** all day.
                                 walking here.

Simple Perfect Present, Past, and Future:
It **has rained** for four days in a row.
It **had rained** in the morning, but it had stopped before the picnic.
It **will have rained** five days in a row if it stops raining tomorrow.

Progressive Perfect Present, Past, and Future:
It **has been raining** somewhere in the world every day since the world began.
It **had been raining** daily in To'anga—until the rain forest was cleared away.
It **will have been raining** all this month if rains for two more days.

GRAMMARWORKS! Forms of the Regular Verb: *To Ask*

Here are the verb forms for the *regular* verb, **to ask.**
Root Word = **ask**   Present Participle = **asking**   Past Participle = **asked**

VERB FORM	PRESENT	PAST	FUTURE
Simple	I ask, do ask; he/she/it asks, does ask; we/you/they ask, do ask	asked; did ask	will ask

GRAMMARWORKS! Forms of the Regular Verb: *To Ask* (continued)

VERB FORM	PRESENT	PAST	FUTURE
Progressive	I am asking; he/she/it is asking; we/you/they are asking	I was asking; he/she/it was asking; we/you/they were asking	will be asking
Simple Perfect	I have asked; he/she/it has asked; we/you/they have asked	had asked	will have asked
Progressive Perfect	I have been asking; he/she/it has been asking; we/you/they have been asking	had been asking	will have been asking

GrammarWorks! Review

*Fill in the blanks with forms of the regular verb **to learn**. Follow this order: simple present, past, and future; progressive present, past, and future; simple perfect present, past, and future; and progressive perfect present, past, and future.*

Root Word = **learn**   Present Participle = **learning**   Past Participle = **learned**

Every day, I _____ something new. Yesterday, I

_____ how to floss my dog's teeth. Tomorrow, I

_____ where Latvia is. At school, I _____

how to make a living. I _____ to play Hearts, but I didn't get it,

so I _____ a different game instead. All together, I

_____ three new card games. I thought I

_____ a lot in my life already, but by the time I graduate,

I _____ a whole lot more. I _____ for twenty

years so far. I _____ before I even realized it. When I am ninety,

I _____ for ninety years.

THE BIG EIGHT BONEHEADS!

- Words Misspelled
- Words or Caps Incorrect
- Sentence Fragments
- Sentence Run-Ons, Spliced or Fused
- Pronouns Confused
- Verbs Misused
- Commas Misplaced
- Apostrophes Abused

FIXING A BONEHEAD PERSONAL STORY
Read the paragraph and then follow the directions below.

I GOT HIT ONCE TOO OFFEN
BY RAMROD R.

(1) Last friday, we was about to play a football game. (2) My coach ask me, "Hay, Ramrod, are we ready for tonight?" (3) I replied, "Me and the team is ready, Coach." (4) Are opponents, Eastside high school, with a record of 0 and 4. (5) We could sure have fun beeting up on them, how could you loose? (6) Our record stands at 3 and 1 Im the only one who knows how to call our offensive plays. (7) We kicked off. (8) On forth down I blitz their punter. (9) The next thing I hear was my coach yelling, "Hey, guys! Were having a meeting in the looker room." (10) I said, "but the games just started!" (11) The coach say, "Ramrod you got hit everything went downhill. (12) We turned the ball over to much, because nobody new what to do. (13) And loss 14 to 20." (14) if your not around you can't pass on information."

Edit the paragraph above. Search for the Big Eight: circle misspelled words, wrong words, and wrong capitalizations. Put an X in front of sentence fragments, run-on, spliced, and fused sentences. Underline misused pronouns and verbs and the comma and apostrophe errors. Each sentence above has a number. On the lines below, write what you've found wrong with each numbered sentence. (Write what you found wrong with sentence (1) on line 1, and so on.)

1. _____
2. _____
3. _____
4. _____
5. _____
6. _____
7. _____
8. _____
9. _____
10. _____
11. _____
12. _____
13. _____

How does the paragraph illustrate the storytelling technique? _____

_____

How does the paragraph illustrate information skills? _____

_____

Now you're ready to revise the paragraph. Write it in your own words on a separate piece of paper.

WORK! WORK! WORK!

Writing Practice

The following prompts will help you pick a topic to show what you've learned about the writing technique studied in this lesson. On your paper, indicate whether the story you are writing is fiction or nonfiction.

"A job isn't finished until the paperwork is done."

Nonfiction

1. A news article tells who, what, where, when, why, and how. Write a 250-word news article about an outrageous or noteworthy circumstance on campus or in your community. Remember: News articles require *headlines!*

Fiction

1. In a narrative of three or more paragraphs, using the *third* person point of view, make up a story about something humorous or life changing that happens to someone.

Fiction or Nonfiction (indicate *fiction* or *nonfiction* on your paper)

A story can be defined like this: *Something meaningful happens to someone.*

1. Write a story of three or more paragraphs—from the *first* person point of view—about friendship or family or a subject of your choice.

2. Write a story of three or more paragraphs—from the *third* person point of view of a goldfish, a mouse, or any animal or insect—about a subject of your choice.

From the newspaper. *None means* not one, *so its verb should be singular, too, right? Find the sentence with the subject/verb disagreement and rewrite it correctly below.*

The bus driver was taken to St. Mary Medical Center. None of the about twenty-five other passengers were injured.

_____

_____

WORK! WORK! WORK!

Lesson Review

The following practices show what you've learned in this lesson.

SCANS Focus

1. Looking up a word in the thesaurus is an example of
   _____ information. Deciding which similar word to use
   is an example of _____ information.

2. When you put addresses in an address book, you _____
   information.

3. When you replace an old address with a new one, you
   _____ it.

4. When you take a phone message and pass it along to the appropriate person,
   you have _____ and _____ info.

Fill In the Blanks Regarding Storytelling, or Narrative Writing

1. In a narrative story, someone (the narrator) says that
   _____ (the plot) to _____ (the main
   character).

2. A story written in whole or part from the writer's imagination is called
   _____. The opposite of this, a true story, is called
   _____.

3. Narrative points of view are generally either _____ or
   _____ person.

GrammarWorks! Review

Fill in the blanks with the pronouns and verb tenses.

1. The third person singular, simple present tense, of the regular verb *to wash* is
   he/she/it washes. Write the third person singular pronouns with the *simple past*
   tense of the regular verb *to wash.* _____

2. Write the third person singular pronouns with the progressive past tense of the
   regular verb *to shop.* _____

3. Write the third person plural pronoun with the past perfect tense of the regular verb
   to love. _____

4. Write the third person plural pronoun with progressive past perfect tense of the
   regular verb *to look.* _____

5. Write the first person singular pronoun with the simple present tense of the regular
   verb *to live.* _____

6. Write the first person singular pronoun with the progressive present tense of the
   verb *to cry.* _____

7. Write the first person plural pronoun with the present perfect tense of the regular
   verb *to cook.* _____

8. Write the first person plural pronoun with the progressive perfect present tense of
   the verb *to inform.* _____

"It was a dark and stormy night . . . "

DRAWING WORD PICTURES—DESCRIPTION

DRAWING WORD PICTURES HELPS US TELL OTHERS WHAT WE SEE, THINK, OR FEEL

One aspect of good narratives is vivid description. Describing things is a method of communicating information. Here are some everyday occasions for descriptions.

- We tell a friend about the clothes we bought.
- We tell a mechanic what's wrong with our car.
- We tell the barber or hairdresser how we want our hair cut.
- We tell a contractor how we want our house remodeled.
- We tell the nurse our symptoms.
- We read about the kinds of cameras available so we can make an informed decision before we buy.
- We tell the server at the restaurant that we want our steak pink, but not *too* pink, with the outside charred and the inside juicy.
- We read the tempting paragraphs on a menu that tell about the house specialities.

"He has a nice car" doesn't tell us much. But if someone says, "He owns a black, convertible, cherry '91 Olds, with white leather seat covers and a rad stereo," *that's a word picture!* Right?

GOOD DESCRIPTIONS DON'T HAVE TO BE LONG ONES

We shouldn't overestimate the depth of our listeners' or readers' interest! **A few words** can describe the texture of the carpenter's fingers: *rough as Velcro.* **One paragraph** might be enough to describe a car you'd like to own. **Many paragraphs** could be written to describe the rooms of your home. The topic almost tells you how big the whole descriptive word picture should be. When describing the benefits of a new computer program to help you at work, you'd want to give the boss *exactly the right amount* of information.

WHAT'S THE BIG IDEA?

Be clear, not vague.
Focus on what's important.

FOCUS ON THE MAIN POINT YOU WANT TO MAKE

Sometimes we have a vague idea of what we want to say. When we're *talking,* we can use a lot of words before we get around to exactly what we want to tell someone. In *writing,* we have to shave away all those extra words. A reader will lose interest if you only give him a *vague* idea of what you have in mind. To help you focus on exactly what you want to say, you can list all the features of the thing you want to describe and then eliminate the less important ones.

WHO CARES? YOU DO!

Keep the reader interested in what interests *you.*

Harcourt, Inc.

YOU WANT TO KEEP THE READERS' INTEREST

Keep this in mind: Each person is his or her own favorite subject! **Writers** want to share something *they're* interested in, to tell something about *themselves*. **Readers** want to read what's interesting to *them*, something that will tell them about *themselves*. Many things we have to say are interesting to us *and* to others because of the universal appeal of common human experiences. If we write about something *very* common, we must have something new to say about it—we must give it our own slant.

Would it be okay with you if your friends wandered off in the middle of what you're saying to them? *No!* You would "hook" their interest so they will listen until you've finished your "story." When you go fishing, you want to *hook* the fish and reel it in. Unlike fish, readers should be *glad* they got hooked! Writing is the attempt to interest others in what is interesting to the writer.

TIRED OLD WORDS ARE BORING TO READERS!

Knock, knock. *Who's there?* Banana. *Banana who?*
Knock, knock. *Who's there?* Banana. *Banana who?*
Knock, knock. *Who's there?* Orange. *Orange who?*
Orange you glad I didn't say "banana"?

DICTIONARIES HAVE HUNDREDS OF THOUSANDS OF WORDS—TRY SOME NEW ONES!

There are many ways to gain and keep the readers' attention. One of them is to choose *fresh* and *vivid* words. The best descriptions are not strung with sparkling adjectives like a Christmas tree is strung with lights. The best descriptions are those in which you convey the main impression the subject has made on you with *powerful* nouns and verbs, but *few* adjectives and adverbs. *"Leo's a really cool actor"* doesn't communicate the extent to which the movie star mesmerizes the writer. Try to express yourself in a way no one else would say it, in a more descriptive way: *"My baby green orbs stick like magnets to Leo every moment he graces the screen."* When you write powerfully, you give your readers the idea you want them to get, and they enjoy the process of understanding you. The object is to connect with the readers so that they relate *personally* to what you have told them.

The meaning changes sometimes when two words are written as one word. Find the bonehead and write it correctly below.

And now, the Superstore—unequaled in size, unmatched in variety, unrivaled inconvenience.

_____

SOME TRICKS OF THE WRITER'S TRADE

Draw Word Pictures with Figures of Speech

Writers use all kinds of tricks to help their readers better understand them. Sometimes they get their thoughts across by painting visual pictures with words, using imaginative **figures of speech** that have implications beyond the meaning of the words themselves. Figures of speech include **similes, metaphors, personification, understatement, hyperbole,** and **analogy.** Using these figures of speech helps draw images for the mind's eye and adds color, emphasis, and clarity to your writing.

Simile (pronounced SIMM-*uh-lee*) *compares* two *unlike* things, using *like* or *as*.

- **Like:** *He stuck* to her **like** *a wet bathing suit.*
  Her *term paper* was so thick it looked **like** *the phone book.*
- **As:** The *little boy* was **as** *muddy* **as** *a pig* in a barnyard.
  The *mayor* was **as** *crooked* **as** *a broken pencil.*

Metaphor (pronounced MET-*uh-fore*) expresses *similar qualities* of *unlike* things, without using *like* or *as*.

- Sunlight turned the *snow* into a *blanket of diamonds.*
- To the cow, *the green wheat in the neighboring field* was *a party waiting to happen.*

Personification (pronounced *purr-SOHN-ifi-CAY-shun*) invests *human characteristics* in a *lifeless* thing.

- Broke and without a job, he knew *hunger sat shivering on the curbside.*
- In the bedroom with the pillow over her head, *she could still hear the chocolate calling to her from the kitchen.*

Understatement uses more moderate words than the facts call for.

- Eric was *slightly upset* when he failed his courses and was put on academic probation.
- The Grand Canyon is a *somewhat large* hole in the ground.

Hyperbole (pronounced *high-PURR-bowl-ee*), the opposite of *understatement, overstates* or *exaggerates* a situation or a thing.

- She was so hungry *she ate everything in the kitchen, including the table.*
- He's pumped iron so long *he could spit nails.*

Analogy makes a point by telling a *parallel* story, often a long story, without mentioning the real subject.

- Facing stress: *If you can't stand the heat, get out of the kitchen.*
- Taking risks: *Don't put all your eggs in one basket.*

When *talking*, have you ever exaggerated to make your story more interesting? Have you used similes or metaphors to draw word pictures—without knowing you were being so clever? Well, you'll find figures of speech very useful when you're *writing*, too.

FIGURES OF SPEECH DRAW WORD PICTURES!

Simile: *Compares* unlike things, using *like* or *as*.
Metaphor: Expresses *similar qualities* of *unlike* things.
Personification: Gives *human* qualities to a *lifeless* thing.
Understatement: *Minimizes* the facts.
Hyperbole: *Exaggerates* the facts.
Analogy: Tells a *parallel* story.

Harcourt, Inc.

Use Common Senses!

Referring to common experience is another device writers use to make their meaning clear. A good way to describe something is to express how that thing affects our *senses*. Authors often use the senses of taste, touch, smell, sound, and sight to influence the reader's understanding. They describe things in ways that we have all experienced them through our **five senses.**

DESCRIBING WITH YOUR FIVE SENSES

How does it *taste?*
How does it *feel?*
How does it *smell?*
How does it *sound?*
How does it *look?*

In writing with word pictures, our purpose is to pass along information about ourselves, other people, things, and circumstances. Because the object of writing is to express what we're thinking, we choose words that will help other people understand us better. Saying "The native music was rhythmic" isn't as effective as saying "The drum beat like a hurried heart ahead of the twanging lyre pursuing it." Don't worry! This is more extreme than what you might try to come up with in your writing exercises. Just remember that the more vivid the description, the better the image for the reader.

Taste: I could taste the salt of the sea in the wind.
Touch: My fingers felt the warm, sticky blood, and I knew my nose was broken.
Smell: The woman had on so much perfume, she smelled like a candle shop.
Sound: The rain made a "rat-a-tat" noise on the tin roof of the shack.
Sight: The sunset was an artist's pallette of orange, purple, and yellow.

These words call up the same sensations in most of us because they are common experiences of taste, touch, smell, sound, and sight. Using figures of speech and references to things commonly known will make your descriptions colorful, interesting, and meaningful.

The following student and professional examples draw good word pictures.

The student author's assignment: Write a brief essay about your vehicle, using the technique of drawing word pictures.
Rosa Granados majored in culinary arts and hopes to become a chef.

Granados 1

Rosa Granados
English 120-8:00
Drawing Word Pictures
Sept. 14, 1999

My 240SX

    We've all imagined the perfect car for us. Actually buying that new "dream car" can be a great experience. After all the financial matters are over, you get to enjoy your new investment in status and image.

    When I first saw the new 240SX, I fell in love with its sleek, sexy shape. Its smooth curves were eye-catching, yet the hatchback gave it a conservative look. When I was at the dealer buying my car, I was trying to decide which color to get. When I saw it in black, I knew that was the color for me. Black gives me the feeling of sexiness, mysteriousness, sleekness, and ferociousness. This is exactly what I saw when I looked at this car. I pictured myself in this sporty vehicle. I felt it suited my personality perfectly.

    When I sat down in the bucket-style seat, I was amazed how comfortable I was. The seat was reclined. I almost felt like falling asleep, but I didn't. I looked throughout the car and was pleased with the dark grey interior and modern, slanted dashboard.

    Finally, it was time for me to drive off. I started the car and pulled away with caution. As soon as I got onto the freeway, I was gone like the wind. My car took off like a bullet out of a gun. I must admit, I've won a few races with my sporty, fast car. Driving my dream car is everything I expected it to be.

WORK! WORK! WORK!

These exercises help build skills by prompting you to express your understanding of what you've read.

Reading Comprehension

1. Descriptive passages convey information about all kinds of things. What does Rosa say about herself while describing her car? _____

   _____

2. What did you like best about Rosa's car? _____

   _____

3. What features would you want in a new car? _____

_____

_____

Writing Analysis

1. In descriptions, authors often use such figures of speech as simile, metaphor, and personification. Write down two figures of speech Rosa used in her last paragraph and identify them by type of figure of speech. _____

_____

_____

2. Throughout the story, the writer describes the car as if it had human qualities. What are examples of these terms, and what is the figure of speech that gives human qualities to inanimate objects? _____

_____

_____

From the Sports section. *Are the mistakes in the last sentence the fault of the coach or the sports writer who quoted him? Rewrite the last sentence to correct the run-on and the two misused words.*

"You're probably not going to win all your games. . . but this is a team that had lost two games at home all year and (then) lost two in one week. So I'm not real happy about that and they players aren't either."

_____

_____

The following professional article makes good use of description to explain how designing and drafting were done before computers facilitated the process.

Computer-Aided Design Drafters and Technicians

DEFINITION

CAD technicians use computer-based systems to produce or revise technical illustrations needed in the design and development of machines, products, buildings, manufacturing processes, and other work.

Harcourt Inc.

HISTORY

CAD/CAM technology came about in the 1970s with the development of microprocessors (computer processors in the form of miniaturized integrated circuits contained on tiny silicon chips). Microprocessors opened up many new uses for computers by greatly reducing the size of computers while also increasing their power and speed.

Amazingly enough, the drafters and designers working to develop these microprocessors were also the first to benefit from this technology. Until that point, designing and drafting were done the old-fashioned way, with pen and paper on a drafting board. To make a circle, drafters used a compass. To draw straight lines and the correct angles, they used a straightedge, slide rule, and other tools. With every change required before a design was right, it was "back to the drawing board" to get out the eraser, sharpen the pencil, and revise the drawing. Everybody did it this way, whether the design was simple or complex: automobiles, hammers, printed circuit boards, utility piping, highways, or buildings.

As the circuits on the silicon chips that the designers were working on became too complex to diagram by pencil and paper, the designers began to use the chips themselves to help store information, create models, and produce diagrams for the design of new chip circuits. This was just the beginning of computer-assisted design and drafting technology. Today, there are tens of thousands of CAD work stations in industrial settings. The use of CAD systems greatly speed and simplify the designer's and drafter's work. They do more than just let the operator "draw" the technical illustration on the screen. They add the speed and power of computer processing, plus software with technical information that ease the designer's and drafter's tasks. CAD systems make complex mathematical calculations, spot problems, offer advice, and provide a wide range of other assistance. Makers of CAD equipment expect their products to continue to sell very well in the years to come, so that by about the year 2000 nearly all drafting tasks will be done with such equipment.

NATURE OF THE WORK

Technicians specializing in CAD technology usually work in the design and drafting activities associated with new product research and development, although many work in other areas such as structural mechanics or piping. CAD technicians must combine drafting and computer skills. They work in any field where detailed drawings, diagrams, and layouts are important aspects of developing new product designs—for example, in architecture, electronics, and in the manufacturing of automobiles, aircraft, computers, and missiles and other defense systems. Most CAD technicians specialize in a particular industry or on one part of design.

CAD technicians work under the direction and supervision of CAD engineers and designers, experts highly trained in applying computer technology to industrial design and manufacturing. These designers and engineers plan how to relate the CAD technology and equipment to the design process. They are also the ones who give assignments to the CAD technicians.

These technicians work at specially designed and equipped interactive computer graphics work stations. They call up computer files that hold data about a new product; they then run the programs to convert that information into diagrams and drawings of the product. These are displayed on a video display screen, which then acts as an electronic drawing board. Following the directions of a CAD engineer or designer, the CAD technician enters changes to the product's design into the computer. The technician then merges these changes into the data file, then displays the corrected diagrams and drawings.

The software in CAD systems is very helpful to the user—it offers suggestions and advice and even points out errors. The most important advantage of working with a CAD system is that it saves the technician from the lengthy process of having to produce, by hand, the original and then the revised product drawings and diagrams.

The CAD work station is equipped to allow technicians to perform calculations, develop simulations, and manipulate and modify the displayed material. Using typed commands at a keyboard, a stylus or light pen for touching the screen display, a mouse, joystick, or other electronic methods of interacting with the display, technicians can move, rotate, zoom in on any aspect of the drawing on the screen, and project three-dimensional images from two-dimensional sketches. They can make experimental changes to the design and then run tests on the modified design to determine its qualities, such as weight, strength, flexibility, and the cost of materials that would be required. Compared to traditional drafting and design techniques, CAD offers virtually unlimited freedom to explore alternatives, and in far less time.

When the product design is completed and the necessary information is assembled in the computer files, technicians may store the newly developed data, output it on a printer, transfer it to another computer, or send it directly to another step of the automated testing or manufacturing process.

Once the design is approved for production, CAD technicians may use their computers to assist in making detailed drawings of certain parts of the design. They may also prepare designs and drawings of the tools or equipment, such as molds, cutting tools and jigs, that must be specially made in order to manufacture the product.

CAD technicians must keep records of all their test procedures and results. They may need to present written reports, tables, or charts to document their test results or other findings. If a particular system, subsystem or material has not meet a testing or production requirement, technicians may be asked to suggest a way to rearrange the system's components or substitute alternate materials.

REQUIREMENTS

CAD/CAM technicians must be able to read and understand complex engineering diagrams and drawings. The minimum educational requirement for CAD technicians is a high school diploma. Interested high school students should take courses that provide them with a solid background in algebra, geometry, trigonometry, physics, machine-shop skills, drafting, and electronics, and they should take whatever computer courses are available to them. They should also take courses in English, especially those that improve their communications skills.

Increasingly, most prospective CAD technicians are undertaking formal training beyond the high school level usually in a two-year associate's degree program taught at a technical school or community college.

Such a program should include courses in eight basic areas: basic drafting, machine drawing, architecture civil drafting (with an emphasis on highways), process piping, electrical, electrical instrumentation, HVAC, and plumbing. There should also be courses in data processing; computer programming, systems, and equipment, especially video-display equipment; computer graphics; product design; and computer peripheral equipment and data storage. Some two-year programs may also require the student to complete courses in technical writing, communications, social sciences, and the humanities.

In addition, some companies have their own training programs, which can last as long as two years. Requirements for entry into these company-run training programs vary from company to company.

Students considering a career in CAD technology should realize that such a career will require taking continuing-education courses even after they have found jobs. This continuing education is necessary because technicians need to know about recent advances in technology that may affect procedures, equipment, terminology, or programming concepts.

Harcourt Inc.

Certification for CAD technicians is voluntary. Certification in drafting is available from the American Design and Drafting Association (ADDA), which invites members and nonmembers regardless of formal training or experience to participate in its Drafter Certification Program. The certification process includes taking a ninety-minute test of basic drafting skills.

Licensing requirements vary. Licensing may be required for specific projects, such as a construction project, when the client requires it.

CAD technicians need to think logically, have good analytical skills, and be methodical, accurate, and detail-oriented in all their work. They should be able to work as part of a team, as well as independently, since they will spend long periods of time in front of video-display screens.

OPPORTUNITIES FOR EXPERIENCE AND EXPLORATION

There are a number of ways to gain firsthand knowledge about the field of CAD technology. Unfortunately, part-time or summer jobs involved directly with CAD technology are very hard to find; however, drafting-related jobs can sometimes be found, and many future employers will look favorably on applicants with this kind of experience. In addition, jobs related to other engineering fields, such as electronics or mechanics, may be available, and they offer the student an opportunity to become familiar with the kind of workplace in which technicians may later be employed.

In addition, high school courses in computers, geometry, physics, mechanical drawing, and shop work will give a student a feel for the mental and physical activities associated with CAD technology. Other relevant activities include membership in high school science clubs (especially computer and electronics clubs); participating in science fairs; pursuing hobbies that involve computers, electronics, drafting, mechanical equipment, and model building; and reading books and articles about technical topics.

METHODS OF ENTERING

Probably the most reliable method for entering this field is through your school's placement office. This is especially true for students who graduate from a two-year college or technical institute: recruiters from companies employing CAD technicians sometimes visit such schools, and placement-office personnel can help students meet with these recruiters.

Graduates of post-high school programs who conduct their own job search might begin with architects, building firms, manufacturers, high technology companies, and government agencies. They can contact prospective employers by phone or with a letter stating their interest in employment, accompanied by a resume that provides details about their education and job experience. State or private employment agencies may also be helpful, and classified ads in newspapers and professional journals may provide additional leads.

ADVANCEMENT

CAD technicians who demonstrate their ability to handle more responsibility can expect to receive promotions after just a few years on the job. They may be assigned to designing work that requires their special skills or experience, such as troubleshooting problems with systems they have worked with; or they may be promoted to supervisory or training positions. As trainers, they may teach courses at their workplace or at a local school or community college.

In general, as CAD technicians advance, their assignments become less and less routine, until they may actually have a hand in designing and building equipment. Technicians who continue their education and earn a bachelor's degree may become data-processing managers, engineers, or systems or manufacturing analysts.

Other routes for advancement include becoming a sales representative for a design firm or for a company selling computer-assisted design services or equipment. It may also be possible to become an independent contractor for companies using or manufacturing CAD equipment.

EMPLOYMENT OUTLOOK

The employment outlook for CAD technicians is excellent. Many companies in the near future will feel pressures to increase productivity in design and manufacturing activities, and CAD technology provides some of the best opportunities to improve that productivity. By some estimates, there will be as many as a million jobs available for technically trained personnel in the field of CAD/CAM technology by the start of the next century.

EARNINGS

Starting salaries for CAD technicians who are graduates of two-year technical programs typically fall in the range of $13,500 to $22,396 a year; however, actual salaries will vary widely depending on geographic location, exact job requirements, and the training needed to obtain those jobs. With increased training and experience, technicians can earn salaries of approximately $25,000 to $42,000 a year, and some technicians with special skills, extensive experience, or added responsibilities may earn more.

Benefits usually include insurance, paid vacations and holidays, pension plans, and sometimes stock purchase plans.

CONDITIONS OF WORK

CAD technicians almost always work in clean, quiet, well-lighted, air-conditioned rooms. Most CAD technicians spend most of their days at a work station. While the work does not require great physical effort, it does require patience and the ability to maintain concentration and attention for extended periods of time. Some technicians may find they suffer from eyestrain from working long periods in front of a video-display screen.

CAD technicians, because of their training and experience, are valuable employees. They are called upon to exercise independent judgment and to be responsible for valuable equipment. Out of necessity, they also sometimes find themselves carrying out routine uncomplicated tasks. CAD technicians must be able to respond well to both kinds of demands. Most CAD technicians work as part of a team. They are required to follow orders, and may encounter situations in which their individual contributions are not fully recognized. Successful CAD technicians are those who work well as team members and who can derive satisfaction from the accomplishments of the team as a whole.

Increasing productivity in the industrial design and manufacturing fields will ensure the long-term economic vitality of the country; CAD technology is one of the most promising developments in this search for increased productivity. Knowing that they are in the forefront of this important and challenging undertaking can provide CAD technicians with a good deal of pride and satisfaction.

————————●————————

Exercise Related to the Professional Article from the World of Work

Reading Comprehension

1. What is the old-fashioned form of computer-aided design? _____

   _____

2. What is the employment outlook for CAD technicians? _____

   _____

3. Briefly describe the work of a computer-aided design technician. _____

   _____

   _____

Writing Analysis

1. The article is divided into ten categories introducing the reader to this vocational

   field. Name five of them. _____

   _____

2. In the history section, how does the author explain how drafting and designing

   have changed from 1970 to the present? _____

   _____

3. Is the format appropriate to other career fields? Why or why not? _____

   _____

GRAMMARWORKS! Irregular Verbs: *To Be* and *to Have*

There are many irregular verbs. You can find a complete list of irregular verbs in a
grammar book in the library.

    *Complete tenses of the irregular verbs **to be** and **to have**.* These are the auxiliary
(helping) verbs for forming perfect and progressive tenses of other verbs.

		PRESENT TENSE	PAST TENSE	FUTURE TENSE
Simple	to have	have (has)	had	will have
	to be	am (is), are	was, were	will be
Progressive	to have	am having	was having	will be having
	to be	am being	was being	will be being
Simple Perfect	to have	have had	had had	will have had
	to be	have been	had been	will have been

GRAMMARWORKS! Some Common Irregular Verbs

Irregular verbs have four parts: *present, past, progressive,* and *perfect.*

    To form the *future tense,* use *will* before the present participle.

    To form *progressive tenses,* use a form of **to be,** and add *-ing* to the *present
participle.*

    To form *perfect tenses,* use a form of **to have** with the *perfect* participle.

GRAMMARWORKS! Some Common Irregular Verbs (continued)

ROOT	PRESENT	PAST	PROGRESSIVE	PERFECT
to begin	begin	began	(to be) beginning	(to have) begun
to buy	buy	bought	(to be) buying	(to have) bought
to choose	choose	chose	(to be) choosing	(to have) chosen
to do	do	did	(to be) doing	(to have) done
to get	get	got	(to be) getting	(to have) gotten
to give	give	gave	(to be) giving	(to have) given
to go	go	went	(to be) going	(to have) gone
to know	know	knew	(to be) knowing	(to have) known
to make	make	made	(to be) making	(to have) made
to see	see	saw	(to be) seeing	(to have) seen
to take	take	took	(to be) taking	(to have) taken
to write	write	wrote	(to be) writing	(to have) written

TO BE VERBS: *I am, he/she/it is, we are, you are, they are*

TO HAVE VERBS: *I have, he/she/it has, we have, you have, they have*

GrammarWorks! Review

Write a correct verb form above every underlined verb. Most writing tells of more than one period of time. The basic story, however, is usually written in the past tense.

Dear Diary, Guess what I <u>done</u>! I <u>beginned</u> a new pastime. Today I <u>gone</u> and <u>tooken</u> a guitar lesson. My teacher, Ms. Strumm, says <u>I will be do</u> a lot of practicing. Already, I <u>had got</u> a bright red star in the music book I <u>choosed</u>. (She <u>gived</u> it to me so I didn't have to <u>bought</u> one.) Ms. Strumm says I <u>maked</u> very few mistakes. I <u>knowed</u> I <u>done</u> a good job; every chord sounded good. Don't be surprised if I <u>don't wrote</u> very often because I practice a lot. <u>I'll be seen</u> you! *Ciao for now!*

GRAMMARWORKS! Subject/Verb Agreement

The verb we use for the predicate in a sentence depends upon the noun(s) or pronoun(s) we use as the subject of the sentence. When the correct form of the verb is used, it "agrees" with the subject.

Subjects in the first and second person singular and plural (**I, we, you**), and third person plural (**they**), all take the same form of the present tense verb.

(*I sing, we sing, you sing, they sing.*)

Only when speaking in the present tense does a third person singular subject take a verb that ends in *-s* (or *-es*).

(*He calls, she sings, it buzzes.*)

WHEN THE SUBJECT IS THIRD PERSON SINGULAR, A PRESENT TENSE VERB ENDS IN *-S*.	WITH ANY SUBJECT *EXCEPT* THIRD PERSON SINGULAR, A PRESENT TENSE VERB DOES *NOT* END IN *-S*.
Gina *likes* apples. **She** *likes* apples.	*I like* apples. *You like* apples. **They** *like* apples.

GRAMMARWORKS! Subject/Verb Agreement (continued)

Be sure the verb agrees with the subject and not with *other words* in the sentence.

The subject *might be* the noun or pronoun *just* before the verb. **GrammarTool:** *Keep the verb near the subject!*

One of the girls *likes* candy.	**Two** of the boys *like* candy.
Ito, but not his friends, *likes* soccer.	**Kyle and Elizabeth,** not Pierce, *like* soccer.

Or or **nor** means **not both.**

If both subjects are singular, use a singular verb.

I forget whether Marty **or** Lauren *likes* rap music.

If both subjects are plural, use a plural verb.

Neither the Joneses **nor** the Johnsons *like* rap music.

If one subject is singular and one is plural, use a verb that agrees with the subject nearest the verb.

I forget whether she **or** they *like* rap music.

Pronouns containing **-one** and **-body** are singular.

Everyone likes popsicles. *Somebody likes* squash.

Present tense verbs frequently used with third person singular subjects: *is, has, does*
Present tense verbs frequently used with third person *plural* subjects: *are, have, do*

Use **here is/there is** to show one: **Here is** a book you may borrow.
Use **here are/there are** to show more than one: **There are** two cookies left.

GrammarWorks! Review

Circle the proper forms of the italicized verbs in the sentences below.

1. The king and queen *take/takes* a stroll every evening.
2. Information systems at our office *include/includes* a bulletin board for messages.
3. *There's/There are* some people I want you to meet.
4. The faster we *gave/gived* Viva the orders, the faster she *had filled/filled* them.
5. *Here's/Here are* some advice for you.
6. When Joel *have/had* evaluated the information, he *gave/gives* it to Duane.
7. Glenda *will organize/will have organized* the computer filing system by this time next week.
8. Norman *had knew/had known* Betsy for ten years when he *asks/asked* for the reference.
9. Jeremy, who usually does the dishes, never *break/breaks* the glasses.
10. All of the women except Wendy *get/gets* cosmetics from Debbyie.
11. Les, who sings in the choir, *play/plays* guitar in a rock band.
12. Jan and Jon *opened/had opened* a family restaurant near the mall last week.

At the end of the following sentences, write the correct form of the italicized verbs.

1. Gretchen *has beginned* training as a flight attendant. _____

2. Howie *buyed* the office supplies yesterday. _____

3. Habib and Yusef *makes* parts for washing machines. _____

4. When you *was* at the gas station, *did you got* a receipt for expenses? (2 verbs)

   _____

5. Sandy *seen* you at the movies last week. _____

6. When I *gets* the information, I *gives* it to Pauline and she *give* it to Jack. (3 verbs) _____

7. Gabriele *gone* to the library and *chosed* some books *to began* his research paper. (3 verbs) _____

8. Antoinette and Alexandra *done* the sales report together. They *had wrote* it up, and they *was distributing* it at the meeting.(3 verbs) _____
_____

9. After Spike *taked* the report, he *knowed* what was necessary to improve sales. (2 verbs) _____

10. Lyle and Herbert *has been working* together for thirty years. _____

FIXING A BONEHEAD DESCRIPTION
Read through the paragraph to determine its purpose and content, and then follow the directions below.

**HOW FRED GOT DISCOVERED
BY FORREST RIVERS**

(1) Once their was a frog named Fred who lifed in a water lily pond. (2) Fred use to make a loud noise all the time it sounded like godzilla whispering, "europe." (3) "Urrupp, urrupp," to scare peoples away. (4) well one day a beg fella from Hollywood a talent scout stopped by the pond to catch some fish. (5) He didnt have no luck at all. (6) He thought it was cause he keeped going, "Urrupp, ur-rupp." (7) He lucked as big as a hippopotamus to Fred. (8)Finly, the hippo guy pulled out a can of beer, he starts drinkin it. (9) Fred watched for a while and all of a suddin he leaped up and grabs the guys beer. (10) Rite outa his hand. (11) The guy started laughin, because he never had saw nothing like that in his live. (12) Well, that's how Fred got to be a TV star

---

Edit the paragraph above. Search for the Big Eight: circle misspelled words, wrong words, and wrong capitalizations. Put an X in front of sentence fragments, run-on, spliced, and fused sentences. Underline misused pronouns and verbs and the comma and apostrophe errors. Each sentence above has a number. On the lines below, tell what you've found wrong with each numbered sentence. (Write what you found wrong with sentence (1) on line 1, and so on.)

1. _____
2. _____
3. _____
4. _____
5. _____
6. _____

7. _____

8. _____

9. _____

10. _____

11. _____

12. _____

How does the paragraph illustrate the writing technique? _____

_____

_____

_____

How does the paragraph illustrate the SCANS skills? _____

_____

_____

_____

Now you're ready to revise the paragraph. Write it in your own words on a separate piece of paper.

WORK! WORK! WORK!

Writing Practice

The following prompts will help you pick a topic to show what you've learned about the writing technique studied in this lesson.

"A job isn't finished until the paperwork is done."

Writing Exercises in Drawing Word Pictures, the Description Technique

Enhance your descriptions by using figures of speech.

1. Write a description of three or more paragraphs about a favorite possession (piece of jewelry, motorcycle, pet, or whatever), or describe a topic of your choice.

2. In three or more paragraphs, describe the typical work environment in which you would do your job. (Examples: A nurse describes the pediatrics ward; a printer describes the shop area.)

3. In three or more paragraphs, describe the most important tools needed in performing the job you plan to obtain upon completing your education.

WORK! WORK! WORK!

Lesson Review

The following practices show what you've learned in this lesson.

Fill In the Blanks Regarding Word Pictures or Description

1. The purpose of description, or word pictures, is to convey _____

   _____

2. In describing something, it helps to tell how it affects our five senses; meaning, tell how it (Answer with five verbs.) _____

   _____

3. In descriptive writing, using _____ helps create images in the mind's eye.

Fill In the Blanks by Putting the Name of the Figure of Speech Next to Its Description

These are the figures of speech we studied: simile, metaphor, understatement, hyperbole, personification, and analogy.

1. Tells a parallel story: _____

2. Exaggerates the facts: _____

3. Expresses similar qualities of unlike things: _____

4. Minimizes the facts: _____

5. Compares unlike things, using like or as: _____

6. Gives human qualities to a lifeless thing: _____

Give Examples of the Following Figures of Speech

▪ A **simile** about your car, your cousin, or whatever you choose: _____

   _____

▪ A **metaphor** about school, life, or whatever you choose: _____

   _____

▪ A **personification** of the sun, a computer, or whatever you choose: _____

   _____

▪ An **understatement** about the state of the world today: _____

▪ A **hyperbole** about a feeling (hope, anger, grief, happiness, etc.): _____

   _____

▪ An **analogy** about justice, making mistakes, or your choice: _____

   _____

Chapter 6

IDENTIFYING WHAT'S IMPORTANT

> ## SCANS FOUNDATIONS: PERSONAL VALUES—SELF-KNOWLEDGE, SELF-RESPECT, SELF-MANAGEMENT
>
> ## SCANS COMPETENCIES: SELF-ESTEEM, RESPONSIBILITY/ACCOUNTABILITY, INTEGRITY/HONESTY, SOCIAL SKILLS
>
> Our relationship with others depends upon who we are to ourselves. We've been getting to *know* ourselves since we were small, often basing our beliefs about ourselves on the opinions of others. Yet, we may well be wrong about ourselves. If we have a false picture of ourselves as not talented, not smart, or too shy, we restrict our ability to take on tasks that we well might perform skillfully.
>
> People who recognize their strengths and weaknesses do not exaggerate their good points or ignore their flaws. People *like* people who have a true picture of themselves, but, more important, people who have a true picture of themselves *like themselves.* When we feel good about ourselves, we have *self-esteem.* We continue to acquire desirable qualities that lead to our *self-respect.* We develop personal values by which we want others to judge us, our *personal integrity.* We are ready to assume *responsibility* in the world, to be accountable for what we do. We are honest with ourselves, and we use *honesty* when dealing with others.
>
> The better we know ourselves, the better we manage our lives and the better we function in the outer world. We have practiced *self-management* throughout our lives as we performed a hated chore at home because it had to be done, showed up for a boring class because we needed the credit, completed assignments that seemed pointless because they were required, and went to work—even though we were tired—because people were counting on us. Self-management and social skills are partners in our getting the job we want and in doing that job well.
>
> In considering personal values, we'll study definition and illustration, two writing techniques that help us identify things as they truly are.
>
> *Let's get to work!*

SCANS FOCUS: PERSONAL VALUES

SELF-KNOWLEDGE AND SELF-RESPECT

We Measure Others by the Standards We Set for Ourselves

Often we're critical of others when they don't measure up to what *we* believe is right. All our lives, we've been subconsciously collecting a set of **personal values.** Our values are our beliefs about the way the world should work. In finding that we don't like it when others are unfair, rude, dishonest, selfish, irresponsible, or when they don't accept blame, we realize we've established our own standards of fairness, courtesy, honesty, generosity, responsibility, and accountability. We are improving our self-knowledge. We are learning how we want to be and how we don't want to be. We recognize that we feel good about ourselves when we live by our personal values.

Gaining Self-Esteem

Feeling good about ourselves based on true self-knowledge is **self-esteem.** Self-esteem is not the same as *conceit,* which is an *exaggerated* sense of self-worth. Self-esteem is an honest evaluation of ourselves, with all our strengths and weaknesses. *Everyone* has strengths and weaknesses. If we have often been criticized for our weaknesses, we might not be honoring our strengths. For some of us, those entrusted with our care in our important early years damaged our self-image. Even the best "caregivers" can be flawed themselves. Parents, brothers and sisters, and teachers all contribute to our sense of self-worth—or our lack of it.

As children, we were too vulnerable to disregard the faulty messages we received. But as maturing adults, we can replace old, inaccurate self-images with true self-knowledge. Self-esteem is a healthy personal quality. It helps us know what is good for us and avoid what is bad for us. Making good choices for ourselves, based on good self-esteem, earns our self-respect.

Who would follow this *ad to the used car lot? Rewrite the ad so it doesn't drive customers in the other direction.*

Used Cars: Why go elsewhere to be cheated? Come here first.

_____

_____

Responsibility and Accountability

In school and in the workplace, people who possess self-esteem exhibit **responsibility.** They work hard to excel at challenging tasks, and they are cooperative even when assigned unpleasant tasks. People who respect themselves set high standards for themselves and pay attention to details while keeping their eyes on the goal. They do their share of the work, and they take pride in what the team accomplishes. Being responsible means doing what is expected of you—*and what you expect of yourself.* These traits illustrate personal responsibility: paying attention, exerting effort and perseverance toward reaching a goal, being punctual and dependable, showing enthusiasm for a task, exhibiting vitality, and expressing optimism.

People who possess self-esteem aren't embarrassed to take credit when they have done something right, and they aren't afraid to acknowledge when they have done something wrong. Acknowledging when you are wrong and taking the steps to make corrections is known as **accountability.**

Personal Integrity

As we come to live by our codes of what is right, we find that we *honor ourselves* by treating others well, even when they do not deserve it. We control our tempers because we dislike it when others lose control; we do our share of the work because we dislike it when others slack off; we forgive others for their mistakes because we dislike it when others don't forgive. We add being honest and trustworthy to our package of high standards of personal behavior because we dislike it when we are treated dishonestly or find that someone else is untrustworthy.

Often, we don't expect to *gain* anything by treating others fairly; we just know that to behave differently would violate the personal pact we have with ourselves. The term for this pact is **personal integrity.** With a firm sense of personal integrity, we are not tempted to violate it for some immediate personal gain. People with personal integrity keep focused on the overall good, the long-term goal, and they gain the self-respect that comes from being true to themselves.

From a newspaper article. *A careless oversight can cause something to be said twice. Cross out the repeated information in this old news article.*

Inside, Chelsea and her friends posed for innumerable snapshots. Later, parents and teenagers went their separate ways—the kids to their prom, the parents to a local restaurant for dinner. Later, parents and teenagers went their separate ways. White House aides were tight-lipped on the big question—whether Chelsea had a date.

Trite but True

Special statements become "old sayings" because they best illustrate a significant point.

> *"This above all: to thine own self be true,*
> *And it must follow, as the night the day,*
> *Thou canst not then be false to any man."*

—WILLIAM SHAKESPEARE

> *"We can't change others; we can only change ourselves."*

—AUTHOR UNKNOWN

> *"First impressions are lasting."*

—AUTHOR UNKNOWN

> *"Do unto others as you would have them do unto you."*

—THE BIBLE

SELF-MANAGEMENT AND SOCIAL SKILLS

Social Skills Go Beyond Waiting Your Turn and Shaking Hands

Valued employees exhibit the **social skills** of friendliness, adaptability, empathy, and courtesy toward both fellow workers and customers or clients. Socially in-tune people take an **interest** in what others say and do. An employee with these skills can be counted on for appropriate behavior when trying situations occur at work. People described as "loose cannons" and "bombs waiting to explode" do not fit in the typical work environment. People described as "shrinking violets" or "quiet as mice" might have trouble contributing and coping on the job.

Socially well-adjusted people assert themselves in both familiar and unfamiliar situations. Such individuals **respond appropriately** as the situation requires. When there is a fire in a metal trash can, neither the person who gets hysterical and shouts "Fire! Fire!" nor the person who says nothing and hopes it will go out is acting appropriately. An appropriate reaction generally lies somewhere between the extremes of alternatives: "I see there's a fire in the metal trash can. I'll get the fire extinguisher I saw in the hall and put it out."

Neither a person who waits to be told what to do until the boss gets in nor one who takes it upon himself to change policy when the boss is away is serving his employer well. While it is important to be a **self-starter,** one who knows what's expected and where to begin, it is equally important not to exceed the responsibilities with which you've been entrusted. No one will be impressed by your changing the filing system or the software program, unless you were asked to do so.

If Your Goal Is to Manage Others, Exhibit Self-Management Skills

Of course you've heard that "Actions speak louder than words." It's another trite but true saying. We don't impress people by telling them how terrific we are; we impress others by doing our jobs well. We don't "fake it"; *we assess our own knowledge, skills, and abilities accurately.* We don't take on more than we can handle or tackle a project for which we are not prepared; *we set well-defined and realistic goals.* We don't hop and skip around our tasks; *we proceed logically and methodically and see our tasks through to completion.* And when systems come crashing down, and they undoubtedly will while we're learning the ropes, we don't "put up our dukes" or "cast a good light on it" or blame others: We *listen to the feedback* unemotionally and nondefensively, and we learn the ropes *better* than we knew them before.

Though perhaps unaware of it, a good employee is learning what good management is. A good manager knows how an employee should behave, understands how best to get an employee to serve well, and exhibits exemplary social and self-management skills.

The Value of Good Personal Values

You've probably noticed that, as soon as we meet people, we begin judging them according to our own standards. While this isn't completely fair, it is a trait of human nature. Although sometimes we're wrong about someone, that person may not get another chance at our attention. In the same way, others judge us on brief acquaintance. We can reveal a lot about ourselves in a short time: our attitudes, our interest in others, our sense of humor, our grasp of what's going on. We can't broadcast what *isn't* inside, and we can't help but broadcast what *is*. We need to fill ourselves with a good sense of self-worth based on self-knowledge, personal standards, and integrity. These aren't just nice traits; they are *life* skills.

Employers want to hire people with good personal values systems. To convince yourself of the truth of this, picture yourself as an employer. You have to decide, after only a few moments, whether or not an applicant has good personal values. Now, picture yourself as the applicant. How do *you* appear to a potential employer?

SCANS Focus Exercise
The following examples are some occasions for employing social and self-management skills on the job. Read the examples and perform the exercise below.
Shipping Clerk: Realizes he has forgotten to fill an order for a good customer. Calls immediately and apologizes. Asks if customer will be inconvenienced if shipment arrives later. Tells supervisor of his error and that company must ship now and absorb premium price.
Clerical Worker: On duty when the office manager isn't there. Decides how to handle important package delivered COD (COD stands for Collect on Delivery. The person who delivers the item is not to leave it with the addressee unless the deliverer collects the amount of money owed to the sender.)
Construction Foreman: Stays on top of schedule. Makes phone calls to be sure important material, if late, will arrive soon. Tells field supervisor that insulation hasn't arrived and company is unresponsive to his calls.

Auto Parts Salesman: When invited to participate in plan to rip off inventory, declines and takes precautions for securing inventory.

Security Company Technician: Stands up for woman being harrassed by others for being in a "man's" job. Won't tolerate sexist, racist, or other prejudicial behavior.

Bookkeeper: Realizes an esteemed client's books show a decided increase in outgo, suspects manipulation of funds, and brings discrepancy to attention of supervisor.

Quality Control Inspector: Does not take on more work than can be accomplished in a reasonable amount of time. Acknowledges unfamiliarity with a particular item. Seeks more information or reads up on type of product.

Equipment Technician: Acknowledges that repairs he has made did not last through warranty and honors warranty. Explores other possibilities. Solicits input from others. Recognizes when to repair and when a product is not repairable.

Customer Service Representative: Does not blame customer for defect. Knows when to call in manager to ease escalating customer tension.

Machine Operator: Recognizes that machine is not operating properly. Does not just complain or refuse to work. Determines source of failure and recommends service or replacement.

In-Class SCANS Exercise

The above examples show how personal values apply on the job. In terms of your own personal values, write a paragraph on how you would handle one *of the following situations.*

1. Your best friend tells you she listed an AA degree on her job application at the place you work. You know she doesn't have an AA degree, and the manager knows she's your friend.
2. You work in an auto parts store. Ten minutes ago, you sold a headlight to a customer for $10. You just found out the price is actually $50. The customer is nowhere in sight.
3. You see a fellow employee steal a $5 bill from the cash register.

"School is a place where they teach you how much more you've got to learn . . ."

GIVING MEANINGS—DEFINITION

SHINE SOME LIGHT ON IT

If we can't identify something in the dark, we turn on a light. When we're *reading* and come across a word we don't recognize, we're "in the dark" about its meaning. A dictionary, which defines words, will cast some light on the word by giving its **meaning,** but definition isn't limited to *words.* Sometimes we want to bring others out of the dark by defining something for them; for example, "Consumer credit is economic servitude in disguise." You'd need to define *consumer credit* and *economic servitude* to write a paper about this topic. The writing technique known as **definition** answers the question, "What is that?"

A MOVING EXPERIENCE, FROM THE
GENERAL TO THE SPECIFIC

A dictionary definition helps us understand how something is *like* something else and how it is *unlike* other things. Take the word *module.* A dictionary gives many definitions, from the **general** meaning of *standard unit* to **specific** meanings in architecture, electronics, computer science, space flight, and education. Understanding the *general meaning* is only the first step toward mastering a word. To get or give meaning, you have to think in terms of the *specific circumstance* of its use. The purpose of definition is to isolate meaning *in its setting,* just as a diamond means more when set in an engagement ring.

For example, you're visiting my house, and I say, "A black feline is in my living room." What do I mean? Looking up *feline* in the dictionary won't tell you enough. You'll just find out that a feline is a cat.

- *Thinking* about it could mean these things to you.
  1. Your friend has a black cat.
  2. You'd better get your allergy medication out of your backpack.
- But seeing that black cat would mean something else to me.
  1. I don't have a black cat, so there must be a door open somewhere; or
  2. My white cat is very, very dirty, and I'd better investigate the cause.

When writing a definition, start with the general meaning and move to the specific. You might want to define your feelings about some *thing* or explain what some *experience* means to you. Be sure you frame your definition in the right circumstances so your meaning will be clearly understood. Stay on track, and don't cross over into other specific definitions that don't apply to the point you're trying to make. When you're through writing your definition, both you and the reader should be "in the light."

The following student and professional examples give meanings, making use of the definition writing technique.

The student author's assignment: Write an essay giving your meaning of family.

Marco Rivera, born in Mexico, works in Reception at a Los Angeles hospital. He plans to be a teacher.

```
Marco Rivera                                    Rivera 1
English 1020-11:00
Definition
February 4, 1998

                      Defining Family


    Family is a word that traditionally conjured up similar
images for most people: a father, a mother, and a couple of
```

Rivera 2

kids—sometimes a pet was in the imaginary scene, too. Though the number of children and type of pets might have varied, a mother and a father were always an integral part of that family portrait. However, our concepts of family are changing. Better said, *families* are changing. No longer can we accept the image of the wholesome nuclear family as a definitive representation of the family unit.

Family now, like the people who make them up, come in different shapes and sizes. Today, many families have only one parent. Usually, but not always, the mother runs the household and supports and nurtures the family. She tries to instill values and teach morals to the children to ensure they grow up to be responsible and productive members of society. In many families, a stepparent assists in raising children from the spouse's previous relationship. Families today consist of a widowed aunt raising her orphaned nephew, a grandmother raising a grandchild, and an uncle who takes in his sixteen-year-old niece, whose father couldn't handle her. Family can be two winos and a seventeen-year-old runaway. Family today is even made up of same sex parents raising adopted children. These are but a few of the countless examples of the variety of family groups that exist in our communities today that, in fact, make up communities today.

As long as the members of the family group love and trust each other, whether or not they share the same blood, or even the same last name, they can be a family. Family is being there for your loved ones, showing them understanding, giving them support or advice. It's being a shoulder to cry on or a sensitive ear to listen without being judgmental. Family is accepting without reservations. It is sharing joy and pain, good times and bad times. Family is being honest with your loved ones. It is accepting the flaws that others have and even loving them for those flaws. Family is something different to us all. What I have written is what family is to me.

WORK! WORK! WORK!

These exercises help build skills by prompting you to express your understanding of what you read.

Reading Comprehension

1. How does Marco feel about wholesome nuclear families? _____

   _____

2. Marco gives seven examples of today's families. Name at least three of the

   heads of these units. _____

3. Does Marco feel bloodline is necessary to the family unit? _____

Writing Analysis

1. How do you think the word "family" is defined in the dictionary? _____

   _____

2. What is Mario's topic sentence? _____

   _____

3. Do you agree or disagree with Marco's premise regarding family? _____

   _____

The following professional article defines the use of computers in the culinary arts field.

Get a Grip on Computer Technology
by Nancy Berkoff

Now that chefs are expected to be managers, purchasing agents, marketers, event planners, public relations agents and customer service gurus, computers have become essential to success in the competitive foodservice market.

Computers assist chefs in a thousand ways, says Andy Feinstein at Hospitality Media Solutions in San Francisco. "From simple time-saving functions, such as ordering by computer or personnel scheduling, to broader applications, such as integrating inventory files with recipe files to create a current menu, computers allow chefs to keep tight control on products, customers and competition."

Culinary educators agree that graduates without computer skills will be lost in today's foodservice world. Nearly every major culinary school in the country has added a computer education component to its basic curriculum.

"There is no question that computers will be an essential part of a chef's job," says Bill Reynolds, director of continuing education at the Culinary Institute of

America's Hyde Park, N.Y., campus. "As more operations turn to computers, it's important that the chef understand and utilize computers to their full potential."

TEACHING OLD CHEFS NEW TRICKS

Chefs who master new technology stay a step ahead of the competition. Without doubt, culinary school grads enter the foodservice world with a bounty of computer skills, which give graduates an edge over other young cooks.

The CIA offers computer-age survival courses for professionals as short-term extension classes. Their popular course "Computers in the Food Business" covers computer applications and cost management, marketing, human resources, sales, performance and training. Other courses cover software operations, such as word processing to create menus, spreadsheets to inventory, databases to store recipes and ingredients, accounting programs, nutritional analysis and surfing the Internet for inspiration.

CIA at Greystone in California's Napa Valley offers several extension courses that allow chefs to learn about computers in a way that is most relevant to foodservice operations, says Greg Drescher, director of education at CIA Greystone.

One of Greystone's professional six-week courses is designed to help chefs to spot daily operational problems and use computer applications to solve them. This course is taught by CIA graduate Susan Schaefer, the creator of the popular ExecuChef software.

Columbia College in Sonora, Calif., demonstrates the benefits of computers with a classroom comparison. First students cost out and convert recipes, take physical inventories and calculate portion size all by hand with paper and pencil. Then the instructor introduces them to software that electronically performs all these tasks in a fraction of the time. "By the time they've completed our course, they will have seen and used programs for spreadsheets, menu writing, costing, inventory, recipe extension and POS systems," says chef Francis Lynch, Columbia's culinary arts program coordinator.

Rather than attend culinary schools, chefs can enroll in classes at consumer-oriented computer training centers. CompUSA, for example, has over eighty locations nationally and can customize computer training for chefs, kitchen staff, and waitstaff. The computer giant offers on- and off-site classes, flexible schedules and gives chefs the opportunity to sample and learn an assortment of systems and software before they purchase anything.

After chefs gain basic computer knowledge, there are exciting educational opportunities online. Distance learning by computer is the up-and-coming method for time-and geographically challenged chefs. Kansas State University in Manhattan, Kan., offers several food science classes by computer, complete with a mini-computer communications seminar. Students need only an IBM-compatible or Macintosh computer and a modem.

The New School in New York City offers classes on its electronic bulletin board on the Internet at *info@dialnsa.edu.* The most recent class was "How to Open a Restaurant."

WHAT CHEFS NEED TO KNOW

Experts agree that basic computer skills will be required of all chefs in the very near future, including basic word processing, desktop publishing (to create menus, wine lists, and newsletters), spreadsheets (to write recipes, manage costs, and to inventory), recipe manipulation, and point-of-sale (POS) systems. Computer-age chefs also understand nutritional analyses, can perform payroll functions and use ordering systems.

In fact, Sheraton Hotel's Cuisine of the Americas recipe program is distributed to the chain's chefs via CD-ROM, which requires chefs to develop skills to access recipes, preparation techniques, ordering and sourcing information on a computer.

"I think it would be fair to say that chefs would have to be computer literate before Marriott would consider them for employment," says chef Steven Ward, a former Marriott executive chef now at Phoenix's America West Arena. "I would spend several hours every afternoon on the computer, ordering, scheduling, performing company-required tasks and revising menus, to name a few things. Without computer skills, a Marriott chef could not perform up to company standards."

Ward continues to use computers at Restaura's America West Arena to publish daily menus for table tents and menu inserts, to manage inventory, to order products, and to communicate internally with employees and with other properties.

SELECT HARDWARE CAREFULLY

Computer hardware choices usually bewilder techno neophytes. "Do your homework before purchasing anything," says Feinstein, who experienced a variety of systems as an instructor at the University of Nevada Las Vegas Hotel Program. "See what's comfortable and have an idea what you'll need from your system in advance. While I don't encourage anyone to mortgage their home for a computer, it's also not worth saving a little and winding up with an underpowered system." Computer hardware with inadequate memory to run the software performs functions slowly and wastes time.

Feinstein suggests a Pentium 9, quad speed with a CD-ROM drive, graphics and sound options, sixteen megabytes of memory, a one-gigabyte memory hard drive, a modem to link to the Internet and to fax and a fifteen-inch monitor. Feinstein uses Windows 3.11 and believes it's a great program for chefs.

"I would recommend my Compaq 486 with 1.2 gigabytes and a backup system for culinary businesses," says chef Ray Mickiewicz, coowner of Joan's Catering in Tampa, Fla., who has been using his computer for daily operations for years. Mickiewicz uses Windows 95 and some Intuit software, such as Quickbooks. He uses his Macintosh to inventory, check registers, for payroll, to track menu items and accounts, and to produce a monthly desktop newsletter. He also has plunged into the World Wide Web to find recipe information and background for culinary articles.

"I use computers during the day for nonfood business and in the evenings with my family for culinary information. I think the Macintosh Performa is easy to learn and Nisus Writer is a great work processing program," says Charlie Pendleton, an independent computer consultant.

SELECT SOFTWARE TO MATCH NEEDS

To stay on top of the explosion of new software programs available, read *PC Magazine* or *Computer Shopper,* recommends Ward. Many software programs also can be sampled via the Internet. The following are some of the most popular software programs among chefs.

ExecuChef is designed by a chef for chefs to write recipes, manage costs, and manage inventory.

System One is a comprehensive foodservice management program to manage inventory, purchase, receive, write recipes, menus, sales reports, and audit trails.

Food Trak and **At-Your-Service** software offer full-system and modules for foodservice operations. At-Your-Service offers recipe and menu management, inventory management, and sales analysis features.

Single-topic software (recipe writing, nutrition analysis, inventorying) can be used on its own or added to an existing system. The **Food Processor,** for example, is a computer nutritional analysis program, which allows chefs to guarantee accuracy of information and personalize recipes without hiring a nutrition consultant.

ResNet is a software system offered to restaurateurs who need to efficiently manage the front of the house with a server database, interactive voice response system, and voice recognition to offer customer reservation access twenty-four hours a day and decrease loss of revenue from "no-shows."

Clarifye, another single-topic software program, is ideal for sommeliers and requires little previous computer experience in order to function as a highly effective wine cellar management tool.

On the Internet

Chefs who have discovered the World Wide Web are like children in a candy store. The Web, of course, is a massive network of computers all linked via phone lines. To surf the Web, chefs need a modem linked to their computers and a subscription to an online host service, essentially a toll both at the on-ramp of the Internet. Subscription costs to one of the online host services (America Online, Compuserve, Prodigy, for example) include a one-time account set-up fee, a monthly fee and a per-use charge based on the length of time spent "surfing." America Online alone expects to have over five million subscribers by mid-1996.

Once on the Web, chefs chat with peers around the country, tap into databases for recipes, order information, and learn about culinary trends. Chefs can find out about the carrot crop in Kentucky, place a dairy order with a local purveyor, chat with a vintner in Sonoma, and tap into a famous chef's recipe collection.

As an unregulated public forum, there's a lot of cyber fraud. There are numerous chat forums, online publications, lists, essays, and catalogs that require a credit card number. Chefs are advised to be very cautious of credit card scams.

Web sites and addresses are a lot like television shows: Some are very short-lived and new ones appear continuously. The most popular ones survive, but don't be surprised to find a favorite Web site no longer on the Net. To keep on top, try downloading the **Food and Wine Online Newsletter** from Van Nostrand Reinhold through **The Culinary Professional's Resource Center** @ *http://www.vnr.com/cul.html.*

Chefs who don't have access to a computer can grab a "cuppa joe" at one of the increasingly popular Internet cafés—actual (rather than virtual) cafés that have computers linked to the Web at each table, such as the **Icon Byte** cafe in San Francisco and the **@ Cafe** in New York City.

Exercise Related to the Professional Article from the World of Work

Reading Comprehension

1. What method does Columbia College in Sonora, California, use to demonstrate the benefits of a computer?

_____

_____

_____

2. Name at least three basic computer applications experts agree will be required of all chefs in the very near future. _____

3. For what purpose does Ray Mickiewicz of Joan's Catering in Tampa, Florida, use the World Wide Web? _____

Writing Analysis

1. As an example of a definition article from the literature of the "World of Work," what is defined? _____

2. What is the topic sentence? _____

3. In validating the need for computer fluency, what method does the author use throughout the essay? _____

4. Name three ways in which computers assist workers in your current position or future career. _____

From the Sports section. *Watch those verb tenses. There's "a hole" in one! Find the incorrect verb form and write the correct verb form on the line below.*

Actually, it's not all that surprising to everyone else, basically because Leonard [a golfer] isn't really the excitable type. He's just a preppy Dallas kid who probably wouldn't notice if you set fire to the tassels of his loafers or get too upset at the restaurant if they had just ran out of chicken-fried steak.

_____

GRAMMARWORKS!   Those "!(.:,—);?" Punctuation Marks: The Comma ,

The most used (and misused) punctuation mark is the comma. It separates words, phrases, and clauses and pops up wherever a writer desires a reader to pause.

THE TWO GREAT RULES OF THE COMMA

1. *If you need a comma, use one!* Commas signal the reader to pause. Besides the usual reasons for commas, sometimes you need a comma for clarity or flow.
2. *If you don't need a comma, don't use one!* Each pause disrupts the reader. If you use a comma, you'd better have a good reason. *Here are some good reasons.*

COMMAS ARE *REQUIRED* IN THE FOLLOWING CONSTRUCTIONS

1. SIMPLE SERIES (USE A COMMA BEFORE THE FINAL CONJUNCTION)	You can't run a business without pens, paper, paper clips, staples, tape, telephones, computers, office machines, personnel, and customers or clients. (Newspapers generally *omit* the comma before the final conjunction.)
2. TO SET OFF TWO OR MORE INDEPENDENT CLAUSES	Elisa goes to school in the morning, she works as a security guard at night, and she studies on weekends.
3. PARENTHETICAL EXPRESSIONS	Eduardo, hoping to be promoted, gives a lot of thought to solving problems.
4. DIRECT ADDRESS	"Les, did you know that the meeting was canceled?" Wendy asked.
5. APPOSITIVES	Carolyn, a writer, sells her written work to magazines and journals.
6. TO SET OFF INTRODUCTORY AND NONESSENTIAL PHRASES AND CLAUSES	*Introductory Phrase:* Besides borrowing my car, Lara borrowed money for gas. *Internal Phrase:* Zack goes to bed, as a rule, after the eleven o'clock news. *Clause:* I saw Kevin at the market, and, if you ask me, he looks great.
7. FOR DATES AND ADDRESSES	The CEO of the company was born August 13, 1939, in Kansas. Debbie lives at 11111 South Jeremy Street, Phoenix, Arizona.
8. IN DIALOGUE	(**Note:** Quotation marks go outside commas and periods.) "I'm waiting for the customer's order," Phil said. Paula answered, "Too late! He ordered from our competitor." "That's awful!" he said. (**Note:** In quotes, don't put commas after question marks and exclamation points.)

GRAMMARWORKS! Review

Using the above guidelines, insert the twenty-six missing commas in this paragraph.

LaWanda Taylor is a bright twenty-year-old part-time community college coed who lives with her mother aunt and five sisters. She has worked for five months in a Ralph's Supermarket bakery. Five mornings a week she arrives at 4:00 o'clock to bake bread cookies sweet rolls and muffins for the customers. LaWanda is a hard-working committed friendly person but she is often late to work and she sometimes forgets work assignments such as clearing cash registers ordering supplies and turning off the ovens. When a supervisor position opened LaWanda decided to apply for it. Aware of her strengths and weaknesses she approached the store manager with a plan to conquer her shortcomings. In one breath she said "I'm moving in with a girlfriend next door to the store one who has a giant alarm clock and I've started using a 'to do' checklist for tasks at work boss." The manager a wide smile crossing his face said "The job is yours."

FIXING A BONEHEAD DEFINITION PARAGRAPH

Read the paragraph and then follow the directions below.

DEFINING A PROBLEM AT WORK
BY MAX SENS

(1) I work at a Movie Theter I tell my friends "no you cant come in with no ticket" (2) Besides taking peoples tickets I'm responsable for sweeping up the theater. (3) They dropped popcorn cartoons candy boxes ice cream wrappers and soda pop cups on the floor. (4) This is how I define the problem: they're is to much mess in the theater for myself to clean it all before the next show. (5) How to get costumers to help out? (6) I know! (7) "Mr. perkins," I said, to my boss, "can we have a 'clean-up-the-theater' contest"? (8) I esplained my idea to give chances for free tickets to people that throw trash away and he gave me his blessing. (9) The customers cooperated, I was permoted to ass't manager.

Edit the paragraph above. Search for the Big Eight: circle misspelled words, wrong words, and wrong capitalizations. Put an X in front of sentence fragments, run-on, spliced, and fused sentences. Underline misused pronouns and verbs and the comma and apostrophe errors. Each sentence above has a number. On the lines below, tell what you've found wrong with each numbered sentence. (Write what you found wrong with sentence (1) on line 1, and so on.)

1. _____

2. _____

3. _____

4. _____

5. _____

6. _____

7. _____

8. _____

What does "gave me his blessing" mean? _____

9. _____

How does the paragraph illustrate the writing technique? _____

_____

What personal values are illustrated in the story? _____

Now you're ready to revise the paragraph. Write it in your own words on a separate piece of paper.

WORK! WORK! WORK!

Writing Practice

The following prompts will help you pick a topic to show what you've learned about the writing technique studied in this lesson.

"A job isn't finished until the paperwork is done."

Exercises in Giving Meanings, the Definition Technique

1. Define your job, family, art, humor, entertainment, or a topic of your choice. Use your own words, not the dictionary definition.
2. Write a memorandum to your (present or future) supervisor defining a personnel problem in the workplace and explaining how you would solve it.
3. Consider your own personal values. Assuming you have both self-esteem and personal integrity, define the strengths and weaknesses you would bring to a prospective employer.
4. Give your own definition of integrity, responsibility, accountability, fairness, or any other personal value, as it applies in your work.

Maybe the price is half off, too. Rewrite the following ad to avoid giving the wrong impression.

Our bikinis are exciting. They are simply the tops!

_____

_____

---

*"Faster than a speeding bullet,
more powerful than a locomotive . . . "*

USING EXAMPLES—ILLUSTRATION

ILLUSTRATION IS EXPLAINING YOUR MEANING BY GIVING EXAMPLES

Illustration is a technique that helps others understand you better. Suppose your little brother Wally finds a tick sucking blood from your dog. He removes the bug with a pair of tweezers, and the next morning Wally takes the tick and some other items to school for "show and tell."

He says, "What is a tick? What does it do? The tick is a tiny black insect with six legs and pointy lips that stick in you and suck your blood."

Wally holds up the plastic bag with the tick in it. He knows the tick is too small for the kids to see how it works, so he uses an example. He calls his best friend "Tank" up to the front of the class and gives him a glass of tomato juice and a straw.

"Please drink the juice, 'Tank.'" As his friend sucks on the straw, Wally says triumphantly to the class, "This is an example of how a tick sucks your blood!"

YOU CAN USE AN ILLUSTRATION TO HELP SOMEONE UNDERSTAND WHAT YOU MEAN

Illustration conveys information by giving specific **examples** that help others understand us. We clarify broad, vague, hard-to-visualize terms by naming an individual or object, *known by the person to whom we are speaking,* that is similar to the meaning we are trying to express.

strong	We call him "Rambo."
courageous	She would run into a fire to save a child.
foolhardy	He was the first one to bungee-jump off the bridge.
stupid	She thinks stop signs don't apply to her.
dull	I fell asleep while he was telling me his name.
boring	His story seemed as long as a flight from L.A. to Denver.

It is easy to see how examples help make meaning clear. They also make writing and reading a paper more fun.

The following student and professional writings use examples to illustrate their meaning.

The student author's assignment: Write an essay giving examples of a good manager.

Maria Evans, who came to the United States from Mexico, is the happily married mother of three. Her career objective is to become a physician's assistant, and her motto is: "I never give up."

```
Maria M. Evans                                    Evans 1
English 100-8:00
Using Examples
May 2, 1999

           Great Management Makes the Difference

     Many companies are successful, thanks to productive
employees. Lots of them are going bankrupt every year due to
the poor quality of their employees or managers. Tampico
Spices and Herbs Company was in danger of going out of
business in 1996, but thanks to Mrs. Cecilia Santibanez, her
management skills, and her dedication, this company was saved
from disaster. How did an efficient manager save the Tampico
```

Company from going out of business? Well, here are some examples of what the new manager did.

Mrs. Santibanez arrived one hour before the rest of the workers and checked every station. She examined the orders and inspected the supplies. Later, when the workers arrived to work, she counted them and went over every station to make sure it was covered. She also observed the routine of the workers for one week. She noticed a lot of deficiencies among the workers. For instance, some of them arrived late but were punched in on time by a colleague. In the production department, most workers were talking half the time. They didn't bother making the orders of the day. The workers in charge of the deliveries didn't check the shipments, and, many times, they sent the wrong orders.

When the day had finished, Mrs. Santibanez stayed another hour or more to go over the shipping and receiving orders. Without hesitation, the new manager discovered a deficit in the inventory department. The purchase of raw herbs didn't match with the production. Where were the profits? Perhaps they walked away inside those extra large lunch bags at the end of the day. She was right; most workers returned home every day with their lunch bags full of herbs.

With all this information, she started making some changes. First, she called a meeting to get to know the workers better. She moved personnel from one station to another, making it more difficult for "old friends" to engage in social conversations. She set up three breaks in each shift to make the environment more friendly. She hired a new security company to patrol inside the building and outside. When the workers finished for the day, the new security guard had to inspect every "trash can" and those extra large lunch bags. The use of the parking lot was restricted to staff only, and frequent trips to the workers' cars were discouraged. Finally, Mrs. Santibanez established an incentive program wherein workers with high achievements for the company received a financial bonus at a monthly recognition meeting. There were prizes for perfect attendance, increased production, and zero mistakes in each station.

People started working happily and with more enthusiasm. As a result of the changes, the production increased forty-five percent. After three months of very hard work, the manager delegated some of the responsibilities to selected workers. Nevertheless, Mrs. Santibanez was always alert,

Evans 3

supportive of the employees, and attentive to every detail of the company.

In recognition for her outstanding job, the owners of the Tampico Spice and Herbs Company gave her a new Lincoln Continental and a two-week paid vacation. Mrs. Cecelia, as the workers called her, accepted the car, but she refused to take time off because she didn't want to spoil what the company had already achieved. Thanks to her excellent management and dedication to her employers and employees, this company went back to being a successful business.

WORK! WORK! WORK!

These exercises help build skills by prompting you to express your understanding of what you read.

Reading Comprehension

1. Name at least two deficiencies Mrs. Santibanez discovered. _____
   _____

2. What caused the deficit in the inventory? _____
   _____

3. For what activities could an employee receive a prize on recognition day? __
   _____
   _____

4. Was Mrs. Santibanez' decision not to take the reward of a two-week paid vacation an illustration of personal integrity, self-respect, and/or self-management? _____
   _____

Writing Analysis

1. What is the topic sentence of this article? _____
   _____

2. In which sentence does the author better illustrate the topic? _____
   _____

3. The article is organized into five paragraphs. In brief step-sheet fashion, list the
   reasons for each paragraph. _____
   _____
   _____

The following professional article has been included because it serves as a good example of how an author treats a technical subject in a professional journal. All readers, as consumers, should be aware of the potential danger of their gas heating systems.

Gas Furnace Maintenance Keeps the Heat On
by Craig J. Barnett

It is somewhat ironic that I'm writing an article about gas furnace maintenance after I just finished a blower motor change-out in a 135° F attic! Actually, by the time this issue is in your hands, technicians in many parts of the country will be mentally gearing up to deal with the 'H' in hvacr.

In some instances, a blast of unseasonably cold weather may persuade an equipment owner to fire up the furnace before you arrive to conduct your heating season startup. Even if the owner says that everything is working fine, you should check each gas furnace for safe and reliable operation. This article will focus on yearly maintenance/performance checkups (M/PCs) on residential and small commercial gas furnaces.

CHECK FOR GAS LEAKS AT CONNECTION POINTS

Every furnace should be tested for natural gas leaks starting at the connection to the supply pipe and finishing at the gas valve connection to the burner manifold. This, of course, includes the flexible connector and pilot gas tubing connections. In many cases, your nose will inform you of a problem and the use of a soap bubble solution will confirm the exact source of the leak(s).

Never use an open flame to search for gas leaks. Additionally, do not use your electronic halogen leak detector to find escaping natural gas. Although many sensing tips will activate the detector's electronic circuitry in the presence of this fuel, the high voltage potential across the electrodes, plus oxygen in the air may cause an explosion. It is best to use an electronic detector

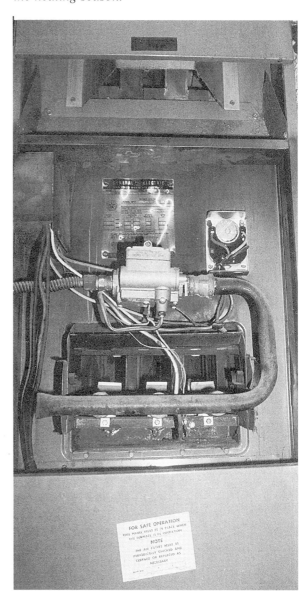

Even a fossil like this can be kept in a safe and reliable working condition if a thorough maintenance/performance checkup is done at the beginning of the heating season.

designed to safely "sniff" fuel gases. All leaks must be repaired immediately after detection and location.

If the owner or tenant of the residence or building is present when you are doing your M/PC, ask if they are satisfied with the performance of their furnace. Any complaints about headaches or nausea during the heating season, primarily within the confines of the building, should be taken seriously. These symptoms may indicate mild carbon monoxide poisoning, resulting from a cracked heat exchanger, the introduction of combustion by-products into the circulating air or by another method.

CARBON MONOXIDE TESTING

If my customers mention symptoms of carbon monoxide in the circulating air, I strongly recommend they allow me to test for the presence of this offending gas. For a number of years, I have been using a manually operated, pump-style air sampler, which uses glass sensing tubes (Figure 1) that contain a chemical that darkens in the presence of carbon monoxide.

The concentration of carbon monoxide, in parts per million (ppm), is shown by the width of the dark band in the tube. I prefer this type of instrument because each tube is fresh and hermetically sealed until the ends are broken, which is immediately prior to sampling. There are no sensors to wear out and no recalibration is necessary. Generally, I energize the system prior to arriving to a heating call and ten minutes later begin the test by pulling one hundred milliliters of supply air through the sensing tube.

When carbon monoxide is noted, I record the amount on a special data sheet that I create on my computer. In addition to the ppm number, I shade in the width of the band on an outline of the tube. I keep the original data sheet(s) and make a copy for the customer.

Any reading greater than one ppm gets my immediate attention, initiating my search for the causes(s). One fairly common reason for the existence of circulating carbon monoxide is a damaged heat exchanger in a gravity vented furnace.

Figure 1   *A manually operated pump with attached sensing tube tests for the presence of carbon monoxide. A data sheet is shown above the pump.*

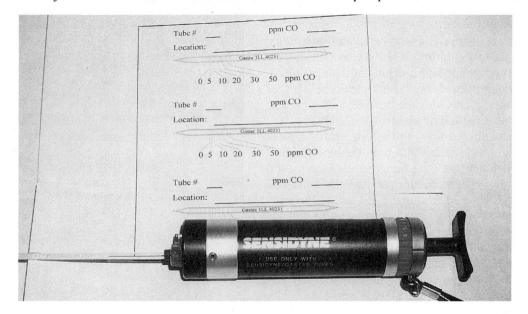

INSPECT THE HEAT EXCHANGER

I always use a powerful flashlight to inspect the burner assemblies and lower combustion chamber segments (Figure 2) of older generation furnaces such as those that rely on gravity to vent combustion by-products. If I see rust on the top of burners or on the bottom of heat exchange cells (modules), I will look for the source of the rusted metal with a rectangular, three-inch-by-two-inch telescopic handle inspection mirror and a trusty Mag-Lite.

A severely rusted heat exchanger (Figure 3) might actually have a hole or crack through which combustion by-products may be aspirated into the circulating air, thus introducing carbon monoxide into the occupied space. I have replaced furnaces with such large gaps in the heat exchanger segments that the circulating air actually blew into the combustion side of the module, extinguishing a portion of the furnace flame.

Never repair rusted heat exchangers. When I encounter a furnace with a perforated heat exchanger, I shut off the gas and the electrical power to the unit, and inform the customer as soon as possible. Advise your customer that the cost of replacing a heat exchanger in an old furnace may cost as much in labor and materials as the installation of a brand new furnace. I usually recommend a furnace replacement.

EXAMINING AIRFLOW

If this section seems like déjà vu, it should. I wrote about the importance of proper airflow regarding servicing and maintenance of air conditioning (cooling) systems in the March issue of the *RSES Journal* ("How to Make A/C Servicing a Cool Breeze") and the subject is no less important when dealing with heating systems.

Figure 2   *The large openings above the burners allow for the inspection of excessive rust or cracks in the metal of the heat exchanger.*

Figure 3   *A badly rusted heat exchanger in an eighteen-year-old rooftop gas/electric package unit alerts the technician to the possibility of cracks or holes.*

Most gas furnaces create a temperature rise of 40° F to 65° F through the heat exchanger, depending on the design. Many gas furnaces will have this information stamped or written on the name-plate. A dirty filter obviously impedes air circulation through the furnace and may cause excessive discharge in air temperatures, high heat exchanger temperatures, and decreased "throw" once the circulating air leaves the supply registers. Filter changes or filter cleaning should be a part of any heating M/PC.

Dirty evaporator coils also reduce airflow and are commonly overlooked, even in systems that have easily removable access panels. Pet hair and other fibers can block airflow through the furnace, leading to premature failure (i.e., cracking) of the heat exchanger and possible introduction of carbon monoxide into the conditioned space. All evaporator coils on units belonging to first-time customers should be inspected for cleanliness and, if necessary, a thorough cleaning should be performed.

Examine the blower motor carefully and notice if the ventilation holes are clogged with dirt and fibers. A thorough manual cleaning with a shop vacuum and rag may be required. Remember, a motor that can't "breathe" is doomed to premature failure.

Furthermore, inspect supply and return registers, making sure they are fully open to allow maximum airflow. Be sure that furniture and interior decorations don't block the return air grille or the supply air stream.

FIRE IT UP

If proper airflow is indicated, move the set point lever to call for heat and standby as the equipment goes through its programmed operation sequence. An experienced technician should pay attention to any unusual sights and sounds that may occur during the M/PC. Ten minutes after the indoor blower motor energizes on low speed, check the supply and return air temperatures (i.e., the delta-T), looking for a temperature rise of 40° F to 65° F.

If possible, check the operation of the high (temperature) limit control by temporarily deenergizing the blower motor before or during burner operation. Lack of circulating air across the heat exchanger will quickly raise the temperature at the location of the high limit switch. It should open the control voltage circuit to the gas valve or electronic control module, stopping gas flow to the main burners. An inoperative high limit control should be replaced before the furnace is allowed back into service.

INDUCED DRAFT FAN MOTOR CAUTION

It is hard to believe that we are approaching the twentieth anniversary of the introduction of 80+ percent efficiency gas furnaces. Although I commend any and all improvements in the efficient use of fuel, I dislike the continued use of the shaded pole, induced draft fan motors (Figure 4) that have between a part of these units since their inception.

Figure 4 *The lack of provisions for lubricating induced draft fan motors may result in a partial flame roll-out condition. Always inspect the burners during furnace operation.*

My chief complaint is the lack of oil holes for lubricating the motor bearings. In many instances, the motor shaft and the shaft bearing encounter temperatures in excess of 350° F.

Over months and years of operation, the oil in this "in-board" bearing vaporizes and the motor revolutions per minute (rpm) decreases. Under this condition, the pressure differential switch may sense satisfactory airflow and energize the gas valve or control module. However, the induced draft blower is not pulling all of the combustion by-products through the serpentine heat exchanger. Therefore, a partial flame roll-out condition occurs.

In some early 1980s models of downflow/horizontal model furnaces, flame roll-out protection was not provided in the form of fusible links for both horizontal positions. If you observe oily control wires at the front of the furnace, especially above or in front of the burners, watch the furnace carefully during three or four on/off cycles. Oily wire insulation usually indicates the presence of excessive heat, possibly generated by a flame roll-out condition.

All M/PCs should include checking the appearance of the burner flames during furnace operation. If the furnace is located in a closet, close the closet door so you can observe the condition of the flames through a $\frac{1}{4}$-inch crack between the door and door frame. This will simulate typical operating conditions and indicate if the combustion air passages to the outside are blocked with fiberglass insulation or other material. Both of the passages (high and low) should be unobstructed to allow adequate air to feed the combustion process.

ADDITIONAL CONSIDERATIONS

There are hundreds of thousands, perhaps millions, of older gravity venting furnaces that use either thermocouples or pilot generators as safety and operating controls. In my experience, five years of continuous pilot flame impingement makes both types of these direct current generators prone to failure or unreliable operation.

Since thermocouples and pilot generators are relatively inexpensive compared to today's sophisticated electronic controls, it is best to replace them after five years of service or when the customer can't remember when the furnace was last serviced. This is a small expense to pay for five more years of trouble-free operation.

When the owner of a furnace shuts off the pilot flame to conserve resources and to keep the home a little cooler during the summer months, the pilot orifice may become the abode of a tiny spider that is attracted to the odorant in natural gas. The spider will spin a web that completely blocks the orifice, making the relighting of the pilot flame difficult or impossible. Fortunately, the web is quite sticky and can be removed by inserting the point of a small sewing needle into the orifice and twirling it a few times to unobstruct the gas pilot.

The venting of combustion by-products in older generation furnaces is simple and straightforward. Hot gases rise within the heat exchanger and collect in a vestibule called a downdraft diverter, before rising through the vent stack to the outdoors. If the vent becomes blocked by a rusted vent cap, a bird's nest or other objects, combustion gases will spill out the downdraft diverter into the closet, attic, or garage. This phenomenon causes a localized buildup of carbon dioxide, water vapor, and even carbon monoxide.

A simple test for proper venting consists of bringing a lit match up to the bottom of the downdraft diverter after the main burner has been on for three minutes or more. If the match flame is pulled into the diverter toward the vent stack, the vent is working properly. If, on the other hand, the flame is extinguished as it approaches the diverter, the vent is blocked and a potentially dangerous condition must be remedied.

This test also may be conducted with a match that has just been blown out by paying attention to the direction the smoke travels. Smoke pulled into the diverter indicates proper venting; smoke pushed away from the diverter indicates a blockage.

A regularly scheduled maintenance and testing program will enable a gas furnace to operate nearly trouble-free for decades. Remember, natural gas is a fairly high energy fuel and fuels are potentially hazardous if handled improperly. All of our customers deserve the protection that a conscientious M/PC program affords.

---●---

Exercise Related to the Professional Article from the World of Work

Reading Comprehension

1. Is the responsibility for heating equipment that of the owner or the maintenance provider? _____

_____

2. How are gas leaks best detected? _____

_____

3. Why does the author advise his readers to replace rather than repair rusted heat exchanges? _____

_____

4. Why should gas furnaces undergo regularly scheduled maintenance and testing programs? _____

_____

Writing Analysis

1. In what two ways do the four figure examples help in understanding the article?

_____

_____

2. This article is from a professional journal especially published for members of the Refrigeration Service Engineers Society. Members also work with air conditioning and heating systems. Name at least three professional publications in your chosen field of endeavor. _____

_____

3. In the section on examining airflow, the author uses the term *déjà vu*. What does this mean? _____

_____

From the Sports section. *This quote from a professional basketball player shows he didn't know that double negatives are as bad as double dribbles! Since two negatives* do *make a positive, rewrite the second sentence to mean it's as bad as it can get.*

"We've got to improve. It can't get no worse."

_____

GRAMMARWORKS!   Those "!(.:,—);?" Punctuation Marks:
The Period . The Question Mark ?
The Exclamation Point !

THE PERIOD .

The most powerful punctuation mark is the period. The period ends every declarative sentence.

> Donna cried.
> Theo said, "Do it today, or you'll be sorry tomorrow."

NOTE: Quotation marks go *outside* commas and periods.

> "If you come to work for us," he said, "you'll have to leave your 'snookie-wookums' with a sitter."

THE QUESTION MARK?

Is the simplest punctuation mark the question mark? The question mark ends every question.

> Why did Donna cry?
> Can you do it, or shall I show you how?

THE EXCLAMATION POINT!

The most overused punctuation mark is the exclamation point. Save it! The exclamation point indicates joy, surprise, grief, anger, insistence, and so on.

> You made Donna cry!
> I cringed when the client yelled, "Do it now, or I'll go elsewhere!"

NOTE: Question marks and exclamation points that *are* part of the quotation go *inside* quotation marks (whether single or double quotation marks).

> My coworker asked, "Would you like to come over for dinner, Erin?"
> Willem said, "Brooke actually shouted, 'Eek, a mouse!' What a hoot!"

NOTE: Question marks and exclamation points that *are not* part of the quotation go *outside* the quotation marks.

> Did you laugh when the customer referred to the salesclerk as a "gross dude"?
> Imagine a grammar teacher saying "I ain't"!

GrammarWorks! Review

Using the above guidelines, insert the periods, question marks, and exclamation points.

"Holy poop__" the foreman shouted__ "We have until five o'clock to finish this paint job, and two of our crew left early__" Brad said, "I won't quit on you__ We'll fulfill our responsibility__" Two healthy-looking young women walked by__ "Hey, ladies, can you help us out__ We'll pay you fifty dollars for twenty minutes' work__" The redhead asked, "What do we have to do__" Brad asked, "Have you ever ironed a dress__" The brunette said, "Yes, but we've never done any painting__" Brad gathered ladders, paint, and rollers__ "Put on these overalls and baseball caps," he said__ "All you have to do is 'iron' this wall before five o'clock__" The young women laughed__ "We'll do it," they said__ "You saved us__" shouted the foreman__ "That's my job," said Brad__

FIXING A BONEHEAD ILLUSTRATION PARAGRAPH
Read the paragraph and follow the directions below.

THE ZOO'S A TRIP
BY N. M. OLIVER

(1) I'm a apprentice animal feeder at the boston Zoo I like my job a lot. (2) The chef feeder trusts me with the keys to the cages, and I lock it up to protect the animals from the vistors. (3) Jokingly, I say I work for peanuts. (4) What kinds of animal do I like the most. (5) The colorful ones—like leopards, cheetahs tigers zebras giraffes and snakes. (6) Why do I like snakes. (7) Well they don't bark they don't growl they don't screech and they don't nag you aboat food. (8) Because they eat every little thing that crawels. (9) Snakes is cheap to keep and there quite as a mouse. (10) Which is part of there diet. (11) I just had a grate idea. (12) Some day Ill open my own snake zoo. (13) I call it the "Snoo."

Edit the paragraph above. Search for the Big Eight: circle misspelled words, wrong words, and wrong capitalizations. Put an X in front of sentence fragments, run-on, spliced, and fused sentences. Underline misused pronouns and verbs and the comma and apostrophe errors. Each sentence above has a number. On the lines below, tell what you've found wrong with each numbered sentence. (Write what you found wrong with sentence (1) on line 1, and so on.)

1. _____
2. _____
3. _____
4. _____
5. _____
6. _____
7. _____
8. _____
9. _____
10. _____
11. _____
12. _____
13. _____

What animal does the "animal lover" use to illustrate something about snakes? _____

_____

How does the paragraph illustrate one of the personal values studied in this chapter?

_____

_____

Now you're ready to revise the paragraph. Write it in your own words on a separate piece of paper.

WORK! WORK! WORK!

Writing Practice

The following prompts will help you pick a topic to show what you've learned about the writing technique studied in this lesson.

"A job isn't finished until the paperwork is done."

Writing Exercises in Using Examples, the Illustration Technique

1. You think a coworker deserves a raise. Write a memorandum to his or her supervisor giving examples of the good work he or she has done.

2. Write an essay giving examples of problems that need to be resolved at your workplace.

3. Write a essay giving examples of your personality quirks. How do you illustrate one of the following personality features: intelligence, common sense, friendliness, charm, sense of humor, warmth, conceit, or wickedness?

4. Write an essay illustrating the personal values of a good employer or a good employee. Be sure you know which is which!

5. Write an essay giving examples of ways in which dogs have better social skills than people.

THE BIG EIGHT BONEHEADS!

- Words Misspelled
- Words or Caps Incorrect
- Sentence Fragments
- Sentence Run-Ons, Spliced or Fused
- Pronouns Confused
- Verbs Misused
- Commas Misplaced
- Apostrophes Abused

WORK! WORK! WORK!

Lesson Review

The following practices show what you've learned in this lesson.

SCANS Focus

Fill In the Blanks Regarding Self-Knowledge/Self-Esteem and Self-Management/Social Skills

1. Our set of beliefs about what is right is called our _____.

2. _____ is feeling good about ourselves, based on true knowledge of our strengths and weaknesses.

3. When you do what is expected of you and what you expect of yourself, you are showing _____ . When you acknowledge your mistakes and take steps to make corrections, you show _____ _____ .

4. A pact we have with ourselves that keeps us true to our high standards is our _____ .

5. _____ are important to help us fit in in the world of work.

6. Two examples of self-management you've shown in the past are _____ and _____ .

7. The _____ lies somewhere between the possible extremes of reaction to a given circumstance.

8. When we know what it is we are supposed to do and do it without being told, we are said to be a _____ .

9. Four examples of social skills are _____

_____ _____

_____ .

Fill In the Blanks Regarding Giving Meanings (definition)

1. In defining something, we move from the _____ to the

_____ .

2. _____ are helpful tools to illustrate meaning.

Fill In the Blanks Regarding Using Examples (illustration)

1. Another word for example is _____ .

2. In using examples, we illustrate broad, vague, hard-to-visualize terms by naming _____ that will get our meaning across.

GrammarWorks! Review

1. Written punctuation represents spoken _____ and

_____ .

Fill in the missing commas and periods. The number at the end of the line indicates the number of missing punctuation marks.

1. If you see Rebecca tell her I live at 215 Spruce Rd Los Angeles (4)

2. Be back by nine I have a doctor's appointment and I need the car (3)

3. When you go the market get tuna celery onions and potato chips (5)

4. Ms. Robbins my teacher brought her dog Rex the Magnificent to school (5)

5. Different methods of written expression include giving meanings using examples making categories and showing similarities and differences (4)

6. "Good attendance Kim is a sign of responsibility" said the professor (4)

Chapter 7

SORTING THINGS OUT

SCANS FOUNDATIONS: THINKING, MAKING DECISIONS, AND SOLVING PROBLEMS
SCANS COMPETENCY: ALLOCATION OF RESOURCES

Getting from here to there takes the ability to think. *Here* is the first tee of the first hole on the golf course; *there* is putting the ball into the eighteenth hole. *Here* might be behind the fast-food counter, and *there* can be achieving your career goals.

Thinking is the process we use to make decisions and solve problems. From that process, we take action to accomplish our goals—the actual allocation of time, material, and our own (or others') resources. To develop necessary job skills, we read attentively to gain the knowledge on which we'll base our decisions.

To practice organizing our thoughts, we will explore these methods of written expression: making categories (classification) and showing similarities and differences (comparison and contrast).

Let's get to work!

SCANS FOCUS: THINKING

MAKING DECISIONS AND SOLVING PROBLEMS TO ALLOCATE RESOURCES

When Juggling School, Work, and Family, Remember Not to Drop the Baby

We've all been making our own **decisions** and solving our own **problems** since we were children. *Should I share my doll with Bridget, or will she keep it forever? Willie kicked me. Should I kick him back or tell the teacher?* But, the older we get, the more complicated life becomes. More decisions become critical; and the problems become more difficult to solve. However, we also all have acquired the basic skill to access the information we need to move forward—our ability to *think*. We use the skill of thinking to weigh the advantages and the disadvantages of alternate ways of doing things. You can think of any decision you have to make as a problem to be solved.

A very wise man said, "The harder a decision is to make, the less it matters which alternative you choose." Think about it! If one choice will make you rich, famous, and happy, and the alternative will keep you poor, unknown, and sad, the decision would be *easy* to make! But, when we must choose between two *acceptable* courses of action, we sometimes are unable to decide. We ask our friends, we ask our family, and still we can't decide.

Say you're deciding whether to buy a Snickers or a Hershey bar. You have "done your homework" and know the two candy bars are about equal in fat and calories. There's no use agonizing over which one to buy. *It doesn't make any difference.* Make a decision to buy one—or both, *and get on with it.*

DECISION MAKING SOLVES PROBLEMS!

- Define the Problem
- Classify the Components
- Consider the Alternatives
- Take Action

THE KEY WORD IS "HOMEWORK"

If you're hung up on whether to have a hamburger or a hot dog, the impact of making the "wrong" choice is minimal. There's not much point in delaying the decision by doing research. If, however, the decision will affect your whole life, you need to do some *thinking*. Making a final decision is like solving a problem. First, we **define** the problem. Then, we **classify** its components. Finally, we **compare** the like qualities and **contrast** the different ones. A key element in making our decision or solving our problem is considering our **resources.** We go through these thought processes automatically, every day, without even realizing we're *thinking*.

These Are the Things You Need to Know How to Do

Learn how to address problems and decisions so you only have to worry about what is worth worrying about. Keep your eyes and energies on what's important.

STEPS TO MAKING A DECISION AND SOLVING A PROBLEM

Analysis	Situation	Thinking Process
Define a problem that will require making a decision.	It's Friday night, and I deserve to have some fun! But what shall I do?	*I'll think about the options.*
Broadly *classify* the choices.	What are the possibilities? A movie or a sports event; going out to dinner; throwing a party; ~~studying at the library; doing the laundry~~.	*I automatically reject the last two because they do not answer the question, What shall I do to have fun?*
Find *examples* to guide your reasoning.	When I made plans at the last minute before, I couldn't find a parking space at the ballpark, and the restaurant cost too much money.	*These examples help me decide not to go to the ballpark or a restaurant.*
Compare the similarities.	The remaining choices involve the allocation of time (time making plans and time I'll spend), material (money), and human resources (friends).	*This helps me focus on the features of the remaining choices.*
Contrast the differences.	Do I want to spend more or less time making plans and carrying them out, to invest more or less money on the fun, to divide my attention among more or fewer friends?	*I see some big differences now. I'll choose in the direction of the least expenditure of my time and money.*
Take Action!	I quickly call my best buddy, who I know will agree to pizza and the cheap show at the AMC. We always have fun together, and the two of us can decide how to spend *Saturday* night!	*Voila! I've come to a conclusion! Problem solved. Decision made.*

THINK OF YOUR PROBLEMS AND DECISIONS AS MENU CHOICES

At a restaurant, menu items are orderly and categorized. It would be harder to decide on what to have for breakfast, if breakfast items were mixed in with the salads and entrees instead of grouped together. Imagine that you're in a hurry to eat lunch and you go into Cooke's Coffee Shop.

If you don't want an appetizer, knowing that the appetizers come first on the menu makes it possible for you to omit that phase from your decision-making process. Then you notice that the sandwiches are listed by price, from lowest to highest. How soon can you find something that appeals to you before you get out of your price range? Don't spend your precious time thinking about whether to get Bacon on a Bagel or Tuna on Toast! The sooner you decide, the sooner you can order, eat, and leave. And, hey, this is only one meal in your life. How important is this decision? Do you need to spend fifteen minutes making it?

Learning how best to allocate time, material, and human resources is a necessary skill for life in the world of work. Here's a typical example.

If we finish sooner, we will get a bonus from our client. But, will the overtime wages cause an outgo of money greater than the income from the bonus?

The employee who has trouble making minor decisions will never be appointed the task of making major decisions. The employee who is unhinged by small problems will not be promoted to solving large ones. Maybe you've heard this not-so-old saying: "If you're not part of the solution, you're part of the problem."

PRACTICE, PRACTICE, PRACTICE

The more familiar we become with a process, the easier it is to perform. "Getting from here to there" can mean giving up writing your papers in longhand and learning to use a word processor. Word processing means you have to use a—gulp!—computer. A computer is mysterious! You're afraid you'll push the wrong button, causing the whole thing to melt on the spot. But, after someone helps you a few times, you're ready to try working on the computer alone. In a few months, you'll be able to turn in a research paper with footnotes and tables! All it takes is practice.

The objective is to become as comfortable with our skills at solving problems and making decisions as we are with any learned skill. We practice problem solving and decision making so that we can have a trusted routine to rely on, a valuable tool among our personal resources.

Do they really want what they're asking for? Rewrite the first sentence so the school will look as smart as the students.

Three-year-old teacher needed for preschool. Experience preferred.

_____

_____

SCANS Focus Exercise

The following examples show opportunities for using decision making and problem solving on the job. Read the examples and perform the exercise below.

Fashion Designer: Decides if the cost-range of the product will suit the targeted purchaser. Thinks how to get a quality fabric at the lowest price.

Electrical Technician: Decides how best to place wiring to accomplish desired results. Thinks how to cause least interference with existing construction.

Caterer: Decides what foods can be kept on hand and which must be purchased at last moment. Thinks how to prepare hot food for one hundred guests in a home with only one oven.

Office Manager: Decides who is best available person for job. Thinks how to maximize performance of payroll department.

Medical or Dental Receptionist/Secretary: Decides whether to recommend that Mrs. Delaney be served before Mrs. Hasenpfeffer because of Mrs. D's apparent pain. Thinks how to group insurance forms for fastest processing.

Freight Company Router: Decides order of loading items for best order of unloading of items. Thinks about scheduling time and human resources.

In-Class SCANS Exercise

The above examples show how problem-solving, decision-making, and resource-allocation skills are involved in the jobs mentioned. Choose one of the following topics and, on a separate piece of paper, give a brief example of how these skills apply to the work you're doing or training for. Remember to include the name of your job.

1. Describe a typical *problem* you had to solve and how you solved it.
2. Describe a typical *decision* you had to make and how you made it.
3. On what project or service would you need to make a decision about the allocation of time, material, or human resources?

Advertisement in a university extension catalog for a workshop on spirituality. *You can fix the fragment below by omitting a few introductory words.*

Spend a weekend with XXX and discover how to tap your personal source of spirituality. So that even in the midst of daily challenges, you can be more loving.

"This little piggy went to market, this little piggy stayed home . . . "

MAKING CATEGORIES— CLASSIFICATION

DIVIDE AND CONQUER

Dividing a large mixed group into smaller parts or subgroups makes more manageable units. If your task is to order the school's sports team uniforms, you can't just go from that large problem to the telephone and say, "Send me 350 red and white uniforms." You need to sort things out. You need **categories!** You need to **classify!**

How many kinds of teams are there?

How many members are on each team? What are their sizes?

What do they wear for practice?

Does each sport need home and away uniforms?

Whew! You get the idea. But, you'll notice that each *small* unit is a simple question to answer. Making each small decision in its turn solves the big problem. In writing, this technique can turn a large, complicated topic into small, simple, separate units that help explain the whole.

YOU NEED TO KNOW THE REASON FOR BREAKING DOWN THE LARGE GROUP

There are many ways to break down large groups into smaller ones. The laundry can be sorted by types of materials, colors of fabrics, or by clothing and towels and sheets. It depends on whether your goal is to have the fewest loads or loads with items or colors that are alike.

If the boss asks you to sort the mail, you can be pretty sure she doesn't want it sorted by the sizes of the envelopes! You need to know what groups to sort the mail *into*. You don't want to spend three hours sorting the envelopes by the fifty states' postmarks if what she wanted was for you to make four categories: orders, bills, letters, and everything else. The boss may very well benefit from knowing which states are responding to the advertising and which are not. You might even suggest categorizing the orders by states. Of course, today that task would be done more easily by computer, and you'll know how to accomplish that, won't you? Meanwhile, you'll want to ask what categories the boss wants.

The purpose of the writing technique called *classification,* or making categories, is to deliver information in clear, concise groups *that fulfill the purpose of the procedure.*

The following are student and professional examples of the category-making technique.

The student author's assignment: Write an essay sorting a large group into smaller categories.

Minnie Choi is a Chinese American who is majoring in business and has been working in her parents' restaurant for several years.

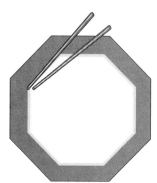

```
Minnie Choi                                    Choi 1
English 103-1:00
Making Categories
July 18, 1999

                        Paul's Menu


    Paul's Kitchen, my parents' restaurant, is a renowned
Chinese restaurant that serves many different kinds of
Chinese food. You've probably noticed on menus at American or
```

Mexican or Italian restaurants that food items are grouped according to first course selections, entrées, and desserts, and entrées sometimes come with one kind of soup or salad. At Chinese restaurants, you can choose all your courses yourself from many entrée categories and from separate lists of noodle and rice dishes and soups. There are many dishes in each category on the menu at Paul's Kitchen, and in each category there is at least one "customers' favorite."

In the first section, we have seafood dishes. The item ordered most is Shrimp Cantonese. This dish contains large, whole pieces of shrimp—without the shells, of course. The shrimp are cooked in lobster sauce, which contains a little bit of black bean sauce, pieces of minced pork, as well as lobster and egg whites. There are other great-tasting items in the seafood section, including dishes with scallops, rock cod, and prawns.

In the next section, we have beef. The item ordered most in this section is Beef with Broccoli. The tender beef in this dish is cut in thin slices, then stir-fried with the American broccoli in a light sauce. Some other dishes include Pepper Steak, Ginger Beef, Beef with Snow Peas, and many other savory beef dishes.

In the chicken section, we have Paul's Kitchen's most famous dish, Crispy Fried Chicken. The chicken is prepared whole, with a very light batter, fried to perfection, and cut into pieces topped with seasonings and shrimp chips. Of course, we serve Kung Pao Chicken and Chinese Chicken Salad, which are also favorites with the customers.

Another menu section is for pork dishes. One of the favorites is Sweet and Sour Pork. The pork is cut into bite-size pieces and covered with a special batter, then fried to a golden brown. The pork is topped with bell peppers, onions, pineapple chunks, and sweet-and-sour sauce. Other pork dishes include Minced Pork with Tofu and Barbecued Pork with Chinese Broccoli.

Our barbecue section contains the customers' overall favorite dishes: Barbecued Sausage, Barbecued Pork Ribs, Chanshu (barbecued pork), and Barbecued Chicken. These meats are not cooked with tomato-based sauces like the ones at Western barbecues. Paul's Kitchen barbecue dishes are prepared with special Chinese sauces and seasonings.

Noodle dishes come next on our menu because some people like to eat them as their entrée instead of as a companion dish. Chow Mein noodles can be cooked in different ways. Most often, customers order our House Special Chow Mein— soft noodles, sort of like Italian spaghetti, stir-fried in a light sauce, with pieces of barbecued pork, chicken, shrimp, shiitake mushrooms, snow peas, and bok choi. Lo Mein and Mun Yee Mein are soft-noodles dishes, prepared with just one selection of meat and vegetable. Some customers prefer chow mein dishes served with crispy noodles instead of soft ones.

The next category on the menu would be rice dishes. What's Chinese food without rice? On our menu, we have fried rice and just plain, steamed white rice. The fried rice is cooked in several different ways: with just vegetables; with pork, shrimp, chicken, or beef; or with all the meats mentioned. There is also a fried rice dish cooked with a mixture of shrimp and barbecue pork and bean sprouts. This popular dish is called Yan Chow Fried Rice. Would you be surprised to know that plain steamed rice is the most popular rice dish?

Last, we have our soup section. We serve Egg Flower Soup and Seaweed Soup as our soups of the day. We also have specialty soups such as Tofu Soup, Hot and Sour Soup, Chicken Corn Soup, and Wonton Soup. Egg Flower and Wonton are the customers' two favorites.

We prepare many other dishes at Paul's Kitchen that I have not mentioned, and we have even more categories on our menu. I didn't describe any of our delicious appetizers or desserts. All the food is prepared well, and the dishes are so tasty, they're fit for a king or queen. After two years of working at my parent's restaurant, I have tried just about all the items on the menu. I have my own favorites. If you always order the same dishes from the menu, you'll never know what wonderful things you're missing! If you come to Paul's Kitchen, I'll help you decide what new dishes to try.

Harcourt, Inc.

WORK! WORK! WORK!

These exercises help build skills by prompting you to express your understanding of what you read.

Reading Comprehension

1. Minnie mentions many of the customers' favorite dishes. What category includes their overall favorites? (Remember, the word *section* can indicate categories.) _____

   _____

2. What is the main ingredient of Chow Mein? _____

3. Does Minnie mention your favorite Chinese dish? Name your favorite Chinese dish. _____

Writing Analysis

1. To write a paper showing categories, you begin with a broad issue. In the first paragraph, in the topic sentence, you state the subject you're going to sort out. What is Minnie's topic sentence? _____

   _____

2. Paul's kitchen has a physical location with a kitchen and a seating area, employees, and an inventory of food and recipe ingredients. On what other key resource does Paul depend to sustain his restaurant business and guarantee his success. _____

   _____

3. Besides menu items, name three other broad subjects that can be broken down into sections or categories. _____

   _____

From a Sports section. *The writer left out a comma and added a letter where none belongs. Can you find his mistakes and correct them?*

[Mr.] Evans' home phone number is listed in the Oxford directory and he attempts to answers all his calls—crank, praiseworthy, racist, or otherwise.

The following professional article uses a common way to classify items, numerical listing. All information pertaining to one idea, or subject, is grouped under one number.

Watch for the Warning Flags Customers Wave
by John Witkowski

People can be an incredible source of entertainment—if you take the time to observe carefully, that is. They can act with such profound stupidity, it's incredible. And I say "they," of course. You and I may have the occasional slip-up, but we never come close to the follies of others, do we? Have you ever watched a salesperson blow an excellent chance to make a sale? It's more profitable to learn from the mistakes of others rather than paying for the experience ourselves!

Have you ever watched someone lose a good customer for good? We often can see it coming. The "other guy" is walking right into it, eyes wide open, and *bam!*—another opportunity bites the dust. Shaking his head afterwards, the salesperson may blame the "stupid" customer. Amazing! If only others had the good sense and clarity of vision that we have, right? It must be an ego preservation instinct that we possess—it's easy to spot someone else's mistakes right away. The "other" guy has the disadvantage of being immersed in the developing circumstance, while we can stand back from a situation and see it unfolding before our eyes. It's that "can't see the forest for the trees" thing. But our own mistakes? What's our excuse?

If we watch for the warning flags that signal that someone else is about to botch a sales opportunity—or worse, turn off a customer for good—we'll discover things that will likely crop up in our own customer relationships. One of the best tests for whether we are building a positive rapport with a customer or not is to imagine ourselves in their shoes. How does it feel? Would you like to deal with a salesperson like yourself, or would you rather walk out the door?

Here is a list of warning flags that customers will wave as certain situations approach—especially if they feel that they're being shortchanged in the process. Picture yourself as the customer. Do you recognize the feeling? What if you are the person trying to make the sale—do these situations deliver a sense of déjà vu? If they do, try to prevent *your* customers from feeling that way—before it costs you more money!

WARNING FLAG NO. 1: "I HAVE THIS SKETCH OF A LOGO. . . ."

This means that the customer probably has some emotional attachment to the sketched design, no matter how terrible it is. Insult the sketch, and the customer walks.
Avoid: "What's this? There's no way I could use it; it's very unprofessional. Did your plumber do this?"
Say: "Are there some particular parts of this design that you feel are very important to you?"

WARNING FLAG NO. 2: "COULD YOU JUST GIVE ME A BALLPARK PRICE OVER THE PHONE?"

This means that the customer is not sure what price to expect. They want to "test the waters" to see if they can afford the type of sign they have envisioned. They are shopping around. And they want to do it with some anonymity. If they tell you their price range up front, they run the risk of appearing "cheap" or, even worse, feeling embarrassed if their price expectations fall short of reality. Force them into naming their price first and if it is way too low, you may never hear from them again.

Avoid: " A decent sign will cost a thousand bucks, at least. Oh, you can only afford two hundred, you say?"
Say: "Our flexibility in materials and types of signs allows us to provide good value for most price ranges. What price range did you have in mind?"

WARNING FLAG No. 3: "I TALKED TO FLY-BY-NITE SIGNS, AND THEY GAVE ME A PRICE 25 PERCENT LOWER THAN YOURS."

This means that the customer wants to get the best possible value for their money. You would, too, right? So don't treat them as if they have no right to shop around. Educate them about what makes a good sign. Try to find out if they are comparing apples to apples. Maybe two-year vinyl on plastic sheeting is all they really need. Find out!
Avoid: "Well, is that so? And what kind of rubbish are they trying to sell you at that low price?"
Say: "Well, tell me what you need in terms of impact, durability, and quality, and then we can make a good comparison between what they have offered and what I can do for you."

WARNING FLAG No. 4: "I'VE WAITED A WEEK FOR SOMEONE TO CALL ME BACK FROM NO-CALL SIGNS."

Here is a most glorious opportunity to win over a customer's precious loyalty. Your competition has handed you a touchdown pass in a silver basket—don't drop it! The customer has offered you the opportunity to do business. All they have asked for is to be treated with deserved respect. Treat them like a king! Kiss the ground they walk on! What do they want? Deliver, deliver!
Avoid: "Sure, I'll just make an important phone call, then I'll call you back."
Say: "Is right now a convenient time to talk about what you need?" Or, if you must make another call, say, "I must return another call first, then I'll call you right back and we can take the time to discuss what you need."

WARNING FLAG No. 5: "I NEED THIS SIGN BY THURSDAY."

This means that the customer may or may not really need the sign by Thursday, but they are giving you an important test. Don't flunk out! They probably expect you to say, "Fine, no problem, I promise"—and then fail to deliver on time.

Have you ever had a salesperson break a promise? Who hasn't? Be honest. If you cannot guarantee to deliver on time, tell them when you can be sure of delivery.

If you cannot ensure meeting their time schedule, tell them up front. If they absolutely must have it by Thursday, call up one of your competitors and refer the job to them—but only if you know from prior experience that they won't let you and the customer down. You should receive a referral fee from your competitor for this. If nothing else, you will gain the customer's respect, and that could pay off big-time in the future.
Avoid: "Next Thursday? On, *this* Thursday—sure, no problem, heh, heh! Friday at the very latest—I promise!"
Say: "Let me check our work schedule to see if I can guarantee the date you need. I'll call you right back in a few minutes."

WARNING FLAG NO. 6: "I WOULD GIVE YOU A DEPOSIT, BUT I DON'T WANT TO IMPACT MY CASH FLOW."

There is no cash flow. Do you like to gamble? Go ahead—spend your time, money, and effort. And then see if you get paid in full, on time!
Avoid: "Well, okay, I'll just go ahead and cover the $3,000 vinyl cost out of my own pocket!"
Say: "Because of the cost of quality materials that cannot be used over again, we need a deposit to confirm that you have given us the go-ahead for your work."

WARNING FLAG NO. 7: "CAN I JUST TAKE THIS COLOR PRINTOUT HOME TO SHOW MY SPOUSE/PARTNER/HOUSE CAT?"

You might as well send a copy to every sign shop within one hundred miles, with the explicit instructions to "Please feel free to copy and/or use any or all parts of this design to undercut my price for this customer." The professional shops that do see the sketch will let you know; the others will use it without regard for your work. Anyway, what's the cat going to say about it? It's purrfect?!
Avoid: "Sure, go ahead, but don't use it to get a better price from a sign shop that doesn't have to include a cost for design, layout, and the time we spent discussing what image you wanted to project, okay?"
Say: "I'm sorry, but all of our designs and layouts belong to us until they are paid for. If you wish, you can pay for this now, and if you choose to have us do your sign work, the cost will be credited towards the overall price of the signs."

WARNING FLAG NO. 8: "I USED TO USE TRIED-HARD SIGNS, BUT THEY DIDN'T DO WHAT I WANTED."

Communications may have broken down somewhere along the line. Maybe no one kept a record of the sign copy or the exact colors to be used. Perhaps specific instructions for delivery or payment were not clear. Maybe the customer changed his mind at some point. Whatever. Use a clear, concise work order form to record all the pertinent details in writing. (See past issues of SignCraft *or the* SignCraft *business forms pack for some excellent ideas.) Have the customer sign the work order. And if in doubt, call the customer to verify the details! See what poor or sloppy communications can do? Your competition just lost a customer, and you gained a new one!*
Avoid: "Whatsamatter, don't you speak clearly? Listen, you tell me once, and I'm gonna do it!"
Say: "Let's go over all the details. We'll write them all down, sign it, and give you a copy. I don't want to disappoint you because of a misunderstanding!"

WARNING FLAG NO. 9: "CAN YOU DO THIS?"

The customer has a specific request in relation to their sign. It will involve a feature that is very important to them. Don't trivialize their request. It may involve reproducing a certain logo, using a specific color, or providing a material that meets a specific performance criteria. It might require specific skills or experience. Whatever the customer is asking you to do, don't play around. If you can provide what they want, show examples as proof—it will boost their confidence in you. Not sure if you can do it? Be

honest with the customer. Don't take on work that is obviously beyond your capabilities. Don't practice with a paying customer's money!
Avoid: "Sure, we can do it—we can do anything—take my word for it!"
Say: "Yes, we can provide that—here is an example." Or: "We haven't completed a sign using that technique before, but I could prepare a sample for you to see on Friday." Or: "I'm sorry, but we don't do that type of work at the present time. However, I will call you back with the name of one of my colleagues that can help you out." (Try to get a referral fee from your colleague if they do business with the customer.)

WARNING FLAG NO. 10: "I'M JUST CALLING TO SEE HOW THE TRUCK LOOKS!"

The customer is getting pumped. They can't wait to see how their new vehicle looks. They are excited about the layout you showed them—and they did spring for a bit extra for the airbrushed color fades. Keep that excitement going—now is the perfect time to remind them to bring a check along!
Avoid: "Bummer, Joe. It just didn't turn out like I thought it would." This is one of Jackie's and my favorite "inside" jokes about the sign business. Virtually everybody asks how the finished job looks when they call to arrange a pick-up time. Now, really, what are you going to say? But sometimes we just can't resist the "Bummer" line–but *only* when we know the customer *really* well!
Say: "Terrific! It looks even better than the color sketch you saw. And when you pick the truck up at 5:00, could you send a check along for the balance? Thanks, Joe!"

———————●———————

Exercise Related to the Professional Article from the World of Work on Classification (Categories)

Reading Comprehension

1. In the article, the author uses warning flags to divide his subject into ten different categories. Paraphrase three of these warning flags. _____

   _____

   _____

2. After each category, the author suggests two alternatives. What are they? _____

   _____

   _____

3. This article relates directly to sign painting. Is it appropriate to other trade services as well? _____

Writing Analysis

1. What is the author's purpose in using italics after each warning sign? _____

   _____

   _____

2. The author takes a difficult subject yet presents it in a positive manner. What is his

   topic sentence? _____

   _____

3. The author has a sign business in Ireland. Can you note any cultural differences between customer approaches in Ireland and in this country? Explain your answer.

_____

_____

Even when you get the spelling right, your meaning may be misunderstood. Rewrite the ad so that dynamite doesn't appear to be the means of travel.

Man wanted to work in dynamite factory. Must be willing to travel.

_____

_____

GRAMMARWORKS! A Battle of Words

Can versus May versus Might

CAN/*expresses ability*   I **can** open the can.
MAY/*seeks permission*   Mother, **may** I?
MIGHT/*expresses possibility*   I **might** fight if the prize is right.

If you **can** find them in the attic, you **may** borrow my disco duds.
You **might** even change your mind about what to wear to the costume party.

Which versus That

WHICH   Use *which* when a clause *can be omitted* from the sentence without changing the meaning of the sentence. If a clause *is* set off by commas, **which** are little curlicue things, the clause *is not* essential to the meaning of the sentence.

THAT   Use *that* when a clause *cannot be omitted* from the sentence without changing the meaning of the sentence. A clause **that** is not set off by commas is essential to the meaning of the sentence. (Sometimes, the word *that* is omitted, but understood.)

Kim told me a rumor **that** circulated through the office. The rumor **(that)** she heard was **that** all office personnel will receive a 10 percent raise.
Kim's rumor, **which** sounded too good to be true, was started by the office prankster. I heard a rumor **that** wages will be cut by 10 percent, **which** also proved false.

Good versus Well

GOOD   Adjective/*opposite of bad*   We had a good time.
WELL   Adverb/*satisfactorily*   Well done.
WELL   Adjective/*healthy*   Get well soon.

We are all glad that Kate feels **good** again and has a **good** attitude.
She is now doing **well** in all her courses and is **well** enough to complete the research paper.

Bad versus Badly versus Ill

BAD	Adjective/*opposite of good*	What bad luck!
BADLY	Adverb/*poorly*	I need money badly.
ILL	Adjective/*sick* & Adverb/*scarcely*	He can ill afford a new car.

When Lucas feels **bad**, he gets in a **bad** mood and writes **badly** on his term paper. He was too **ill** to complete his term paper last week. He can **ill** afford to miss the deadline.

Certain verbs (sometimes called *verbs of being*) link subjects to modifiers: *be (am, is, are, was, were, etc.), become, appear, seem; feel, look, smell, sound, taste; continue, grow, keep, remain, stay.*

Since a subject is *always* a noun (or pronoun), the modifier is *always* an adjective, *never* an adverb. Example: I felt **bad** (*not* **badly**) when I hurt his feelings.

GRAMMARWORKS! Review

Circle the correct italicized words. Each word studied is used correctly at least once in the sentences below.

1. I *can/may/might* move to Ohio. I *can/may/might* find a job there. You *can/may/might* visit me.
2. We rented a movie *which/that* frightened me, *which/that* Stephen King wrote.
3. Whether my mood is *good/well* or *bad/badly*, I do *good/well* in English.
4. When I feel *bad/ill* with a cold, I do *bad/badly* in all of my classes.
5. Is this the book *which/that* you told me I *can/may/might* borrow?

GRAMMARWORKS! One Word or Two—which Will Do?

ALOT	*There is no such word!*	
A LOT	Noun/*a great deal* Adverb/*much*	*A lot* happened since he left. I'm *a lot* happier now that he's back.
ALLOT	Verb/*apportion*	Gregory *allotted* the candy equally among the trick-or-treaters.
A WHILE	Noun/*a short time*	*A while* has passed since Phil saw JoJo.
AWHILE	Adverb/*for a short time*	Grandma said, "Come and sit *awhile*."
ALL READY	Adverb phrase/*totally prepared*	The Smiths are *all ready* to move.
ALREADY	Adverb/*before now*	The moving van is here *already*.
ALL RIGHT	Adjective or adverb phrase/*safe, acceptable* *satisfactorily*	He called to see if I was *all right*. Blueboy ran *all right*, but he tired out.
ALRIGHT	A corruption of *all right*. Many authorities say there is no such word. Its use is acceptable only in informal writing, such as personal letters. Business and student writing assignments call for the preferred form . . . *all right*.	

ALL TOGETHER	Adjective phrase/*as a unit, in one place*	The packages were *all together* in the corner of the warehouse.
ALTOGETHER	Adverb/*entirely*	Deni's grades were *altogether* too low to get her into the university.
EVERY DAY	Adverb phrase/*daily*	Oliver wrote Rosemarie a letter *every day* that he was in Santa Fe.
EVERYDAY	Adjective/*commonplace*	Aisha's *everyday* dishes were good enough for the family gathering.

GRAMMARWORKS! Review

Circle the correct italicized word or words in each of the following sentences.

1. Dad bought *a lot/allot* of old marbles at the garage sale.
2. The heirs are going to *a lot/allot* her personal items as equally as possible.
3. I haven't watched that sitcom in quite *a while/awhile*.
4. Are you *all ready/already* for your final exam?
5. Elvis has *all ready/already* left the building.
6. Is everything *all right/alright* since Sue and Henry made up?
7. Our family was *all together/altogether* for our parents' fiftieth anniversary.
8. Forget the idea of winning the lottery *all together/altogether*!
9. You can't wear your *every day/everyday* clothing to the job interview!
10. After his surgery, Clyde got better and better *every day/everyday*.

GRAMMARWORKS! Difficult Distinctions

I will **accept** the job of explaining these distinctions on any day **except** Sunday.

ACCEPT	Verb/*receive*	Jane *accepted* the Emmy for her ailing father.
	Verb/*acknowledge*	It's hard to *accept* that nobody's perfect.
EXCEPT	Preposition/*excluding, not counting*	Take everything off the bed *except* your hat.
	Occasionally a verb/*exclude*	Everyone's crazy—present company *excepted*.
AMONG	Preposition/*referring to more than two*	The six sisters split the dinner bill among them.

(GrammarTool: Correct plural pronouns always sound correct. *Among they* doesn't sound right!)

| BETWEEN | Preposition/*referring to only two* | *Between* you and me, Gary's an awful cook. |

(GrammarTool: If *us* sounds correct, *me, him,* and *her* are correct. You wouldn't say, *between we!*)

Among us sticklers, there's a clear difference **between** these two words.

Remember! Prepositions always take the objective case pronouns: *me, him, her, us, them.*

| LIE, LYING, LAY, LAIN | Verb/*rest, recline, or remain* (no object) | Present: If I have a migraine headache, I **lie** down. In Progress: Jill is **lying** on the couch watching TV. Past: The papers **lay** on the desk overnight. |

LAY, LAYING, LAID, LAID	Verb/*to place* (an object)	Perfect: The man **has lain** in the clinic three days. In Progress: Viva is **laying** *flowers* on the grave. Past: Yoko **laid** her *head* on her arms and slept. Perfect: Duane **had laid** the *briefcase* on the chair. Present: Everyone knows chickens **lay** *eggs*.

I cannot tell a **lie**! You can either **lie** down or **lay** *your head* on the desk.

While you are **lying** on the couch, you are **laying** *the TV listings* beside you.

The papers **lay** on the desk for two days because Stan **laid** *them* there.

The briefcase **had lain** on the chair because Charlie **had laid** *his coat* on the table.

You'll get **less** criticism and **fewer** complaints if you know when to use **less** and when to use **fewer**.

LESS	*Use this adverb only when the quantity is as a unit.*	Tori ate **less** *peanut butter* than Dave. During a drought, we use **less** *water*.
FEWER	*Use this adverb when you can count the units.*	Tori ate **fewer** *peanuts* than Dave. During a drought, we take **fewer** *showers*.

(GrammarTool: Plural words require **fewer**: **fewer** classes, chairs, flowers, people, men, women.)

GrammarWorks! Review

Circle the correct italicized word in each of the following sentences.

Among/Between health authorities, *less/fewer* men than women *accept/except* the idea that emotional health affects physical health. However, the evidence doesn't lie. Besides ill health, a bad mood can make you sick or cause a rift *among/between* two people who love each other—*accept/except* when they're angry or frustrated. So when things are going *bad/badly* and you're feeling *bad/badly,* don't just *lie/lay* around making yourself sick because you think that love is lost! *Lie/Lay* down your head and have a good cry. There will be *less/fewer* tension in your life, and you and your sweetie can *lie/lay* health issues aside—emotionally *and* physically!

THE BIG EIGHT BONEHEADS!

- Words Misspelled
- Words or Caps Incorrect
- Sentence Fragments
- Sentence Run-Ons, Spliced or Fused
- Pronouns Confused
- Verbs Misused
- Commas Misplaced
- Apostrophes Abused

FIXING A BONEHEAD CLASSIFICATION
Read the paragraph and then follow the directions below.

(1) SORDID SCREWS by Homer Knott

(2) My father axed me to sort the screws in his toolbox box which had a tray with four squares. (3) First, I poured everything out of the box. (4) you never seen such alot of things. (5) I put the shinny screws altogether in one square, well use those last. (6) Sorting screws were hard and they had flat heads and round heads and pointy bottoms and flat bottoms. (7) I throwed away the ones with the flat bottoms cause them had the points busted off. (8) The ones with little exes in one sqare, and without exes in another. (9) I had one square left I filled it with m&ms. (10) All done. (11) Wont' Dad be suprised at how good I done my job? (12) I'm a big help to he and Mom.

Edit the paragraph above. Search for the Big Eight: circle misspelled words, wrong words, and wrong capitalizations. Put an X in front of sentence fragments, run-on, spliced, and fused sentences. Underline misused pronouns and verbs and the comma and apostrophe errors. Each sentence above has a number. On the lines below, write what you've found wrong with each numbered sentence. (Write what you found wrong with sentence (1) on line 1, and so on.)

1. _____
2. _____
3. _____
4. _____
5. _____
6. _____
7. _____
8. _____
9. _____
10. _____
11. _____
12. _____

How does the paragraph illustrate the writing technique? _____

_____

How does the paragraph illustrate the SCANS skills? _____

_____

Now you're ready to revise the paragraph. Write it in your own words on a separate piece of paper.

WORK! WORK! WORK!

Writing Practice

The following prompts will help you pick a topic to show what you've learned about the writing technique studied in this lesson.

"A job isn't finished until the paperwork is done."

Exercises in Writing Categories, the Classification Technique

1. Most classifications solve a large problem by breaking it into small categories. Here's a large problem most of us would enjoy: You have inherited one million dollars that you must *spend* within thirty days! Write an essay of three or more paragraphs classifying four or more ways in which you would spend or distribute the money.

2. Write an essay of three or more paragraphs classifying the rides at Disneyland, television shows, tools used around the house, types of candy, or any topic of your choice. Consider choosing a topic concerning your field of study or work.

3. Look again at the SCANS chart "Steps to Making a Decision and Solving a Problem." Following the steps in the example, and using an experience from your own life or work, write an essay of three or more paragraphs in which you define a problem, outline the alternatives, and show the decision you would reach.

4. We make many decisions in our lives, and we learn a great deal from our mistakes. In 250 or more words, recall a wrong decision you made. Define the problem and write about the steps you should have taken in making the right decision.

Caveat emptor is Latin for "Buyer beware!" Correct the comma splice and rewrite the ad so that a prospective customer might want to try the shop's service.

Auto Repair Service. Try us once, you'll never go anywhere again.

_____

_____

"Although they were all teen-age girls, Cinderella was very nice and very pretty, while her stepsisters were wicked and ugly . . . ."

SIMILARITIES AND DIFFERENCES— COMPARISON AND CONTRAST

IF YOU WANT TO BORROW A DIME, FIRST DEFINE YOUR TERMS

When things **compare,** we say they are *similar to* each other. When they **contrast,** we say they are *different from* (not different *than*) each other. We group **similarities (comparisons)** and

differences (contrasts) together because these are opposite ways of looking at the same things. This technique helps us make analyses and draw conclusions.

Imagine two dimes, both face up. They *compare* in that their face values, sizes, and weights are alike, and each has a ziggedy edge. They *contrast* in that they have different years on them and different letters that represent where they were minted. If one is very old and the other very new, they may have different pictures on them, be of different material (all silver or part copper), and exhibit different wear and tear. But, a really old, mint-condition, silver dime has a value *far* in excess of ten cents! Don't stick that one in a parking meter!

COMPARATIVELY SPEAKING . . .

Often in the world of work, we make decisions based on comparisons. However, when things are comparable (a lot alike) a decision is difficult to make. It is in the *contrasts* (the differences) between items that we find the bases for making decisions.

WHAT WE NEED HERE IS A LITTLE CONTRAST

Some people seem always to be looking for something new and different—for things that contrast with what they're used to. "Been there; done that" leads them to seek new sights. They think, *yes, that's good, but might something else be better?* That's another example of seeking contrasts. However, when you are in a position to manage your own or other people's resources, you will often look for the *differences* between your options. Maybe you've thought of a new way to perform a task at work. How do you determine if it is better than the old way? You need to get more light into your study area. What are the differences in cost and effectiveness that would cause you to choose a hanging lamp, a pole lamp, or a stick-on flourescent lamp? It's the ability to see the differences clearly that makes our problems simpler and our decisions easier. This is a good tool to stash among your personal resources.

KNOW WHAT TO ORGANIZE

If you're asked to organize the shoes at the store where you work, you wouldn't put all the left shoes in one place and all the right shoes in another or *some* of the blue shoes together. But would you put *all* the blue shoes together, or all the shoes by one manufacturer, or all the size nines? To make the decision, you need to keep the objective in mind: to arrange the shoes in a way that will make it easy for the salespeople to find what the customers want. Salespeople will tell you they like the shoes by the manufacturer's styles—because if someone wants to try on two sizes or two colors of the same shoe, they are right next to each other in the storeroom.

You might keep your closet in a state of chaos, but you *must* organize your comparisons and contrasts! Parallel structure and balance are necessary to make the best use of the information you have gathered. Give attention to the important similarities of *every* item you are comparing and the important differences in *every* item you are contrasting. The material should be easy to follow and should lead to a responsible conclusion. Like the stock clerk, be consistent and logical in organizing your comparisons and contrasts. Written information should be as easy for the readers to find as shoes are for salespeople.

TWO METHODS OF ORGANIZING COMPARISON AND CONTRAST PAPERS: BLOCK INFORMATION AND ALTERNATING INFORMATION

Block information balances a block of all the features of one item against a block of all features of another item. **Alternating** information parallels each feature of each item (like rows and columns). You can even combine them. Your goal and the material should help you decide which method to choose.

The Block Information Method

One *item* with *all* its features is shown in one block, *followed by* the other *item* with *all* its similar, or different, features in a separate block.

> ### BLOCKS SHOWING SIMILARITIES BETWEEN GEORGE AND MITZI
>
> **George** is a six-foot tall, African American with a copper-toned face topped by curly black hair. He has a warm, friendly personality and an infectious laugh. George is a student in visual communications. (**All of George's features that you want to mention.**)
>
> **Mitzi** is also six feet tall, also African American. Mitzi has honey-almond skin, and her dark brown hair curls tightly. Her personality is as appealing as George's, and she is known for her good sense of humor. Mitzi is in the visual communications field also. (**All of Mitzi's features that you want to mention.**)

The Alternating Information Method

One *feature* of one item is shown *next to* the similarities or differences in *that feature of the other item.*

> ### ALTERNATING INFORMATION SHOWING DIFFERENCES BETWEEN GEORGE AND MITZI
>
> **George** wears a closely trimmed Vandyke beard on his jutting chin, while **Mitzi's** chin features a dimple. **He** has a prominent, distinguished nose, bushy eyebrows, and dark brown eyes. **She** has a dainty nose that turns up slightly. Her eyebrows are hardly noticeable, and her brown eyes are flecked with gold. (**Facial features of each.**)
>
> **George's** body is that of an athlete, as muscular as a weight lifter's. **Mitzi's** build is softly feminine, like Oprah Winfrey's. (**Body features of each.**)
>
> **George,** who is a twenty-five-year-old man, wants to be a graphic artist. **Mitzi,** who is thirty-five, is studying photography. (**Age and career interest of each.**)

Alternating Blocks of Similarities and Differences.   It is not likely that two things will be *only* alike or *only* different. Example:

Nikki and Maura are nonathletic line-dancing fans who love reading cookbooks. It's no wonder they enjoy each other's company. (**Similarities.**)

Nikki works part time in a pet store, and Maura works in the day care center. Even though Nikki doesn't enjoy young kids and Maura is allergic to animals, they enjoy hearing about each other's experiences at work. (**Differences.**)

Alternating Similarities or Differences within the Same Paragraph.   Sometimes the information is not enough to require more than one paragraph. As long as the information is orderly and easy to follow, you can combine it.

Ricardo, a Latino man, is thirty-two years old and six feet tall. **Toby,** a Canadian, is ten years younger and a foot shorter. **Ricardo** and **Toby** are both computer fanatics who met on the Internet. **(One block with parallel differences and parallel similarities.)**

The above examples intentionally lack the flair of polished writing so that you can easily understand the methods. You do not have to be so strict in your writing! Be relaxed. Enjoy telling similarities and differences. Just be sure to include the same features of both subjects when you make your comparisons and contrasts.

WRITING ABOUT A LARGE TOPIC

In a long paper, some aspects of the topic might lend themselves to block comparison and contrast, and other aspects might better be compared and contrasted in the alternating format. In combining the methods, the important thing is to structure your material so the reader can easily follow your points.

The following are examples of student and professional articles using the comparison and contrast technique of writing.

Large brass sign at upscale shopping center. *They might not have had enough room to spell out every word, but they had plenty of room for correct punctuation. Cross out the incorrect punctuation and add periods where necessary. Rewrite below.*

Cross the Blvd to more shopping, & dining at Plaza de Oro Use our new crosswalk.

_____

_____

The student author's assignment: Compare and/or contrast two people.

Dedrick Brown is a college night student, the father of three. He's employed by the City of Los Angeles and a carpentry hobbyist.

```
Dedrick Brown                                    Brown 1
English 104-10:30
Compare/Contrast
Dec. 5, 1999

                        Craftsmen

    Let's talk about tools. I like tools. No, I'm a tool
fanatic! As a "do-it-yourself" builder, I identify with two
```

other tool fanatics—Homer and Tim. The thing is, neither of them is real, and they're not much alike. Homer is a cartoon character that is printed on Home Depot's ad pages. Tim Allen, the television personality, uses his real name for a fictitious character who has a fictitious TV show called *Tool Time*. Both clowns keep me in stitches, partly because they remind me of myself.

When I think of tools, I first think of Homer, Home Depot's mascot. He is a "local yokel" type. Overalls, red striped shirt, and a denim cap are his basic attire. Homer is a "Jack of all trades." He reminds me of a shade-tree mechanic. In other words, he looks like an average Joe. His persona is cool, calm, and collected—in a bumpkin kind of way. Homer is a happy guy with a rough voice. He gives me the impression that he is content walking around the store testing every product in sight. This behavior may seem odd to people unlike Homer and me, but we gain a lot of knowledge in the process. Homer collects tools of all types, for no reason. Well, for no immediate need. Maybe Homer thinks it's better to have a tool and not need it than not to have it at all. One thing is for sure: he does keep safety in mind. At the closing of his endorsements, he gives safety tips and offers craftsmen's techniques.

Many cartoon ad characters have negatively influenced my life—that camel, for example, but Homer has made a positive impact on my life. The store ads are very informative. Being a carpenter by trade, I find that reading Homer's advice enhances my skill level. However, Homer gets only a small amount of commercial airtime to endorse products for Home Depot. It's not close to the thirty minutes Tim is given to perform his wacky craftsman satire.

Tim is more a "city slicker" type guy. He is a wild man who portrays himself as a handsome devil. His primary mission is to build a better mousetrap. Tim also has a rough voice, which he employs to make ape sounds when he is pleased with himself. His forte is inventing tools or enhancing them to do outrageous feats, such as operate at speeds ten times faster than their normal capacity. Tim is not much of an on-air shopper, although he owns a wide variety of tools. He seems to want them, not for use, but for the prestige of being the first of our kind to acquire a particular gadget. He is a "wanna be." If this guy came to your house to repair

Brown 3

anything, the entire building would be in jeopardy. Even though he has good intentions, his craftsman skills are not up to par. He's a show-off, with no knack for safety.

Even though Tim-the-Tool-Time-guy is a TV character, there's a bit of him in all craftsmen. When Murphy's Law is overruled and every detail turns out right, we all experience craftsman's euphoria. Every one of us has some quirky thing we do to signify this joy. Tim hoots like an ape. I dance like a ballerina. My friend Mark makes long-distance calls from California to Florida just to tell his dad he drove a nail straight.

Because I love my job, I am mindful to stay current with new trends and technology. I achieve this by spending hours in the hardware store, meticulously browsing each department. I tend to call myself "Homer" because I have gained much knowledge by roaming Home Depot's aisles. I enjoy watching Tim because of the hilarious blunders he makes when attempting to make repairs in his home. After laughing at his mistakes, my mistakes don't seem so bad. Identifying with these two jokers has its advantages.

WORK! WORK! WORK!

These exercises help build skills by prompting you to express your understanding of what you read.

Reading Comprehension

1. In what way does Dedrick identify with Homer? _____

_____

2. In what way does Dedrick identify with Tim Allen? _____

_____

3. Are the tool fanatics real or invented characters? _____

_____

4. The author refers to Murphy's Law. Explain that "law." _____

_____

Harcourt, Inc.

Writing Analysis

1. Is the block or alternating method of comparison and contrast used? _____
   _____

2. Homer is identified in five descriptive ways. Name them.
   _____

3. Dedrick uses hyperbole when referring to Tim's potential in home repair. What is it? _____
   _____

Be sure you understand the want ad before you apply for the job! Rewrite the ad so the health benefits don't sound directly connected to the work.

Girl wanted to assist magician in cutting-off-head illusion. Salary and Blue Cross.

_____

_____

In the following professional article, the author compares and contrasts a relatively new product to products that have been on the market for some time.

APS: Advanced Photo System
by Rob Sheppard

Along the top are three formats of the Advanced Photo System, from left, "C," "H," and "P." These formats

Unless you've ignored the photo magazines and haven't read a newspaper or watched TV since February, you've probably heard of the Advanced Photo System (street name APS, although that's not an official title). The system gets broad distribution beginning April 22. (It won't be in stores until then.)

A lot of questions come up, such as: Does it replace 35mm? Will I need all new equipment? Will pros use it?

We want to make two things clear from the start: The Advanced Photo System is a serious effort at making photography easier and more fun for many people, and it doesn't in any way replace 35mm (although it does relate to 35mm). The companies involved in engineering this new format would be in serious trouble if it replaced 35mm because it would mean their huge development costs would have to come out of existing business. They want to make photography appeal to a broader audience and to add a format that inspires new uses of photography.

WHAT IS IT?

Five companies have come together to develop a consistent standard for the Advanced Photo System: Canon, Fuji, Kodak, Minolta, and Nikon. Other photo companies are licensing the use of the format, such as Agfa, Pentax, and Olympus. The actual creation of the format was based on extensive research with consumers who weren't heavy-use photographers in order to understand what would help them better use photography. The engineering specifications also demanded that the format make use of modern technological advancements.

The system is based on a smaller-format negative about 60 percent the size of 35mm (which results in everything being smaller, though it makes focal lengths more magnified, i.e., based on the diagonal of the film, lenses magnify the image about 1.25 percent, but this varies depending on the compositional format).

It features a leaderless film cassette for very simple drop-in loading; three instantly changeable framing formats; a convenient negative storage system; a magnetic coating over the film that allows recording of a variety of information; enhanced back-printing of information on prints; smaller camera; and mid-roll film change.

Obviously, a smaller image won't enlarge as well as larger formats (this is especially noticeable in the most enlarged element of the system, the panoramic compositional format). But it has also made film manufacturers go back to the lab and make higher quality films, technology that will certainly make the larger film formats better

offer a great opportunity to have fun with composition, including a long, tall P shot as a vertical.

as well. In standard 4x6 prints and moderate enlargements, you'd be hard pressed to see a quality problem with the excellent films available for the Advanced Photo System. (Although the system is heavily slanted toward print film users, there will be transparency films available to take advantage of the size benefits of the format.)

THREE COMPOSITIONAL FORMATS

One of the most exciting parts of this system is its ability to change framing formats for every shot. The choices are "C" for classic (similar proportions to traditional 4x6 prints), "H" for HDTV (an interesting wide format based on HDTV) and "P" for panoramic. Every frame is actually exposed to cover the whole image area (the largest on the film, "H"), but the framing in the viewfinder changes, which is then recorded electronically on the film so the printer knows what to actually print out.

Some people feel this isn't a big deal. Anybody can crop a 35mm or any other film size into these proportions. That's true. The difference is that the viewfinder blocks out the areas not included with a particular framing choice so that *the photographer specifically composes for that unique framing format.* This forces you to be very aware of the whole of the composition and especially the edges.

This feature alone is a great tool for many photographers. It helps beginners see the world in different ways and encourages them to find new compositions (a good panoramic image isn't simply the middle of a standard shot). For advanced photographers and even professionals, it can be a fun way to break established patterns of seeing—try some new compositions for a renewed vision.

OTHER BENEFITS

The small cassette size makes it very easy to produce tiny cameras, especially of the point-and-shoot variety. This will become more obvious as SLRs are produced for the system (Fuji's and Minolta's are the first ones available). For the backpacker or traveler, an Advanced Photo System camera can be an ideal alternate camera for use when space or weight is really at a premium.

SLRs are being designed to handle this new format. Manufacturers are taking two approaches: Either make a totally new system, new lenses and bodies, or make a new body that will accept standard 35mm lenses. There are advantages and disadvantages to both.

The totally new system allows lenses to be made for minimum size and weight, and zoom lenses can have focal lengths appropriate to the format (remember that the smaller film size

means lens focal lengths are actually about 1.25× as an equivalent in 35mm terms—a wide-to-short-tele zoom for 35mm might be a normal-to-tele zoom in the new format). A new body that takes old lenses allows a great diversity of lenses to be used with the new format, and you gain 1.25× in power, so longer lenses become even longer, a boon to wildlife shooting.

The film cassette is designed to hold the film after processing. The manufacturers have come up with ultra-thin films that easily fit inside these small cassettes. With the small cassette and an index print (described below), you gain a convenient storage system.

Mid-roll film exchange is very easy. The magnetic coating allows the camera to remember where it left off on a roll, so a traveler could photograph the exterior of a town with one film, change to a faster speed to go inside a church, then change back to the slower film when outside again, and nothing would be lost.

The magnetic coating has the potential of actually holding megabytes of information, ranging from exposure records to short messages and more. This all depends on the capability of the camera. The coating also helps in processing because it allows the film and processor to "communicate" for optimum printing and reprints. This information can be printed on the back of prints.

In addition, the Advanced Photo System is set up for making an index print, a small print that includes thumbnail-sized images of all shots on a roll of film. This is very handy for finding images for reprinting, finding the right negatives from storage (the film cassette and index print will have the same number code) and comparing a series of images as a learning experience (you won't be able to compare exposure or look at fine detail).

DIGITAL POTENTIAL

The Advanced Photo System is definitely designed to merge photographic and digital technologies together. The magnetic film coating alone allows a great deal of digital information to be potentially recorded before, during, or after exposure and processing.

A number of manufacturers are working on special system scanners designed to mate with this new format (Fuji is the first to actually demonstrate a model). These scanners will allow drop-in loading of the cassette with processed film enclosed and will then remove the film to the desired frame based again on information recorded on the magnetic coating. You'll then be able to add data to the magnetic coating (for example, location or plant/animal names) that will stay with the desired frame.

Although digital cameras are quickly making gains in image quality, the more affordable models still can't come close to recording the information possible on the Advanced Photo System film. You'll be able to purchase the camera, lens, and scanner for less than the price of most digital cameras and gain higher resolution and better color when you want to put an image into the computer.

The average person won't use this for some exotic image manipulation, but rather to add photos to family newsletters, make birthday cards or postcards, bring in photos to a brochure, and other desktop publishing uses. This holds a huge potential to make photography more accessible for everyone. Obviously, people can already do this with existing formats—the Advanced Photo System makes it so easy and convenient that more people will be encouraged to try.

PRODUCTS

More new products for the Advanced Photo System are being announced every day, so we can't hope to be all-inclusive at this point. But this roundup should give you an idea of what will be available for the new format.

The Advanced Photo System uses a very small film cassette, allowing designers to come up with some very compact cameras. The Nikon Navis 125i includes a 30-100 zoom (approximately 38-125mm in 35mm terms); the Canon Elph features a 24-48mm zoom (roughly 30-60mm in 35mm terms); and a splash-proof Minolta Vectis S-1 SLR offers a lineup of interchangeable lenses.

Agfa has a single-use camera and two new films. Agfa Futura 100 and 400 are 100- and 400-speed print films that incorporate the new Surface Enhanced Multistructured crystals to significantly improve definition with the smaller format.

Canon has one camera ready for the April 22 launch of the system, the appropriately named Elph, but it's one of the most compact zoom cameras that can be found anywhere—it can literally fit in a shirt pocket. Its very modern design includes a 24-48mm lens. An SLR camera will be added by fall and will take existing Canon EF lenses.

Fuji is introducing five Endeavor cameras, two single-use cameras and three films. The Fujifilm Endeavor 4000SL is a 4×, fixed-zoom (25-100mm), multi-mode SLR with a sleek, compact body. The new system films are the Smart print films and include film speeds of ISO 100, 200, and 400 and incorporate the new Super Uniform Fine Grain, which reduces grain size by one-third to one-half.

Kodak's new Advantix product line will have six cameras ready by April, more later, and three new films. The Advantix 5600MRX camera is a highly compact point-and-shoot camera with a 30-120mm zoom range. Advantix films will include 100, 200, and 400 print films (using Kodak's T-grain technology, combined with new cubic grain technology for enhanced sharpness and grain structure). A 200-speed pro film is due by fall.

Konica continues its tradition of fine point-and-shoot cameras with the introduction of three new very small Advanced Photo System models, including the ultra-compact BMS-100 with 28mm lens. Its JX400 film is a newly designed 400-speed print film.

Harcourt, Inc.

Minolta offers one of the most diverse product lines for the new system, including five point-and-shoot Vectis models and an SLR. The Vectis S1 SLR promises a lot for the outdoor photographer—a compact, splash-proof body, flash and set of lenses (including a 50mm macro and zooms from 22mm to 240mm, equivalent to approximately 28-300mm in 35mm). We'll try to review it as soon as we can get a production model.

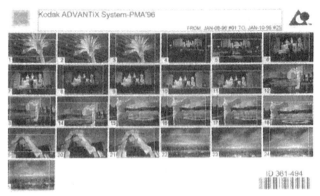

The system's index print makes it easy to find the right image for reprints and to keep a reference print with the negatives.

Nikon is introducing a set of six Nuvis compact point-and-shoot cameras that, because of the format, are extremely small. The Nuvis 125i offers a 30-100mm zoom, close focusing to 2.6 feet and a multi-mode built-in flash. Nikon also promises an SLR that will use existing Nikkor lenses along with some specially made system lenses later this year.

Pentax will be offering its Advanced Photo System cameras later this year.

Yashica has two new system point-and-shoots, both very compact models. The Acclaim 200 features a 30-60mm zoom lens and built-in flash.

What's probably most exciting about the Advanced Photo System is that it has stimulated some very creative responses to making photography better and more accessible for everyone. This is sure to enhance photography at all levels and for all film formats.

●

Exercise Related to the Professional Article from the World of Work on Comparison and Contrast

Reading Comprehension

1. In the beginning of the article, the author uses the term "35 mm." What does that mean? _____

2. Is the new system designed for amateur or professional photographers? _____

   _____

3. What are the four major features of the new APS cameras? _____

   _____

   _____

   _____

4. What major decision influenced camera companies to develop APS? _____

   _____

Writing Analysis

1. The author is dealing with a difficult subject. First, he must introduce the reader to new information. Does he use the alternating or block method to present the information? _____

_____

2. Does the author compare or contrast the cameras? _____

3. Besides comparison, the author (who is both an editor and a professional photographer) uses another writing technique in introducing the material. What is that technique? _____

From the Sports section. *Improve your Grammar Game! Cross out that extra comma!*

Their games showed the improvement . . . Garces excelled on defense, and grabbed eighteen rebounds at Seton Hall.

GRAMMARWORKS ON SENTENCES!

THE ONE GREAT RULE OF WRITING SENTENCES: INSERT PAUSES!

If someone asked you which came first, speech or punctuation, you might say speech. After all, people can communicate without grammar. Well, the fact is, speech and punctuation were invented about the same time.

Birds and beasts make noises of alarm and contentment to communicate with each other. Maybe that's how ancient men and women got the idea of trying out their lungs and vocal chords. Their first sounds of communication were grunts that, through repetition and acknowledgment, grew into recognizable, understandable language. But, even those first noises were "punctuated" with **pauses** and **voice inflections**—the equivalent of commas, periods, question marks, and exclamation points. Even today, don't we pause pertinently in our flow of words? Don't we raise our voices at the end of questions? When the first person wrote down the first words, if he didn't use spaces or some sort of indication of pauses, the first person who read them would have said, *"Moogla!"* (or whatever meant "This doesn't make sense to me") Read the following example without pausing for a "breath."

Mary Jo Ann Peggy Sue Billy Jack and I got in my Volkswagon Beetle my little brother needed a ride but there was plenty of room in the van we were only going for the day and had no luggage rack 'em up I said when I got to the pool table tennis and table tennis players outside hurry this one day vacation is thanks to our boss who has employees day once each summer tomorrow we go back to our jobs not playing working here

When a speaker pauses, that helps the listeners keep up with and absorb what they're hearing. And (here's the *big* point) in *writing*, pauses are marked by **punctuation.** See where the pauses are now?

Mary Jo, Ann, Peggy, Sue, Billy Jack, and I got in my Volkswagen. Beetle, my little brother, needed a ride, but there was plenty of room in the van. We were only going for the day and had no luggage.

"Rack 'em up," I said when I got to the pool table. "Tennis and table tennis players outside. Hurry!"

This one-day vacation is thanks to our boss, who has Employees' Day once each summer. Tomorrow we go back to our jobs—not playing—working here.

MOST PEOPLE CONSTRUCT SENTENCES BETTER WHEN THEY SPEAK THAN WHEN THEY WRITE!

Try writing the way you speak. Pause where you would naturally pause if you were talking, and put the sort of punctuation called for at that place in your sentence. You will find that your written grammar improves and that people understand you better.

Of course, not punctuating correctly isn't the only cause of troubled sentences. The following GrammarWorks table contains some hints to help you recognize common errors in sentence construction.

GRAMMARWORKS! **Please, Don't Put It in Writing! Some of the Big Eight—and Other Errors to Avoid When Writing Sentences**

SENTENCE FRAGMENTS	My brother, who moved to New York.
RUN-ON SENTENCES	My brother moved and he lives in New York.
COMMA SPLICE	My brother moved, he lives in New York.
FUSED SENTENCES	My brother lives in New York he moved 3,000 miles away. Correct: *My brother moved to New York, which is 3,000 miles away.*
PRONOUN/ANTECEDENT NONAGREEMENT	Karen went to the doctor for a checkup. He checked everything–your heart, your lungs, and so on. Correct: *Karen went to the doctor. He checked her heart, her lungs, and so on.*
NONPARALLEL CONSTRUCTION	Monica is learning to sing and dancing. Correct: *to sing and to dance* OR *singing and dancing.*
NONAGREEMENT OF SUBJECT MODIFIER	Whether small or large, a fashion show coordinator works hard. Correct: *Whether a fashion show is small or large, the coordinator works hard.*
DOUBLE NEGATIVES (NOT, NEVER, NO, NONE)	He doesn't have no paper. (Two negatives cancel each other out.) Correct: *He doesn't have any paper.* OR *He has no paper.*
REDUNDANCY (REPETITION)	The *moonless night* was very *dark.* Boy, was it *black outside!* Correct: Say it once, OR say *Not a sliver of moon lightened the night.*
MISPLACED MODIFIERS	(Be sure what you *say* is what you *mean!*) *I asked* only *Nico (no one else) to get books from the office. I asked Nico to get* only *books (not tablets) from the office. I asked Nico to get books* only *from the office (not from the store).*
VAGUE, UNCLEAR SENTENCES:	Opinions on life help you form plans that create future successes. Correct: *Knowing what you want from life helps you make career decisions.*

GRAMMARWORKS! Review

In the following exercise, identify sentence construction errors. See the following examples of how to revise the sentences to form complete, correct sentences. You may abbreviate the errors: Frag. for Sentence Fragment; Run-On, Splice, or Fused for Run-on Sentences, and so on. NOTE: Each incorrect "sentence" can be rewritten in several ways. Make your revision clear and simple and as close to the apparent meaning as possible.

Incorrect: *When you called and I was at work and my brother didn't tell.*

Correct examples:

Acceptable: Sentence fragment/*When you called, I was at work, and my brother didn't tell me.*

Better: Frag./*My brother didn't tell me you called while I was at work.*

Incorrect: *Things were difficult in the old days, life was harder then.*

Correct Examples:

Acceptable: Run-on sentence/*Things were difficult in the old days. Life was harder then.*

Better: Run-on/*Life was harder in the old days.*

Below, you'll find at least one of each sentence-construction error described in the grammar table. Identify the error, then revise the words to form complete, correct sentences. Follow the previous examples, making your sentences as simple and close to the apparent meaning as possible.

1. If you have a poor self-image, you don't have to carry it forever you can decide you're okay. _____

   _____

2. List these among your personal values: being fair, courtesy, honest, responsibility, and accountable. _____

   _____

3. If you're well trained, you don't have to worry about not getting a job ever. _____

   _____

   _____

4. We can make better decisions if we classify our choices, we can contrast the difference. _____

   _____

5. Allocating our resources is necessary. It's important to allocate our time and money and materials. _____

   _____

6. Students should read their papers before turning them in so you can find your accidental mistakes. _____

   _____

7. Barking and getting into mischief, I am in trouble because of my dog Perky always. _____

   _____

8. We solve problems based on thinking that's how we solve our problems.

9. If I can't find it and my supervisor gets really mad at me. _____

10. While they were under the bed, Brian thought Chris took his sneakers.

11. A person should never cheat on their income tax. _____

12. Even though someone is wrong about us and they might not give us another chance. _____

13. Knowing how to get along with others, the application lists as important to the employer. _____

14. Most employers won't hire nobody who doesn't have no well-defined, realistic goals. _____

15. The snow was white and freezing, and my feet got cold walking outside in the winter air. _____

FIXING BONEHEAD SIMILARITIES AND DIFFERENCES
Read the paragraph and then follow the directions below.

(1) WHY WIENER FACTORY CHILI DOGS IS BETTER THAN PUNK'S by Connie Sewer

(2) My goal is to buy the Wiener Factory to get its chili dog secrets. (3) I relly like chili dogs, I have ate more chilly dogs than you believe me. (4) That the Factory's are best. (5) Punk's buns are to hard and he does'nt great your cheese. (6) His' chili isn't hot enough too melt their cheeze neither. (7) Punk's dont refill you're drinks. (8) Whether spicy or Polish the employees heap onions on the dogs you can't hardly eat it without a lot droping. (9) When the Factory give you all the coke or mabey its pepsi you want. (10) The Weiner Factory sine says "We have sold over 4 hotdogs this year" but its kidding because the employees act nice to people and friendly because they sell a lot and good food.

Edit the paragraph above. Search for the Big Eight: circle misspelled words, wrong words, and wrong capitalizations. Put an X in front of sentence fragments, run-on, spliced, and fused sentences. Underline misused pronouns and verbs and the comma and apostrophe errors. Each sentence above has a number. On the lines below, tell what you've found wrong with each numbered sentence. (Write what you found wrong with sentence (1) on line 1, and so on.)

1. _____

2. _____

3. _____

4. _____

5. _____

6. _____

7. _____

8. _____

9. _____

10. _____

Write sentence 5 with parallel construction. _____

_____

How does the paragraph illustrate the comparison/contrast technique? _____

_____

Would this article help you make a decision about where to buy your chili dogs?   ___

_____

Now you're ready to revise the paragraph. Write it in your own words on a separate piece of paper.

WORK! WORK! WORK!

Writing Practice

The following prompts will help you pick a topic to show what you've learned about the writing technique studied in this lesson.

"A job isn't finished until the paperwork is done."

Exercises in Writing Similarities and Differences, the Comparison and Contrast Technique

On your paper, identify the format you choose.

1. Write an essay of three or more paragraphs comparing and contrasting the wasteful and efficient allocation of your (present or future) employer's time, material, and human resources, using either the *block* or the *alternating* format.

2. Write an essay of three or more paragraphs in the *block* format, *comparing the similarities* and *contrasting the differences* between your parents, your siblings, two friends, two singers, or any two people who form a logical "pair."

3. Write an essay of three or more paragraphs using the *alternating* format, *comparing the similarities* and *contrasting the differences* between two products, two cars, two cities, two schools, or any two things that form a logical "pair," and decide which is better.

4. Write an essay of three or more paragraphs comparing and contrasting a good employer and a bad employer.

Impossible! *Do you want to make a small profit on many items, or do you want to limit the quantity sold now so you can sell the merchandise later at full price. Decide which you want to do and then rewrite the ad so it doesn't contradict itself.*

Laundry detergent bargain! Stock up and save! Limit one per customer.

WORK! WORK! WORK!

Lesson Review

The following practices show what you've learned in this lesson.

SCANS Focus

Fill In the Blanks Regarding Decision Making and Problem Solving

1. _____ is the process we use to make decisions and solve problems.

2. Three things we need to allocate are _____

_____ .

3. Three (or four) steps to making a decision are _____

_____ .

Fill In the Blanks Regarding Making Categories, the Classification Technique

1. Classification breaks a _____ into

_____ .

2. The most important thing to know before starting a classification paper is __

_____ .

Fill In the Blanks Regarding Similarities and Differences (Comparison and Contrast)

1. Comparison shows the _____ between or among things; and contrast shows the _____ between or among things.

2. In writing a comparison/contrast paper, _____ is necessary to make the best use of information.
3. The method of organizing a comparison/contrast paper that parallels information, as if in rows and columns, is called _____.
4. The method of organizing a comparison/contrast paper that balances all features of one item against all features of another item is called _____.

GrammarWorks! Review

Complete each sentence showing you understand the use of the word studied in the lesson.

1. I can _____ .

2. I may _____ .

3. I might _____ .

4. Will you accept _____ ?

5. Except for _____ .

6. At night, you lie _____ .

7. You lay [present tense] _____ .

Write sentences showing that you understand how to use the words correctly.

1. all ready _____

2. already _____

3. all together _____

4. altogether _____

5. every day _____

6. everyday _____

7. fewer _____

Chapter 8

THINKING THINGS UP

IN THIS CHAPTER

SCANS FOUNDATIONS: VISION AND CREATIVITY

SCANS COMPETENCY: MANAGING TECHNOLOGY

SCANS FOCUS: VISION AND CREATIVITY

REASONS FOR RESULTS—CAUSE AND EFFECT

GRAMMARWORKS!
Timely Advice: Affect and Effect

STUDENT PAPER
"Seamed Ends" by Mimie Hanson

PROFESSIONAL ARTICLE
"Why Do Cabinet Shops Fail" by Danny Proulx

GRAMMARWORKS!
When *Do* We and When *Don't* We Use an Apostrophe with a Pronoun?

GRAMMARWORKS!
Another "!(.:,—);?" Punctuation Mark: What's an Apostrophe, Anyway?

FIXING BONEHEAD REASONS AND RESULTS
"Essay Requesting an Incomplete Instead of a Fail" by Patsy Buck

Harcourt, Inc.

> ## SCANS FOUNDATIONS: VISION AND CREATIVITY
> ## SCANS COMPETENCY: MANAGING TECHNOLOGY
>
> The competencies we've studied until now have been primarily skills of the left brain, by which we gain knowledge of language and numbers. Processing information, allocating resources, and managing systems require an eyes-open, mind-focused approach.
>
> In exercising those skills, however, we often get new ideas. These represent the stimulation of our right brain—the source of *imagination* (thinking things up) and *creativity* (bringing new ideas into reality). In pursuing ideas, we activate an *inner vision* that functions with closed eyes and wandering minds. In a creative state, we release ourselves from any concern about making mistakes. We pursue *any* train of thought that might lead to a desired result.
>
> All inventions and all of modern *technology* occurred because people's minds wandered from the regular ways things were done to ways in which they could be improved. Old methods are given new applications; old problems find solutions. One thing leads to another . . . .
>
> To get an idea of how current technology works and how new technology comes to be, we look at *cause and effect*. The human mind can consider cause and effect in two different ways. With our analytical left brain, we can trace an effect back to its cause. With our creative right brain, we can think upon a desired effect and figure out what would have to precede it to make it happen.
>
> *Let's get to work!*

SCANS FOCUS: VISION AND CREATIVITY

WORKING WITH TECHNOLOGY

We Can Think about Technology as a Ladder of Infinite Height

We are standing somewhere on the ladder of technology. Someone's *vision* inspired someone's *creativity,* enabling us to climb up to our current technological level. We can't go higher on the ladder until someone develops new technology. As we *select, apply, maintain,* and *troubleshoot* existing technology, our minds drift toward the next rung of the ladder, *improving technology.*

Few Things Are an End unto Themselves

When we begin a task, there is invariably an outlet for the finished product. If we keep our eye on the objective—what it is we want to accomplish—we will be better able to **select** the technology to produce the desired results. A world of information in both experience and books teaches what we need to know in order to get from square one to the goal.

Square One: Applying Technology

The objective is to assemble the little boy's tricycle before Christmas morning. The manufacturer has provided a wrench and a booklet showing which bolts connect which parts. The booklet isn't foolproof, but it's a place to start. So you **apply** the wrench and the booklet to the task. With no parts left over and the trike behaving as a trike should behave, you've successfully applied technology.

Oh-Oh! Sometimes Things Go Wrong

The instruction booklet didn't mention that the fender goes on before the handlebar brace. When you figured that out yourself, didn't you feel *smart?* You were **troubleshooting** technology. Write the company to correct its directions, and they'll send you a financial reward. Okay, maybe they won't—but when you identify a flaw in the directions for your *employer's* product, or you locate a worn part on a machine so it gets **maintenance** instead of breaking down, you'll be seen as someone using both sides of the brain, someone climbing the ladder.

Use Your Imagination!

To improve any technology, of course, we first need to know the causes and effects that led to current technology. We learn to operate a computer, to **select** the right programs to accomplish our tasks, and to **apply** the results. We **maintain** our equipment, investigating its full capability. When things work fine, we may not think about other possibilities; but when they don't, we seek new and better ways of doing things. We explore our **creativity** by projecting the way we want things to be and by having a **vision** of what would cause such effects.

- Martin Luther King Jr. had a dream of his children living peacefully in an integrated society.
- General Eisenhower wanted an end to World War II with victory for the Allies.
- AIDS is curable, and researchers are envisioning ways to find the cure.

Ideas can happen at unexpected moments. *You're brushing your teeth, and the toothpaste falls off the toothbrush and into the sink—like every morning before you're fully awake. You squeeze more toothpaste onto the brush and wonder: Could I make this process better? You think up a new toothbrush, one that screws onto the toothpaste tube so toothpaste will squirt directly into the bristles.* That's vision. *Hey, it might sell, you think—and you decide to figure out how to build it.* That's creativity!

When you want a certain outcome, and you look above you on the technology ladder to figure out how to accomplish it, you are experiencing the wonder of human creativity and vision. What will *you* see?

SCANS Focus Exercise

Following are some examples of how creativity and vision apply to jobs. Read the examples and then perform the exercise below.

Rental Property Agent: Creates a file-card system for keeping property records, and later recommends an available computer program that would make reporting income and expenses to the property owners easier and better.

Hairdresser: Realizes customers have trouble curling their hair with a brush and blow dryer and invents a hot-air brush that can be handled more easily.

Mechanic: Invents a way to remove those darn lug nuts pneumatically.

Copy Machine User: Thinks a copy machine that would collate copies would be a real time-saver.

Mom: Rigs up a retractable wrist harness to protect her toddling son while not making him feel so restricted.

Movie Projectionist: Tells his boss about a new looping technology that lets a theater run one film in more than one theater at a time.

Harcourt, Inc.

In-Class SCANS Exercise

The above examples show how selection, application, troubleshooting, or maintenance skills are involved in the jobs mentioned. Choose one of the following topics, and on a separate piece of paper, give a brief example of how these skills apply to the work you're doing or training for. Remember to include the name of your job.

1.   List three or more examples of technology used in your job (i.e., computers, measuring devices, etc.). Choose one technology process and briefly explain how it is used.

2.   You have been asked to create "the office of the future," the type of office that will exist ten years from now. What technological aids will workers have at their disposal?

"You naughty kittens, you've lost your mittens, and you shall have no pie . . . ."

REASONS FOR RESULTS—CAUSE AND EFFECT

> *Causes* are *Reasons*
> *Effects* are *Results*

THINK OF HOW OFTEN YOU USE THE WORD BECAUSE

"It's your fault the boss is mad at me *because* you made me take two hours for lunch!" That's **explaining** the cause for the effect (though that explanation denies accountability). "*Because* I am allergic to peanut butter, I will break out in hives if I eat it." That's **predicting** an effect from a cause. *Causes are reasons; effects are results.*

The main thing to remember is that your reasoning has to work: at the end, all the reasons for actions have to add up to the results. The effect has to be the sum of all the causes; otherwise, you are guilty of fuzzy thinking. "Why did he run out of gas on the freeway? *Because* his gas gauge was broken, and he didn't have the money to fix it." That adds up. "What will happen if we spend every dime we've got on fun? We'll really be happy." That doesn't add up.

> ## THREE TYPES OF CAUSES
>
> - Sufficient
> - Necessary
> - Contributory

IF YOU HAVE JUST CAUSE, SPEAK NOW OR
FOREVER HOLD YOUR PEACE

Answers to questions like *why* and *what if* can go to extremes. So how do we manage an assignment about cause and effect? First, we decide whether we want to start with a cause or with an effect; then we consider the three types of causes: **sufficient, necessary,** and **contributory.**

A *true, **sufficient** cause* is the only one that can produce an effect by itself. (Not every effect has a sufficient cause.)

If an avalanche hits a house, that is sufficient cause for the house to fall down.

A *required, **necessary** cause* is one that must exist for the effect to occur, but it cannot cause the effect by itself.

For the house to be hit by an avalanche, it is necessary for it to be at the bottom of a snowy mountain—say, in the Alps.

A *supplemental, **contributory** cause* is not essential for the effect to occur and cannot produce the effect by itself, but it takes part in the effect.

Someone yodeling in the Alps contributed to the house's collapse by creating sound waves that triggered the avalanche.

Not all effects have all three kinds of causes. Most causes are either necessary or contributory. The key to a good cause and effect essay is knowing what kind of cause each cause is.

CAUSE FOR CONCERN!

Fuzzy, vague thinking stands out in an essay on cause and effect. While you might be able to wander thoughtlessly through other assignments, a causal analysis is a minefield. To mistake a **contributing** or **necessary** cause for a **sufficient** cause will blow up your thesis (your statement of intent). Do you remember the story of Little Red Riding Hood? We'll use it to help you understand the kinds of causes.

You must make your purpose clear from the start. *If Red Riding Hood's grandma hadn't been sick, Red wouldn't have gotten into trouble with the wolf.* Is this logical thinking? *Buzzz,* nope! Red got into trouble *not* because Granny was sick (**contributory cause**) but because Red met the wolf in his territory (**sufficient cause**). Had she remained on the path as she was told, the wolf wouldn't have seen her, known where she was going, and tried to eat both her *and* her grandmother. The wolf might not even have talked to Red had she not appeared to be such a delectable tidbit (**necessary cause**).

From the Sports section. *Quoting actual conversation without tidying up the grammar can lead to mistakes. Rewrite the sentences, correcting the punctuation, restructuring the awkward run-on sentence, correcting its pronoun/antecedent error, and omitting the unnecessary comma.*

"He's extremely busy and I understand that," Alford says. "It's just good to hear from his assistants, because I know that's an extension of what he is."

_____

_____

_____

_____

COMMON PROBLEMS IN CAUSE AND EFFECT PAPERS: LOFTY TOPICS, MINOR AND DISTANT CAUSES, AND UNSUPPORTED STATISTICS

It's a common mistake for students writing cause and effect studies to choose huge, **lofty topics,** like *"Humanity will make itself extinct within fifty years because . . . "* If you want to address a philosophical topic, cast about for a smaller-scale thesis statement, like *"Men are unlikely to stop and ask directions when they are lost because . . . "*

Avoid getting sidetracked on **minor causes** and **distant causes.** If your topic is "Why I got a poor grade on the math quiz," don't go into *distant* causes, like your great aunt's inability to balance her checkbook, or *minor* causes, like a splinter in your finger. Stick with **direct causes,** *real* main reasons called **proximate causes:** your little brother kept bothering you while you were studying; the TV was too loud, and you couldn't concentrate; you fell asleep; and so on.

GOOD CAUSE AND EFFECT PAPERS SHOW . . .

Manageable Topics.
Major and Proximate Causes.
Supported Statistics.

If you quote statistics, acknowledge the sources! Statements like "it seems" or "in my opinion" aren't adequate compensation for facts. *"It seems nine out of ten marriages end in divorce"* doesn't cut it. *"Of my ten best friends, nine have divorced parents"* is acceptable. Even better sources are books, magazines, and other reference works.

NO CAUSE FOR ALARM

Let the subject matter help you decide on one of two ways to organize your paper.
You may state the cause first and then explore the effects.
"Television is the source of many of America's problems." To explain why you believe that TV is a powerful negative force, you will explore TV's affect on the decline of education and individual IQ and the increase in violent crime. After you've given your reasons that TV is the root of all evil, briefly sum up your causes and effects, ending with a restatement of your, now proven, thesis.
You may state the effect first and then explore the causes.
Mack's thesis is: *"The world is getting worse."* Mack gives the many reasons he sees for the world's worsening condition. Jack's thesis is: *"The world is getting better."* To come to his conclusion, this optimist mentions all the causes he sees for the world's improvement.

Watch that pronoun/antecedent agreement! Rewrite the ad so that customers will want to patronize the establishment, not stay away from it.

Laundry and Dry Cleaners: We do not tear your clothing with machinery. We do it carefully by hand.

_____

_____

Harcourt, Inc.

NO CAUSE FOR TEARS

Whether you start with the cause or with the effect, whether you explore what *has* happened or what *could* happen, choose a manageable topic, use proximate causes, and avoid fuzzy thinking. Remember to identify the sources of your information.

GRAMMARWORKS! Timely Advice: Affect and Effect

AFFECT	EFFECT
Affect is *always* a verb! It can mean *to change:* My head cold **affected** the sound of my voice.	*Effect* is *usually* a noun. It can mean *a result:* I suffer the miserable **effects** of my allergies.
Affect is *always* a verb! It can mean *to act upon:* One weak link **affects** the strength of the chain.	*Effect* is *sometimes* a verb. It can mean *to cause:* Constant loud noise can **effect** deafness.

GrammarTool! AF-fect is a verb. A verb usually comes AF-ter a noun.
*The special computerized **effects** in the movie **affected** the audience.*

The following student and professional examples show reasons and results, using the cause and effect writing technique.

The student author's assignment: Write a story illustrating cause and effect.

Mimie Hanson emigrated from Ghana, Africa, but she says she has become completely "Americanized."

```
                                              Hanson 1

     Mimie Hanson
     English 1200-9:30
     Cause and Effect
     April 8, 1999

                        Seamed Ends


         I was still bemoaning the loss of my friends, my school,
     and my teachers when I met Jim. I had just arrived in
     Chicago from Ghana where I had lived with my grandmother for
     about ten years. I was only six years old when my parents
     left Africa to work in the United States. My grandmother was
     wonderful; she adored me and almost worshiped the very earth
     I walked on. Somehow, I always thought joining my parents and
     my two younger brothers in the States would be heaven. It
     turned out to be very disappointing. I was lonely and longing
     for a friend.
```

My parents were both working very hard and were almost
never at home. My two brothers turned out to be two horrible
"made-in-America" brats. They found something wrong with
whatever I did or said; they laughed at my accent and teased
me for dressing decently; they said I was not "hip" or some
other stupid word. School was worse. I did not understand
what the teacher said and made very bad mistakes on my class
exercises. I shall never forget the day I made a mistake
working on a math problem on the chalkboard in front of the
class. The whole class booed, jeered, and laughed at me. I had
never known such humiliation in all my life. I wished I
could die. A few minutes later, everyone left for the lunch
break except me. All I wanted was to be left alone to sink
deeper into self-pity.

I had been sobbing quietly for five minutes when I felt a
hand touch me gently on the shoulder. I lifted my head from
the desk, now wet with my tears, and looked into the blue
eyes of a boy who sat a couple of tables behind me. I had
seen him being teased badly the day before. It had taken the
arrival of the teacher in the classroom to prevent a fist
fight. Presently, he offered me some Kleenex and told me his
name was Jim Baccarach. It was the beginning of a friendship
that would last for decades—and one that created some
confusion in my household.

Jim gave me rides to and from school every day from then
on. He came to my house to help me with my math homework, and
sometimes I helped him with other subjects that came more
easily to me. Later, I noticed the taunting and name calling
that Jim suffered at the hands of our classmates had
worsened. Only this time, he seemed stronger, pretending they
did not exist. I was curious to find out why he was teased
and called names.

What he told me was shocking. He said that he was gay
and went on to explain what it meant. Jim said he preferred
intimacy with persons of the same sex. "What?" was my shocked
response. I had never heard of such a thing in the land
where I came from. There, intimate relationships were between
members of the opposite sex only. Jim went to great lengths
to explain the biology, the chemistry, and the sociology of
being gay. He also said that he was not the only one like
that. There were lots of people in the world with the same
problem—that is, if it was a problem. Well, I had a lot to

learn about American social issues, more so than of academic issues.

"Well," I said, "There are no people like that in my country, or my grandmother would have told me." She had taught me everything I knew about life.

He mentioned something about people being in the closet and a whole lot of what I thought was rubbish. What a rude awakening this was for me! I had entertained briefly the fantasy of our friendship developing into something beyond the platonic level. That was not ever to be.

I told my mother about Jim. Needless to say, it sent her into shock, followed by fury. When my father heard about it, he took a worse stand. He did not want Jim around me ever again. For two days, I refused Jim's offer of rides to school and back, not so much because of my father but because I did not know how to relate to Jim anymore. By the third day, I missed his friendship badly, not to mention his masterful control over my math problems. I finally rationalized that what he did in his, or anyone else's, bedroom was none of my business. I had taken my stand, and Jim was going to remain my friend.

The following Saturday was my birthday, and I had invited Jim to my party. He arrived at my house three hours early bearing flowers, a card, and a birthday present. My parents were pretty civil with him. He did not seem to notice their restrained civility. He helped my father arrange the chairs and finish the decorations. After that, he went into the kitchen to lend a helping hand to my mother with the cake decorations. Just as the guests (mostly teenage children of my mother's friends) started arriving, I came down the stairs and extended my hand to greet one of my mother's friends. All of a sudden, the zipper on my beautiful tight-fitting birthday dress broke open exposing my slip. I ran quickly into the kitchen to my mom, and there was Jim.

I was practically in tears. My mother took one look at the open zipper and told me to go upstairs to change. *This can't be,* I thought. *Even my seventeenth birthday is spoiled!* Jim seemed to have heard my thoughts. He examined the mechanics of the zipper and said he needed a needle and thread. I don't know what Jim did to the zipper, but it carried me and my dress through the party. From then on, my parents started to treat Jim with respect. The needle and thread not only mended my zipper; they seemed to have mended Jim to my family.

WORK! WORK! WORK!

These exercises help build skills by prompting you to express your understanding of what you read.

Reading Comprehension

1. Mimie mentions several causes and several effects. Name the causes of Mimie's misery. _____

   _____

   _____

2. Name the causes of her parents' change of heart regarding Jim. _____

   _____

   _____

3. What effect do you think being treated unkindly had upon Mimie and Jim?

   _____

   _____

Writing Analysis

1. What sentence in the first paragraph does the author use to "hook" the reader?

   _____

   _____

2. The author uses four paragraphs to deal with the subject of Jim's being gay. Why doesn't she combine them in one paragraph? _____

   _____

3. What analogy does the author use in her concluding sentence? _____

   _____

   _____

Restaurant ad in newspaper. *This ad appears to be a question, but where's the question mark? Edit the advertisement so it has parallel construction and good punctuation.*

G.G. Restaurant
   The New Restaurant people are telling their friends about!
Did you know . . .
- Unlimited Champagne Brunch is served Sundays from 10 a.m. to 2 p.m.
- Our new Garden Patio is now open daily
- Now Featuring new lower priced menus
- Reservations at (G.G.) are welcome
- That a 20% discount on your entire bill is available from July 10-17th with this ad

———————●———————

The following professional article illustrates cause and effect by giving the reasons that can result in the failure of a small business.

Why Do Cabinet Shops Fail?
by Danny Proulx

There are unlimited sources of information on how to successfully operate a small business. Home study programs, video training, college courses, government services, and the Internet all offer the most in-depth information available. One TV commercial offers a course that will let you "be your own boss and enjoy the good life." If all the answers are there for the taking, and it's all so easy, why are there so many business failures?

Maybe we should start the journey into small business from the other end of the road and look at the reasons for failure instead of how to be successful. The lessons learned may very well be just as educational—and probably more practical.

I operate a small, one-person cabinet shop and my target market is kitchen cabinets. The focus of these articles will be on the small woodworking operation with a definite leaning toward custom and semicustom kitchen cabinetmaking, as that is my area of knowledge. But, most of the topics can be applied to any small or medium-sized shop.

In this series of articles I'll explore some of the reasons for business failures—the "why and what happened." And, more importantly, try to determine the mistakes to prevent the same thing happening to you and me.

SMALL MISTAKES

All too often, it's not just one major mistake, but a series of poor decisions that—added together—contribute to the downfall of a small business. There are very well-defined issues, the so-called business commandments, that must be addressed in all operations, both new and old. Most, including financial management, operating licenses, accounting, and future planning are well known to everyone.

However other areas, like researching target markets, determining the shop's location, and maintaining momentum, are very often not given the attention they deserve. I'll briefly describe major topics that will be discussed in this series.

Their order is not meant to suggest that any one issue is more or less important. Each is dependent on the other and together they form the building blocks for a solid foundation.

THE BUSINESS PLAN

Writing a business plan is the first exercise that should be completed. It's the road map to success or failure. All too often this map is quickly written for the sole purpose of getting start-up capital and then forgotten.

As with any map, refer to it constantly to make sure you're headed in the right direction. Reviewing this important document is a worthwhile exercise and should be undertaken on a regular basis.

CASH FLOW

Mismanaging financial affairs is the leading cause of business failure. The accountants tell us that poor old Bob failed because he had a cash flow problem. So, what is this all-too-common problem? Simply put, the failed business didn't have the cash on hand to pay the bills. But why? We'll look at some of the reasons and try to learn from others who've experienced this sad situation first hand.

LOCATION

As the real estate agents say, the three most important reasons for a successful business are location, location, and location. Their views are biased because they're in the business of selling property, but nevertheless it's a very important issue. One failed kitchen cabinet shop decided to open the business in a fairly new subdivision where the majority of homes were less than five years old. When I asked him why he decided to locate in an area that probably wouldn't need new kitchens for the next five years or so, he replied that the shop rent was very reasonable.

That may have been valid, but the bulk of his work would be in other areas and towns with older homes that were located far from his base of operations. He couldn't establish a reputation in his own area because there wasn't a need. Additionally, the added cost of time and travel raised his project estimates. He soon found himself in serious financial trouble.

SPECIALTY MARKETS

Specialty or niche marketing should be determined from day one. What type of work are you most comfortable with, and is there a market? Your decision should be based on exhaustive research with data including market size, location, investment requirements, and your own woodworking abilities.

Failure often results when someone opens a shop, waits to see what the demand will be, then decides on a specialty. Quite often time is not a luxury and before we determine the business style, costs have increased to a point where they're out of control. However, original plans don't have to be cast in stone.

NEW MARKETS

If a new niche market appears you can head in a different direction, but it should be an addition to your start-up plans until one specialty becomes the dominant force. Setting up shop includes many important issues. These include determining the shop floor plan, customer service/reception area, stationery, signs, and shipping and receiving, as well as the process of establishing supplier accounts.

Seemingly simple decisions, such as the number and style of public washrooms that are regulated by the local municipality, can be missed and drive you over the edge.

Failing to address the basics of a retail operation can often mean thousands of dollars in added costs, to say nothing about the lost time correcting the situation. A business I was familiar with failed to investigate the noise and hours of operation bylaws in the industrial condominium where it was located and was seriously affected by the restrictions. That's a classic example of taking too much for granted.

Setting up shop also involves the establishment of a workforce, or at least, the potential availability of that workforce. Too many times businesses have failed

Harcourt, Inc.

because they couldn't meet production demands when there wasn't enough trained help available. As well, you must analyze productivity in the new shop by designing a plan that doesn't include you working sixteen hours a day. Hundreds of business failures are recorded each year because the owner worked to the point of exhaustion. The workflow plan can detail simple tools like the computer to manage the hours of accounting, quoting, and drawing that are a fact of life in any woodworking shop.

ADVERTISING

Many times, thousands of dollars are spent creating an image, raising a profile, and still the business fails. What went wrong? There are many examples of failures by well-known operations. Often it appears that the advertising was directed at the wrong target market. The classic examples of advertising refrigerators in Alaska or heating systems in Hawaii seems basic, yet happens too frequently. We'll examine some of the failed campaigns to see if there are lessons to be learned.

A kitchen cabinetmaker in my area routinely photographed all his completed projects for a promotional album. It's a basic and well thought out plan to promote your work. However, he took it a step further and ordered an extra set of prints that he gave to the client in a presentation album. It was very effective, as most customers enjoyed showing off their new kitchen project to family and friends. The contractor received many calls based solely on others seeing these pictures.

When I recently spoke to him, he complained that things were very slow. The conversation eventually got around to his photo album promotion, which he said he had discontinued. He said he had almost three albums of projects to display and didn't need any more pictures. By not realizing that the client's album was the important issue, not his album, much of his word-of-mouth referral business was lost. It's worth taking the time to analyze what's working well and fine tune the process as much as possible.

MAINTAINING MOMENTUM

Once the shop is established reasonably well, how do we maintain the momentum? We certainly can't forget everything that got us to this point. A monthly review of advertising, types of jobs completed, how we got the work, and where it came from must be done. Simply put, what actions were effective and what was a waste of time and money?

Many factors combine to make one business unbelievably successful, and another a failure. What is the common thread? Is it simply luck and being in the right place, with the right product, at the right time?

I don't believe that's the case. Success in business is directly related to the quality of your research data, formulation of a good business plan, adequate sensible financing, a good product, a lot of hard work, and yes, maybe a little luck.

Starting a new business is a tremendous risk. Many have invested all their savings into the operation and suffer greatly when failure occurs. A couple of hours spent analyzing this data each month might very well mean the difference between success and avoiding failure.

Finally, I'll be the first to admit that I don't have all the answers—I don't believe that anyone can provide everything needed to guarantee success. Most of the time the process involves setting goals and reviewing the results, seeking out areas of failure and acting on the situation. As an old proverb states "Correction is good administered in time."

Exercise Related to the Professional Article from the World of Work on Reasons and Results (cause and effect)

Reading Comprehension

1. According to the author, what is the leading cause of business failure? _____

_____

2. What do real estate agents say are the three most important reasons for a successful business? _____

_____

3. Why is it important to start a business with a business plan? _____

_____

_____

Writing Analysis

1. The author uses such terms as "poor old Bob," and "advertising refrigerators in Alaska or heating systems in Hawaii." Why does he do this? _____

_____

2. What idea is the author attempting to convey in his concluding sentence, "Correction is good administered in time"? _____

_____

3. How does this article illustrate the Cause and Effect technique of writing? _____

_____

_____

From an article about the attractions in the town of Paso Robles. *Huh?? Try to rewrite this sentence so it would make sense to a potential visitor.*

"But there's more to Paso Robles than just what you can get to from there."

_____

_____

GRAMMARWORKS!   When *Do* We and When *Don't* We Use an Apostrophe with a Pronoun?

Whose lesson is this, anyway? *It's* for anyone *who's* confused by the italicized words in this paragraph. *There* is a good reason *their* spelling is difficult: *they're* sound-alikes. *You're* confused because of *your* good habit of showing **noun possession** by adding an apostrophe *(')* followed by an *s* (Bob's ear). Also, **pronoun possession** gets confused with **pronoun contraction**. *It's* easier to give each word *its* proper spelling if *you're* aware of *your* rules.

Do not use an apostrophe with *possessive pronouns!* (**your** = belonging to you)
Use the apostrophe only in *contractions* with pronouns. (**you're** = you are)

Contraction occurs when two words get shoved together and a letter pops out. An apostrophe goes in place of the missing letter.
GrammarTool: When two words become one, they wear an apostrophe—like a wedding ring.

Confusion arises because possessive *nouns* take an apostrophe. However, possessive *pronouns* do *not* take an apostrophe, which distinguishes them from *contractions*.
The apostrophe goes where at least one letter's been omitted.
If *no* letter has been omitted, *do not* use the apostrophe.

ITS   Possessive Pronoun/*belonging to it*
The cat watched as the humming bird sipped at **its** feeder.
(*Possessive pronouns his and hers have no apostrophe either.*)

IT'S (contraction)   Pronoun and Verb/*it is, it has*
When it's time to wake up, my alarm goes off. **It's** been ringing too early.
(Contractions *he's* and *she's* have an apostrophe, too.)
Joe leaves the dog a lot of water in **its** big dishpan when **it's** this hot out.

WHOSE   Possessive Pronoun/*belonging to whom*
The professor asked Connor if he knew **whose** backpack was left on Kendal's desk.

WHO'S (contraction)   Pronoun and Verb/*who is, who has*
Who's the better pitcher, Sandy or Nolan? (who is)
Who's been sleeping in my bed? (who has)
Sally, **whose** role in the play is Ophelia, is the one **who's** always early for practice.

YOUR   Possessive Pronoun/*belonging to you*
The travel agent said **your** tickets should arrive in the mail tomorrow.

YOU'RE (contraction)   Pronoun and Verb/*you are*
Call and let Daneesha know whether **you're** able to go to the party.
Your research paper is due next week; **you're** smart if **you're** almost finished.

THEIR   Possessive Pronoun/*belonging to them*
Hansel and Gretel lost **their** way in the woods.

THERE   Pronoun/Adverb/*in, at, or to that place*
Chris saw Kacie's book **there** on Kelly's desk.

THEY'RE (contraction)   Pronoun and Verb/*they are*
Patti and Jim said **they're** trying to start a business.
Brenda and Darrell like the video arcade. **Their** parents take them **there** when **they're** good.

GRAMMARWORKS! Review

In the following exercises, write a brief sentence correctly using each word shown.

1. Its _____

2. It's _____

3. Whose _____

4. Who's _____

5. Your _____

6. You're _____

7. Their _____

8. They're _____

9. There _____

GRAMMARWORKS! Another "!(.:,—);?" Punctuation Mark: What's an Apostrophe, Anyway?

An apostrophe (pronounced *uh-PAH-struh-fee*) is a punctuation mark that looks like a comma above the line. It often appears between letters.

- After a noun, an apostrophe followed by an *s* ('s) shows possession or ownership: for example, Ted's car. (After a noun ending in *s,* often only the apostrophe is used: for example, *the Smiths' dog*—not *the Smiths's dog.* It depends on how it sounds. *Mrs. Jones's house* sounds better than *Mrs. Jones' house.*)
- An apostrophe sometimes indicates that two words have been combined by omitting part of one word (thus forming a contraction): for example, *haven't, she'll, I'm, you've.*
- Apostrophes are also used, in facing pairs—like "small parentheses," as quotation-within-a-quotation marks: for example, I asked, "Did you read your name in the magazine article called, 'Hot Hunks at the Heigh-Ho Hangout'?"

GRAMMARWORKS! Review

Fill in the blanks following the words with *or* without apostrophes. *Tell why they are used (or not used). These are your choices: Contraction, Pronoun Contraction, Pronoun Possession, Noun Possession, and Quotation within a Quotation. You may abbreviate your answers.*

Don't (_____) you feel smart? You know that only nouns claim

their possessions by adding an *'s.* You also know all about a contraction's

(_____) wedding ring! You even read this: "Apostrophes are

used, . . . like 'small parentheses,' . . . " (_____) The apostrophe

has its (_____) tricks, but it's (_____) not as

hard as you thought!

THE BIG EIGHT BONEHEADS!

- Words Misspelled
- Words or Caps Incorrect
- Sentence Fragments
- Sentence Run-Ons, Spliced or Fused
- Pronouns Confused
- Verbs Misused
- Commas Misplaced
- Apostrophes Abused

Harcourt, Inc.

FIXING BONEHEAD REASONS AND RESULTS
Read the paragraph and then follow the directions below.

Essay Requesting an Incomplete Instead of a Fail
by Patsy Buck

(1) I couldnt get to school on time to take the final. (2) I was in the rong place at the rong time I'm in alotta trouble. (3) If I hadn't been on Olympic at 9:00 a.m. in the morning last Tuesday I would of almost been at school on time for the test. (4) I had got a ticket for speeding and running a red light and the cop run my license and found out about my fourty unpaid parking tickets. (5) He noticed that my registration, its two years out-of-date. (6) Just because my doderant smells like Booze. (7) They made me touch my nose with my fingers and eyes closed and whose able to do that even if your sober? (8) Now I'm doing time. (9) All because I wasnt in the right place on time. (10) I shoulda told the cop I was colored blind. (11) There just not fair to students.

Edit the paragraph above. Search for the Big Eight: circle misspelled words, wrong words, and wrong capitalizations. Put an X in front of sentence fragments, run-on, spliced, and fused sentences. Underline misused pronouns and verbs and the comma and apostrophe errors. Each sentence above has a number. On the lines below, tell what you've found wrong with each numbered sentence. (Write what you found wrong with sentence (1) on line 1, and so on.)

1. _____
2. _____
3. _____
4. _____
5. _____
6. _____
7. _____
8. _____
9. _____
10. _____
11. _____

How does the paragraph illustrate cause and effect? _____

_____

_____

How does the paragraph illustrate vision and creativity? _____

_____

_____

Now you're ready to revise the paragraph. Write it in your own words on a separate piece of paper.

WORK! WORK! WORK!

Writing Practice

The following prompts will help you pick a topic to show what you've learned about the writing technique studied in this lesson.

"A job isn't finished until the paperwork is done."

Exercises in Writing Reasons for Results, the Cause and Effect Technique

1. Write an essay of four or more paragraphs on the causes of air pollution, traffic congestion, divorce, homelessness, or any other social ill you choose.

2. Write an essay of four or more paragraphs about the effects of prejudice: against race, religion, or political beliefs; or against smart kids; or against unusual-looking, ill, or disabled people; or against any other group or individual.

3. You were late with your English assignment! Write an essay of four or more paragraphs explaining each of the three types of causes for your tardiness: sufficient (true), necessary (required), and contributing (supplemental). You may use another circumstance (auto accident, broken leg, outcome of a ball game), but list the three different types of causes.

WORK! WORK! WORK!

Lesson Review

The following practices show what you've learned in this lesson.

SCANS Focus
Fill In the Blanks Regarding SCANS Focus

1. Thinking things up is a phrase for using our _____.
   Bringing new ideas into reality is called _____. Vision and creativity lead to new inventions or _____.

2. For technology to work for us, we must know which technology to _____; then we must _____ it. To avoid problems, it's best to give a system the proper _____. When something does go wrong and we try to find the problem, we call that effort _____.

Cause and Effect
Fill In the Blanks Regarding Cause and Effect

1. The reason for something is the _____; the result is the _____.

2. A cause that can produce an effect by itself is called a _____ cause.

3. A cause that must exist but does not cause the effect is called a _____ cause.

4. A cause that can't produce an effect by itself is called a _____ cause.

GRAMMARWORKS! Review

Where given a choice, circle the correct word(s). Put in the correct punctuation on the short lines throughout the paragraph. On the long blank lines, write the correct contraction of the preceding bold words.

Stop shouting at me ___ *Your/You're* hurting my feelings. This will *affect/effect* how I feel all day. **That is** _____ *the affect/effect* a headache has on you. It happens every time **you are** _____ stressed ____ it happens every time you lose *your/you're* glasses. **Do not** _____ get upset about losing them __ they **are not** _____ in outer space. If **you will** _____ get a grip, **I will** _____ help you look for them. *Its/It's* okay. I forgive you __ as always __ I know you get upset because not having your glasses *affects/effects* how well you _____ Where were you using them last night ____ Oh, *they're/their/there* they are ____ under the crossword puzzle book! Crossword puzzles _____ *they're/their/there* just the thing for someone *whose/who's* got a temper like yours __ People **should not** _____ lose *they're/their/there* tempers so easily as their glasses! *Your/You're* welcome, dear.

Chapter 9

THINKING THINGS THROUGH

SCANS FOUNDATIONS: LEARNING AND REASONING
SCANS COMPETENCY: UNDERSTANDING, MONITORING, AND IMPROVING SYSTEMS

Whether you are at home, at school, or on the job, education is the opportunity to acquire knowledge. With knowledge, we can think and reason for ourselves. *Learning* is the process of taking information into our memory and making it part of our personal resources (our "mental library"). Some people learn best by *seeing*, some by *hearing*, and some by *reading*. *Reasoning* is applying our knowledge to a problem or goal and drawing conclusions.

The more information we store within us, the greater our understanding of new information. We are able to discover connections between pieces of information. We recognize *systems*–the procedures or organization we use to perform our tasks. In our daily lives, we create and follow systems of our own. At work, we use *learning* to *understand* the job systems; we use *reasoning* to *monitor* the systems (to see that they continue to work well) and to draw conclusions about how to improve them.

To acquaint ourselves with systems, we explore the step-by-step writing technique called *process*. In this method, we present information as a series of steps to instruct or inform.

Let's get to work!

SCANS FOCUS: LEARNING AND REASONING

MANAGING SYSTEMS

Whatever Works!

This trendy comment often follows someone's description of a certain routine, or system, of doing something. A **system** is a step-by-step method of action, from beginning to end. Catherine starts her day with a Big Gulp from 7-Eleven in her lap as she drives to school. Ray keeps a jar of instant coffee in the bathroom; as soon as he wakes up, he mixes some with hot tap water and drinks it. Each person has a system for getting the body's engine started in the morning. While Catherine would never use Ray's system, she acknowledges that it works for him. A system is just a way to do things.

Systems are common to us all. A system can just happen; it can be developed through trial and error; or it can be thought out in advance in great detail. There are **social systems** (the family, a circle of friends, the church, the government); **organizational systems** (as in a business—where the biggest boss is at the top); and **technological systems** (which have products, or goals, like going to the moon). A job-ready person recognizes that systems are essential and knows how to work within them.

A System Needs to Be Understood

The place where Regina first worked had an "Office Bible"—a book of methods for doing every task in the company. The bible made it easy for Regina to **understand** the proven methods of doing work in that office, and for all employees to learn their jobs and to find information on hard-to-remember or seldom-performed activities. That bible was a *system* of teaching *systems*.

A System Needs to Be Kept Current

People who use systems need to keep them up-to-date. A tiny change, like a short circuit, can affect systems down the line. The supply place that the Office Bible says to call could have changed its name; that listing needs to be cross-referenced to its replacement in the company's Service Resources system—its phone book. The person who knows that the old messenger service went out of business needs to inform the person who is responsible to **monitor,** or **maintain,** the Service Resources system. If the system isn't kept current, an employee could waste precious time trying to find Zippo Depot instead of calling Fast-Feet Express.

Sometimes a System Needs to Be Improved

Don't think that the system that's in place will work forever. When the method isn't accomplishing its objective, the system needs to be faster, or simpler, or somehow better. If you know what's wrong and how to fix it, say so. Sometimes the new person on the job sees things in a way that's different from the ways of people accustomed to the old system. New people in the workplace bring new resources that can **improve** an organization's systems.

WE'VE ALL HEARD IT: LIFE IS A LEARNING EXPERIENCE

In any new work position we enter, we must figure out what is expected of us and how to fulfill the expectations. After we understand the systems in place, we can contribute our ideas for the betterment of the *technological system* and maybe for the betterment of the *organizational system*. If the changes improve the morale of the workers, the *social system* may improve as well.

SCANS Focus Exercise

The following are some occupations and the systems-oriented tasks related to those jobs. Read the examples, and then perform the exercise below.

Manicurist: Uses procedures for applying acrylic fingernails that must be performed in specific order.

Office Worker: Prepares monthly or quarterly government or union reports that require collection of information, filling out of forms, attaching payments, and submitting the combination to the proper authority.

Photo Processor: Gets that film into a securely dark place before opening the can! Has to apply the chemicals in a specific order to develop the negatives and get the prints.

Traffic Engineer: Counts the traffic at an intersection before recommending a special left-turn phase be added to the traffic light there.

Computer Telephone Tech Support: Takes the computer user through various steps to determine what the problem is and how to fix it.

Airplane Pilot: Has cockpit checks to make and procedures to follow before each flight.

In-Class SCANS Exercise

On a separate piece of paper, describe a system, or routine, you use at work or will use in a future job. You might try to include answers to one or more of the following questions.

1. How is the company organized, and where do you fit in?
2. How do you carry out your tasks?
3. How does one of the machines assist in the workload?

Manager's message. *Try editing the many mistakes in this notice actually sent to employees at one company. There are wrong words, two words erroneously combined as one, a run-on sentence, missing punctuation, and too many words.*

I think it is safe to say that no one won and no one likes the new unionization, but it happened and now we all have to accept it deal with it and make it work. We have suddenly lost some very capable service staff but we have fired new staff or promoted existing staff and while they are adjusting, service will fluctuate. Anyone of these changes could easily be perceived as overwhelming however we are fortunate to have the desire and willingness to deal with it and prevail. Everyone has the organizations best interest at heart. As stare as I know my name there will be more challenges and changes ahead.

"This is the chimney that sits on the roof that covers the house that Jack built."

LISTING THE STEPS—PROCESS

PROCESS IS A METHOD USED TO . . .

- **Instruct** How to Do Something Step-By-Step.
- **Inform** by Providing Your Point in a Logical Sequence.

JUST FOLLOW THESE SIMPLE STEPS

Only a hermit living in a cave for the last fifty years would not be familiar with "how-to books." These self-help books made the term so popular that an adjective (a *how-to* book) and a noun (a *how-to* on filing income tax) have been added to our dictionaries. How-to books follow the **step-by-step,** or **process,** technique of writing. *Any* writing that sets out to **instruct** or **inform,** and follows steps from beginning to end, uses the process technique.

PURPOSE: INSTRUCTION OR INFORMATION?

Instruction

Do you plan to *give instruction* (how to do something) or *tell information* (how something happened)? Instruction is the simpler one (unless you're trying to write an essay on how to tie your shoes). You state what you're going to teach, list the steps, and finish by assuring your readers that they can now accomplish what you've taught them. "This is how to swat a fly" leads to **listing steps that will** *instruct.*

1. Get a fly swatter.
2. Locate a fly.
3. Move stealthily until you're within arm's reach of the fly.
4. Move the swatter swiftly into contact with the fly.
5. If you've perfected following these instructions, get a tissue and dispose of the dead fly.

Information

For an essay that gives information, state your thesis or topic statement (the sentence that tells what you will prove) in the first paragraph. In the middle paragraphs, explain the process in a logical, orderly way, step-by-step. In your final paragraph, restate your thesis and summarize what you have proved. Mission accomplished! *"I will show that marriage leads to catastrophe"* is a thesis that requires **listing steps that will** *inform* to prove a point.

> *Mr. and Mrs. O'Leary got married. They had a baby. Mrs. O'Leary bought a cow. The cow kicked over her lantern—starting a fire in the straw that burnt down all of Chicago. This proves that marriage leads to catastrophe!*

Of course, your **reasoning** should tell you that the above summary of points really didn't prove the essay's thesis! The process essay *you* turn in should make much better sense than the *informational* steps in "marriage leads to catastrophe," and *your* essay should be more detailed than the *instructional* steps in "how to swat a fly"!

The following student and professional examples use the step-by-step, process-writing technique.

The student author's assignment: Write an essay describing a process or system you follow.

Shakei Quinn, currently a security guard, is pursuing a career in the computer sciences. She declares, "I'm a hard worker, and I plan to achieve all my goals."

```
                                                    Quinn 1
   Shakei Quinn
   English 100-8:00
   Process
   March 16, 1998

                    How to Drive a Car

       Learning to drive a car is a matter of three main steps:
   learning the rules, getting familiar with the car, and
   following a series of procedures. First, you have to learn
   your signals, signs, your "do's and don'ts," and your
   right-of-ways. The most important rule to remember is that
```

Quinn 2

pedestrians have the right-of-way at all times. Of course, it is initially necessary that you have a car so you can practice the other steps. Once you have a car, the steps to driving begin before you even turn on the engine.

When you sit in the car, you first prepare to drive. Make sure your seat is adjusted properly so you can see to your advantage. Put your seat belt on and make sure your passengers are strapped in their seats correctly. Check if you can see clearly out of your rearview mirror and the two side mirrors. Once you're in a comfortable driving position, locate the car's safety features. Every vehicle is different. Be sure to find the knobs and buttons and switches that control the important safety features in the car you're driving.

The most important of all is your emergency brake. Make sure it is working properly so that, if your brakes decide to give out, you can pull or step on your emergency brake to slow your vehicle and come to a stop. Also, use your emergency brake when you park. Next, make sure that your turn signals are working properly. You use them when you make left or right turns and also to indicate that you want to change lanes. Make sure you know your hand signals, too, so that if your turning signals or brake lights are not working, you can use your hand signals to help indicate whether you're going to turn, slow down, change lanes, or even come to a stop. Next, locate the switch for the hazard lights. They indicate when your vehicle is not in proper working condition and notify other drivers to take precautions when approaching you. Next, locate the windshield wiper switch. Windshield wipers are used during rain, of course, but they also remove condensation or wash away any type of debris on your windshield. People often forget to locate the defroster. The defroster is used to remove any type of frost, fog, or dew on your windshield that may keep you from seeing the road clearly.

Next, you start the car. While you are turning the ignition key, give the vehicle a little gas and it should fire right up. Check and see if any of the warning lights on the dashboard are lighted that tell if you need gas or oil. Finally, you've completed the preliminary steps.

Now it's time to actually drive the car. Place your foot on the brake and put the car in Drive. Before leaving the

Quinn 3

curb, look in the mirrors to see if there are any vehicles in your path. Pull out from the curb very slowly as you watch what's in front of you, in back, and on the sides. When you are driving, make sure you are not driving faster than the posted speed limit. When you want to switch lanes, always remember to use your turning signals, your side mirrors, and your rearview mirror to make sure you are in the clear to switch lanes. When approaching a stop sign or red light, slow up and come to a complete stop. When you've reached your destination, you're ready to park. Put your foot on the brake and shift the gear into Park. On hills, turn your wheels toward the curb, and then set the emergency brake so that your vehicle will not go speeding downhill. Whenever you park, make sure you shift into the parking gear and set your emergency brake. Then turn off the engine.

You've learned the rules, familiarized yourself with the vehicle, and driven from here to there safely. This completes your first lesson in driving. Did you enjoy it?

WORK! WORK! WORK!

These exercises help build skills by prompting you to express your understanding of what you read.

Reading Comprehension

1. According to Shakei, what are the three main steps in learning to drive a car?

_____

_____

2. What does Shakei suggest you do *after* you turn on the engine but *before* you drive? _____

_____

3. Name some of the features Shakei says you should locate in the car. _____

_____

4. What is the most important rule in learning to drive a car? _____

_____

Writing Analysis

1. In using the process writing technique, does Shakei provide information or instruction in learning to drive? _____

_____

2. The essay is organized into six paragraphs. What is the purpose of the short fourth paragraph? _____

3. What is the purpose of the sixth paragraph? _____

_____

Be careful what you ask for; you just might get it. Rewrite the ad, rewording the message so that the antecedent of the pronoun can't be misunderstood.

Housekeeping Service: Tired of cleaning yourself? Let me do it.

_____

The following professional article gives the steps in the process of becoming a paramedic.

A Career to Consider—Paramedic
by Ronald A. Reis

Even with eighteen years experience as a Los Angeles City Fire Department Paramedic, Captain Stephen Johnson stood awestruck by the disaster unfolding before him. A three-story apartment building, in the predominately Latino immigrant district of Westlake, was totally engulfed in smoke and flames.

"People were leaping from windows, clambering down fire escape ladders, and lowering themselves with sheets tied to balcony railings," he told me. "At one point, I found myself cradling an infant brought out in full arrest, pupils fixed and dilated, asystole on the EKG."

Of twenty-nine individuals treated at the scene in that early May 1993 calamity, eighteen had to be hospitalized. Tragically, nine people lost their lives, six of them children.

Nevertheless, the one hundred firefighters and sixteen ambulances dispatched to the scene were able to save many, among them an eight-months-pregnant woman who went into labor as paramedics administered cardiopulmonary resuscitation. Yet, as Stephen continued: "When you lose a child, as in this case, it's a traumatic experience. As paramedics we have our routine, mundane days. This, most certainly, was not one of them. Emotionally, it was the worst."

ALL IN AN EMERGENCY

Nonetheless, paramedics are trained to handle whatever comes their way. From knee scrapes to flu symptoms, traffic accidents, stabbings, and heart attacks, when a 911 call is taken, paramedics respond to provide prehospital emergency care.

According to Alan Cowen, Deputy Fire Chief, Los Angeles City Fire Department, in a first response setting: "Paramedics control bleeding, open airways, treat for shock, immobilize fractures, bandage, and manage emotionally disturbed patients.

"In addition, they can be called upon to provide advanced life-support, such as defibrillating a patient, administering solutions, both orally and intravenously, and interpreting EKGs (electrocardiograms)."

What they don't do is intervene surgically. But short of that, the timely medical aid paramedics provide can, and often does, save lives.

To the Drill Tower for You?

To become a paramedic with the Los Angeles City Fire Department, you must first become a firefighter. That's no easy task. Of the literally thousands who, in Chief Cowen's words: "Circle City Hall each year for applications," only five hundred or so will, after an extensive written exam, physical agility test, medical screening, psychological review, preliminary background check, and interview, be given an "academy date." Even then, only thirty-five to forty of the five hundred applicants will actually begin the arduous 16 weeks of "Drill Tower" preparation they hope will lead to rookie firefighter.

As part of that four-month paramilitary firefighter training, you'll spend approximately 130 hours becoming an Emergency Medical Technician (EMT) Level 1D. Thus every Los Angeles firefighter can, at the least, extricate people pinned in vehicles, do advanced first aid, administer oxygen, and perform cardiopulmonary resuscitation.

Upon graduation from the academy, you're rotated through three fire stations in the first year. At each, you are exposed to engine, truck, and ambulance duties.

Two years after becoming a firefighter, you may apply to attend paramedic school. If chosen, you're in for a grueling five- to six-month commitment. Two months will be didactic (in the classroom), two months at a hospital, and forty-five days in the field. It's a total of one thousand hours in an intense, competitive, environment. The reward? If you pass, you're a state licensed firefighter paramedic (EMT3). Also, you get a 17 percent pay raise.

While the Los Angeles City Fire Department has close to six hundred paramedics (over eighty women), becoming a paramedic does not require you join a fire department. "There are a number of private ambulance services hiring civilian, single-function paramedics," Alan explained. You'll need to attend the same paramedic schools firefighters do, of course, and obtain your state license.

The Paramedic Way of Life

Is running the paramedic training gauntlet, subjecting yourself to the Darwinian selection process, worth it? Stephen Johnson, now District Commander, thinks so.

"The environment is exciting. When you arrive on the scene, you're confronted with a puzzle you have to put back together. Someone is injured, how do we fix this, how do we help them, I ask myself. It may be minor in our eyes, but to them it's an emergency. We help, they're happy, it's a great feeling."

"The time off is good, too," Stephen continued. "With four days off between three twenty-four-hour platoon duty shifts, I have time to water ski, hike, do the active sports thing."

What about burnout, I wondered? With all the stress, surely mental fatigue must be a factor?

"It is," Stephen explained. "But now that paramedics are also firefighters, there are places to go within the organization. You can become a dispatcher, inspector, do fire prevention, or be promoted up through the ranks, for example. A lot of options."

Alan Cowen took advantage of that last option. Starting as a paramedic in 1967, he has worked his way to the very top, holding all ranks in the Emergency Medical Service (EMS) hierarchy. He regrets nothing. "I don't consider this a job, being a firefighter, a paramedic," he told me, at the conclusion of our interview, "it is a way of life."

"It's people going out and helping someone they've never met, someone they don't know, someone they'll probably never see again. And they will lay down their life for that person—without thinking. Why? Because they are trained to do so. They are there to render care, to ease suffering. It is a noble, grand profession."

Exercises Related to the Professional Article from the World of Work on Listing the Steps (process)

Reading Comprehension

1. According to the article, what are three procedures that para-medics perform? _____

   _____

   _____

   _____

2. How many of the thousands of applicants get "academy dates"? Of these, how many actually begin the sixteen weeks of "Drill Tower" preparation? _____

   _____

3. What does "EMT" stand for? _____

4. What are two functions that every Los Angeles firefighter is able to perform? ____

   _____

   _____

   _____

Writing Analysis

1. How does the article apply to the step-by-step writing technique? _____

   _____

   _____

2. Does the article inform or instruct? _____

   _____

3. Why did the author begin the essay by describing a "tragic" occurrence? _____

   _____

   _____

4. Why does the author use a quotation to end his article? _____

   _____

   _____

GrammarWorks! Those "!(.:,—);?" Punctuation Marks: The Semicolon ; and the Colon :

The Semicolon;

The semicolon is an enhanced comma; it serves better than the comma in complex sentences and in the presence of other internal punctuation.

The semicolon is most commonly used to separate two or more closely related independent clauses.	Britt Roberts was elected president; Ralph Andrews was elected vice president; Skip Lewis was elected treasurer; K. B. Connor was elected secretary.
The semicolon serves wherever punctuation stronger than a comma is needed for ease of understanding.	The brothers were born January 3, 1961, in Poland; and April 2, 1962, in Ireland. Tim teaches math in Daly City; Mark, English, in Long Beach.
The semicolon separates clauses containing words or phrases marked by many commas, or dashes or parentheses.	Most people agree that the states—not the federal government—should decide maximum road speeds; while others, notably sports car drivers, want a national speed limit set at seventy mph.
The semicolon separates elements in a complex series.	On the form, put your name, address, and telephone number; driver's license and social security numbers; and date of birth.

The Colon:

The colon is like an arrow: It directs attention to the phrase or clause that follows it.

The colon follows an independent clause (a complete sentence) that introduces a complex series.	On the field trip, bus seating will be as follows: the teacher will sit behind the driver; the girls will sit on the left side; and the boys will sit on the right.
The colon points to an important statement or lengthy passage.	This is the law of the work day: Be there on time and don't leave early!
The colon introduces enumerations and series of items, whether in text or outline format.	Here's my schedule: (1) write insurance company; (2) call painter; (3) drop off dry cleaning; (4) get gasoline; (5) pick up kids; (6) buy milk.

The words that precede the colon should form a complete sentence.

NOTE: While quotation marks go outside commas and periods, *quotation marks go inside semicolons and colons!*

Ted said the words are "the home of the free and the land of the brave"; however, everyone else knew the words are "the land of the free and the home of the brave."	Marin keeps these in her "secret stash": twenty dollars in cash and a bag of "Gummy Nummies."

GRAMMARWORKS! Review

Refer to the GrammarWorks!' rules and the following examples to identify the purposes served by the semicolons and colons used below.

Semicolon Example: *My recipe for Caesar salad calls for romaine lettuce, oil, egg, lemon juice, garlic, and parmesan cheese; the egg isn't really necessary.* Used to separate clauses containing words or phrases marked by many commas.

1. For every A on his report card, Bejan gets a dollar; for every B, fifty cents; and for every C, a quarter. _____

_____

2. Kath turned seventeen last month; Colleen will turn nineteen next month. _____

_____

3. Jeanne lives at 725 South Citrus, Newport, California; Brian at 860 South Hudson Street, Bozeman, Montana; and Teresa at 795 South Cochran Avenue, North Salem, New York. _____

_____

4. Tomas told Pablo—not Jamil—to get the hamburgers; but the guys ended up with six burgers instead of three (from two different fast food places)!

_____

Colon Example: *Lincoln's Gettysburg Address begins: "Four score and seven years ago, our fathers brought forth on this continent a new nation, conceived in liberty and dedicated to the proposition that all men are created equal."* Used to point to a lengthy passage.

1. The crudely written road sign said: BEWARE! BRIDGE OUT! _____

_____

2. Whenever Dad hears car keys jingle, he always reminds us: (1) lock the doors; (2) roll up the windows; and (3) don't pick up hitchhikers. _____

_____

3. A big wedding requires the participation of many people: the bride and groom are essential; attendants act as legal witnesses; someone organizes the ceremony and the reception; and guests make it a party. _____

_____

4. Fonya set out what she'd need to make her kids' lunches in the morning: bread, peanut butter, corn chips, apples, and cookies. _____

_____

In the following sentences, insert a period, question mark, colon, or semicolon in the correct blank before or after the quotation marks.

Example: Chris asked, "Who ate the cake *?* " *;* the little boy said, "It was I *.* "

1. Abdul shouted, "Hold the elevator!__ "__ but, by mistake, we pushed the button marked "Close Door__"__

2. Ms. Burns listed these flowers that are "purple__"__ lilacs, orchids, and violets.

THE BIG EIGHT BONEHEADS!

- Words Misspelled
- Words or Caps Incorrect
- Sentence Fragments
- Sentence Run-Ons, Spliced or Fused
- Pronouns Confused
- Verbs Misused
- Commas Misplaced
- Apostrophes Abused

FIXING A BONEHEAD PROCESS PAPER, STEP-BY-STEP

Read the paragraph and then follow the directions below.

**(1) HOW TO PLANT BULBS
BY O. "TUBBY" A. GARDENER**

(2) Planting bulbs is a good thing to do in winter if you want flowers in spring. (3) First you dig a whole and put in the bulb it looks like a Garlic. (4) then you cover it up with dirt. (5) Be sure you're bulb is right side up. (6) The pointy end. (6) The things that looks like dry worms is roots; it goes on the bottom of the hole. (7) A good place to by blubs is a nursary. (8) They sell all kindsa bulbs tulips daffodils iris and onions. (9) Oh You should have put some planter mix in the whole too. (10) In servile months time your gonna to sea green coming out of the dirt. (11) If you watered them right and put them in a sunny plaice. (12) Right down these steps you'll have a good system for planting bulbs next spring.

Edit the paragraph above. Search for the Big Eight: circle misspelled words, wrong words, and wrong capitalizations. Put an X in front of sentence fragments, run-on, spliced, and fused sentences. Underline misused pronouns and verbs and the comma and apostrophe errors. Each sentence above has a number. On the lines below, tell what you've found wrong with each numbered sentence. (Write what you found wrong with sentence (1) on line 1, and so on.)

1. _____
2. _____
3. _____
4. _____
5. _____

6. _____

7. _____

8. _____

9. _____

10. _____

11. _____

12. _____

Is it an orderly or disorderly illustration of the step-by-step technique? _____

_____

_____

How does this "system" represent a management of resources? _____

_____

_____

Now you're ready to revise the paragraph. Write it in your own words on a separate piece of paper.

WORK! WORK! WORK!

Writing Practice

The following prompts will help you pick a topic to show what you've learned about the writing technique studied in this lesson.

"A job isn't finished until the paperwork is done."

Exercises in Step-by-Step Writing, the Process Technique

On your paper, identify whether you are instructing or informing.

1. Write a step-by-step essay of four or more paragraphs *instructing* someone on how to wash windows, play a game, do a crafts project, build a birdhouse, buy a used car, get a financial-aid grant, or make your favorite dinner; or choose your own topic for *instruction.*

2. Write a step-by-step essay of four or more paragraphs *informing* someone of how you became the terrific (or terrible) person you are today. Or write four or more paragraphs *giving information* regarding the steps you will take to complete your college major, the steps you took to get your current job, or the steps you will take to get your future job.

3. Choose any system you want—your work, your family, your church, or a system from any place of your choice. Identify at least three ways by which the system can be improved.

WORK! WORK! WORK!

Lesson Review

The following practices show what you've learned in this lesson.

SCANS Focus

Fill In the Blanks Regarding SCANS Focus

1. _____ is the process of taking information into one's memory.

2. _____ is applying knowledge and drawing conclusions.

3. A way of doing things is called a _____. We must understand systems in order to _____ and _____ and _____ them.

Step-By-Step Writing Technique

Fill In the Blanks Regarding the Step-by-Step Writing Technique

1. Another word for the step-by-step technique is _____.

2. The process technique is used to _____ or _____.

Exercise your knowledge of periods, colons, and semicolons. Using the information that follows, put the final punctuation to each item in the following outline.

I. The topic becomes *roman* numeral I (a capital i).*

A. Each subtopic is indented and denoted by a capital letter, in alphabetical order__

B. If a subtopic has subsections, there must be at least two of them, indented under the alphabetical section, and numbered with arabic numerals (1, 2, 3, etc.).**

   1. Each numbered subsection usually ends with a semicolon__

   2. The exceptions are the following__
      a. When a sentence is not connected in thought to the previous and next item, it ends with a period__

      b. When subsections are one or two words, each line ends in a comma__

      c. When the subsection is the final one, it ends in a period__

C. Sentences in subtopics usually begin with a capital letter and end with a period__

D. Occasionally a subtopic ends with a colon; for instance__

   1. When the subtopic line introduces the items that complete a thought__

   2. When the subsections below are in list form__

E. Be consistent: Subtopics should be either all sentences or all phrases (or clauses); subsections should be all phrases or clauses_____

---

*A *short* outline may begin with *either* the letter A (followed by numerals) or the *arabic* numeral 1 (followed by lower case letters). Each letter or number is followed by a period.

**Subheadings thereafter alternate between beginning with a letter or a number, differentiated as follows: I, A, 1, a, 1), a), (1), (a). Each letter or number is followed by a period.

Chapter 10

LOOKING OUTWARD

IN THIS CHAPTER

SCANS FOUNDATION: COOPERATION

SCANS COMPETENCIES: TEAMWORK AND CULTURAL DIVERSITY, TEACHING AND SERVING, LEADERSHIP AND NEGOTIATION

SCANS FOCUS: COOPERATION, TEAMWORK, LEADERSHIP, NEGOTIATION

DIALOGUE—CONVERSATION

SCANS FOUNDATION: COOPERATION

SCANS COMPETENCIES: TEAMWORK AND CULTURAL DIVERSITY, TEACHING AND SERVING, LEADERSHIP AND NEGOTIATION

The ability to interact well with people, whether they are known to us or strangers, is especially important in the world of work. We have to "get along with" (move forward together with) our fellow workers and with the clients and customers of our employers.

Cooperation is the key to getting things done that can't be done by one person alone. *Teamwork* is working together to accomplish a mutual goal—whether it is winning a game, completing a science project, or designing someone's house. At home and in school, we might have had limited contact with people whose backgrounds differ from our own. In the work environment, we will have daily opportunities to interact with people of all cultures, races, creeds, and nationalities. Respect for others' ideas and opinions, simple courtesy, and commitment to the business at hand "grease the wheels" of the job machine.

In the course of our contact with other people, we take part in conversation or dialogue. We need *to teach* a fellow worker how to do a task. We engage in conversation in the effort *to serve* clients and customers. As we grow within our work environments, we have continued opportunities to show and develop our skills at *negotiation* and *leadership*.

Often, the purpose of conversations is to persuade someone to do something new or to convince someone to believe something we believe in. We continue to grow and mature as we try new and different things, discuss new ideas, and acquire new goals or objectives. In this chapter, we explore the writing techniques of *dialogue* and *influencing people*.

Let's get to work!

SCANS FOCUS: COOPERATION, TEAMWORK, LEADERSHIP, NEGOTIATION

IT ALL BEGINS AND ENDS WITH TALKING

Chances are, if you are with friends, you're exchanging words with them. You're having a **conversation.** We can't maintain a friendship or do business without conversation. A conversation is like a game of basketball: the "conversational ball" passes often from one person to another.

In the workplace, it's a good idea to keep notes of conversations. *Who* said *what* to *whom*—and *when*—can play an important part in the history of a task or transaction. Notes help you remember important information you can easily forget. This is especially true with telephone conversations. Notes taken of telephone conversations should always include the dates, telephone numbers, and names of the people spoken to. With this information, you, or anyone who reads your notes, can reconstruct the chain of people who placed orders, made promises, quoted prices, and so on. Making notes helps keep the game rolling according to the rules and helps you communicate information to your coworkers, your team members. Conversations are important because they facilitate teamwork.

Harcourt, Inc.

YOU MIGHT NOT HAVE THOUGHT OF THIS . . .

Coaches have *to learn how to teach* their players. We *all* serve as teachers in life. When you teach your kid brother to ride a bike, you're a *teacher*. You also *learn* something from the experience. When, later on, you teach your little sister to ride a bike, the task is easier than before. As a student writing descriptive or informative essays, you are teaching others about things that interest you. More important, you are *learning valuable job skills.* Whether teaching a coworker a system at work or providing information to a customer, everybody benefits if you can pass the conversational ball in a direct and team-spirited manner.

GIVE SERVICE WITH A SMILE

There is a general, but special, word to describe what a business provides its clients and customers: **service.** Whether you're a repairperson, a dental technician, a postal worker, a food server, a hairstylist, a pharmacist, or a salesperson, you are providing a service. Even when you *can't* say, "Yeah, we have that," if you refer the customer to another business, you have given service. Good service earns the good will of the customers. Good service means repeat business.

Let's look again at the analogy of a business conversation being like a basketball game. We can think of the people who work together as "the home team" and the people who make use of their services as "the visiting team." The two teams come together because without two teams there's no game. In the work environment, however, the intention is *not* for one team to defeat the other. Each team must get something in return for what it puts out.

When businesspeople feel they have been well paid for the services they provided, and customers or clients feel they have received what they want for the money they spent, it's called a **win/win situation.** Giving good service is what people in business aim for. *Satisfying* customers and clients means providing what's wanted in a businesslike way, identifying and correcting misunderstandings, and dealing with problems fairly and promptly. Happy customers spread the word and attract new customers to the business.

> ### IT'S TEAMWORK THAT . . .
>
> - Wins Ball Games.
> - Makes Win/Win Work Situations.

WIN/WIN WORKS *WITHIN* THE HOME TEAM, TOO

For every person to do his or her job on the team, there must be cooperation among the players. **Teamwork**—working together to achieve the goal—is a satisfying human experience. Whether people have common or different backgrounds, deciding how best to get things done can often cause clashes. The trick to resolving workplace conflict is to be aware that **conflict doesn't mean combat!** When there is a task to be accomplished, each of us thinks of a plan. But when we focus only on our *own* way, we don't recognize that a fellow worker might have a way to complete the task that benefits *both* of us. *Conflict can be an opportunity to discover better ways of doing things.* But remember, you don't have to *create* conflict; it occurs naturally, without help!

The teamwork way to handle the conflict is to discuss all the ideas without anyone trying to be "the winner." If there can be only one winner, everyone else loses. For our team to win, everyone on our team must win. Every player on every team must contribute ideas and effort to the group. Not everyone plays the same position on the team, but by supporting and encouraging each others' ideas, we find out where each player serves best.

HOW TO BE THE HOME TEAM'S MOST VALUABLE PLAYER

Negotiation is the art of resolving conflict. Conflict means *disagreement*. Disagreement can delay the making of decisions and the completion of tasks. A good negotiator is quick to recognize a deadlock. Call it what you will—a stalemate, an impasse, the cessation of forward movement—when things come to a screeching halt, you need a good negotiator. To resolve conflict, the negotiator traces disagreements to their roots; hears all sides; and presents the facts and arguments calmly and accurately, clarifying problems, proposing and examining options, and participating in compromises. One who can negotiate well and keep the ball rolling is the most valuable player to the team and the coach alike.

Be part of the solution, not part of the problem! Respect for others' opinions, tolerance of people's differences, and patience in reaching decisions—all these virtues come into play in the work game.

A FUNNY THING HAPPENED AT WORK

As you go about doing your job—helping your coworkers, satisfying the clients, and resolving disputes on both sides of the counter—there is a side effect. Instead of attracting attention by the chaos around you, you draw attention because things around you are always running smoothly. Your boss singles you out because "the coach" knows he can depend on you to handle a sticky situation or accomplish a difficult task. *You're up for team captain!* **Leadership** comes from being a good team player.

A GOOD TEAM PLAYER IS AN EMPLOYEE WHO . . .

Is able to communicate thoughts, feelings, and ideas;

Is self-motivated and skilled in motivating others;

Is able to persuade and convince others for the good of all; and

Recognizes when to go along with the crowd and when to step forward and take a stand.

A GOOD LEADER IS A PERSON WHO . . .

Sets realistic and attainable goals;

Follows the rules or negotiates new rules;

Establishes credibility through competence and integrity; and

Takes others' viewpoints into consideration.

A good leader knows this: **cultural diversity** is a valuable source of new ideas, just as *variety in diet* is a valuable source of nutrition for ball players and business people alike. A good leader knows the score, and it's always win/win.

Harcourt, Inc.

SCANS Focus Exercise

The following are some opportunities for cooperation and working together on the job. Read the examples, and then perform the exercise below.

Chef: Trains others and compliments them on the performance of their preparation tasks, apportions work fairly, satisfies the special requests of the waiters, and fulfills the patrons' expectations.

Electrician: Cautions others in dangerous situations. Explains to clients how lighting and other wiring systems work. Gets his crew back to work after lunch.

Nurse: Makes sure everything is in order for next shift. Reassures patient when doctor is delayed. Instructs volunteers in proper way to serve staff and patients. Encourages others when hours are long and late.

Printer: Performs his share of the work in a timely fashion. Tactfully handles dispute as to who is responsible for cleaning equipment. Acknowledges fault in error and makes good for client.

Fashion Manufacturer: Takes orders carefully and passes them along to cutters clearly. Arranges for workers to contact families when overtime is required and assures boss it is not *workers'* fault that work is incomplete.

In-Class SCANS Exercise

The above examples show how cooperative skills are involved in the jobs mentioned. Write a brief paragraph on how one of the following cooperative skills may apply in the job you're doing or training for.

1.   In what way are clients or customers served?
2.   When does the work force function as a team?
3.   Are there problems or conflicts that repeat themselves? How are they resolved?
4.   If you were in charge of workers on your current or future job, list three examples of leadership qualities that you should display.

"Little pig, little pig, let me come in!"
"Not by the hair of my chinny-chin-chin!"

DIALOGUE—CONVERSATION

WRITTEN CONVERSATION IS CALLED DIALOGUE

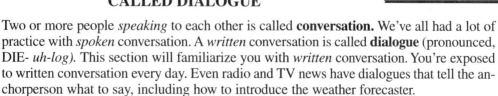

Two or more people *speaking* to each other is called **conversation.** We've all had a lot of practice with *spoken* conversation. A *written* conversation is called **dialogue** (pronounced, DIE- *uh-log).* This section will familiarize you with *written* conversation. You're exposed to written conversation every day. Even radio and TV news have dialogues that tell the anchorperson what to say, including how to introduce the weather forecaster.

ARTHUR: And now to Maria Vega with the weather. Where's that rain, Maria?
MARIA: Thank you, Arthur. Yes, the forecast rain didn't materialize today, but . . .

There are many differences between spoken conversation and written dialogue. There are even different kinds of written dialogue.

From a national magazine. He admits that he couldn't see clearly, but is his sense of touch defective, too? Circle that adverb that should be an adjective and write the correct word above it.

Sitting over lunch in his local Elks Club, Det. John Ingram shook his head in regret and puzzlement. "I feel badly that I couldn't see through this," he reported.

DIALOGUE IS OFTEN AN ASPECT OF STORYTELLING

In telling stories, we often write down conversations between or among people. A true story is called *nonfiction*. A story we make up is called *fiction*.

When Written Dialogue Is *Nonfiction*

We refer to *real* people in *nonfiction dialogue* as **speakers.** The above example is a *nonfiction* dialogue. Here are two other examples of nonfiction dialogue: a news story—about something that actually happened, where real people are being quoted; and a letter—for example, to a business that quotes a conversation between you and their employee.

When Written Dialogue Is *Fiction*

We refer to *fictional people* as **characters.** Examples of *fiction dialogue* can be found in novels, short stories, television series, and films.

TWO TYPES OF WRITTEN DIALOGUE

- Narrative
- Scripted

For those guests who never know when to leave. . . . Using a wrong word can give someone the wrong idea. Find the misused word and write the correct word below.

Vacation special: Have your home exterminated. Get rid of aunts.

THERE ARE TWO FORMATS FOR WRITTEN DIALOGUE

Narrative format is used in long and short *fiction and nonfiction* stories. In a *narrated* story, dialogue weaves through the literary descriptions of characters and situations to bring a story to a reader's mind. Narrative dialogue is set off with quotation marks.

Scripted format is used in *fiction and nonfiction* theatrical productions, television scripts, and screenplays. In a *scripted* story, dialogue is conversation for characters who will be portrayed by live actors. Scripted dialogue stands apart from the descriptions and information for the director, technicians, artists, and craftspeople who bring the story to life on stage or screen.

 From a magazine article on getting along with difficult people (DPs). *Cross out the extra word in the first sentence and correct the verb form in the last sentence to show that using correct verbs isn't a difficult proposition. Also correct the pronoun/antecedent error.*

Show the DP you've heard the him or her by repeating the DP's words. Knowing they been heard will begin to defuse the DP's anger.

Narrative dialogue, between speakers or characters in your writing assignments, is set off by quotation marks. The written conversations are part of the story you are unfolding, or they are necessary to the information you are providing. Here is a brief example of the narrative format used in a story about the fictional Marta and her boyfriend Julio, who begin to argue at dinner in Marta's parents' house.

> Marta said with disgust, "Oh, no! You spilled red wine all over my new blue dress! I was going to wear it to my awards dinner tonight! Why do you eat like such a pig?" Marta rushed to the kitchen sink to wash out the stain.
>
> Julio belched. "So why'd you leave your precious dress next to me if you think I'm such a slob? Is this table for eating, or were you gonna use it for an ironing board?" He threw down his fork and left.

Narrative dialogue is an important part of your story, and it flows through the narrated emotions and actions of your characters. The reader uses his imagination to fill in much of the background, but the writer must fill in the words. We will get to the mechanics of narrative dialogue later in the chapter. But first, let's look at the above narrative in scripted format.

Scripted dialogue is the written format for television, motion pictures, radio, stage, and musical theater productions. Scriptwriters, playwrights, and screenwriters provide not only dialogue. They must also describe who the characters are and their relationships, the emotions or feelings with which the dialogue is spoken, the time of day and location of the scene, and stage directions to describe what action takes place. The following example of a scene for a television show is *scripted dialogue* for the *narrative dialogue* above.

FADE IN

Interior. 5:30 P.M. kitchen of modest one-story bungalow of the Morales family in Hollywood. Kitchen is painted soft pink, modern, with all new appliances and a silver urn for utensils.

Marta Morales, eighteen, is an intelligent, very attractive college student. She wears Levis and a T-shirt with "UCLA" on it. Her hair is in pigtails, and she wears no makeup.

JULIO OBELLES, twenty-three, is a construction laborer. He wears dirty one-piece overalls, his hair is disheveled, and he needs a shave.

Marta stands at open refrigerator. Julio sits at table. It is cluttered with school books. A plastic bag with a blue dress folded on top of it sits near Julio. Julio pushes a huge portion of spaghetti into his mouth. Beside him are a bottle and a glass of wine. Julio knocks over the glass.

JULIO: *(chewing calmly)* Oops. Hey, you wanna get a rag?

MARTA: *(turning from refrigerator, surprised and dismayed)* Oh, no! You've spilled red wine all over my new blue dress! I was going to wear it to my awards dinner tonight! *(Grabs dish towel and rushes to table.)* Why do you eat like such a pig? *(Disgusted, takes dress to sink and turns on tap water.)*

JULIO: *(belches)* So why'd you leave your precious dress next to me if you think I'm such a slob? Is this table for eating, or were you gonna use it for an ironing board? *(Tosses fork and angrily stomps out.)*

You can readily notice the differences between these two methods of writing dialogue. The *narrative* form contains only enough detail for the reader to get a mental picture of the scene taking place. *Scripting* includes detailed directions, or suggestions, for all of the other people responsible for bringing the script to life: the scenery and props people, the lighting and sound technicians, and the costume designers. The writer also includes information so that the director will know how to cast the parts and stage the scene. For the actors, the dialogue is set off separately so that it will stand out, along with detailed guidelines so the actors know how to speak their lines. There are many books available on script writing.

From a newspaper article. *This was a model paragraph for construction and punctuation . . . until the last sentences. Rewrite the last two sentences correcting the pronoun misuse and the sentence fragment.*

Estrich, who began as a substitute host in 1990 and had been Jackson's major fill-in, disclosed Tuesday that Green asked her "to secretly negotiate a contract and not tell Michael. And I said, 'That's not how I play baseball.' I just wouldn't do it. I spoke to both Michael and his wife. I said, 'Michael, go sign your contract.' That really forged a strong relationship between Michael and I. And he did sign."

_____

_____

_____

RULES FOR NARRATIVE DIALOGUE

In Narrative Dialogue, Each Person Who Speaks Must Be Identified. Reading dialogue is something like listening to the radio. But on the radio, we can recognize different voices. Since we can't *see* the characters in a written story, the writer tells us who is speaking. First, writers always *begin a new paragraph each time a different character begins speaking.*

With only two characters, you can change speakers a few times without saying who is speaking. But when narration interrupts the dialogue, or when *not* identifying the speaker would be confusing to the reader, the writer will *use an identifying phrase.* Sometimes names identify who's speaking *(Owen said);* sometimes *he said* or *she asked* is sufficient; and sometimes the character is described *(the tall man said* or *the model asked). Said* or *asked* is all the reader needs. *She shrilled, he cried, Isaac hooted,* and so on, are not acceptable. And, unlike scripted writing, avoid using adverbs to describe *how* the speaker spoke unless the words don't match the emotions. *He said harshly, she asked angrily,* and so on, are not examples of good writing. The dialogue *should* carry the emotion to the reader. For example:

"I love you," he said. (We get the idea.)
"I love you, too," she said *with sarcasm.* (We needed help to get the idea.)
Better: "I love you, too," she said, crossing her eyes and sticking out her tongue.

Set Off the Spoken Words with Quotation Marks. Special punctuation goes around each set of words spoken by one person. Perhaps the *most important thing* about writing dialogue is to learn to use quotation marks correctly. (GrammarWorks! will help you.) **Double quotation marks** look like mirror image, double apostrophes. The first ones are *opening* quotation marks, and the end ones are *closing* quotation marks. For example:

As she entered the den, Tisha said, "So, who's *not* coming to this party?"

Quotation marks "face" each other, like parentheses. (On typewriters, and some word processors, there are only one type of quotation marks, which point down.) Usually, quotation marks are used in pairs. The exception is when a person speaks for *more than* one paragraph. Then, opening marks begin each new paragraph, and closing marks go only where the person stops speaking.

Quotations within Quotations. People in dialogues sometimes quote other people. This is called a quotation within a quotation. Since it would be very confusing to have multiple sets of *double* quotation marks, the quotation *inside* the double quotation marks is set off with **single quotation marks.** For example:

Jonah answered, "Jackie said she'd be at the party 'unless something more fun came up.' I told her to forget it."

Punctuation for Interruptions. In dialogue, two people can't talk at once. To signal an interruption in a speaker's words, use an ellipsis. (You'll study the ellipsis later in this chapter's GrammarWorks!) Use the ellipsis rarely; the reader wants to believe that everything the characters have to say is important.

Tisha said, "I'll bet Jackie didn't like hearing . . . "
"Oh, she laughed it off," he said.

Internal Dialogue. What the characters *think* is called internal dialogue. It is written in italics without quotation marks. (If you cannot use italics, underline internal dialogue.)

Jonah extended his hands to Tisha, to invite her to dance. *Jackie'll probably show up anyway,* he thought.

NARRATIVE DIALOGUE

- Identifies Speakers
- Uses Quotation Marks
- Has Special Punctuation Rules
- Is Sometimes Internal, Not Spoken Aloud

THE BOTTOM LINES

You'll need to balance dialogue with narration in your stories to flesh out your characters and the action. If readers wanted *only* dialogue, they'd listen to radio drama programs.

Plan to pay close attention to the punctuation as you read the following examples of student and professional use of the dialogue writing technique.

The student author's assignment: Write a true story about someone you respect, using dialogue.

José de Dios, somewhat older than the average student, spent four years in a Cuban prison because of his political views.

---

de Dios 1

José de Dios
English 120-10:00
Dialogue
Sept. 19, 1999

The One Who Loves and the One Who Hates

"Men can be classified in two types, the ones who love and build and the ones who hate and destroy." It was 1883 when José Marti, a Cuban revolutionary fighting for his country's independence from Spain, wrote this phrase.

In 1976, I met Pablo, a seventy-year-old man with the belly of a bishop and a face like Mother Teresa. It is difficult to understand why some people ask stupid questions in prison, like "How are you today?" or "How is your family?" Obviously, I could not find a more polite or better way to approach Pablo, my new cellmate.

"How is your family?" I asked him.

His face lit up slowly, the way a candle does when one first lights it. He told me about his wife and two sons and how his life changed after he became sterile.

"How did that happen?" I asked, unable to hide my curiosity. "Oh, I'm sorry. I didn't mean that." At this point in time, I was ashamed of my question.

"It's okay," he said, as he walked toward the door of our prison cell and took hold of the steel bars. He rested his head sadly against the metal door, and, after a short pause, he began his narration.

In 1957, when Fidel Castro's supporters were fighting to overthrow the government of General Batista, Pablo was one of the members of an urban guerrilla band. His function in the group was to hide the weapons in a secure place. At that time, his two sons were eleven and twelve years old, and he

was living in a two-story house with them and his wife.
Behind a false wall in the house's basement, he kept all the
weapons and ammunition he was hiding for his group.

One day, General Batista's soldiers captured one of the
group members. After he was tortured, the poor guy told them
that Pablo was assigned to keep the weapons. The soldiers
went to Pablo's house, but, after what they thought was a
thorough search, they found nothing.

Pablo resisted the interrogators, and they punched and
kicked him in front of his family until his body was blood-
reddened flesh. Hundreds of times they asked Pablo for the
weapons, and he did not answer a word. Then, everything
happened in a second.

A brutal hit with a rifle in his groin made Pablo lose
consciousness. When he regained his senses, he was still
lying on the floor, wet with his own blood. He turned his eyes
toward the soldiers, and what he saw turned him to ice. A
furious soldier, eyes red with anger, held Pablo's sons by
the backs of their shirts with his left hand, holding a
pistol ready to be fired in his right hand.

Pablo's sons screamed, "Daddy! Daddy!"

"Son of a . . .! I'm going to kill these boys right
now," the soldier cried, pointing his gun to the head of one
of the frightened boys.

With great effort, Pablo, close to death, complied, "No,
I'll talk. Leave my boys alone. They are not responsible."
He told the soldiers what their torture could not get out of
him—where the weapons were.

The soldiers took the arms and ammunition, and Pablo was
conducted to a hospital. His family, after the soldiers had
left with Pablo, went to the Mexican Embassy where they
received political asylum. Once recovered, Pablo was sent to
jail.

After being in jail and learning that his family was
living in Mexico, Pablo managed to escape to the Mexican
Embassy and was able to join his family. In Mexico, doctors
told him he was sterile as a result of the beating he had
received from the Cuban soldiers.

I learned at this time that this man could be considered
in the first group, of which Marti said, "The one who loves
and builds. . . . "

So why was he in prison with me now? I was there for
opposing Castro's government, but Pablo was a Castro
supporter. What was going on?

de Dios 3

I learned that Pablo and his family decided to return to Cuba after Castro gained power, and, several years after they had arrived, his sons decided they wanted to join Castro's army. One of them was sent to Russia for training as a missile specialist; the other was trained in Cuba for military intelligence. At the time of this story, 1976, both were army commanders.

Pablo explained to me that he was recently arrested and sent to prison because someone accused him of volunteering information in 1957 to Batista's soldiers about the weapons he was hiding. The accusation was related to the past incident in his home when he and his sons almost lost their lives.

But now, twenty years later, his sons were Castro's army commanders. With their testimony, Pablo knew that Castro's government would acquit him. The day after our conversation, a guard came to our cell seeking Pablo. The guard had spoken with the investigator on Pablo's case and had been reassured that his two sons would be at the interview that day. As he left our cell, Pablo said, "Good luck, José, in case I do not return. It is possible that I will go home with my sons."

"Good luck to you, Pablo," I replied.

The guard opened and closed the cell door as rapidly as an automatic one. After they left, the silence in my cell could be cut with a knife. I was thinking how good it was to love the way Pablo loved and how he had built such an extraordinary family based on that love.

It is difficult to say how long I had been talking to myself. In prison, you do not measure time in hours but in years. My running dreams and thoughts stopped with the sound of a door opening. From my bed, I moved my head to see what was happening. Crossing the cell and collapsing on the bed, hands covering his face, fingers clutching his hair, a man was sobbing. It was Pablo.

"What happened?" He seemed paralyzed in the same position, not moving his hands from his face. After a few minutes, which seemed to me like a hundred years, he slowly answered my question.

"My sons," Pablo said sadly, "told the investigator, if the Revolution needed to kill me for what I had done, they would accept it. There is no place in the Revolution for traitors."

I felt stupid standing silently in front of Pablo. The rest of Marti's phrase came to my mind, " . . . the ones who hate and destroy."

WORK! WORK! WORK!

These exercises help build skills by prompting you to express your understanding of what you read.

Reading Comprehension

1. José's story shows excellent use of dialogue. He also uses a quotation to advance his story and to tie it up at the end. What are the two types of people José Marti speaks of? _____

    _____

2. The student assignment was to write about someone you respect. Why did José respect this fellow prisoner? _____

    _____

    _____

3. Why is Pablo in prison twenty years after the revolution? _____

    _____

Writing Analysis

1. Where does the author repeat the title, and why does he repeat it? _____

    _____

2. Why does the author use dialogue in telling this story? _____

    _____

3. Why does the author weave Marti's phrases into his essay? _____

    _____

●

The following professional article involves a most unusual use of "dialogue" in that the writer quotes what his dog might say. This is not the sort of conversation that you would be expected to write, with alternating speakers; it is one long, uninterrupted quotation. You will see that, when quoted conversation extends for more than one paragraph, opening quotation marks are used at the beginning of each new paragraph, and closing quotations are not used until the speaker is finished. Notice also that when a speaker quotes someone else, as the dog quotes his master, the quotation within a quotation is marked by single quotation marks.

Phenomena, Comment, and Notes
by John P. Wiley Jr.

For a good part of this century, while the behaviorists ruled, science gave animals little or no respect. They were thought to be automata or, as we would say today, "hardwired." Dogma had it that animals could not think, that they did not even have consciousness. Case closed.

In recent years, however, a few intrepid souls, inspired perhaps by Donald Griffin of Harvard University, have started to take another look. Papers that would have been sneered at a generation ago are being published in research journals. "The Problem of Animal Consciousness in Relation to Neuropsychology" is printed in *Behavioural Brain Research*. Science magazines are not far behind: "The Emotional Chicken" appears in *New Scientist*. And Smithsonian ran an article in March 1985 that showed animals not simply acting consciously but apparently with Machiavellian intent.

All this is exciting, but it is not surprising to those members of the population who share their lives with what are now known as companion animals. There's no doubt in my mind, for example, that dogs not only have consciousness but also a sense of humor. It is very nice to see animals at last getting some respect from the cold hearts of science. But it also makes me nervous . . . very, very nervous.

At the moment a dog named Gizzie shares my life, not to mention my food and a substantial fraction of my bed. He seems content but who can say? My great fear is that we will not only concede that animals have consciousness, we will find ways to piece together at least a general idea of what they think.

It could be a rude awakening. My dog loves to go for long walks across pastures and into the woods (I think), but recently I've begun to worry about what he's thinking as we wend our way together. Suppose, just suppose, he sees a typical walk as something like the following. (Having no idea of how a dog might actually think, I've given him a mostly human vocabulary.)

"They're so hard to deal with. Disappear upstairs for hours until in desperation I have to give my strangled-puppy yelp. He looks down the stairs and says 'Just a minute.' Yeah, sure. Finally he comes down and takes forever to put those heavy things on his feet and then layer after layer of pelt. It must be so tedious to be a two-foot.

"Outside I have to walk toward the back gate over and over to show him the way. He doesn't see the flier sitting on the fence, its feathers all puffed out against the cold, until it flies. Something wrong with his eyes. 'Bluebird,' he says. So what, I say. It's too hard to catch and too small to eat.

"The wind is coming from where the sun goes down. It is heavy with the smell of the oversized grass eaters. But the smell of fresh manure makes me feel warm. I run this way and that, getting the kinks out. He straggles. As we walk across the field I have to stop every fifty yards to make sure he is still coming.

"When we come to the creek, I just walk across. What else? He stops, sticks out a foot, makes a big deal of stepping from rock to rock, finally gives a little jump to the other side. Why is he so afraid of water?

"Then the ground starts going up toward the sky. Big deal. I just keep walking. He comes up on an angle so he has to walk twice as far to get to the top. He is breathing hard like he has been running, but he has barely been moving. I'm feeling so good I can hardly keep my feet on the ground. So I race along the side of the hill, back and forth, in sheer exuberance. He finally makes it to the top, to the end of the pasture, to a fencerow that has come straight up the hill. Now I'm getting good smells, fresh ones. In and out of the bushes. Mice. Foxes. Weasels. Dogs trying to mark my territory.

"Across the top of the hill. On one side of us now are the trees that always stay green. I can smell the leaping wild ones. They're here; I know they're here. Sometimes I find places full of their scent where the grass is all mashed down: the places where they sleep.

"We're alongside the naked trees now, walking easily where eight-foot-high flowers made it tough in the summer. He always crosses the barbed wire at the same place, where a rotting log makes it easier for him to step over. Being vertical must be a drag. I can walk under the fence in a hundred places.

"As we make our way through the bushes on the other side of the fence, we emerge into another pasture. He follows a grass-eater trail that descends the hill on an angle, moving slowly down. I go straight down (the slope isn't that steep!) and get to the bottom in one-fourth of the distance. Here there's a truly tiny stream, and yet he looks for a shallow place to cross.

"Red alert! A hot scent fills my being and I'm off, running effortlessly with my nose only inches from the ground. I start the wrong way and feel the scent cooling. Reverse direction, and the scent gets warmer and warmer . . . and then ends in that same little stream.

"Across this pasture we come to the big stream and the pond below the dam. He always stops here and looks around, but I know there is nothing of any interest because we have walked into the wind and I would have smelled it. To go upstream we have to climb over a stone wall that extends out from the dam. I walk up and jump down on the other side and start to walk. Oops, no two-foot. I look back and there's Old Clumsy, carefully putting one foot on a rock in the wall, then another foot on another rock. The wall only comes up to his shoulders, but he acts like he'd be killed if he slipped. Finally he's on top and drops down to the other side, which is only a little jump.

"It's so much easier now than it was in the summer. But still the long skinny green stems catch in his outer pelt (fur is so much easier); sometimes he actually cuts a path. Across the stream a flier is making a sound just like a two-foot laughing.

"We're both alert now, because we're coming to where the underwater animals live. A furry face silently pops up out of the water; the animal swims slowly to no place in particular, dragging that flat, hairless tail behind it. Then it makes a loud slapping sound and rolls under the water. A few minutes later it is up again, swimming just as slowly. Old Clumsy always looks at me to see what I'm going to do. I watch it for a while, and then look away and pretend it's not there. He surely can't expect me to retrieve something as big as that, especially while it's still alive.

"The sun is beginning to feel warm now. Clumsy is taking the extra pelt off the top of his head.

"We get to where the ground is collapsing and there are lots of dens, some of them almost big enough for me to walk into. But most of them have no fresh scent, so I move on. Clumsy never checks them. Across the stream a flier is hitting its head against a tree.

"I climb down the bank and swim across to the other side. Another hot scent: I'm off, nose to ground, coursing back and forth up the hill through the trees. But up on top I lose the scent, come back, swim back across and have a good roll. He watches.

"Ever so slowly, we walk farther up the stream, past the place where last summer the underwater animals had built a dam clear across a shallow part of the stream. It's not there now. Ice hangs down from the roots of trees that have blown over. In one place the stream pushes us into a grass road that smells of gasoline and oil; this is where the two-feet play on their noisy carts that are too small for them. We go about a mile and then come to where wire stretches across our path. There are only a couple of strands, and I go under them like they're not there and try to lure him farther up the stream. But Clumsy always turns around here. There's so much more stream to explore . . . I really don't get it.

"On the way back I try to lure him into going in another direction, but nothing doing. He just kind of slogs along. I hear one flier singing and another singing the same song right back at him. Another one flies down the stream, making a rattling sound. The big fliers that swam where the underwater animals do and honked at us all the time are gone. The big dark ones that just glide around all day are in the sky, though.

"Climbing back up the hill to where the log is under the wire fence, I hit pay dirt. A hot den entrance. I dig my fastest, but it's tough going, with all the roots and rocks. I keep pushing my head in the hole and sure enough, the scent gets hotter and hotter. But the digging gets tougher and tougher, and so I break off.

"Under and over the fence, through the naked trees and past the green ones, and then down the hill again. Clumsy takes his same path; I gallop up the ridge just for fun. I time it just right so when he gets to the creek I come racing out of nowhere and cross just in front of him. It takes him just as long to get back over. Through the gate and back to the house. We both head for the kitchen: it's time for a biscuit. Then I climb up on the couch for a quick nap, while he touches the magic box and sits down to watch the flickering images."

Now I'll cheerfully stipulate that Gizzie is faster, has a better sense of smell, and seems immune to cold. I'll certainly bow to his night vision, which allows him to run across pastures on moonless nights while I stumble along. But does he really think of me as Old Clumsy? If I could find out, would I really want to know? The sensible thing, perhaps, is to let sleeping dogs lie.

---●---

Exercise Related to the Professional Article from the World of Work on Dialogue (conversation)

Reading Comprehension

1. What is the name of the author's dog? _____

2. The dog refers to "he" in his personally told story. Who is "he"?

   _____

3. What does the dog describe in its "thinking out loud"? _____

   _____

Writing Analysis

1. Why does the author use dialogue instead of just telling a story about the dog? __

   _____

   _____

2. Quotation marks are used at the beginning of each paragraph except the next to last one. Why? _____

   _____

3. Do you think telling the story from the dog's point of view is an effective choice of writer's strategy? Explain why or why not? _____

   _____

From a book review in a newspaper. *Did the commas just fall off the page? Fill in the missing commas and a missing hyphen.*

"The horses the adolescent riders and the sometimes cruel trainers and neurotic parents are primarily viewed through the clear eyes of forty-year old Lex Healey."

GRAMMARWORKS! Those "!(.:,—);?" Punctuation Marks: "Quotation Marks"

Quotation marks look like a pair of "double apostrophes" around words.

Narrative Dialogue Is Set Off with "Quotation Marks"

- Dialogue begins with a capital letter. When *one quoted sentence is interrupted* by an identifying phrase (she asked/said he), the sentence resumes with a small letter.
- When an identifying phrase that's part of the sentence follows the quotation marks, the *identifying phrase* begins with a small letter, not a capital.
  "Let's go for a walk," she said, "before it rains." *Not:* Let's go for a walk," She said, "Before it rains."
- Quotation marks go *outside* commas and periods.
  "Don't forget your umbrella," her mother said. "It's going to rain." *Not:* "Don't forget your umbrella", her mother said. "It's going to rain".
- Question marks and exclamation points that *are* part of the quotation go *inside* quotation marks.
  The police officer asked, "Where's the fire?"
  Robin said,"Holy houseboat, Batman!"
- Question marks and exclamation points that *are not* part of the quotation go *outside* the quotation marks.
  Can you speak "pig latin"?
  Marian knows all the verses of "The Star-Spangled Banner"!

Other Uses of "Quotation Marks"

- To set off *Quotations!* Any time you write word for word what a book or person has said, that is a *quotation.* Set it off with quotation marks, with one paragraph per speaker. (A quotation longer than four lines, such as a long quote used in a research paper, is *not* set off with quotation marks. Offset the whole quote one-half inch from both margins, and double space before and after.)
- To set off "titles of small works" that are parts of *large works with italicized* or *underlined titles:* "chapters" in a *book;* "articles" in a *magazine* or *newspaper;* and "songs" in a *musical. Example:* I like the song "Hair" from the musical *Hair* (or <u>Hair</u>).
- *Also:* To set off *slang, unusual* or *unfamiliar words* or *phrases,* and *nicknames. Examples:* You "talk the talk," but can you "walk the walk"? "Shortie" is six feet tall.

Don't use quotation marks with indirect or summary dialogue unless stressing some of it.
  Prissie told Miss Scarlett she didn't know anything about "birthing babies."

'Single Quotation Marks'

- Use single quotation marks when words that would *ordinarily be marked with double quotation marks* occur within a group of words *already* marked by double quotation marks.
  "Hey, 'Snail,'" Dex called to his buddy. "What does 'hasten' mean?"

GRAMMARWORKS! Review

In the following exercise, write the corrected sentence after each incorrect sentence. Use GrammarWorks! as a guide.

1. Max asked, "Who finished the milk"? _____

_____

2. "Slow down, Doug. Do you want to be "road kill?"" his sister asked. _____

_____

3. Did you read the article *"A Changing World"* in "Newsweek"? _____

_____

4. "If you really love me, she said, You'll take out the trash". _____

_____

5. "The boss picked up the bomb and yelled, Get out of here before this thing blows up"! _____

_____

6. Steve said, "I don't need to be a team player." "I am my own boss." _____

_____

7. The customer asked Michell "if she could make the decision." _____

_____

From a detective novel. *Who's the culprit who put a period where a comma should go—leaving behind a fragment—a sentence that starts without a capital letter, and a disagreement between pronouns and antecedent? Rewrite the following sentences correcting those errors.*

"When you want someone to tell the truth," Mason said. "you put them in a comfortable chair and give them every assurance of stability, sympathy, comfort—that is, if they're cooperative."

_____

_____

FIXING A BONEHEAD DIALOGUE
Read the paragraph and then follow the directions below.

WHEN SARIE MET HALLIE
BY RONNIE RETRO

(1) "Holy guacamoly"! Sarie squeeled to Hallie. (2) "Your wearing the same outfit as me!

(3) "Thats really no surprise you silly girl, said a smiling Hallie."

(4) Yes, but there are one too many of them at this party and I'm embarressed. (5) Said Sarie. (6) "Who'd have expected two people to ware shinny lime green shirts, skin-tite orange pants, and Black Boots to a wedding. (7) I thoght I'd stand out in the crowd, now I don't?

(8) Why are you so upset Sarie, Hallie asked? (9) Everybody knows that were twins."

(10) "But, Hallie," Sarie whined dramatically, "you're a *guy!*"

(11) "Hey, sis, guys liked to stand out in a crowd to, said Hallie."

Edit the paragraph above. Search for the Big Eight: circle misspelled words, wrong words, and wrong capitalizations. Put an X in front of sentence fragments, run-on, spliced, and fused sentences. Underline misused pronouns and verbs and the comma and apostrophe errors. Each sentence above has a number. On the lines below, write what you've found wrong with each numbered sentence. (Write what you found wrong with sentence (1) on line 1, and so on.)

1. _____

2. _____

3. _____

4. _____

5. _____

6. _____

7. _____

8. _____

9. _____

10. _____

11. _____

How is this story told? _____
How might the brother and sister illustrate teamwork or negotiation in this matter?

_____

Now you're ready to revise the conversation. Write it in your own words on a separate piece of paper.

WORK! WORK! WORK!

Writing Practice

The following prompts will help you pick a topic to show what you've learned about writing personal stories.

"A job isn't finished until the paperwork is done."

Exercises in Writing Conversation, the Dialogue Technique

1. Write a 750-word fiction story as if three animals are talking together about their masters, conditions in the barnyard, their hard or easy life, or a subject of your choice.
2. Write a 750-word fiction *script* using dialogue between a social worker and a single mother, or two strangers who meet on a bus or standing in line, or a subject of your choice.
3. Write a 750-word, double-spaced letter to a business quoting a satisfactory or an unsatisfactory conversation you had with one of its employees.
4. Write a television commercial in which there is a dialogue between a representative of your company and a happy customer.
5. Rewrite the Bonehead dialogue "When Sarie Met Hallie," using scripted dialogue.

"Or I'll huff, and I'll puff, and I'll blow your house in!"

INFLUENCING PEOPLE— PERSUADING AND CONVINCING

FIRST COMES THE DIFFERENCE BETWEEN *ARGUE* AND *QUARREL*

"Argue" is a fine word that has a bad rap. It originally meant *to discuss with the intent to resolve disagreement.* Over the generations, "argue" drifted in meaning from one extreme to another: from *influence*—when one person tries to change another's mind; to *quarrel*—when people exchange angry words. Don't you hate it when word meanings get ruined like that? In this section, we will explore the idea of writing for the purpose of *influencing others to change their minds.* Written argument is necessarily lopsided. Only the arguer, the one trying to change minds, has a say, as he tries to *persuade* or *convince* others.

PERSUADING SOMEONE TO *DO* SOMETHING

Some people are good at changing other people's minds. They are skilled in **argumentation.** The buddy who talked you into jumping into the ocean on the coldest day of the year may well grow up to be in the persuasion business, talking people into *doing* something.

There are plenty of everyday examples of people *persuading others to do something.* An advertising executive talks BoxCo into hiring *him* (instead of someone else) to get consumers to buy BoxCo's boxes (instead of another company's). An automobile salesperson tries to talk you into buying The Speedo Special because it has the greatest profit margin or awards the biggest commission. A boss tries to talk an employee into working unpaid overtime by promising a big bonus. Except for parents and coaches maybe, the persuader usually has more to gain than the one being persuaded. Our relatives are often great persuaders.

TO INFLUENCE PEOPLE

Persuade Someone to *Do* Something
Convince Someone to *Believe* Something

CONVINCING SOMEONE TO *BELIEVE* SOMETHING

Politicians are a different kind of mind-changer from the persuader; they are into *convincing people to believe* something. If the people a politician speaks to will believe that their programs are better than the worthy opponent's, they will get elected. The buddy who could always make you believe in his dreams of the future may have the skills to be a politician. Others involved in convincing people to follow beliefs are ministers, leaders of causes (civil rights activists and union organizers), and parents (who keep trying to convince you that you can do whatever you set your mind to).

Harcourt, Inc.

From the Entertainment section of a newspaper. *A TV pilot that didn't sell won an Oscar?! Rewrite the sentence so that it's clear that Bebe Neuwirth won the Oscar.*

Bebe Neuwirth appeared in the pilot for "Dear Diary," which wasn't picked up by ABC but won an Oscar.

_____

_____

_____

WRITING CAN INFLUENCE PEOPLE TO CHANGE THEIR MINDS

There are four critical elements to include when writing a paper to influence someone's thoughts or actions—to convince or to persuade them.

Credibility.   To be able to move someone to do or to believe something, you must be believable yourself. Having credibility means you *show why you're knowledgeable about the subject you've chosen.* You earn credibility through personal **experience** in the subject and by researching **evidence** to support your stand. When giving your argument, you refer to your experience and evidence.

Logic.   Maybe the most important element of a good mind-changing essay is logic, or common sense. As we exercise our *reasoning,* we are better able to *use arguments that make sense,* and we are better able to recognize when arguments *don't* make sense. When Chicken Little said "The sky is falling," he had the bump on his head to prove it. But while the bump was evidence of *something,* the smartest critter in the barnyard knew it wasn't evidence that the sky was falling. That didn't make sense because other evidence, like the sky still being up there, weighed more heavily. Beware of giving evidence that doesn't prove your point. Where cause-and-effect writing is like a mine field, arguing with fuzzy thinking is like quicksand. If you don't make sense, your argument will sink, along with all the credibility you established.

Appeal.   Another necessary part of a good written argument is appeal. Whatever it is that interests you, so strongly that you would try to persuade someone to do it or convince someone to believe it, it had better *interest the readers you have in mind.* For people to listen to what interests you, they also need an interest in it. As we said before, more often than not it's the persuader or convincer who has something to gain. An obvious exception to this statement is Dr. Martin Luther King Jr., who wanted to influence people toward actions and beliefs that are equally good for all people.

You want to pick a topic that will be interesting to others. However, if you pick a topic of extreme popularity, you will look like you don't know what else is going on in the world. You may have heard the saying "preaching to the choir." That phrase means you're trying to convince someone who already believes what you believe. If you use a topic that all students and teachers agree with, your audience might leave for choir practice.

Purpose.   To choose a mind-changing writing technique, you need to have your purpose in mind. What do you want people to *do* after they read your paper? What do you want them to *believe* after they read your paper? If all you want is to inform or instruct about something, you would choose the *process* approach or the *cause-and-effect* approach we studied in previous lessons. To use the *influencing* approach, you have to want to *move others to do or to believe something they didn't do or believe before.* You have to select a potent topic and write with passion, using strong, moving words. Don't write as though you're just letting off steam!

> ## FOUR CRITICAL ELEMENTS TO PERSUADE OR CONVINCE
>
> - Credibility
> - Logic
> - Appeal
> - Purpose

HERE'S A SAMPLE OUTLINE FOR PERSUADING SOMEONE TO DO SOMETHING

Topic: Quit smoking!

Credibility

I know how addictive it is. I smoked for ten years before I quit two years ago. I was sick and coughing all the time. Now I'm fine.

The Surgeon General, American Cancer Society, and American Heart Association all agree that smoking kills.

Research shows smoking to be the number one preventable cause of cancer and heart disease.

Logic

The sooner you quit, the sooner you will heal.

Your parents had heart and lung diseases.

You're setting a bad example for your children.

Appeal

You won't get lines around your mouth and a gravelly voice.

Your breath, body, and clothes will smell better.

What you don't spend on cigarettes is money you can use elsewhere. It's better than getting a $100-a-month raise in pay!

Purpose

You'll add years to your life so you can see your children grow up.

You'll add years to *my* life so I can see *my* children grow up.

Your children may not start smoking if they see you quit.

You can make a similar outline for a paper that convinces someone to *believe* something. But, you'll have to think of some *other* topic for your paper!

The following are student and professional examples of writing that influences others to change their minds.

The student author's assignment: Write an essay persuading someone to do something.

Frank Stovall is an African American in his forties, majoring in Computer Information. He plans to become a computer programmer.

Frank Stovall
English 120-2:00
Persuasion
May 2, 1999

Register to Vote

It is every American's duty to vote because voting is exercising our right to take part in the political process. Voting is the sacred trust of a free society. Being a well-informed voter is an American's right and duty, and you cannot vote if you do not register. Registration begins the most active process of citizenship.

Registering to vote is not hard: all you have to do is get a voter registration application, fill it out, and mail it to the County Registrar of Voters. You can find voter applications at post offices, at the DMV, and at some supermarkets. About two weeks after you mail in an application, you will receive a Voter Registration Card that tells you that you are registered to vote. Now you are eligible to exercise your right to vote according to the American political system—to say who you want to govern you and to express how you stand on the issues placed before you.

Before the next voting day, you will get a Sample Ballot in the mail. This contains the date to vote and the location of the polling place near you, the names of the people running for offices, and brief descriptions of the issues that you will vote on. The Voter's Pamphlet provides more detailed information on the candidates running for office and arguments for and against the various federal, state, and local ballot measures and initiatives. You will also receive political mail from various candidates urging you to vote for them and from proponents or opponents of the ballot measures. This information helps you make wise and informed decisions in preparation for casting your ballot.

Too many people take the right to vote for granted, and they do not exercise it; a look at voter turnout in elections can tell you that. People who do not exercise the right to vote shouldn't complain or cop an attitude about anything that happens on the political scene. I take offense when somebody says that a person's vote doesn't count or that the politicians will do what they want to do anyway. Voting is a privilege, a right to be exercised at every opportunity. The voting process gives tangible proof that a

Stovall 2

person can make a difference. It's the people who go out and vote who make the decisions. An old commercial said, "Vote and the choice is yours; don't vote and the choice is theirs." That is the truth of it.

I feel so strongly about the subject that I cannot say enough about people exercising their right to vote. I take pride that since I registered to vote more than twenty years ago, I have voted in almost every election. No one forces me to do it; I just know it is the right thing to do. Registering to vote is the important first step in gaining a sense of belonging to the American society.

WORK! WORK! WORK!

These exercises help build skills by prompting you to express your understanding of what you read.

Reading Comprehension

1. What four types of information does Frank say the Sample Ballot contains?

   _____

   _____

2. Why does Frank take offense when a person says his or her vote doesn't count? _____

   _____

3. When did Frank register to vote? Have you registered? Why or why not? ___

   _____

   _____

   _____

Writing Analysis

1. Does the author open each paragraph with a topic sentence? _____

2. Even though the author is attempting to persuade the reader to vote, does he consider the argument against voting as well? _____

3. Which of the four critical elements of persuasion does the author use most effectively: credibility, logic, appeal, or purpose? Explain your answer. _____

   _____

   _____

   _____

From the Features section of the newspaper. *Do you suppose they mean the trunk of a tree, or perhaps the trunk of a car, or an old-fashioned steamer trunk? Scissors, pants, scales, and similar "two-part" items are plural. Find the word that should end in s but doesn't, and write it below.*

Here in the world swimwear capital, it seems a man could find any style of trunk imaginable. Even if he hasn't exercised since George Bush was president. _____

In the following professional article, the author convinces *and* persuades. She wants printers (her audience) to believe what she tells them and to be vigilant in following trademark laws.

Printers Beware!
by Caroline R. Clark

Trademarks are a big business, and not just for the trademark owner. We see trademarks, not only on the genuine products that made them famous, but also on knockoffs of the genuine article, as well as on novelty items such as coffee mugs, T-shirts, buttons, bumper stickers, and posters.

Trademark law prohibits the unauthorized manufacture and sale of products bearing a trademark owned by another. It is no less an infringement knowingly to aid and abet the infringing manufacturer or seller.

For example, firms that print labels or decals bearing trademarks for placement on nongenuine articles and novelty items profit from sales to infringing users who, in turn, divert sales from the trademark owner. The sale of such labels, and their subsequent use on bogus goods and unauthorized novelty items, deprives the trademark owner of the right to control the trademark and to shape the public's perception of the goods whose source the trademark identifies.

Even honest printers must be ever vigilant to ensure they are not dragged into civil litigation or criminal investigations due to circumstances not of their own making.

SCENE ONE: THE INFRINGER

There are, in fact, printers who advertise and sell ready-made trademark decals on the open market to any and all customers—not just the trademark owner. For illustration, imagine the fictitious trademark, "Sonaip," of an imaginary well-known piano maker. A decal printer sells Sonaip decals to customers who could be manufacturers or rebuilders of pianos who plan to affix the Sonaip decals to the fallboards. One such customer's intention is to pass off his own new or rebuilt pianos as the genuine article and hence increase his sales and profits by exploiting the brand-name recognition that the Sonaip trademark enjoys in the marketplace.

The manufacturer or rebuilder thus becomes a direct infringer whom the trademark owner can sue under federal and/or state law. The trademark owner may sue not only the manufacturer or seller for direct infringement, but also the printer of the decals for contributory infringement. Contributory infringement occurs when the decal printer induces the customer's direct infringement and also when the printer simply knows or should know that its customers misuse decals, and yet the printer continues to supply decals to such customers.

If the printer supplies decals without knowledge of the customer's infringement, then the trademark owner's sole remedy under federal law will be an order prohibiting future printing of the offending decals. But when is a printer, to use the statutory term, "innocent"?

Monetary liability for aiding and abetting trademark infringement, including counterfeiting, will be imposed on anyone who knows that his actions would facilitate the violation of trademark law. However, "willful blindness" is no defense in an infringement suit. In Polo Fashions Inc. vs. Ontario Printers Inc., a case involving a printer of labels, a federal court in Ohio ruled that printers may not "be like ostriches and put their heads in the sand and ignore obvious facts that should be readily apparent to a reasonable business person." If the facts indicate a reasonable expectation that infringement would result, then a printer may not sell unauthorized decals without incurring monetary liability for the trademark infringement resulting from his customer's use of them.

If the printer in our example knows that Sonaip is a famous trademark, then he would likely not be deemed an "innocent" infringer under federal law. Notably, however, federal law places the burden of proving innocence on the infringing printer, not the trademark owner.

SCENE TWO: THE DILUTER

Imagine the same decal printer, but a different customer. The customer manufactures cardboard boxes for storing office files and wants to sell them under the mark Sonaip by affixing Sonaip labels bought from the printer.

Have the customer and the printer engaged in trademark infringement? Not necessarily. Trademark infringement occurs when unauthorized use of a mark causes a likelihood of consumer confusion; that is, a likelihood that a prospective purchaser would think that the source of the allegedly infringing goods is affiliated, connected, or associated with the trademark owner, or that the allegedly infringing goods were in fact produced, sponsored, or approved by the trademark owner. If the trademark owner's products and those of the alleged infringer are totally different in nature, such confusion might not occur.

But the customer may be liable for trademark dilution, that is, the erosion of a trademark's distinctiveness and hence its ability to denote the source of the goods. The law recognizes that a trademark's distinctiveness may be "whittled away" by its use on goods that are unrelated in kind to those of the trademark owner. For example, if Sonaip were perceived as being a trademark for storage boxes, soap, bicycles, cigars, and calendars, then its value in distinguishing Sonaip pianos might be diminished.

More than half the states offer legal protection against trademark dilution. In January of 1996, another level of protection has come into force: the Federal Trademark Dilution act.

There is a catch, however. To be eligible for protection under federal or state antidilution laws, the trademark must be "famous." Certainly, famous marks would include McDonald's, Chrysler, and Sony. But as to others less well-known, there is uncertainty as to what "famous" really means.

SCENE THREE: THE LICENSEE

Finally, consider the printer who, in each of the above scenarios, has a supply contract with the trademark owner to print Sonaip decals and sell them to authorized manufacturers of promotional products, or to the Sonaip Company for use on its pianos. Is the contract a defense to liability for the printer's sales of decals to each of the customers described in the scenarios above? No.

The existence of a contractual relationship with the trademark owner is no bar per se to a suit against the printer for unlawful use of the mark. In our example of the licensed decal printer, the license by its nature only authorizes the printing company to make the Sonaip decals for the trademark owner or to make authorized sales of the trademark. Any other use might trigger liability for trademark infringement, dilution, and breach of contract.

As demonstrated in these scenarios and in the case law, printers may—unwittingly or not—facilitate trademark infringement and dilution by supplying counterfeiters and merchandisers with unauthorized trademark labels.

Last, I should point out that I have used printed labels as an example in each of the scenarios presented, but the guidelines provided here extend to all forms of printing. Printing on stationery, boxes, T-shirts or any other medium is covered under the laws as discussed above.

———————●———————

Exercise Related to the Professional Article from the World of Work on Influencing People

Reading Comprehension

1. What does the author suggest that printers be aware? _____

   _____

   _____

2. What is a trademark? _____

   _____

3. Why is it unlawful for one business to use another's trademark?

   _____

4. The example the author uses for a trademark is "the famous Sonaip." For what product is Sonaip a trademark? _____

   _____

Writing Analysis

1. Does the author attempt to persuade you to do something, or does he attempt to convince you to believe something? Is the author successful? _____

   _____

2. What adds credibility to the author's dealing with a legal issue in the article? _____

   _____

3. What process must authors follow to protect their works? _____

   _____

 From the newspaper. *There are so many prepositional phrases, it's hard to know who thinks what. No wonder "Mr. Kay" is weak in defending his actions! Decide who did and who didn't think the president should be restored to power, and revise the sentences for clarity. You might make two sentences out of the first one. Isn't a capital letter missing also?*

"Mr. Kay" strayed from "Mr. Dee's" position on the issue of U.S. intervention in Haiti two years ago to restore the elected haitian president to power after a coup. "*Clearly*, it was *maybe* the right thing to do," Mr. Kay said.

_____

_____

_____

_____

GRAMMARWORKS! Those "!(.:,—);?" Punctuation Marks (Parentheses), [Brackets], Hyphens-, Dashes—, and Ellipses . . .

Parentheses (looking like half circles) enclose side thoughts and nonessential information.

The Two (or so) Great Rules of Parentheses

1. Parentheses set off information that is worthwhile but not essential to the meaning. Avoid enclosing a long parenthetical sentence within another sentence. (Beginning capitals and ending punctuation occur inside parentheses only when a sentence stands alone within the parentheses, like this one.)
2. Parentheses come *between* the previous word and the punctuation that would follow that word if there were no parentheses. (Avoid using parentheses wherever possible.)

Not: When Ko left, (before I did) he took the cat.

But: When Ko left (before I did), he took the cat.

Not: Ko left (before I did,) and he took the cat.

But: Ko left (before I did), and he took the cat.

Not: Karla leaves Sunday for Rome (not Paris).

But: Karla leaves Sunday for Rome (not Paris).

Not: Flo is driving to Reno. (Flying makes her ill.)

But: Flo is driving (not flying) to Reno. *or:* Flo is driving to Reno. (Flying makes her ill.)

The Hyphen, a short line with no space before or after it, is used to separate a word between syllables at the end of a line, and between compound adjectives (In-class exercise) and words (mother-in-law).

The Dash—is very disruptive. Use it sparingly—like a dash of salt. Make it by typing two hyphens with no space before, between, or after them.

Use the dash to set off an explanation occurring in mid-sentence.	Combine three flavors of ice cream—cherry, chocolate, and pistachio—to make spumoni.
Use the dash between a list of items and the first word of the independent clause.	Frogs and snails and puppy dog tails—that's what little boys are made of!
Use the dash when a change in direction takes place in the sentence.	He said he knew he could get hit by lightning in the electrical storm if he went golfing—but he went golfing anyway.

The Ellipsis . . .

Three periods with spaces before and after each one form the ellipsis . . . but if what you've omitted comes after a period that *ends a sentence*, you end up with four dots like this. . . .

Use an ellipsis to show interrupted thought.	I saw . . . did you know Sam's back in town?
Use an ellipsis to show hesitation.	Let's go to a movie this evening . . . unless you were planning to do something else.
Use an ellipsis when you omit something from a quotation.	*"[A] new nation . . . dedicated to the proposition that all men are created equal."*

Half-squares, called **brackets,** are used for parenthetical expressions parentheses (used [if necessary] like this). They are also used by authors and editors to enclose information [beyond the scope of the text].

GRAMMARWORKS! Review

In the following exercise, complete the sentences, inserting a phrase or clause that would be offset by the punctuation marks studied. Then explain the reason for using that punctuation.

(Parentheses) Example: *I called Tony (instead of e-mailing him) to ask him what the assignment was.*

Reason: information worthwhile but not essential to the sentence

NOTE: Punctuation marks go *after* the parentheses except when a whole sentence stands alone in parentheses.

1. Lisa is captain of our Neighborhood Watch (_____), but she is moving.
   Reason: _____

2. Drop me off at the store on your way to see the editor-in-chief (_____), and pick me up on your way back.
   Reason: _____

Dash—**Example:** *Henry likes to study every evening—except when he has the chance to do anything else!*

Reason: To signal a change from the direction the sentence seemed to be going

1. "Snips and snails and puppy dog tails—_____."
   Reason: _____

2. That woman in the red-violet dress has been staring at you—_____ and I think she's coming over to our table.
   Reason: _____

3. The cooped-up children, tired of being at the baby-sitter's, were excited about the trip— _____.
   Reason: _____

Ellipses . . . Example: *Mom said, "I'll make roast beef, garlic mashed potatoes, and . . . you did go to the store, didn't you?"*
Reason: interrupted thought

1. "I pledge allegiance to the flag . . . _____ . . ."
   Reason: _____

2. (Complete this sentence to show an interrupted thought.) We were all packed and ready to go when Clarysse . . . _____

3. (Complete this sentence to show a hesitation.) I'm going to donate my brain to science . . . _____

THE BIG EIGHT BONEHEADS!

- Words Misspelled
- Words or Caps Incorrect
- Sentence Fragments
- Sentence Run-Ons, Spliced or Fused
- Pronouns Confused
- Verbs Misused
- Commas Misplaced
- Apostrophes Abused

FIXING A BONEHEAD INFLUENCE PARAGRAPH
Read the paragraph and then follow the directions that follow.

BUGS OF THE WORLD, UNITE!
BY KENNY BYCHU

(1) I'm a bed bug. (2) I live in a house with a lot of other insects ---- flies fleas termites moths moskitos crickets and spiders. (3) When the windows or doors left open (only once [or twice] in awile) we have a cockroch or two visit us. (4) Ive ben elected chief-insect-in-charge by our household colony. (5) All of the insects speack different languages they came to this house from different places. (6) We sleep in different parts of the house and we are interested in different types of activities but we all like different things to eat. (7) Like clothing materials blankets wood food crumbs .... and human skin. (8) Recently a female Purple Cockroch has stopped by, he asked to join our organization? (9) Before we take a vote to decide if well let em join. (10) Ill persuade everybody to vote yes becouse we all get along fine.

Edit the previous paragraph. Search for the Big Eight: circle misspelled words, wrong words, and wrong capitalizations. Put an X in front of sentence fragments, run-on, spliced, and fused sentences. Underline misused pronouns and verbs and the comma and apostrophe errors. Each sentence above has a number. On the lines below, tell what you've found wrong with each numbered sentence. (Write what you found wrong with sentence (1) on line 1, and so on.)

1. _____

2. _____

3. _____

4. _____

5. _____

6. _____

7. _____

8. _____

9. _____

10. _____

The paragraph speaks about persuasion, but it doesn't illustrate the influence writing technique. What technique does it represent? _____

_____

How does the paragraph illustrate multicultural diversity and cooperation skills? _____

_____

_____

Now you're ready to revise the paragraph. Write it in your own words on a separate piece of paper.

WORK! WORK! WORK!

Writing Practice

The following prompts will help you pick a topic to show what you've learned about the writing technique studied in this lesson.

"A job isn't finished until the paperwork is done."

Exercises in Persuading and Convincing Using the Influence Technique

1. Write an essay of five or more paragraphs convincing someone to believe something you believe in, such as love conquers all, computers waste more time than they save, it should always be daylight savings time, or a topic of your choice.

2. Write an essay of five or more paragraphs persuading someone to do something, such as change the sheets every day, take vitamins, register to vote, or to do an activity of your choice.

3. Write a business memo of five or more paragraphs persuading the people in your department to donate blood to the Red Cross, go to the annual picnic, organize a company softball team, or to do an activity of your choice.

4. Write a two-page notice to the people who work at your current or future place of business convincing them to believe that employees will accomplish more working ten hours a day, four days a week, than working eight hours a day, five days a week, or that everyone should join a union, or that everyone should wear uniforms.

WORK! WORK! WORK!

Lesson Review

The following practices show what you've learned in this lesson.

SCANS Focus
Fill In the Blanks

1. _____ is working together to accomplish a mutual goal.

2. _____ is what businesses provide their customers and clients. When both the business and the customers are satisfied, it is called a _____ situation.

3. _____ is the art of resolving conflict. One who is able to persuade and convince others for the good of all is a _____.

Dialogue/Conversation-Writing Technique
Fill In the Blanks

1. Two examples of nonfiction dialogue are _____.

2. Two examples of fiction dialogue are _____.

3. Dialogue that uses quotation marks and flows through the story is _____.

4. Two means of showing who is speaking are _____.

GRAMMARWORKS! Review

Choose the correct word to complete the following sentences about quotation marks.

1. *Narrative/Scripted* dialogue is set off with double quotation marks.

2. Quotation marks go *inside/outside* commas and periods.

3. Exclamation points and question marks that **are not** part of the quotation go *inside/outside* the quotation marks.

4. *Underline/Italicize/Use quotation marks around* titles of short works that are part of long works.

5. *Double space before and after and double indent/Use quotation marks around* quotations that are longer than four lines.

Influence, or Mind-Changing, Technique
Fill In the Blanks

1. Written argument is used to _____ someone to *do* something or _____ someone to *believe* something.

2. The four elements of a written argument are _____ _____

_____ _____

3. I wasn't *convinced/persuaded* that Ike could *convince/persuade* Ira to lose weight.

Fill In the Blanks to Form Accurate Sentences

1. The ellipsis [. . .] shows _____ or

_____.

2. Punctuation *follows* parentheses except when a whole sentence

_____.

3. The dash [—] sets off an _____ or a change in

_____.

4. The ellipsis [. . .] shows that something has been omitted

_____.

3

Opportunities

Chapter 11

WRITING A REPORT

IN THIS CHAPTER

REPORT WRITING

THE SEVEN STEPS OF THE REPORT WRITING PROCESS

THE REPORT PACKET

REFLECTING ON YOUR REPORT

BIBLIOGRAPHY FOR REPORT WRITING

REPORT WRITING

Everybody knows what a report is. It's a writing task that a teacher gives you as a special project, a term paper, or a research assignment. Academic reports, the work done by students in colleges and universities, range from a simple undergraduate research paper to masters' theses and doctoral dissertations. Reports also are written in the business and government worlds to develop plans, prepare proposals, make decisions, and sum up the year's activities.

REPORTS ARE INFORMATION-GATHERING ACTIVITIES

Some written reports, like book and theater reviews, can reflect your personal observations, your feelings about a certain situation, or even your opinion about how a problem should be solved. However, most reports require information based on facts, evidence, experience, authorities, or surveys. Such information must be collected, examined, and summarized. The level of difficulty of the task depends upon the depth and breadth of the subject.

You don't need to create a paper monster for yourself—a project that seems to have no beginning and no end. Choose a topic you can get your arms around, something very specific, something that really interests you. Instead of writing about the history of baseball, describe the process of how a baseball is made, define the job of the first baseman, or compare and contrast pitchers Nolan Ryan and Sandy Koufax. Don't research the life of the Beatles. Write about what made them so popular in the 1960s, categorize the various messages of their music, or illustrate the social consciousness of Paul McCartney. Keep your subject simple, specific, and "doable."

Research shouldn't be a frightening word. We often think it refers to a complicated, statistically accurate, extremely long study of momentous proportions. It isn't always like that. Actually, all of us conduct research frequently, in very simple ways. When we want to watch television, we pick up the *TV Guide,* find the time when we'd like to view a program, and choose from the listings. Isn't that research? Selecting a movie by comparing reviews and ratings, deciding which clothes to buy that both appeal to you and fit into your budget, comparing labels on food items in a market—that's research. Researching is analyzing and sorting information and reaching a conclusion, not on our own spontaneous opinions or feelings, but on the basis of what the information suggests. Remember this: Let the information lead you, not the other way around.

REPORTS REQUIRE SEARCH, RESEARCH, AND RECORDING INFORMATION

In discussing report writing, you might encounter terms that are new to you: search and research, resources and sources, references, citation and plagiarism. We all know that **search** means to look for or to investigate.

To look for: Search the beach! I lost my keys down there somewhere.

To investigate: Police search a crime scene for clues.

Research means to *search again,* to look at what others have discovered about a subject.

Scholars research ancient Greek writings to discover the location of the lost continent of Atlantis.

Resources are libraries and other places you acquire information, and **sources** are the publications and authorities you use as references to compile information for your report. **References** can mean either the sources you use or the citations of the sources.

In writing reports, **search** requires looking for a subject to write about and locating the information you'll need. A library or the Internet are examples of *resources* for information. *Research* requires investigating the facts, theories, and information you gather. Once you've gathered sources of information, you'll research the various similar and conflicting opinions of others in order to formulate your own conclusions. The books and expert opinions you actually use in your report are your *sources* of information. The information will support the thesis and the conclusion of your paper.

Recording information *from the sources you investigate is the key to preparing a report.* Every time you identify something useful to your report, you will want to keep a record of it. Your record will have two parts: (1) facts about the source—the author, title, and page numbers, and the publication details; and (2) the information you wish to use (such as statistics and authors' opinions), whether paraphrased or copied exactly for use as a direct quotation. You keep the record so that you can make a proper *citation* for the source of the material in your paper. A **citation** identifies the source of your information and gives credit to the author.

Too many students mistake research with copying material from several books the night before their reports are due. They submit a jumble of information plagiarized directly from a few sources. **Plagiarizing** is using information that another person has gathered without identifying that person as the source. When students use another's materials as if they themselves had originated the information, they are guilty of **plagiarism,** which is the theft of someone else's work. Don't be confused. There is absolutely nothing wrong with using material from books, newspapers, magazines, journals, or other publications *as long as you give credit in your paper to the sources from which you obtained the material.* In properly citing others' material, students illustrate the time and effort they have spent in researching the subjects of their papers.

REPORTS CAN BE REAL WORLD STUDIES

Reports can be supported by real world happenings, such as your own or other people's experience or observation. You don't have to be a research scientist to know that Mark McGuire and Sammy Sosa hit a record total of 136 home runs between them in the 1998 baseball season or that Senator John Glenn orbited the earth in the space shuttle Discovery forty years after his first space flight. You can count the number of people lined up to see the latest popular movie. You can watch a marathoner cross the finish line or learn about fashion trends as Elsa Klensch introduces designs from Milan on CNN. Real world experience is a resource, too. Information gathered by observation, experience, or experiment is termed **empirical evidence.**

"WORLD-OF-WORK" REPORTS

In business, industry, and government, results of studies making use of empirical evidence are often called *reports*—sales and marketing reports and environmental impact reports, for example. Other reports based on observation include termite reports, soils reports, and news reports. Elected politicians make major decisions based upon researched information, such as reports to state legislatures about education and reports to congress about the success of health care in other countries.

In the everyday world, every major decision—from relocating an automobile factory, to building a forty-home development, to selecting a computer system for the finance department—requires careful study. Deciding whether or not to start a new business, preparing a proposal for a skateboard park, evaluating the management efficiency of the city government—all sorts of future and existing projects require study and analysis of important research endeavors, which someone composes in the form of reports. The ability to write effective reports in your job might lead to more challenging work opportunities for you. These are some examples of work-related projects that require research and report writing.

Compare and contrast health care insurance plans for your organization.

Determine the cause for the breakdown of an expensive machine.

Survey past motel guests to determine the most popular colors in towels and bed linens.

Investigate the process for starting your own home-maintenance business.

Categorize options for providing a Metro station shuttle service for employees.

Study the effects of the new employee-training methods.

From the Sports section. *Oops! Edit the sentence below to insert the missing word and the missing letter.*

William Burke, the founder the 26.2-mile race that takes place next Sunday on the streets of Los Angeles and a man noted for hs promotional acumen, admits that the average Joe isn't interested in the elite runners.

COLLEGE REPORT WRITING

Report Resources.   The primary resources of **scholarly research** for college and university students are libraries and laboratory facilities and occasionally oral interviews or questionnaires. In English, psychology, history, or social science courses, the most common report resource is library research—using books, journals, newspapers, and magazines as source information. In addition to printed publications, libraries provide computer access to the Internet, where huge quantities of reference materials—from abstracts to full copies of literary works—are archived.

An additional resource is the opinions of experts—people with personal experience in a particular area of study. You acquire such information by interviewing the experts or by having them complete a questionnaire—a series of questions you prepare for their response. You can accomplish this in person, by mail or e-mail, or over the telephone. If you approach experts by mail, write a courteous letter that explains your purpose and mentions your deadline, and be sure to enclose a stamped envelope, addressed to you, to make it convenient for them to reply.

In the social sciences and humanities, scholars study previous research and document new information about the true authorship of Shakespeare's plays, the major tactical strategies of World War II, and the theories of Sigmund Freud. Scholarly research in the laboratory sciences can involve conducting studies regarding the cloning of animals, the testing of new psychological techniques on human volunteers, and the recent DNA testing that proved Thomas Jefferson, the father of our country, also fathered offspring by one of his slaves. Graduate students perform so much research they jokingly say that Ph.D. refers to research **P**iled **H**igher and **D**eeper.

Similarities and Differences between Reports and Essays.   Writing a research report or term paper is very much like writing an essay. The similarities are that they both have a topic, a thesis you want to prove about the topic, supporting information as the body of the paper, and a conclusion based on the information you have discussed. There are five key differences.

A research report is usually longer than an essay.

For a research report, you must collect information from outside sources.

In a research report, you must acknowledge, with an accurate citation, the source of each item of material you use.

Harcourt, Inc.

For a research report, your own experience is not an acceptable reference.

In a research report, your opinion is not mentioned until you reach the conclusion.

Don't panic! We're not suggesting that you read one hundred books and write a twenty-page manuscript. To show that you understand the report writing process, you need to write a paper only six- to ten-pages long. The purpose is to introduce you to the report writing process so that you can apply it to future research and writing, whether in school or in the workplace.

Now we'll take you through the basic report-writing steps, to demonstrate what effective report writing is all about. Most important, you'll see how to document your research. Remember, in research, the *re* means that you're putting together material that others have searched for. However, you're creating your own original and authoritative document.

Be careful when translating words! Rewrite the ad in complete sentences that will make a toaster sound like a good gift, not a bad one.

Toaster: A gift that every member of the family appreciates. Automatically burns toast.

_____

_____

THE SEVEN STEPS OF THE REPORT WRITING PROCESS

There are seven steps in the report writing process.
1. Choose a topic

2. Locate informational sources

3. Record information on note cards

4. Prepare an outline

5. Write the first draft

6. Edit each draft

7. Prepare the final draft, and submit the formal report packet

1. CHOOSE A TOPIC

What will I write about? This is always the major question asked by students writing reports. If a teacher hasn't recommended a topic, should you chose a broad subject like "How the Allies Won World War II"? or "Five Hundred Ways the United States Benefits from Immigration"? No, definitely not! Don't pick a topic that will never end. Selecting a topic of limited scope makes the tasks of researching information and writing the report more manageable.

In a college English class, an instructor often provides a list of topics or a specific topic and purpose for your paper. The instructor might ask you to test a *hypothesis,* which is a statement to be proven or a question to be answered. Here are some examples of hypotheses.

"Shakespeare wrote for the common man, not the intellectual."

"Were women a more critical influence in pioneering the West than men?"

"The novelist Alice Walker chronicles the mental growth of her characters primarily through dialogue."

If your instructor does not assign a topic, you can choose one of the topics at the end of the chapter from ClassWorks! or you can ask your instructor to approve an original topic that particularly interests you. Once you've zeroed in on a topic, where do you find information about your topic?

2. LOCATE INFORMATIONAL SOURCES

Whether at a library or on the Internet, begin your initial research by gathering **general information** about your topic. Keep a record of your **general sources** because you will include them in the bibliography section of your report. Encyclopedias, dictionaries, newspapers, and magazine articles can provide general information. General sources are not adequate for report writing. They are comprehensive in scope and tend to lack depth. Some general references, like biographical works, contain lists of books and other publications that can direct you to the specific information you will need for your report.

For **specific information** that will become the heart of your report, use **primary sources.** At the library, indexes, abstracts, card catalogues, and the *Reader's Guide* will help you locate specific information in journals, magazines, newspapers, and books. Reference librarians can aid you in finding difficult-to-locate material. Computer searches on the Internet can reap abundant information on most subjects. (Remember to record the full Web site address of each source for the citation so you'll be able to find the information again later, if necessary.) People who have expertise in a field or who might be affected by the results of your report also serve as primary informational sources.

Make lists of all the potential information sources for your further investigation—the names and location of books, magazines, and other materials; the subjects you might want to research on the Internet; and the names of people you might want to interview. When you consult the library and Internet materials and the people themselves, it's essential that you keep a record of each informational source on a separate note card.

3. RECORD INFORMATION ON NOTE CARDS

Research reports differ fundamentally from other English papers because they include reference sources from which information has been obtained. You, as the information gatherer, must remain as neutral as the bee seeking pollen to make honey. Collect as many information specimens as possible, from wherever you can, to add to your research honeycomb. As you accumulate more information about your topic, let that information guide you. You're collecting sources of knowledge that dictate the direction of your report. That's what research is all about.

The written words of your sources formulate the content of your report. As the creator of a research report, you are like the writer and producer of a play. Sources of information are like the actors that tell your story; they give substance to your meaning. All the sources of information in your paper deserve credit, just like the actors in a play—only complete with all identifying details. We identify each source of information in our report on a note card, so that later we can prepare the list of credits. Recording the facts of all of your sources of information might seem complicated and overly detailed, but this is what credibility is all about.

Preparing the Note Cards. Keep a **note card** for each primary source you plan to use in your report. On each note card, record the **bibliographic reference** and the **topic material** you want to refer to later. The **bibliographic reference** includes the following items:

The name of the author

The title of the book or periodical

The subtitle of the specific chapter or article

The page numbers

The location and name of the publisher

The date of the publication

The topic material you transfer to the note cards should be meaningful to your report. We suggest you record two kinds of information on your note cards for later use in your paper: (1) copy verbatim (word-for-word) any sentences you wish to quote in your paper exactly as they appear in print; and (2) paraphrase (put in your own words) any material that you want to refer to in your paper but do not want to quote verbatim.

Label Subtopics on Your Note Cards. Your report is based on one major topic or subject, which is supported by a number of subtopics. Sometimes called *labels* or *slugs,* subtopics help you organize the note cards from your various references. You can arrange the note cards into logical groups that flow according to your outline and your report.

Note cards serve as your resource documentation. As you write your drafts, you'll refer to them for the quotations and information you include in the body of your report. Also, it is from the note cards that you'll prepare your working bibliography, which is the list of all the sources you've consulted in preparing your paper. You must be able to give full bibliographic citations for every directly quoted and paraphrased reference in the body of your paper. The bibliographical information gives your paper credibility—believability. *This is the core of research.* Further, you document your sources for others who might want to investigate the same or similar topics.

Researchers find that index cards are most useful for recording information. Typical index cards are white, lined on one side, and measure 3-by-5-inch (or 5-by-7-inch), like recipe cards. Completed note cards should follow the form suggested in the following examples. (*Note:* The sample note cards are based on a fictitious report on the automobile business in Costa Rica. They are provided as illustrations only and do not represent actual sources.)

On the *first* note card from a published source, write the complete bibliographic information. Below the bibliographic information, write the quotation or information you have selected, circling the page numbers where you found the information. Label the subtopic at the top of the note card, so it will be easy for you to organize the cards later. All information from one source *on the same subtopic* can be written on the same card, with the different page numbers circled. Each source will have a separate card, and each subtopic from each source will have a separate card.

When one source addresses *more than one subtopic,* prepare a separate card for each subtopic. Your single-source note cards can be numbered in the order you gather the information (i.e., $\frac{1}{4}$, meaning the first card of four cards from one source; $\frac{2}{4}$, $\frac{3}{4}$, etc.). On the subsequent cards from one source, you need to record only the author's name. Label the note cards with their subtopics, write the information you select, and circle the page numbers of the material.

Book Example

(Subtopic)

(Source)

(Pages of information)

Card $^1/_3$ *U.S. Car Advertising Fails*

Hall, Ralph J., <u>Auto Industry Failures Circa 1990–1995</u>, Bentley Publishing, New York, 1996.

(28) *The author suggests that the millions spent in advertising American-made cars in the Costa Rican media was money down a rat hole. Ford, GM, and Chrysler all tried to out-promote one another, and many of their ads didn't even make sense in Spanish. Most of the advertising was "redone" from the U.S. versions and didn't translate well in Costa Rica.*

(39) *"Several Costa Rican auto dealers bought American used cars in the United States, drove them to Costa Rica, wrecked them, and left them to rust on major highways. The police cooperated and didn't even tow them away." Quote from reporter John Saunders, <u>Tico Times</u>, San Pedro, Costa Rica, January 5, 1998.*

Magazine Example

(Subtopic)

(Source)

(Pages of information)

$^1/_2$ *Japanese dealerships in Costa Rica*

Thompson, Paul L., "Buying Cars by the Shipload," <u>Motor Trends Magazine</u>, Vol. 1, No. 6, April 6, 1998, pp 17–24.

(20) *The magazine reports that in 1993, foreign automakers made the following sales of new automobiles in Costa Rica: Honda (40%), Toyota (20%), Hyundai (15%), Nissan (12%), General Motors (2%), Ford (1%), all others (10%).*

(22) *"I'd never buy an American car," said Pedro Garcia, Costa Rica's Minister of Trade, January 7, 1993.*

(23) *"The United States never believed that there was a market for their automobiles in Costa Rica. Japan did, and opened car dealerships as early as 1965." Raul Sanchez, Honda dealership owner, 1993.*

Since these cards are for your use, record the data in the manner that is easiest for you. For example, you might identify three note cards from the same article using the following format.

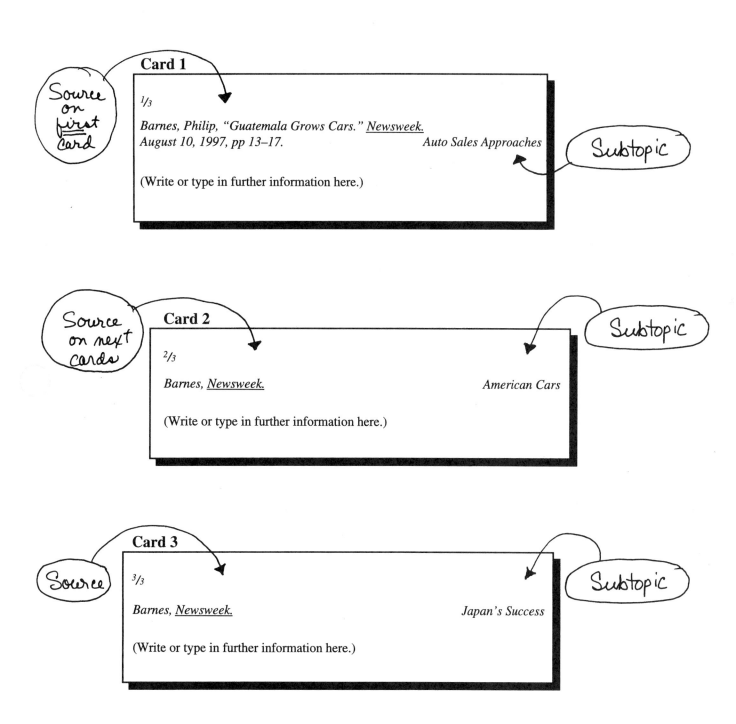

If you interview knowledgeable people as sources of information, you'll prepare a separate note card for each interview, showing the person's name and title (or why the individual is an expert on the topic), the date and place of interview, and the information they provided you. Label subtopics and number subsequent note cards.

Interview Example

one of
five
cards

reference
source

1/5

Roads in Costa Rica → subtopic

Ramos, Carlos, Yakima Valley College, Yakima, WA, student from Costa Rica. Interview, September 7, 1998.

Reported that the roads are quite narrow in the country, also mostly dirt roads with potholes and huge boulders. The best cars are small with four-wheel drive and stick-shifting mechanisms. Because the basic economy is growing coffee beans, bananas, and other crops, as well as raising livestock, "roads" include the fields, mountain trails, and rocky terrain. "American cars would fall apart on a typical Tico road."

When you have completed the research for your report, you can easily organize the note cards according to the subtopic labels. Arrange and rearrange the note cards until they are in the order you want the information, and use the subtopics as items for your initial outline. After you complete your outline, you'll write about the information on each note card in the "rough draft" of your report.

Writing Technique. At this point, you are ready to select the appropriate writing technique for composing your report. To decide the technique that is best for the thesis you're considering and the material you've gathered, review the approaches you've studied: comparison/contrast, cause and effect, classification, narration, definition, description, or illustration. As you prepare your outline, keep in mind the technique you've chosen.

From the Entertainment section of a newspaper. *Some of us reach our peak early in life; and some peak(?) behind(?) covered(?) windows at a club for only one kid! You can do a better job writing the lead and sentences in this article. Try it on a separate piece of paper.*

HEADLINE: Disney's New Realm . . .

LEAD: Kid's club in Westlake promises high-tech attractions for small fry and their parents.

ARTICLE: Passersby tried to peak behind the curtains that for weeks covered the windows of the new Club Disney at the Promenade at the Westlake shopping center.

4. PREPARE THE OUTLINE

Having an outline is a very important step in preparing your report. Arrange and rearrange your note cards to decide the best order for organizing the information you collected. Once you've grouped your note cards according to subtopic and placed them in the order you plan for your report, you are ready to prepare an outline. This outline later becomes the foundation for the table of contents of the report, in which the page numbers of the subtopics appear. The original outline can be a detailed one, with subheadings under each major topic, or a simple straightforward plan like the following example.

Sample Outline

(Note: Prepared by using note cards)

The Automobile Business in Costa Rica

1. Abstract of Research Paper
2. Introduction to Costa Rica
3. Overview of the Automobile Business in Costa Rica
4. Introduction of Japanese Cars
5. American Car Companies in Costa Rica
6. Competitive Approaches to Auto Sales
7. Japan's Success
8. Conclusion

Appendices
    Appendix A: References Cited
    Appendix B: Bibliography

5. WRITE THE FIRST DRAFT—THE ROUGH DRAFT

Before you start the initial draft, review your note cards to be sure you're satisfied that you've arranged them in the order in which you want to address the subtopics. To move the information along from point to point, adhere to one or more of the writing strategies you have learned. Let the information you've collected and organized lead your report to a logical conclusion. Remember that *only in the summary* does the researcher express a personal opinion regarding the conclusions suggested by the collected material.

By now, you should have a good idea of what your paper will be about and you're ready to start writing. First concentrate on your thesis paragraph, making sure to express clearly what your topic is and what the information you've chosen will prove about the topic. Once your thesis is clear, you'll add the subtopic information from your note cards and formulate your conclusion about the information. Your report might be rather short at this point. The text of the report will expand as you flesh out the information, making it flow smoothly from subtopic to subtopic, exploring the material through the writing technique you've decided on. When your fleshed-out first draft is complete, it will contain the beginning thesis paragraph, the supportive subtopic information, credits for your sources (the citations), and your conclusion or summary paragraph. This rough draft might not be perfectly organized, but it will look like a report.

While the pages of the final draft text *must* be numbered, it is good practice to number your pages in every draft, beginning with the first one you prepare. Numbering the pages is called **paginating.** Paginating will help you locate the places in your text where you referred to your source material. You need to number your report pages for two other purposes: to prepare an accurate table of contents for the final draft of the paper, and to prepare the references cited page for the appendix of the paper.

About Footnotes—References

The term *footnote* was originally used when the source of quoted or paraphrased information was credited at the bottom, or foot, of the page where the information appeared. As research report writing became more sophisticated, academics decided that footnotes interfered with the flow of the written material. In addition, it was considerably easier for the writer, and more useful to the reader, to have all of the references together at the end of a paper. Now, we credit sources briefly in the body of the text and make

Harcourt, Inc.

full bibliographic references at the end of a report. However, you may sometimes hear the word footnote to denote the new style of in-text reference, just as we still say we "dial" a telephone number.

The detailed references are usually listed as an appendix titled *References Cited.* List your sources in alphabetical order by the author's last name. If readers are interested in further investigating the topic about which you've written, they'll know where to locate available information. In the text, you'll refer to just the author and page number. The information is shown in parentheses following the last sentence of the referenced material, like this: (Abbicromby 3). That is the citation. (Abbicromby 3) means that the information can be found on page 3 of a book written by Abbicromby, which is described in detail at the end of the report. For information that came from an interview, merely indicate the name of your source in your footnote and the details in the appendix.

About *Not* Referencing—Plagiarism

Not referencing—that is, using other people's information but not giving them credit—is called **plagiarism.** The name of the president may be common knowledge, but a statement like this is not: "The United States lost four million dollars in a bond exchange with Cuba." When a fact that is not common knowledge shows up in a report, the instructor knows the information didn't just pop out of the student's head. The source of the statement must be given credit, or the student is guilty of plagiarism. Maybe the writer didn't take the trouble to identify the source, or maybe the writer is just trying to sound very knowledgeable. Either way, to use someone else's words as one's own is cheating—and for no gain. Giving credit to other sources lends credibility, authenticity, and power to one's own work. If you don't support the information used in your report by naming your sources, your report is unacceptable.

Plagiarism destroys the essence of research—the furtherance of the body of knowledge. In accordance with recognized academic research standards, always credit all sources completely and accurately.

6. EDIT EACH DRAFT

In preparing a typical report, you should follow your rough first draft with at least two more drafts. The second draft incorporates the editing notations you made on the first draft. Your second draft clarifies and refines meaning, smooths out organization and transitions, and validates references. Be sure you've applied the Big Eight Bonehead criteria to ensure that your report is free of errors. After editing the second draft for punctuation, spelling, and grammatical shortcomings, you're ready to type the final draft.

7. WRITE THE FINAL DRAFT

The final draft of the report should reflect your best possible effort. Your formal submittal will include the body of the report and all the supplemental pages indicated in the report packet: the title page, the table of contents, the abstract, and the appendices. Format the parts of the report according to the illustrations on the following pages.

About the Appendices

The appendices are sections *appended,* or added on, at the end of a report. The main appendices identify in detail all the sources used by the writer. Maps, graphs, photographs, and other material may be grouped together in one appendix or placed in separate appendices, depending upon the type and quantity of the supplementary material. Sources must be identified for each item contained in an appendix. Appendices are titled alphabetically: Appendix A, Appendix B, and so on. Your report needs only two appendices, references cited, and bibliography.

Appendix A, References Cited, gives the details of the sources used for your in-text references—*only the sources of information used in the body of the report.* **Appendix B, Bibliography,** includes the works listed in the references cited appendix, as well as any encyclopedias, books, and other sources consulted but not cited—*all of the references consulted in the pursuit of information.*

If you interviewed people and referred to the information they provided, include names, subtopics, and dates of interviews in both appendices. Many times, a report writer looks at possible references that do not contain usable or reliable material. The fact that these references were explored, in addition to the ones you actually used, is important and should be documented. The bibliography allows reference to every single source that you consulted in the pursuit of your information, general or specific, and shows how much effort you put forth.

The references cited page, which identifies the material cited in the text, will be shorter than the bibliography, which shows the extent of the research conducted.

From the Entertainment section. *It looks like these three actors are sharing one source of strength. Are* two *colons necessary? Rewrite this blurb to express what you think the author meant to express.*

Wanted: New Heroes: Schwarzenegger, Stallone, and Seagal lose their box-office muscle.

THE REPORT PACKET

Your final draft will have five sections that comprise the report packet:

Title Page: This is the announcement of the report

Table of Contents: This table lists the subtopics and page numbers

Abstract: This briefly suggests what your report is about in a few sentences

The Report: The body of your report will be from six to ten pages, with sources, identified in parentheses, following the information used

Appendices, Including References Cited and Bibliography, Plus Other Supportive Information (i.e., graphs, lists, charts, and maps, if any)

The following examples will give you an idea of how to prepare the supplementary pages of your report. Your actual pages will measure 8½-by-11 inches; the items will be spaced neatly on the page, with no less than one-inch margins.

Note: Rather than provide the often confusing academic formatting of such style guides as the Modern Language Association (MLA) or the American Psychological Association (APA), we illustrate student papers using a simplified format.

1. Sample Title Page
(Shows approximate placement of items on 8½-by-11-inch paper.
Leave wide margins at top and bottom of page.)

The Automobile Business in Costa Rica

Submitted in Partial Fulfillment of
the Requirements of English 28

For Professor William G. Thomas
By Martha Johnson
English 28, 8:00 A.M., M,W,F
May 12, 1999

2. Sample Table of Contents Page
(Shows format. Actual page is 8½-by-11-inch with one-inch margins.)

Table of Contents

The Automobile Business in Costa Rica

(And so on . . .)

3. Sample Abstract Page
(The abstract is a brief description of what your research paper is about. Actual page is 8½-by-11-inch with one-inch margins.)

Abstract

This research paper is about the automobile industry in Guatemala and why the Japanese have cornered the market through early entry, superior sales technology, quality service, and economies of scale.

4. Sample Research Paper Page
(Shows format. Actual page is 8½-by-11-inch with one-inch margins.)

American Car Companies Enter the Picture

The American car industry never had a chance in Costa Rica. Since the Japanese first entered the automobile market in 1965, they were far ahead in establishing a merchandising network in the Central American country. (Thompson 23) Public sentiment was also not in favor of the U.S. auto product. Pedro Garcia, Costa Rica's Minister of Trade, reflected this negative attitude when he was quoted as saying, "I'd never buy an American car." (Thompson 22)

Also, the Costa Rican terrain was not conducive to automobiles built for modern freeways and paved streets. Narrow dirt roads filled with potholes and huge boulders, and the necessity to drive off the regular roads (into the fields, on mountain trails, and in rocky territory), require smaller cars with four-wheel drive and stick shift mechanisms. (Ramos Interview)

Besides being a late entry into the auto market and not manufacturing cars that really fit well into the requirements of the uncooperative Costa Rican environment, American companies ran "rehashed" advertisements in the newspapers and on radio and television. Instead of creating appealing, persuasive ads relating to Costa Rican transportation needs, advertisements were merely translated from English to Spanish and rerun. (Hall 28)

(Actual page will be numbered in center at bottom.)

4

5A. Sample References Cited Page
(Shows format. Actual page is 8½-by-11-inch with one-inch margins.)

Include References Cited in Bibliography

Appendix A

References Cited

Anderson, Charlotte. "Costa Rican Auto Trade." <u>Motor Trends Magazine</u>, Vol. 3, No. 8, April 6, 1998.

Borellas, Carlos. Costa Rica Tourist Agency, San Francisco. Interview, November 17, 1998.

Carson, Andrew. <u>Rising from the Embers: Costa Rica's Emergence in the Third World.</u> NewYork: Prentice-Hall, 1993.

(And so on . . .)

5B. Sample Bibliography Page
(Shows format. Actual page is 8½-by-11-inch with one-inch margins.)

Appendix B

Bibliography

Allen, George. <u>Problems in the U.S. Automobile Industry.</u> New York: Macmillan, 1990.

Anderson, Charlotte. "Costa Rican Auto Trade." <u>Motor Trends Magazine</u>, Vol 3, No. 8, April 6, 1997.

Automobile Association of America. <u>The Encyclopedia of the Automotive World.</u> Miami, FL: Zenith Co., 1990.

(And so on . . .)

Harcourt, Inc.

REFLECTING ON YOUR REPORT

Once your corrected report has been returned to you, be careful to note all of the comments and editing marks. Consider the different approaches you might have taken in presenting the material initially. Especially ensure that you thoroughly understand the process of report writing. It will be useful the rest of your life.

ClassWorks!   *Assignment*

If the instructor doesn't suggest a topic, choose one topic from the following options.

Report Topics Concerning Your School

1. Write on a subject about another culture represented by a student in your class, interviewing the student as a reference. Consider customs, traditions, education, culture, sports, or a topic of your own choosing.
2. Describe the potential effects of replacing the centralized campus cafeteria with food stands at convenient locations.
3. Illustrate the necessity for creating increased on-campus parking for students.
4. Classify options to increase student loan funding on your campus.
5. Your choice, to be approved by your teacher: _____

Report Topics Concerning the Business World

1. Study the feasibility of starting a new business.
2. Determine how employee working conditions can be improved.
3. Recommend methods to improve customer service.
4. Describe the benefits of a flextime program for employees.
5. Propose ways in which cash flow can be increased.
6. Your choice, to be approved by your teacher: _____

BIBLIOGRAPHY FOR REPORT WRITING

Harnack, Andrew. *Writing Research Papers,* Second Edition. San Diego, CA: Greenhaven Press, 1998.

Holcombe, Marya W. and Judith K. Stein. *Writing for Decision Makers.* Belmont, CA: Lifetime Learning Publications, 1981.

Markman, Robert H., Peter T. Markman, and Marie Waddell. *10 Steps in Writing the Research Paper,* Fifth Edition. New York: Barrons, 1994.

Mulkerne, Donald J. D. and Donald J. D. Mulkerne Jr. *The Term Paper.* New York: Anchor Press/Doubleday, 1983.

Murdick, Robert G. and Donald R. Cooper. *Business Research.* Columbus, OH: Grid Publishing, Inc., 1982.

Roth, Audrey J. *The Research Report: Form and Content.* Belmont, CA: Wadsworth Publishing Company, 1971.

Chapter 12

WRITING STANDARDS FOR DEVELOPMENTAL ENGLISH

IN THIS CHAPTER

WRITING STANDARDS: WHAT TEACHERS LOOK FOR IN ENGLISH PAPERS

THE BENEFIT OF WRITING STANDARDS

Knowing your teacher's expectations of student performance at your English class level should help you establish what to expect of yourself in writing paragraphs, essays, and other papers. You can see by consulting the standards where you are and what you have to do to improve. The higher the goals you set, the more self-esteem you will have when you reach your goals, or even come close. Improvement in your skills and your confidence is what your teacher wants for you, too.

THE VARYING BACKGROUNDS OF STUDENTS

Because each student has a different background in English, it's impossible for everyone to write from exactly the same knowledge and experience base. Some did well in their high school English classes, and others did not do so well. Some students have been out of school for several years before entering or returning to college. Others have been studying English as a second or third language and are still working hard to improve their vocabularies and learn a very difficult language. The objective of the class is not that all students perform on the same level, but that each individual student will improve significantly from his or her beginning level.

American English originally followed the patterns of British English, but it has been greatly influenced by many other languages. Since the United States evolved as a democracy that welcomes newcomers from all over the world, its spoken language is mixed with foreign accents and dialects from different parts of the world. Regional U.S. accents and speech patterns, like those found in Maine, New York, Boston, the deep South, and Texas are difficult to understand. Some communities even have words and pronunciations common only to them, such as Brooklynese, Amish, Ebonics, Spanglish, and Creole. Lawyers are said to speak "legalese," computer programmers talk in bits and bytes, and medical personnel communicate in "doc talk." Where backgrounds are different, problems with English are different.

Knowing about how you are "different" and what your particular writing problems are can help both you and your teacher to understand your individual needs.

FOCUSING ON THE PURPOSES OF WRITING WELL

Developmental English teachers, while acknowledging students' many different English-language backgrounds, pretty much agree on common acceptable writing standards. Whether students enter the world of work immediately upon graduating or continue their education, all will be expected to have attained English competency.

- **Our job market requires that employees read and write literately.** Accomplishing work within our factories, offices, department stores, hospitals, markets, and government and service agencies depends on people understanding one another. This means you must be able to speak, read, and write English well to be employed.

- **Completion of first-year college English is a requirement in more than one thousand colleges and universities in the United States.** Entry into freshman English classes requires that all students be adequately prepared. Developmental English prepares students for freshman English. Successfully passing such a cornerstone college class can predict a person's future success in college or on the job.

For purposes of organization and understanding, we've identified *six areas for evaluating English papers* and *five levels,* or *standards, of writing performance* upon which your work will be graded.

ENGLISH WRITING EVALUATION AREAS

Teachers usually use these six areas of evaluation for student papers:

1. Significance of topic
2. Organization and support of the topic
3. Sentence use and structure
4. Word use and vocabulary
5. Use of outside sources
6. English grammar

SIGNIFICANCE OF TOPIC

Topics should be **important!** They should be of interest, meaning, and concern to you. It's far better to succeed in writing about subjects you know and understand, or for which you can readily obtain interviews or conduct research, than to fail in exploring the unknown. This doesn't mean you should pick weak and general topics. Throughout this book, prompts that relate to writing techniques and vocational disciplines are provided, as well as different aspects of student life, to give you ideas for topics. Writing about what you had for dinner last night or what you watched on television has less value than your thoughtful opinion about racism, unionism, love, heroism, civil rights, and work safety guidelines, or what to do about the homeless situation or about gas station panhandlers.

Topics should be **specific,** not general. For a short essay, writing about how a piece of machinery is used in a print shop is better than tackling the entire media industry. Unless you're writing a full-length research paper, how one actor prepares for a part is a better topic than how movies are made.

Topics should be **meaningful**—interesting both to you and to your readers, whether faculty or student peers. The importance will be apparent in the creative title you have chosen, which suggests the content, and in your statement of purpose, which is the thesis or topic sentence. Choosing a significant topic shows that you know what's worthwhile to think about and that you can think about such things in meaningful ways.

ORGANIZATION AND SUPPORT OF THE TOPIC

To **support** your opinion or point of view in writing, you need to state facts, reasons, examples, and other details that provide the foundation on which your opinion rests.

Writing a paper is like building a house. If you have no foundation, a house isn't going to pass inspection or survive inquisitive probing, and neither will a college paper. Each of the details you include in what you write must be relevant and provide evidence and information that help develop the meaning of what you are writing. Details should be ordered logically, from least important to most important, or separated according to the subtopics into which you may have divided your main topic—ice cream into flavors, football teams into positions, and so on.

A good rule of thumb is to have at least three items or reasons that lend solid support for your opinion on your topic. For example, you have said this in your first paragraph: "The three primary reasons I chose fashion merchandising for a career are creative opportunity, promotion by performance, and unlimited potential." Each reason then becomes the main topic in its own supporting paragraph, and each has its own set of three reasons.

Organization includes the outline or plan of the material, as well as the technique—or approach—used in writing your material, from storytelling, to comparison and contrast, to the use of dialogue. Does the design of your paper help in projecting its overall meaning? Have you put the *tail* or the *head* before the body of the horse? Is everything laid out and presented in logical and sensible order? Poor organization is like telling what the punch line is before you set the scene for a joke. Good organization is hardly noticeable. The writing flows from beginning to end easily and with meaning and congruity.

SENTENCE USE AND STRUCTURE

Did you ever hear about Dick and Jane? They were two imaginary characters in reading textbooks children used to study in the primary grades. Each of the Dick and Jane books was written in short, simple, complete sentences.

> *Dick sees Jane. Jane sees Dick. They see a hill. A house is on the hill. They go up the hill to the house.*

Boring! Boring! Boring! These books may have helped children learn to read, but they never communicated a meaningful thing. Your sentences must be complete thoughts, with nouns and verbs, subjects and predicates, *but you don't want your writing to sound like a "Dick and Jane" book!*

To make sentences readable and understandable, we use punctuation that indicates pauses, divides series of words, and notes the endings of complete thoughts. We avoid incomplete sentences, which we call *fragments*. We also try not to put too many topics into one sentence nor to use commas where periods belong, creating run-on sentences. To make our nouns and pronouns more interesting, we use descriptors.

> *Handsome, well-built, enormously wealthy Dick winked at the most attractive goddess he'd ever seen. In return, Jane blessed Dick with a heart-warming smile. Hand in hand, they climbed the path to a mountain cabin, where a For Sale sign waved on the post in the breeze.*

Now, isn't that more interesting than "Dick and Jane liked each other and got married"?

Sentences carry the messages for the messenger—*you*. In sentences, you carefully place the facts, opinions, reasons, and details that support the meaning of your written effort. *Any sentence that doesn't focus directly on achieving your purpose is unnecessary.* All your sentences must apply to the topic. They must be effective and well written. If not, the reader loses track of what it is you want to say. Your message is important, and it deserves to be delivered in clear, well-structured sentences. The smart Third Little Pig built his house with bricks; you build your essay with strong sentences.

WORD USE AND VOCABULARY

The words you place in your sentences indicate your thought processes and your level of ability to reflect what's in your mind. If you don't know the meaning of a word, look it up in the dictionary or ask someone reliable what it means. That's how we all add to our vocabularies, from childhood to senior citizenship. Could Uhg, a caveman, be projected here from the fifth century B.C.E., get hired immediately by Home Depot, and start working in the hardware department? It's doubtful. He wouldn't be able to communicate.

Psychologists tell us that we think conceptually; that is, we put ideas together in our heads, store them, and use the concepts and information later in our spoken and written words. But words form images in our minds. We know that people who have broad, expressive vocabularies appear to be intelligent. The real value in increasing your vocabulary is in expanding your mind's ability to form thoughts and ideas. Think conceptually and your power of understanding expands.

We shouldn't believe that people who use long or unfamiliar words we don't understand are showing off or being snobbish. In fact, those speakers would be handicapped if restricted to using small, common words. The *specific* words they use show their depth of knowledge and understanding of the subject, their level of interest in it, and their intelligence. In the same way that what we wear tells a considerable amount about our personalities, how we speak and write provides a good idea of what's going on in our minds. Writing well implies a person is smart and focused. Lazy, sloppy writing suggests that the writer's mind has been somewhere else, or he doesn't care, or she can't express herself well.

Your word usage is like a sign you carry that tells others what's in your head. Effective word selection and arrangement is a creative act, well illustrated by poets, authors of the classics, playwrights, and advertisers. However, we can learn the words necessary to get our ideas across and to understand others.

One mistake that's easy to avoid is repetition. Just because you've found a good, meaningful word doesn't mean a reader wants to see it in every other sentence. Even using common words like *I feel, then, usually*, and *because* over and over in an essay is tiring to the reader. Overuse of written words rubs the wrong way; the irritation is the same as when someone uses "you know" and "like" before every spoken phrase.

A *thesaurus* is a fine tool for writers. It's a great vocabulary builder, and it helps you express yourself more precisely. Using a thesaurus can help you liven up your sentences, but don't use a thesaurus word if you don't know its meaning! A student once wrote that he "bequeathed for work at 7:00 A.M." He thought it made him sound smarter than to say that he "*left* for work at 7:00 A.M." However, if he'd looked up the unfamiliar word *bequeath* in the dictionary, he'd have known it means *to leave something to someone when you die,* not *to leave a place!* And he might have selected the word *depart* from the thesaurus instead.

USE OF REFERENCES

You have to give credit where it's due. Since a writer places in written form what's already in his head, he is allowed to take it for granted that most people know the sky from the ground, air from water, and the difference between a dog and a cat. This is termed **general knowledge** or **common knowledge.** Sometimes information may come from places and people other than your own mind.

The information may be from **written material,** or in the form of **verbal statements** from knowledgeable students or other experts on a topic. As a writer, you must, and the word is *must,* credit any source from which you obtain information for your writing. Books, magazines, newspapers, movies, television programs, and other people are all acceptable sources. *To include in your paper anything that comes from a source other than yourself, that source must be given proper credit in the form of a footnote or an explanation (sometimes indicated within parentheses) in the written text.* Many examples of crediting information are in this book, and the topic is covered in chapter 11, Writing a Report.

Remember, if you use the words of others without acknowledging them in the paper, you're committing a crime called *plagiarism.* Using another's words as if they are your own is illegal; it's thievery, and, in English classes, it's a major "no-no." Credit your sources; then you can't be accused of being a "copy machine," *and* you'll get credit for properly researching your topic to support your statements.

USE OF ENGLISH GRAMMAR

Good grammar usage follows the rules and standards of the English language. Applying mechanics to meaning, grammar combines proper sentence structure, syntax, punctuation, spelling, word use, and semantics. Improvement in the use of the English language is what the person who moves to the United States from a foreign country strives for, while many native-born students seem to make no effort at all. It's hard to understand why people who've spoken, read, and written a language all their lives make mistakes in forming sensible sentences and misspell so many words. Fine-tune your grammar, and your thoughts will flow more smoothly for your readers—and for anyone *listening* to you.

When properly using language in your writing, you can be confident that you are communicating what you want to convey. The signals you send out from your writing antenna must be clear, meaningful, and well constructed. There are many examples of good use of the English language in the student and professional papers included in this workbook. Look carefully at the Boneheads. Figure out *why* they're Boneheads. They're excellent examples of what *not* to do to the English language.

THE STANDARDS FOR GRADING CRITERIA FOR STUDENT PAPERS

STANDARDIZING GRADING CRITERIA

In any field, **standards** represent the result of agreement among people who have interests in common. The standards they agree on make it possible for them to understand one another and for the outside world to understand them. Standards make it possible for people to communicate effectively. Student writing is graded on one of five levels, according to what skill level it represents.

ACCEPTABLE LEVELS DEFINED

Level 1—Clearly Superior

This criterion applies to papers that are clearly superior because of their compelling development and mature voice. The paper may not be flawlessly proportioned or even absolutely error-free. However, in a Level 1 paper, the writer accomplishes most of the following:

- Engages an important, specific **topic** meaningfully and intelligently
- **Supports** strong points with significant details, **organizes** coherently
- Writes interesting, complex, pertinent **sentences**
- Chooses appropriate **words** carefully, creatively, and sometimes with flair
- Selects excellent **references** and skillfully paraphrases and cites outside material
- Demonstrates mastery of most **grammar** and **usage** conventions of standard English

Level 2—Effective

Effective papers show good understanding of the assignment and sincere effort in its completion. In Level 2 papers, the writer accomplishes most of the following:

- Engages a worthwhile, specific **topic** in an interesting and thoughtful manner
- **Supports** good points, with significant details **organized** in logical paragraphs
- Writes interesting, complex **sentences** that are effective and focused
- Uses appropriate **words** thoughtfully, using some new words
- Chooses good **references** and adequately paraphrases, quotes, and cites them
- Observes the conventions of English **grammar,** with few errors in sentence structure, punctuation, capitalization, or usage to distract the reader—although work may contain occasional awkwardness

Level 3—Competent

Competent papers communicate clearly, but they lack the purposeful development demonstrated by better papers. In a typical Level 3 paper, the writer accomplishes most of the following:

- Adequately engages a **topic,** but it may be too broad or narrow or loosely focused
- **Supports** good points adequately, with clear if rigid sense of **organization**
- Writes complete, focused **sentences,** though not powerful ones
- Uses generalized, everyday **words** correctly, but with occasional misspelling or inappropriate colloquial language
- Selects and cites average **references,** understanding direct quotation and paraphrase, but handling them sometimes awkwardly
- Commits some distracting, minor, random **grammar** errors in mechanics and usage, such as poor sentence structure, nonagreement, or dangling modifiers

UNACCEPTABLE LEVELS DEFINED

Level 4—Significant Deficiencies

Significant deficiencies show that the student is not ready for freshman English. The papers lack the logic and development of Level 3 papers and exhibit significant deficiencies in their writers' abilities to handle written English. The writer of a typical Level 4 paper accomplishes most of the following:

- Responds with minimal effort, ineffectively, or vaguely to a general **topic**
- **Supports** statements weakly; may state a major idea clearly but develops it inadequately, with poor **organization** or with questionable logic
- Writes **sentences** that are hard to follow or too simple, dull, or repetitive
- Uses no new **words,** misuses and misspells some words, or chooses inappropriate, too general, or idiomatic vocabulary
- Selects few **references,** using quoted material in an inept or confusing manner; exhibits unacknowledged copying
- Makes repeated **grammar** mistakes in sentence structure, punctuation, and word forms that cause the reader serious distraction

Level 5—Serious Weaknesses

This classification applies to papers that show very serious weaknesses in almost all areas, demonstrating extremely severe difficulties with reading and writing standard English. The writer of a Level 5 paper is deficient in the following ways:

- Distorts or misunderstands the **topic;** is unfocused and generalized
- **Supports** inadequate points with few relevant details, using poor **organization**
- Writes incomplete or run-on **sentences** that may be markedly incoherent, or uses too few words to convey the intended message
- Employs too basic a vocabulary, misuses and misspells many simple **words** throughout, has very little sense of English idiom
- Uses few **references** and does not distinguish between sources and the writer's own points, copying large chunks without attribution
- Shows little **grammar** skill, making repeated, distracting errors of all kinds

TRANSLATING NUMERICAL GRADES TO ALPHABETICAL GRADES

DIFFERENCE BETWEEN LETTER GRADING SYSTEM AND NUMERICAL PAPER GRADES

For most of their educational lives, students have been measured by letter grades that average *all the work* in each course. They become categorized as *A* or *F* students, nerds or failures, with a *C* student assumed to be "merely" average. In an attempt to break a rigid grading identification system, some English courses, notably Developmental English courses, sometimes use a *numerical* system. The numerical method of evaluation permits the teacher to consider *the level to which the student has improved* in determining the final *alphabetical* grade for the course, rather than using an average of all grades. Some teachers allow low-level papers to be revised once, to give conscientious students the opportunity to raise the level of a paper's grade.

- **Acceptable levels** represent the standards of writing ability essential for higher-level English classes or for the world of work. A student whose final papers consistently receive Level 1 grades at the end of the term will receive an *A* for the course, despite a weak beginning.
- **Unacceptable levels** are beneath the standard accomplishments of an entry-level college student. A student whose papers consistently receive low-level grades will receive a *D* or an *F* in the course.

The outline and chart, on the following page, define the applicable numerical grades for papers at five levels of work.

AN ENGLISH IMPROVEMENT PLAN

THINKING ABOUT THE FUTURE

You're going to be using English the rest of your life. After your Developmental English class is finished, it would benefit you to continue improving your reading and writing skills. The English Improvement Plan helps you to *establish specific objectives* and *place them within a time frame.* At the end of this chapter is a form for the English Improvement Plan. You can use it to list both the activities that will help you achieve your objectives and the target dates for achieving them.

A few ideas for you to pursue in each of the six English Evaluation Areas follow. The authors hope you will develop a number of your own ideas.

DEVELOPMENTAL ENGLISH WRITING STANDARDS				
	Acceptable Levels			Unacceptable Levels	

Assignment Evaluation Area	1 Superior	2 Effective	3 Competent	4 Deficient	5 Weak
Topic	Important, specific, meaningful	Worthwhile, specific, thoughtful	Adequate, broad or narrow, focused	Minimal, general, vague	Distorted, general, unfocused
Supporting Points/ Organization	Strong, significant/ coherent	Good, significant/ logical	Good, acceptable/ clear, if rigid	Inadequately developed/ questionable logic	Weak, irrelevant/ illogical
Sentences	Interesting, complex, pertinent	Interesting, complex, focused	Generalized, complete, not powerful	Hard to follow or too simple, dull, repetitive	Run-on or incomplete, incoherent
Vocabulary	Appropriate, careful, creative, with flair	Appropriate, thoughtful, some new words, efficient	Everyday words without misuse, some new words, colloquial misuse	Inappropriate, some misuse, few new words, general, idiomatic	Inappropriate, misuse of simple, basic words, no new words
References	Excellent, skillful paraphrasing, good citation	Good, adequate paraphrasing, good citation	Average, some mishandling, understands paraphrase and citation	Few sources, uses material ineptly, exhibits uncredited copying	Few or weak sources, combines own words with copying, poor, if any, citation
Grammar	Mastery, almost no errors	Good knowledge, few errors	Occasional, random miscellaneous errors	Some repeated errors throughout	Replete with repeated errors

Topic Selection.   Establish a plan to improve your writing by developing brief paragraphs on specific topics that interest you, such as sports, food, clothing, music, sports, or gardening. Browse through newspapers and magazines and select the most descriptive titles. Improve your own knowledge of subjects about which you have general knowledge so that you can discuss or write about them in more specific terms. Another idea is to keep a diary or daily journal to record your major activities and relationships on a regular basis. Under *Activities,* you might write: "To keep a daily work journal." Under *Date,* you might write "December 20—."

Support/Organization.   Just as a firm foundation of evidence supports a verdict in a criminal trial—facts, persuasion, examples, analogies, and comparisons and contrasts all provide a strong foundation for your feelings and opinions. Whenever you write a letter, a report, or a personal story, an outline helps you to decide what to include. You jot down items that fortify your premise in an organized, coherent fashion. One example of potential improvement would be "To outline and write ten short stories to submit to ten different popular magazines." In the date column, write "June 20—."

Sentences.   How often have you heard the axiom, "Practice makes perfect"? It may have become a cliché as far as you're concerned. It's still true, though. To improve the meaning and intent of your sentences, you have to keep writing them over and over

Harcourt, Inc.

again. Using strong nouns and verbs and adding vivid adjectives and action-oriented adverbs can make sentences come alive and make them believable to the reader. Letter writing to friends and relatives is one very rewarding way to practice your sentence writing. It also opens up communication and continues a constant communication opportunity, especially with those who live far away. You might even want to locate a pen pal in a foreign country. Making your experiences and observations interesting to a person who wasn't there is good sentence-writing practice.

Vocabulary. The easiest and most enjoyable ways to improve your vocabulary are to read and to listen to people who have a good command of the English language. For your plan, you might list a number of books that you can digest within a reasonable amount of time. Check out a few audiotapes from the library, whether plays, mystery stories, or nonfiction interests you. You can even improve your language skills level by watching television—if you select any of the quality programs on the Public Broadcasting System, the Learning Channel, the Discovery Channel, A&E, or the History Channel. Set several specific objectives that you want to reach in the next few months or even years. You might choose as your activity: "Learn one new word every day."

References. If you're going on to higher education, read research reports in your field of study. Note how resources are credited. If you're entering the world of work, find out from your supervisor what research is required in your field and identify sources you can obtain in which you can study the challenges that may be present in your vocation. Identify references that may provide you with further information in your personal pursuits.

Grammar. Good grammar, as you know by now, is a combination of vocabulary, sentence structure, organization of thought, and having intelligent things to say or write. Your grammar improves through usage, through good listening and verbal habits, and through constant striving for articulate expression. Exposing yourself to good literature, interesting conversation, public lectures, theater performances, and continuous reading are all enjoyable ways to improve your skills. Open up your world. Set some new grammar development objectives, like studying irregular verbs.

USE A SPECIAL RESOURCE AVAILABLE TO YOU

Sit down with your English instructor or a faculty member in your vocational field of study and discuss each of the items in your English Improvement Plan. Make a verbal contract to accomplish each of the activities you've decided upon by a specific date.

If it's not convenient to have a faculty person's help, find someone else who can validate your future accomplishments. Someone who is skilled in the English language will be glad to help you improve *your* skills.

ENGLISH IMPROVEMENT PLAN

English Evaluation Area	My Level at End of Semester				ACTIVITIES TO ACHIEVE MY OBJECTIVES Things I Can Do to Further Improve My English Skills	
I WANT TO IMPROVE MY:	Achievement*				*TO IMPROVE FURTHER, I WILL:*	Dates Start/Finish
	O	G	F	P		
Topic Selection				X	Keep daily journal Subscribe to City News Subscribe to Newsweek	7-99 / indef. / / /
Support/ Organization			X		Write monthly letter to Grandma Write weekly letter to brother NOTE: Practice organizing by outlining info for letters	7-99 / indef. 7-99 / " / /
Sentences			X		See above Also, pay attention when reading newspapers, magazines, and books.	Always !! / / /
Vocabulary		X			Listen to "Books on Tape" — mysteries and nonfiction Use dictionary regularly for spelling, meaning, pronunciation	8-99 / Indef. / Always !
Referencing			X		Meet with boss to find out best publications about our business. Read articles in those magazines and periodicals	5-99 / / 5-99 / indef.
Grammar			X		Attend six plays Use dictionary for verb tenses and usage. Also check Elements of Style by Strunk & White.	7-99 / 8-99 Always ! / /
Classes to Take	Freshman English American Literature (Santa Barbara, CA or Klamath Falls, OR)					9-99 / 12-99 9-00 / 12-00 /
Workshops to Attend	Check on scholarships available for Writers Conference					1-00/ 6-00/ /
Books to Read	Steinbeck - Cannery Row Walker - The Color Purple or Morrison, Beloved Hemingway - The Old Man and The Sea BUY: Strunk & White's Elements of Style					7-99 / 8-99/ 9-99/ always !

*O = Outstanding   G = Good   F = Fair   P = Poor

Harcourt, Inc.

ENGLISH IMPROVEMENT PLAN						
English Evaluation Area	**My Level at End of Semester**				**ACTIVITIES TO ACHIEVE MY OBJECTIVES** **Things I Can Do** **to Further Improve My English Skills**	
I WANT TO IMPROVE MY:	**Achievement***				*TO IMPROVE FURTHER, I WILL:*	**Dates Start/Finish**
	O	**G**	**F**	**P**		
Topic Selection					_____ _____ _____ _____	/ / / /
Support/ Organization					_____ _____ _____ _____	/ / / /
Sentences					_____ _____ _____ _____	/ / / /
Vocabulary					_____ _____ _____ _____	/ / / /
Referencing					_____ _____ _____ _____	/ / / /
Grammar					_____ _____ _____ _____	/ / / /
Classes to Take	_____ _____ _____					/ / /
Workshops to Attend	_____ _____ _____					/ / /
Books to Read	_____ _____ _____					/ / /
*O = Outstanding		**G = Good**		**F = Fair**		**P = Poor**

Chapter 13

COMPUTER FUNDAMENTALS

IN THIS CHAPTER

SECTION 1—FUNDAMENTALS

WHY LEARN ABOUT COMPUTERS?

It has been said that an invention appears when it is needed. The computer definitely fits that description. In addition, the personal computer has exploded onto the scene during your lifetime. Barring any unforeseen catastrophe, computers are here to stay.

There are people who fear that computers are having a dehumanizing effect. This is a pessimistic view of the computer's impact on society. Optimists believe that the computer will improve the world's cultures by allowing people not only to be more productive but to have more free time to be creative. This means that an enlightened approach to computer technology is a must. It seems clear that students, in order to be prepared for the future, will need four basic skills:

1. Reading
2. Writing
3. Arithmetic
4. Computer literacy (a basic knowledge of computers and their use)

FEAR NOT!

Computerphobia is the fear of computers. According to a study at St. Joseph's University, Philadelphia, at least 30 percent of the daily users of computers have some degree of computerphobia. Victims range from high blood pressure sufferers to a policeman who shot the computer console in his police car. As more computers find their way into schools, workplaces, and homes, we need to combat this fear and frustration with knowledge.

Some fear when using a computer is normal, especially for beginners. It is human nature to be afraid of what we do not know and understand; however, remember the words of Franklin D. Roosevelt:

> *The only thing we have to fear is fear itself.*
>
> *—December 1942*

The more you learn about computers, and the more you use them, the more friendly they become.

THE COMPUTER: WHAT IS IT?

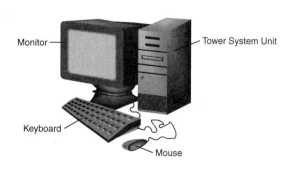

The computer is a remarkable device. Yet, it is just another appliance. A computer is a machine built from plastic, metal, and wires. It is designed to automate routine tasks. Inside the computer there are wires and cables, nuts and bolts, and a whole array of electronic things that you probably will never see or even touch. *That's okay.* The same is true of your radio and TV, and you have enjoyed their use and function.

The physical parts of the computer that you can see and touch are referred to as **hardware.** The monitor, the keyboard, and the "box" that houses the computer system are all hardware items. Computer hardware can include other devices that are connected to the computer, called **peripherals.** Some peripherals are the printer, mouse, scanner, and speakers.

The electronic instructions people write that tell the computer what to do are known as **software.** Although the computer is capable of performing marvelous tasks, it cannot accomplish any of those tasks without the instructions that software programs provide. When the computer is using a particular software program, it is said to be "running the program." Software programs instruct the computer how to interact with the user as well as how to use whatever hardware devices are attached to the computer.

THE CENTRAL PROCESSING UNIT

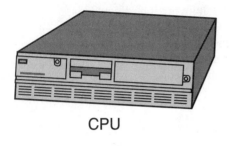

CPU

The **Central Processing Unit (CPU)** is the heart of a computer system. It is the unit that does all the work that you ask the computer to do. The CPU contains all the components with which the computer processes and stores data that you enter and use. It is the brain of the **computer memory.** One way to categorize computer memory is by how you use that memory. Some computer memory chips always hold the same data. The data in these chips can be read only. Since the data cannot be changed, the memory is called **read only memory,** or **ROM.**

Memory that *can* be changed is called **random access memory,** or **RAM.** The purpose of RAM is to store computer programs and data.

Magnetic Storage

There are three common magnetic storage devices:
1. Floppy disk drives
2. Hard disk drives
3. Tape drives

All of the magnetic storage devices use similar techniques for writing and reading data. The surfaces of each device are coated with a magnetically sensitive material, usually iron oxide. Iron oxide reacts to a magnetic field. The **read/write heads** of magnetic storage devices contain electromagnets that charge the particles of iron on the storage medium as the latter passes by the head. The read/write heads record data by altering the direction of the current in the electromagnets.

5 1/4 inch   3 1/2 inch

Floppy Disk Drive. A floppy disk drive is a device that reads and writes data to and from a floppy disk, also called a **diskette.** A floppy diskette is a round, flat piece of plastic coated with iron oxide and is encased in a plastic or vinyl cover. Floppies come in two sizes: $5\frac{1}{4}$ inch and $3\frac{1}{2}$ inch. These sizes refer to the physical diameter of the disk not to the capacity of memory. See figures to the right. (The $5\frac{1}{4}$-inch disk is virtually obsolete.)

Hard Disk Drive. A hard disk drive is the primary storage device for computers. A hard disk is a stack of metal platters, usually made of aluminum, that spins on one spindle. Each platter is coated with iron oxide and is encased in a sealed chamber. The major difference between floppy disks and hard disks is that hard disks are rigid.

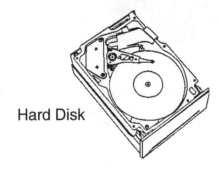

Hard Disk

THE MONITOR

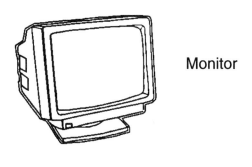

Monitor

The **monitor** is an output device. It looks like a television screen and works the same way. Your TV has a **cathode ray tube (CRT)** and so does the computer monitor. The monitor is also called *the screen, the display,* or *the CRT.* It shows both the information you type on the keyboard and the computer's response to queries. When you press keys on the keyboard, the typed letters appear on the monitor. When you enter a computer command, you see the computer's response to that command displayed on the monitor.

Monitors can be **monochrome,** which means that you see only one color on the background; or they can be **color,** which means that you can see a range of colors.

THE KEYBOARD

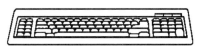

Keyboard

The **keyboard** is an input device. It allows you to give instructions to the computer. The keyboard has all the keys that a typewriter has, plus a few keys that are unique to computer instructions and commands. It contains a set of alphanumeric (letters and numbers) keys for entering text, arrow keys for moving around on the screen, and function keys (F1, F2, F3, etc., through F12) for entering commands. There are also some special function keys:

Alt (Alternative), on some computers "Option"
Ctrl (Con**tr**o**l)**
Esc (Escape), on some computers "Alt"
When used with other keys, these keys assist in the activation of special features.

THE MOUSE

Mouse

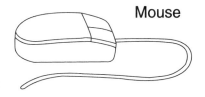

The **mouse** is another input device, like the keyboard. The mouse, on the other hand, can be easier to use than the keyboard since you do not need to remember computer commands and key combinations. You simply place the mouse pointer at an object or command on the monitor and press a button on the mouse to make the selection that tells the computer what to do.

Mouse Anatomy. The mouse comes in different sizes and shapes. They are all designed to fit easily *under* the palm of your hand, and they all have the same input function. On the underside of the mouse is a tracking ball that translates the mouse's movements into input signals that the computer can understand.

Using the Mouse. Like the keyboard, the mouse allows you to communicate with the computer. You move the mouse around on the *mouse pad* to move a mouse pointer around on the computer screen.

Software programs designed for use with the mouse display a *mouse pointer* on the screen. Mouse pointers come in different sizes and shapes. The pointer can be an arrow, an I-beam, a small rectangle, or a small hand with a pointing finger. To move the pointer, you gently slide the mouse around on the mouse pad. When you move the mouse to the right, the pointer moves right; when you move the mouse to

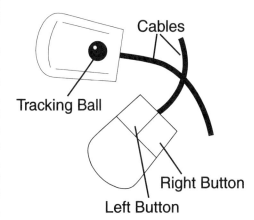

Cables

Tracking Ball

Right Button

Left Button

the left, the pointer moves left, and so on. In other words, whatever the direction you move the mouse, the pointer follows.

- **Pointing.** To point, move the mouse on the mouse pad until the tip of the mouse pointer is on the item to which you want to point.
- **Clicking.** To click on an item, point to it and then hold the mouse steady while you depress and release the left mouse button. A single click is used to select something.
- **Double-Clicking.** To double-click, hold the mouse steady while you quickly press and release the mouse button twice. A double-click initiates a function.
- **Dragging.** To drag, hold down the left mouse button, and move the mouse to a new position. Use "click and drag" to move objects around on the screen.

PRINTERS

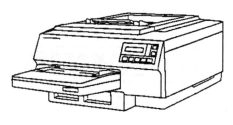

Printer

Once you input information into the computer, you will probably want to get it out. **Printers** are output devices. They let you output information stored in the computer by printing it onto paper. This paper printout is usually referred to as a **hard copy.**

　Before the computer sends data for printing, it checks the printer's status:

- Is the printer turned on?
- Is it ready to accept commands?
- Is it off-line?
- Is it out of paper?
- Is it not working for some other reason?

Only when the computer determines that the printer is online and ready to accept commands can it send data to be printed.

COMPUTER NETWORK

At one time, computers were unique unto themselves. They were designed to be used by one person at a time and for one task at a time. That is why they are called **personal computers (PCs).** However, the world of computing has grown and PCs can be linked into groups called **networks.**

The computers in a network are managed by a more powerful PC called a **server.** (See the illustration on p. 307.) The server stores the software programs and files that those users of the computer system have attached to the network. The server also controls the flow of data. Security systems make sure that only the people who are supposed to access certain data and applications can do so. A network administrator makes certain that the network is running smoothly and that all users have access to the information they need.

When a computer is connected to a network, you will not notice a performance difference during your use. Each computer acts the same as though it were not connected to the network. Each computer performs like it is a stand-alone computer. You will be sharing the same data files as others on the network. You can rest assured that everyone on the network is using the most up-to-date information and programs.

GETTING STARTED

To use a computer attached to a network, you must go through a log-on procedure. Specific log-on and log-off procedures differ from network to network. Once you determine that your computer is on a network, do not hesitate to ask for the log-on process to be explained to you.

Harcourt, Inc.

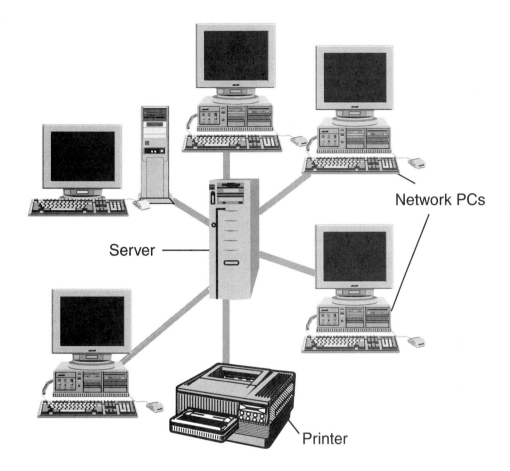

Server

Network PCs

Printer

SECTION 2—WORD PROCESSING

MICROSOFT WORD FOR WINDOWS 6.0

Microsoft Word for Windows is an easy-to-use word processing program designed for creating, editing, and printing documents. Most of the time the product is referred to as **Word** rather than by using its full name, **Microsoft Word for Windows.**

If you have not worked with a word processor, be prepared to be surprised at how easy it is to use the program. The best way to learn how a word processing program works is to use it. Word comes with an assortment of features to prepare your document, dress it up, and print it to paper. In addition to the basics of entering text, making corrections, and printing, you can:

- Change the size of letters and spacing to create professional-looking documents, such as letters, resumes, and reports
- Automatically check spelling and correct mistakes
- Include pictures in your documents
- Display information in tables
- Automatically generate headers, footers, footnotes, and page numbers

The advantage that word processing has over the typewriter is its ability to save documents onto a disk—hard drive or diskette. Documents can be retrieved back onto the monitor so that you can continue working on the document, make revisions, or print it out.

STARTING WORD

You must start Windows before you can start Word. When Windows is up and running, it will display the **Program Manager** screen on the monitor. If you have little or no experience with a mouse or with Windows, you might want to click on the *H*elp option in Program Manager. A menu list will be displayed. The **Windows Tutorial** option will walk you through exercises on how to use the mouse and how Windows works. You may want to go through the tutorial. (In Windows 95, it is even easier to access the Word program. But since many schools still use Windows 3.1, we are giving the instructions according to that format.)

To start Word, the Microsoft Office group window must be open or the Microsoft Office Menu must be displayed. If the **Microsoft Menu (MOM)** is displayed at the top right of your screen, use the mouse to point to the **Word (W) button.** One click allows you to start the program. If the Microsoft Office group window is displayed, point your mouse at the Microsoft **Word** icon and click the screen mouse button twice.

A **Tip of the Day** dialogue box may appear. It might look like the example shown:
Each time the Tip of the Day window opens, it contains a different hint or tip. These tips are designed to help you be more productive while using Word. If a Tip of the Day dialogue box does open, point the mouse pointer to the **OK** button and click the mouse button once to close the dialogue box.

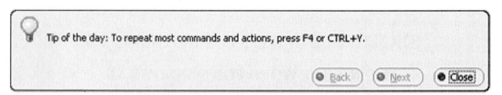

Tip of the day: To repeat most commands and actions, press F4 or CTRL+Y.

Back   Next   Close

PARTS OF THE WORD SCREEN

When you start Word, the screen is displayed as shown below.
The Word screen consists of a variety of features to make your work creating a document more efficient.

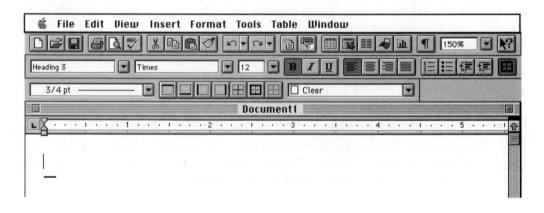

Harcourt, Inc.

The Toolbar

The standard toolbar is a bar across the top of the Word screen. It is just below the menu bar. It contains twenty-one icon buttons or small graphical images. These icons represent frequently used Word commands. Selecting a button on the standard toolbar is a lot faster than pulling down menu lists and choosing the desired commands.

To select a toolbar button, use the mouse pointer to point and click once on the desired icon button.

To find out which command the toolbar button repre-

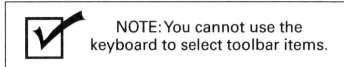

NOTE: You cannot use the keyboard to select toolbar items.

sents, point to the button but do not click. By hesitating on the button, a brief description of the command or task appears. The following ten icons are parts of the standard toolbar.

PURPOSES OF THE TEN BUTTONS OR ICONS
1. Starts a new document
2. Opens an existing document
3. Saves the current document
4. Prints the entire document
5. Previews the full document
6. Checks the spelling
7. Cuts selected items to the clipboard
8. Copies selected text to Office Clipboard
9. Pastes items from clipboard
10. Copies formatting

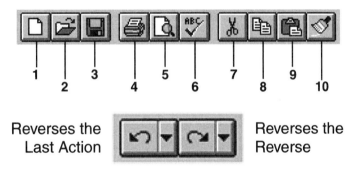

Reverses the Last Action

Reverses the Reverse

PURPOSES OF THE EIGHT BUTTONS OR ICONS
1. Aligns left
2. Aligns centered
3. Aligns right
4. Fully justifies
5. Makes numbered list
6. Makes bulleted list
7. Indents left
8. Indents right

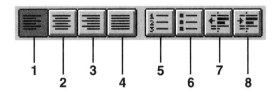

Notice that when an icon button is selected it appears to be pressed. See number 1 above.

Document Preparation

The following is an overview of how to prepare a document using Word.

Entering Document Text.   If the document has a title, you may want to format the title lines. You can center the title, make it bold type, underline, italicize, or enlarge it, or use some combination of these features. Choose the desired format button before typing the title (and deselect it when you finish the title). Begin entering the body of your document as you would if you were using a typewriter. The major difference in using a computer keyboard is that you need not press the return, or enter, key when you come to the end of a line of text. Word will automatically wrap the sentence to the next line. The **enter key** is used when you want to start a new paragraph or create a blank line.

As you enter information on the screen, watch the status line change as the cursor moves across the screen and down. The cursor is the marker that shows the position where data can be entered. It takes a little time to get used to checking and using the status information. It might be hard for you to look at the screen as you are entering text. When most of us learned to type, we were told to keep our eyes on the material we were typing. To become proficient with a word processing program like Word, you may have to modify some of those old habits.

Saving the Document.   If your document has more than one page, it is recommended that you save after each page. The reason is that, if something happens to the computer network, your entire document will not be lost. In addition, you should save after every major change—after spell-checking or adding a graph, a picture, or a table.

To save, use the toolbar button that looks like a diskette. When you save the document the first time, you must assign a **file name** to it. The file name can be eight characters or less. If you do not give your document a name, Word automatically assigns **doc1** as the file name of your document.

Editing the Document.   When you want to make any kind of change to a document, you **edit** it. Editing tasks include correcting errors, replacing old text with new text, copying and deleting text, adding and deleting graphics, and so on. The advantage to using a word processing program like Word to create documents is that you can make changes easily without recreating the document from scratch.

To correct small errors, you can use the backspace key or the delete key. Position the cursor after the error and then use the backspace key. The **backspace** key erases the character **in front** (before, or to the left) of the cursor. The **delete** key erases the character **behind** (after, or to the right of) the cursor.

Printing the Document.   A printed version of your document is called a **printout** or **hard copy.** Perform the following steps to print your document:

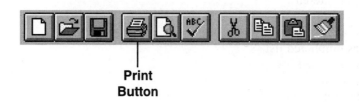

Print
Button

STEP 1: Point to the print button on the standard toolbar.

STEP 2: Click the print button once.

The mouse pointer changes to an hourglass (6) indicating that Word is preparing to print your document. A few moments later the document begins to emerge from the printer.

When you choose the print button on the standard toolbar to print your document, Word automatically prints one copy of the entire document. If you want to print only *one* page, you must select that option in the print dialogue box.

Quitting Word

Once you have created, saved, and printed your document, you may wish to quit Word and return control of the computer to Windows' Program Manager. To quit Word, do the following:

■ Select the file menu by clicking on the word **File.**

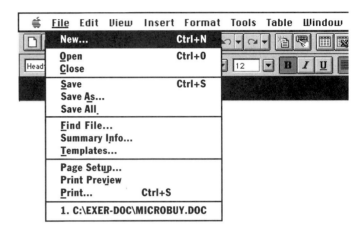

■ Choose the **Exit** command.

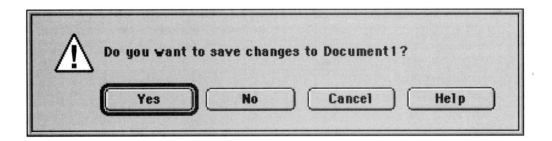

Word displays a message asking you if you want to save the changes. Choose the **Yes** button to save the changes; choose the **No** button to ignore the changes; or choose the **Cancel** button to return to the document.

HELP!

Help is just a mouse click away. To obtain help on an item on the Word screen, click the **Help** button on the standard toolbar. When you click the **Help** Button, the mouse pointer will change to an arrow with a question mark. Move the new mouse pointer to any item on the Word screen and click. Information will immediately be displayed for that item.

Word's online **H**elp feature is powerful and easy to use. The best way to familiarize yourself with this feature is to use it.

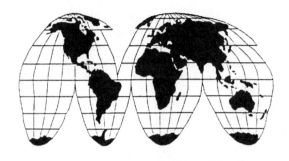

SECTION 3—
THE INTERNET:
COMMUNICATING
WITH THE WORLD

Curious about the latest rage in computer technology? Introduction to the **Internet** is an exciting hands-on tour of the **World Wide Web.** This section exposes you to what the fuss is all about. It also develops the necessary skills for you to navigate the Internet. You will learn some of the terminology and rules of the road. This section is designed for beginners.

There is information galore on the World Wide Web. It is the world's fastest growing computer network. Anyone with the right equipment can connect to the Web from school, work, or home.

IT IS A JUNGLE OUT THERE

The World Wide Web has been compared to an **electronic wilderness.** You never know what you might encounter. Therefore, before you go into uncharted territory of the Web, you should have some survival skills.

It is easier to understand if you think of the Web as a giant library, and the Internet as your access to it. The Web "sites" are like books, and the Web "pages" are specific pages in a book. A "home page" is the starting point for a Web site. It is something like a table of contents.

- **Browsers** are software tools used to look at Web pages. Browsers enable you to search the World Wide Web (i.e., Netscape, Mosaic, and others).
- **Gophers** allow you to burrow and tunnel through menus, directories, and files until you find what you want. In order to perform this service, gophers provide links to many other gophers and information resources on the Internet.
- **TCP/IP** (**T**ransmission **C**ontrol **P**rotocol/**I**nternet **P**rotocol) is like an address label on a package you send through the mail. Internet names and addresses are funny-looking things, for example:
  1. http://www.jpl.nasa.gov
  2. http://www.yahoo.com
  3. http://www.cs.yale.edu

  Everyone must have a different address.
- **FTP** (**F**ile **T**ransfer **P**rotocol) allows you to transfer files from distant computers to your computer or diskette.

INTERNET VOCABULARY

- @ sign = "at"
- (.) period = "dot"
- http = **H**yper**T**ext **T**ransfer **P**rotocol
- .com = commercial domain
- .edu = education domain
- .gov = government domain
- .mil = military domain
- .net = network provider
- .org = organizational domain

SURFING THE WEB

Pages on the Web are interconnected. You connect to other pages by clicking text or graphics that are called **hyperlinks.** Hyperlinks are underlined or bordered words and graphics that have Web addresses, also know as **URL** (pronounced, *u-ral*)—Universal **R**esource **L**ocator. Hyperlinks are easily identified. Their text is a different color from the rest of the text at a Web site. Surfing the Web means following hyperlinks to different Web pages and locations.

CAUTIONS WHILE ON THE WORLD WIDE WEB

When you are using the Internet and communicating with others at another location, keep the following in mind:

> You cannot see them.
>
> You won't know how old or what sex they are.
>
> They can tell you anything.
>
> You cannot be sure they are telling you the truth.
>
> Privacy cannot be guaranteed in the network environment.
>
> Think carefully about what you say and how you say it.

CAUTION

You will be visiting many Web sites. There will be the temptation to download something of interest.
Check for two things:
1. Is there a PRICE for the item?
2. Is the material COPYRIGHTED?

For your safety and the safety of others, exercise extreme caution when you are communicating on the Internet. In addition, you must keep in mind that the Internet is open and insecure. Therefore, everything on the Internet is open to searches and seizures by the snoops of world. In other words, the Internet is a postcard that anyone can read.

GETTING ON THE INTERNET

STEP 1: Double click on the **Netscape** (or your **browser) icon.**

When the GUI Browser starts, it looks for the Netscape home page. It may take a few seconds for the home page to load.

STEP 2: Click on **"What's New."**
Browse the information.
STEP 3: Click on **"What's Cool."**
Browse.
STEPS 4–7: Browse Handbook, Net Search, Net Directory, Newsgroups.

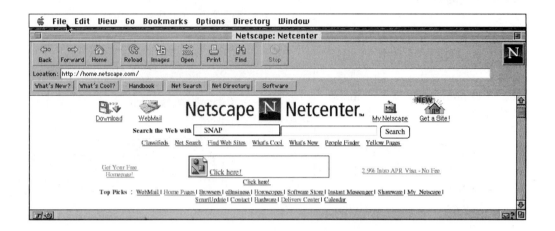

 NOTE: You're probably halfway around the Cyberspace world by now. To retrace your steps, click on the back button at the top of the screen

Popular home pages take a lot of **hits.** A hit is recorded every time someone connects to a home page. There is so much traffic on the Internet, you may get timed out on popular sites. Keep trying or try a different link.

Try the Activity List

1. Click on the Open button.
2. Enter http://www.usps.gov

Browser Activities

Browsers have made using the Internet fun, interesting, and easier to surf. Browsers have changed the way people relate to being online. Browsers allow you to use hypertext links.

Hypertext

Hypertext allows you to select a word with your mouse, then jump to another document that contains more information on the topic you are reading. Hypertext links can also be used with pictures or graphics.

GUI Icons

Netscape has **iconic** or **GUI** interfaces. An **icon** is a picture or a graphic. GUI (pronounced gooey) is short for **G**raphical **U**ser **I**nterface. GUI icons allow you to send your computer commands by selecting graphical icons with a mouse.

Surfing On Your Own

The best way to improve your expertise on surfing the Internet is to experiment on your own. Try it.

NOW YOU'RE READY TO GET STARTED!

Computers have a great many functions and capabilities. There are many books and magazines on computers and on computer programs. So exercise your "wetware"—your brain—and soon you'll find the computer as friendly to use as the telephone, and no more fearsome!

GLOSSARY OF COMPUTER TERMS

application A specific task performed by a computer

boot To start the computer

computerphobia Fear of computers

CPU **C**entral **P**rocessing **U**nit; this is the part of the computer system that does all the work you ask the computer to do

CRT **C**athode-**R**ay Tube; the monitor or screen

cursor A visual indicator, usually a blinking vertical bar on the screen that shows the position where data can be entered

default An assumption made by an application when no specific option is chosen by the user

file A collection of related records or data treated as a unit

floppy disk Also know as a diskette; a small portable device used to store information or programs

font A set of letters, symbols, and numbers in the same type style

gopher An Internet protocol for exchanging data through an hierarchical menuing system model

GUI **G**raphical **U**ser **I**nterface; allows you to send computer commands by selecting graphical icons with a mouse

hard copy A paper copy of material produced on the computer

hard disk A storage device made of rigid magnetic platters or disks

hardware Any physical component of a computer system as opposed to its operating system and software applications

host A network node that supports user accounts

hypertext Allows you to select a word with the mouse, then to another document that contains more information on the topic you are reading or searching on the Internet

icon An on-screen symbol or graphic that represents a program, function, command, or data file

input Information given to a computer or a program running on a computer

Internet A group of networks that use the TCP/IP protocols

keyboard An input device that allows you to give instructions to the computer

login name An identification used for a computer account or workstation, usually in conjunction with a password (also log-in name)

memory Hardware components that provide resources for storing or processing data.

menu A list of options from which a user can choose

microcomputer A personal computer typically used by a single user at a time

modem Stands for **mo**dulator-**dem**odulator; a device that allows the computer to communicate with another computer via a telephone line

monitor Also known as CRT, the screen or the display; it is an output device that shows both the information you typed on the keyboard and the computer's response to queries

mouse A push-button device used for interacting with a computer

network A system of interconnected computer systems

output Information produced by a program running on a computer

password A secret word consisting of a combination of alphanumeric characters used to protect the security of a user account or file

peripheral An external device such as a printer or scanner connected to and controlled by a computer

printers Output devices that allow you to print information and data from the computer to paper

program A set of instructions that tell a computer to perform a specific task or group of tasks

protocol A set of specific rules controlling the transmission and receipt of information over a communication link or network

RAM **R**andom **A**ccess **M**emory; the working space in the computer

reboot To stop and restart the computer operating system again

ROM **R**ead **O**nly **M**emory; holds data permanently and cannot be changed

server A computer that provides services for users of an local area network

site A place where a group of network nodes are located

software The program that directs the operation of a computer

TCP/IP **T**ransmission **C**ontrol **P**rotocol/**I**nternet **P**rotocol. A set of rules used by the Internet to support services such as remote login

toolbar Contains buttons, boxes, and graphics that allow you to perform tasks more quickly than using the menu bar

user friendly A quality of easy-to-use programs or computer systems that provide clear user directions and help

WWW **W**orld **W**ide **W**eb; an Internet information distribution method

WYSIWYG An acronym for **W**hat **Y**ou **S**ee **I**s **W**hat **Y**ou **G**et (pronounced wizzywig)

Appendix A

LEARNING A LIVING

SCANS—FOUNDATION SKILLS[1]

Basic Skills.   Reads, writes, performs arithmetic and mathematical operations, listens, and speaks.

1. *Reading*—Locates, understands, and interprets written information in prose and in documents such as manuals, graphs, and schedules.
2. *Writing*—Communicates thoughts, ideas, information, and messages in writing; and creates documents such as letters, directions, manuals, reports, graphs, and flow charts.
3. *Arithmetic/Mathematics*—Performs basic computations and approaches practical problems by choosing appropriately from a variety of mathematics techniques.
4. *Listening*—Receives, attends to, interprets, and responds to verbal messages and other cues.
5. *Speaking*—Organizes ideas and communicates orally.

Thinking Skills.   Thinks creatively, makes decisions, solves problems, visualizes, knows how to learn, and reasons.

1. *Creative thinking*—Generates new ideas.
2. *Decision making*—Specifies goals and constraints, generates alternatives, considers risks, and evaluates and chooses best alternative.
3. *Problem solving*—Recognizes problems and devises and implements plan of action.
4. *Seeing things in the mind's eye*—Organizes and processes symbols, pictures, graphs, objects, and other information.
5. *Knowing how to learn*—Uses efficient learning techniques to acquire and apply new knowledge and skills.
6. *Reasoning*—Discovers a rule or principle underlying the relationship between two or more objects and applies it when solving a problem.

---

[1]Adapted from *Learning a Living: A Blueprint for High Performance. A SCANS Report for America 2000.* The Secretary's Commission on Achieving Necessary Skills. U.S. Department of Labor, April 1992.

Personal Qualities. Displays responsibility, self-esteem, sociability, self-management, and integrity and honesty.

1. *Responsibility*—Exerts a high level of effort and perseveres towards goal attainment.
2. *Self-Esteem*—Believes in own self-worth and maintains a positive view of self.
3. *Sociability*—Demonstrates understanding, friendliness, adaptability, empathy, and politeness in group settings.
4. *Self-Management*—Assesses self accurately, sets personal goals, monitors progress, and exhibits self-control.
5. *Integrity/Honesty*—Chooses ethical courses of action.

SCANS—WORKPLACE COMPETENCIES

Resources.   Identifies, organizes, plans, and allocates resources.

1. *Time*—Selects goal-relevant activities, ranks them, allocates time, and prepares and follows schedules.
2. *Money*—Uses or prepares budgets, makes forecasts, keeps records, and makes adjustments to meet objectives.
3. *Materials and facilities*—Acquires, stores, allocates, and uses materials or space efficiently.
4. *Human resources*—Assesses skills and distributes work accordingly, evaluates performance and provides feedback.

Interpersonal.   Works with others.

1. *Participates as member of a team*—Contributes to group effort.
2. *Teaches others new skills*—Shares knowledge with others.
3. *Serves clients/customers*—Works to satisfy customers' expectations.
4. *Exercises leadership*—Communicates ideas to justify position, persuades and convinces others, responsibly challenges existing procedures and policies.
5. *Negotiates*—Works toward agreements involving exchange of resources, resolves divergent interests.
6. *Works with diversity*—Works well with men and women from diverse backgrounds.

Information.   Acquires and uses information.

1. Acquires and evaluates information.
2. Organizes and maintains information.
3. Interprets and communicates information.
4. Uses computers to process information.

Systems.   Understands complex interrelations.

1. *Understands systems*—Knows how social, organizational, and technological systems work and operates effectively with them.
2. *Monitors and corrects performance*—Distinguishes trends, predicts impacts on system operations, diagnoses deviations in systems' performance, and corrects malfunctions.
3. *Improves or designs systems*—Suggests modifications to existing systems and develops new or alternate systems to improve performance.

Technology.   Works with a variety of technologies.

1. *Selects technology*—Chooses procedures, tools, or equipment including computers and related technologies.
2. *Applies technology to tasks*—Understands overall intent and proper procedures or set up and operation of equipment.
3. *Maintains and troubleshoots equipment*—Prevents, identifies, or solves problems with equipment, including computers and other technologies.

Harcourt, Inc.

Appendix B

SUPPLEMENTS

EMPLOYMENT APPLICATION

PLEASE PRINT ALL INFORMATION

LAST NAME	FIRST NAME	INITIAL	NICKNAME?

PERSONAL INFORMATION: Date

Address

Phone   Pager   E-mail Address

□ Male   □ Female   □ Married   □ Single   Social Security Number

JOB SOUGHT   □ Part Time   □ Full Time

Position   Salary Desired

Are you currently employed?   May we contact your current your current employer?

EDUCATION (List in reverse chronological order. Include high school if pertinent.)   □ Currently enrolled?

Name, City   Grade Average

Major Subjects Studied   Year(s)

Awards, Degree, Certificates, Activities

Name, City   Grade Average

Major Subjects Studied   Year(s)

Awards, Degree, Certificates, Activities

Name, City   Grade Average

Major Subjects Studied   Year(s)

Awards, Degree, Certificates, Activities

VOLUNTEER EXPERIENCE

Place, City   Year(s)

Supervisor/Phone   Activities

Place, City   Year(s)

Supervisor/Phone   Activities

SKILLS AND INTERESTS

Hobbies and Crafts

Skills and Languages

Complete other side and sign application.

<u>FORMER EMPLOYMENT</u> (List only current job and longest-held jobs, most recent first.)

Name, Address Year(s)

Supervisor's Name, Phone

Duties Reason for Leaving

Name, Address Year(s)

Supervisor's Name, Phone

Duties Reason for Leaving

Name, Address Year(s)

Supervisor's Name, Phone

Duties Reason for Leaving

REFERENCES (List three persons you've known more than one year and your association to them: business associates, educators, friends, etc. Do not list family members here.)

Name, Phone Association Years

Name, Phone Association Years

Name, Phone Association Years

CLOSEST FAMILY MEMBER

Name, Phone Relationship

The statements on this application are true to the best of my recollection. I authorize the employer or his/her agent to contact any of the parties whose names appear hereon.

Signature Date

For company use only:
INTERVIEWER'S EVALUATION
□ Punctual □ Neat appearance □ Courteous □ Good Written Skills □ Good Verbal Skills

REMARKS

Salary Discussed: Interviewer Date

LN/Form 813

Harcourt Inc.

ENGLISH IMPROVEMENT PLAN						
English Evaluation Area	**My Level at End of Semester**				**ACTIVITIES TO ACHIEVE MY OBJECTIVES** **Things I Can Do** **to Further Improve My English Skills**	
I WANT TO IMPROVE MY:	Achievement*				*TO IMPROVE FURTHER, I WILL:*	**Dates Start/Finish**
	O	G	F	P		
Topic Selection						/ / / /
Support/ Organization						/ / / /
Sentences						/ / / /
Vocabulary						/ / / /
Referencing						/ / / /
Grammar						/ / / /
Classes to Take						/ / /
Workshops to Attend						/ / /
Books to Read						/ / /
O = Outstanding G = Good F = Fair P = Poor						

Let's get to work!

REFERENCES

The Chicago Manual of Style. 14th ed. Chicago: University of Chicago Press, 1993.

The Random House Dictionary of the English Language. Unabridged, 2d ed. New York: Random House, 1987.

Copperud, Roy H., *American Usage and Style, the Consensus.* New York: Van Nostrand Reinhold Company, 1980.

Clark and Clark, *How 7: A Handbook for Office Workers.* 7th ed. Cincinnati, Ohio: South-Western College Publishing, 1995.

Diamond, Harriet and Phyllis Dutwin, *Grammar in Plain English.* 2d ed. New York: Barrons Educational Series, Inc., 1989.

Fiske, Robert Hartwell, *Thesaurus of Alternatives to Worn-Out Words and Phrases.* Cincinnati, Ohio: Writer's Digest Books, 1994.

Plotnik, Arthur, *The Elements of Editing: A Modern Guide for Editors and Journalists.* New York: Collier Books, Macmillan Publishing Company, 1982.

Rodale, J. I. *The Synonym Finder,* Rodale Press, Emmaus, Pa., 1978.

Shertzer, Margaret, *The Elements of Grammar.* New York: Collier Books, Macmillan Publishing Company, 1986.

Skillin, Marjorie E. and Robert M. Gay, *Words into Type.* 3d ed. Englewood Cliffs, N. J.: Prentice-Hall, Inc., 1974.

Strunk, William Jr., and E. B. White, *The Elements of Style.* 3d ed. New York: Macmillan Publishing Co., Inc., 1979.

U.S. Department of Labor, SCANS: *Learning a Living: A Blueprint for High Performance. A SCANS Report for America 2000.* The Secretary's Commission on Achieving Necessary Skills. U.S. Department of Labor, April 1992.

LITERARY CREDITS

Barnett, Craig J. "Gas Furnace Maintenance Keeps the Heat On," *RSES Journal.* September 1998. Reprinted with permission of *RSES Journal.*

Berkoff, Nancy. "Get a Grip on Computer Technology." Reprinted by permission of the author. Originally appeared in Chef magazine, February 1996.

Bucci, Bill. "Changing Times." *MicroStation World,* Summer 1996. Reprinted with permission.

Clark, Caroline R. "Printers Beware." *Quick Printing,* April 1997. Reprinted with permission.

"Computer-Aided Design Drafters and Technicians." *Encyclopedia of Careers and Vocational Education,* Tenth Edition, Chicago: Ferguson Publishing Company, 1997. Reprinted with permission.

Jenkins, Kathy. "Six Steps to Avoiding Hiring Mistakes." *Signcraft Magazine,* January/February 1997. Reprinted with permission from Signcraft magazine, P.O. Box 60031, Ft. Meyers, FL 33906.

© Microsoft Corp. "Microsoft Trademark." Redmond, WA 98042-6339. www@microsoft.com or webmaster@msn.com. Copyright © 1998 Microsoft. Used with permission.

Nelton, Sharon. "A Scrappy Entrepreneur." *Nation's Business.* June 1997. Reprinted by permission, Nation's Business, June 1997. Copyright © 1997, U.S. Chamber of Commerce.

Proulx, Danny. "Why Do Cabinet Shops Fail?" *CabinetMaker.* January/February 1997. Reprinted with permission. This article originally appeared in CabinetMaker magazine.

Reis, Ron. "A Career to Consider—Paramedic." *Working World.* November 25–
    December 16, 1996; Ron Reis, Working World. Reprinted with permission.
Sheppard, Rob. "APS: Advanced Photo System." *Outdoor Photography.* May 1996.
    Copyright © 1996 Outdoor Photography magazine. Reprinted with permission.
Wiley, John P. Jr. "Phenomena, Comment and Notes." *Smithsonian Magazine.*
    February 1997. Reprinted with permission.
Witkowski, John. "Watch for the Warning Flags Customers Wave." *Signcraft
    Magazine.* Jan/Feb 1997. Reprinted, with permission, from Signcraft magazine,
    P. O. Box 60031, Ft. Meyers, FL 33906.

PHOTO CREDITS

INDEX